W9-DAE-274

LANGUAGE AS IDEOLOGY

Critical Linguistics, inaugurated in 1979 with the publication of *Language as Ideology* (and its companion volume *Language and Control*), has been widely influential, and successful in documenting the connection of linguistic and social practices. Even now, the book occupies a crucial place in the development of the field, as the first comprehensive account of the theory of language that underpinned the critical discourse enterprise. It still provides the most detailed theoretical study of the operation of power and ideology in all aspects of text.

For this new edition, the authors have updated the critical bibliography and written a new preface and a major new chapter which presents the advances made in the field of critical language study. Through a detailed theoretical discussion of a related set of texts, they present their current position and views on the necessary directions for the field in the future. This book will be of interest to students and teachers of linguistics, education, English language, media, cultural and communication studies.

THE POLITICS OF LANGUAGE

Series editors: Tony Crowley, University of Southampton
Talbot J. Taylor, College of William and Mary,
Williamsburg, Virginia

'In the lives of individuals and societies, language is a factor of greater importance than any other. For the study of language to remain solely the business of a handful of specialists would be a quite unacceptable state of affairs.'

Saussure

The Politics of Language Series covers the field of language and cultural theory and will publish radical and innovative texts in this area. In recent years the developments and advances in the study of language and cultural criticism have brought to the fore a new set of questions. The shift from purely formal, analytical approaches has created an interest in the role of language in the social, political and ideological realms and the series will seek to address these new problems with a clear and informed approach. The intention is to gain recognition for the central role of language in individual and public life.

LANGUAGE AS IDEOLOGY
Second Edition

Robert Hodge
and
Gunther Kress

London and New York

First published in 1979 by
Routledge & Kegan Paul

Second edition published in 1993 by
Routledge
11 New Fetter Lane, London EC4P 4EE

Simultaneously published in the USA and Canada
by Routledge
29 West 35th Street, New York, NY 10001

Reprinted 1996

First Edition © 1979 Gunther Kress and Robert Hodge
Second Edition © 1993 Robert Hodge and Gunther Kress

Typeset in 10/12 pt Baskerville by Megaron
Printed and bound in Great Britain by Redwood Books

British Library Cataloguing in Publication Data
A catalogue record for this book is available from the
British Library

Library of Congress Cataloguing in Publication Data
A catalogue record for this book is available from the
Library of Congress

ISBN 0-415-07001-5

CONTENTS

PREFACE

Disciplines, unlike cows, yield least when most contented. Necessity is the mother of invention and a stimulus to thought – or it can be. The ideas in this book evolved under pressure from outside. We were concerned to develop linguistics in an interdisciplinary school which was divided between history and literature, yet committed to a link between the two. How could a fledgling linguistics justify itself in this context? How indeed? Other institutions have combined the study of language and literature. As literature is mediated through language, the liaison makes sense. Institutionally, history and linguistics are not usually bedmates, though history too is mediated through language. We came to realize that the question 'At what level does linguistics become an essential aspect of the general study of history?' though novel, should at least be put. However, it gradually became clear to us that the particular attempt to link history and linguistics was only an instance of the real task, namely to relate forms of thought to the existence of the producers of those thoughts, as individuals living in a material world under specific conditions in specific societies at given times. Such a study inevitably starts from the study of pieces of language. The role of linguistics and the necessary scope of linguistic theory then became clear: linguistics had to provide the theoretical and methodological framework for the analysis of materials studied by all kinds of intellectual and cultural historian, indeed, by everyone concerned with culture and thought.

We wrote this book over a period of four years at the University of East Anglia, extremely fortunate in the friends and colleagues in different disciplines with whom we worked and talked. We could see how our enterprise made sense in their terms, and our work gained immeasurably from our constant and open discussion. John Nicholls, Ken Lodge, and Andrew Radford read early drafts and commented generously. John Ross read a large chapter during a summer institute in Cairo, where there were many infinitely more enjoyable ways to spend any free time. His extensive and sceptically positive comments were of great help to us. Among linguists, no one has been as continuously and closely involved with the development of our project as Roger Fowler, meticulous and exacting in his criticisms, quick to recognize and acknowledge the fruitful aspects of the theory. The larger theoretical social framework was developed in constant debate and exchange with David Aers; without the contribution of his concerns and theoretical interests, the book would have had a very different form. For us, the demands on linguistics by neighbouring disciplines were represented and articulated most fully by Tony Trew and Gareth Jones, and their ideas and criticism have shaped our thinking. Among contemporary linguists we owe most to the work of Michael Halliday. Our understanding of his ideas forms the background to much of our thinking even where his work is not specifically being referred to. It is hardly necessary to acknowledge the seminal influence of transformational grammar, stemming from the work of Zellig Harris and Noam Chomsky. Of earlier linguists, our greatest debt is to Whorf. Outside linguistics, the work of Marx and Freud has been a decisive and continuous influence, for us as for so many others.

Joy Hardiment typed several versions of this book. By her skill and good humour our work was made a lot easier, and we thank her for that very much. Amazingly, Gwen and Tricia continued to talk to us.

Though it seems merely conventional to say it, we stress that none of those mentioned should be held responsible for the lapses of taste, fact, or theory which no doubt abound. All those who knew us strove to keep us from error.

Perth and Adelaide

PREFACE TO THE SECOND EDITION

The first edition of *Language as Ideology* was published in 1979, although it was written between 1973 and 1976, fifteen years ago as we write the preface to this second edition. In those days it was too innovative for its own good, and it was some time before its merits were appreciated. Most of the early reviews were vitriolic, especially from mainstream linguists of the time; reassuring proof that outraged paradigms strike back, and depressing evidence that they have effective systems of control. Slowly, however, it gained influence, as the enterprise of critical linguistics, or critical discourse analysis as it became known later (see Fairclough 1985, Thompson 1984), gathered momentum. Of the works that enabled this tradition to grow *Language as Ideology* occupies a crucial place, as the first comprehensive account of the theory of language that underpinned the critical discourse enterprise.

Fifteen years later it is out of print, still the only book that attempts this theoretical task. It is curious that this is the case, and worthy of comment as to why. We ourselves in individual and joint publications have continued to work on the theory, and have developed it in a number of directions, but we did not try again to formulate the basic theory of verbal language contained in *Language as Ideology*. We have tried to extend the theory to visual and other semiotic systems, we have emphasized its character as social process, and we have explored further the assumptions about society that were implicit in the project itself, but we tacitly took for granted its basic descriptions of verbal language as structure and system in social use.

But the need for this book was not self-evident for the two main kinds of reader who have found the critical linguistics/critical discourse tradition interesting. The biggest group came from a spectrum of disciplines, – politics, sociology, media studies, legal studies, literary theory – where there was no background in the formal description of language, and a preference for analysis that did not make use of it. This had been one of our target audiences in the initial book. We hoped that they would be stimulated to want more and better descriptions of language, while staying well short of the full apparatus of the technical linguistics of the day. Some of these people used our methodology, attending to linguistic forms in a relatively restricted fashion, usually concentrating on a small number of forms, such as passives or nominalizations that were treated early in our book. But mostly these readers have moved quickly back to the social and political interests that took them to the set of texts in question, showing precisely the opportunism that we had hoped for and expected, but in the end not seduced by a fascination with language as ideology as we had also hoped.

Another group we aimed at started as we thought with a different set of excesses and deficiencies: linguists with more than enough linguistic knowledge, and not enough interest in how linguistic forms functioned in political and social life. They had been our intended audience for an equally important aspect of our project, namely the reform of mainstream linguistics. We had hopes that linguistics could be turned into a socially responsive and responsible discipline. It has to be said that we have not as yet succeeded in this modest aim. In the event most of this second group has remained indifferent to the whole critical discourse approach, preferring the prestige of mainstream linguistics, the funding for (applied) linguistics of various kinds, and the general theoretical and ideological undertaking of the 'scientific' enterprise. Nevertheless, a growing group of people, some of them trained in mainstream linguistics but dissatisfied with its scope and uses, others relative newcomers to the enterprise, have been attracted to critical discourse analysis.

We remain convinced that every powerful critical theory of language and discursive processes needs (among other things) the kind of comprehensive theory of linguistic forms that this book tries to provide. We are also increasingly of the view that this theory cannot simply be taken, unmodified, from any of the existing theories of language, stitching together bits and pieces from the various schools of linguistic theory. Much of the stock of knowledge about language accumulated by different schools of linguistics over thousands of years remains relevant enough, just as apples did not cease to fall even after Newton had proposed the law of gravity; but the way knowledge is organized crucially affects how it can be used, and what it can and cannot do. It is in this sense that we claim there is need for a new theory of linguistic forms. And a theory along the lines sketched out in *Language as Ideology* provides one essential starting point.

We are confident, then, that this book is still useful in what it attempts, and no other book as yet tries to do it. But fifteen years is a long time, and we wanted to take account of the considerable amount of work that has appeared since then, much of which we applaud and use in our own work. No book is beyond criticism, and ours took so many risks that it was more open to criticism than most. There are many points that with hindsight and in the light of our own continuing development of this approach we would now put differently. Initially, therefore, we intended to revise the whole book, section by section and chapter by chapter, turning what was a slim, radical and suggestive book when it was first published, into a solid, explicit and authoritative one in its middle age.

In the end we decided not to do so. Paradoxically, we felt that the book would be more useful if it kept all the excessive speculation and deliberate obtuseness that have troubled even its kindest critics. Even its errors have their uses, like 'virtuous mistakes' for early language learners, and we only wish that we had had the wit to make them on purpose. It was a strategically asymmetrical book when it was published, for good reasons given the context of the time. It contained a well developed theory of how grammar carries social meaning, set in a broadly based programme for the study of language and social meaning, and the two aspects were interdependent. The theory of grammar was motivated by the programme, and the programme projected the form of the theory of grammar.

One way of understanding the contradictions inherent in this enterprise would be to say that this was a theory of grammar that should have connected more strongly and more productively with the work of such writers as Bernstein and Labov, Althusser and Habermas, Foucault and Pecheux, Marcuse and Lacan, Schutz and Bourdieu, Baudrillard and Williams, Kristeva and Tannen, Derrida and Said. The diversity of this still preliminary list establishes it as a field of intertextuality whose boundaries are likely to change continually over time and between different kinds of reader. There is no single theory of society or ideology that is readily available somewhere that we have culpably refused to declare, although many have criticized us for not coming out with our own definitions of these important categories. Our strategy in 1979 was to insert potential points of contact with what was then an inchoate and emerging set of discourses, so that the book's meaning was not contained within its formulations or restricted to a single set of potential allies, but was dispersed throughout an open set of possible uses.

Since it was structured in that way, the easiest way to make it a totally different book in 1991 would be to change not a word, so that the different discourses in which it now circulates can be left free to construct the necessary difference. This is largely what we have chosen to do. But it rests on what is only a half truth. 'Intertextuality' describes an activity of readers but like every social activity it is not unconstrained, and authors who aspire after a rich set of intertextual meanings for their text have to work to help it happen. Our book in its 1979 version did not signal clearly enough how we wanted it to be read against a growing body of texts concerned with the study of discourse and ideology, social and political process. In this second edition we want to clarify this aspect at least of the original project.

What we have done, then, is to reproduce the original text almost unchanged from 1979, and add a new final chapter. This is written to the same kind of format as the rest of the book, though it's twice as long as other chapters. In it we try to do a number of things. We try to articulate the scope of what the book essentially tried to do, in the process taking account of critics who (sometimes with good reason) accused it of seeming to claim to do what it couldn't or shouldn't or didn't attempt. In this final chapter we emphasize the two defining features of the project of the book: the concern with power as the condition of social life, and the need for a theory of language which incorporates this as a major premise.

One impression the original book gave was that we were opportunistic in our choice of texts. This is an impression that we want to confirm. A theory that is not quickly and directly applicable to a new instance is not a good theory, although the novelty of the instance is as important to the development of a theory as its predictability. But in our book we seemed to raid a series of texts from the sixteenth century to the present as though specific contexts and histories could be taken for granted. We did not do justice to the complexity of particular contexts in our concern for a systematic exposition of linguistic forms, and this is not at all an impression that we want to give. On the contrary, linguistic forms do not have a single set of invariant functions and meanings, but are constantly remade by individuals with particular social histories and particular places in social structures. Hence linguistic forms as *signs* constantly change as they circulate in different contexts for different groups with different histories. This variability and the basis that makes it possible and comprehensible are too crucial to be left out of the discussion of language and ideological forms. To make this point we wanted to choose a wider range of texts relating to a single situation and moment which was itself inserted into a series of histories. So we have organized the exposition around a varied set of texts that come from the same situation, the war in the Arabian gulf that was in process during the time we were thinking about and working on the revision of the book.

We chose to look at how language functions in a state of war because war is the best laboratory for studying the kinds of deformations of language that the whole book is about. There is one danger in following this course. The view of language in the original book seemed joyless and paranoiac enough, according to some of our critics, as though no language use could be 'innocent' and there is no possibility of pleasure in the intricate structures of language that are constantly evolving and being used for so many purposes, not all of which are designed only to mystify or oppress.

This chapter seems to take this tendency to its logical extreme, developing a theory of language in which a state of war is the exemplary condition of its existence. But our intention in doing this is the opposite: to limit the scope of the theory that we describe, and to circumscribe its apparent pessimism. The peace movement of the 1960s had the slogan 'make love not war'. From one point of view it can be said that love is just another form of war, and likewise war is just another form of love, but the peaceniks were right to insist that it's possible and even essential to choose between the two. For all its problems, love is definitely better than war. In 1979 we perhaps seemed too unrelenting in searching out examples of mystification and deception, but that was because the kinds of texts and situations we were looking at justified that approach. They still do. But there are many other kinds of text and situation where such analytic suspicion is not so appropriate, where the intentions of the analyst can and should be different. We have not tried to do justice to that aspect of language and that kind of aim in this final chapter, not because it is unimportant or even unassimilable to our basic theory of language but for the opposite reason. It deserves a book, not a section of a chapter.

We owe a debt to many people who have showed us more of the possibilities and problems of the original book than we were capable of seeing ourselves. We indicate in the appropriate place the various published critiques and commentaries that we have found most useful, but here we would like to acknowledge various friends and colleagues who generously shared with us their comments and critiques, and from whom and with whom we have learnt much in the meantime. Among these, special thanks are due to David Birch, Teresa Carbó, Norman Fairclough, Noel King, Jim Martin, Alec McHoul, Stephen Muecke, Michael O'Toole, Horst Ruthrof, John Thompson, Terry Threadgold, and Theo van Leeuwen.

1

THE SCOPE OF LINGUISTICS

A PROSPECT FOR LINGUISTICS

Language is one of man's most remarkable attributes. It is an absolute precondition for nearly all our social life, and it is the medium in which most organized thought and communication proceed. So the study of language, linguistics, ought to be an acknowledged part of any humane education designed to lead to an understanding of one's self and one's world. To meet this challenge, linguistics needs to have an ambitiously wide scope. It must be vitally concerned with the relation between language and mind, since language is only interesting when we see it as a living process. For all humans, language and thought are inextricably bound together. But linguistics must be equally concerned with the relations between society and language, since language is so distinctly a social phenomenon. Language is given to the individual by the society in which he or she lives. It is a key instrument in socialization, and the means whereby society forms and permeates the individual's consciousness. Since language is so important, the insights of linguistics should be generally available: to specialists in other disciplines of course, but also to everyone in society to whom an understanding of the forms and processes of language matters. We have written this book with that as our aim: to describe language from this standpoint for an audience with such interests.

It may be helpful if we set our undertaking in the framework of the theories and concerns of linguistics as it has developed over the last two decades in England and the USA. Within theoretical linguistics itself there have been a number of attempts to provide unified and comprehensive theories of language and behaviour. Names to mention in this connection include Pike, Halliday and Lamb, whose theories are intended to be extendible into all areas of signifying social behaviour. Outside linguistics, valuable contributions have been made by people with an interest in language but with a theoretical and methodological base in other disciplines within the social sciences. Some individuals, like Dell Hymes from anthropology and the philosopher Austin, have had a significant impact on thinking about linguistics. However, in the period since the mid-fifties, the major thrust in linguistic theory has been in the theory of syntax. Without question the outstanding name here has been that of Noam Chomsky. His theory, transformational generative grammar, has dominated the linguistic scene almost since the appearance of his *Syntactic Structures* in 1957. Even non-transformational theories had to come to terms with the challenge of Chomsky's work, and measure their insights against Chomskyan notions such as generative grammar and transformations, taking account of the goals of formality and explicitness which he asserted.

The 'Chomskyan Revolution' ran right through linguistics and affected the work done by every linguist. However, the very power and influence of Chomsky's ideas and the preciseness of the theory had some unfortunate effects. Linguists came to assume that theoretical linguistics meant syntactic theory, and, for many, syntactic theory meant purely transformational theory. Inevitably this led to a drastic narrowing of the scope of linguistics. Recently there has been a widespread and diverse reaction against such narrowness. Over the last seven or eight years an increasing number of linguists have begun to take an interest in the study of extended discourse and the language of social interaction. Sociolinguists look closely at the relations between language and social class. There is an increased concern to study actual language used in actual contexts: speech, conversations, and various kinds of written discourse. Chomsky's famous dictum that linguistics is a branch of cognitive psychology gave a massive impetus to research in psycholinguistics, and some valuable work is being done on the production, memory, decoding, and perception of sentences.

What is needed now is for these disparate impulses and developments to be given unity and coherence through a subsuming theoretical framework. Although there is no longer a Chomskyan orthodoxy, this tradition has left its imprint on conceptions of the discipline. So while linguists in general would not now see sociolinguistics or the study of discourse as marginal, they would still regard these phenomena as falling outside the scope of theoretical linguistics because pure (real) theory is still syntactic theory, as it was in the sixties. So, although there is much more work being done in areas such as discourse analysis and sociolinguistics, these subjects are given names to indicate that they are distinct areas, outside the central field of theoretical linguistics. The theory that is required for the new situation must have a reconstituted scope, abandoning the equation theoretical linguistics = syntactic theory, while retaining both syntax and theory. The requisite theory must encompass the study of syntax and the basic rule systems of the language along with the social uses of language, that is, the relations between language and society and between language and mind, in a single integrated enterprise.

Some readers, both linguists and non-linguists, may feel uneasy about the scope of linguistics we propose. It sounds like academic imperialism, a linguistics which seeks to encroach on other disciplines like psychology and sociology. But disciplines exist for the sake of their subjects, not the other way round. If the boundary that has been drawn round a discipline proves a hindrance to the proper study of that subject matter, then it is the boundary that must change. If language is intrinsically a social and psychological phenomenon, then students of language must take account of the work of psychologists and sociologists. Conversely, psychologists and sociologists will need to know about language phenomena as part of their competence in their own fields.

Some theoretical linguists will also object that the expansion we propose can only be achieved at the cost of loss of rigour and precision. This objection comes out of a set of beliefs and assumptions about linguistics and the nature of scientific enquiry which many linguists hold. These assumptions have been the target of Chomsky himself, who gives the following critique:

> Modern linguistics shares the delusion – the accurate term, I believe – that the modern 'behavioural sciences' have in some essential respects achieved a transition from 'speculation' to 'science' and that earlier work can be safely consigned to the antiquarians. Obviously any rational person will favor rigorous analysis and careful experiment; but to a considerable degree, I feel, the 'behavioural sciences' are merely mimicking the surface features of the natural sciences; much of their scientific character has been achieved by a restriction of subject matter and a concentration on rather peripheral issues. Such narrowing of focus can be justified if it leads to achievements of real intellectual significance, but in this case, I think it would be very difficult to show that the narrowing of scope has led to deep and significant results.
>
> (*Language and Mind*, 1968, p. xi)

Chomsky was then, and arguably still is, the most influential living linguist, writing at the height of his authority.

Chomsky here pinpoints a major problem of strategy, how far a deliberate narrowing of focus can be the source of insight otherwise unobtainable, and how far it reduces the possibility of significant discoveries. The history of the physical sciences shows the value of a sharpened focus and remorseless concentration on particular phenomena. The linguist similarly will have to attend rigorously and scrupulously to aspects of language that may be taken for granted by the man in the street. But Chomsky is right to insist that this strategy is a means to an end, to 'achievements of real intellectual significance', 'deep and significant results'. These are the criteria by which to judge a discipline. Chomsky in 1968 found modern linguistics deficient by these criteria, but he was optimistic that a new, more productive phase was about to begin: 'I think there is more of a healthy ferment in cognitive psychology – and in the particular branch of cognitive psychology known as linguistics – than there has been for many years' (*Language and Mind*, p. 1). What he saw or hoped for was a dissolution of the barriers between linguistics and psychology, the ending of 'the rather artificial separation of disciplines' through the unity of the subject matter, language and thought. Linguistics, in this view, is not connected to psychology through an intermediate hybrid sub-discipline, psycholinguistics. Linguistics *is* part of psychology, and 'psycholinguistics' has no separate existence apart from linguistics itself.

Chomsky advocates returning to a time when a more generous conception of the subject prevailed, in which important issues were explored. Here is Whorf, writing in about 1936, out of a different linguistic tradition:

> The investigator of a culture should hold an ideal of linguistics as that of a heuristic approach to problems of psychology which hitherto he may have shrunk from considering – a glass through which, when correctly focussed, will appear the TRUE SHAPES of many of those forces which hitherto have been to him but the inscrutable blank of invisible and bodiless thought.
>
> (*Language, Thought and Reality*, p. 73)

Whorf here sees linguistics not as an autonomous discipline, but as an indispensable aid in a project of immense importance, the investigation of cultures, the uncovering of profound and inaccessible levels of thought. To be ancillary to this enterprise would be far more exciting than autonomous irrelevance, and might produce the 'deep and significant results' Chomsky also desires. Such a linguistics will be a branch of anthropology or sociology as well as psychology: or, to put it another way, linguistic analysis will have to proceed hand in hand with an understanding of mental and social processes.

LANGUAGE, SCIENCE, AND IDEOLOGY

Whorf's work has raised in an acute form the relation between language and thought, and between language and perception. Psychologists of perception have shown conclusively that there is no 'pure' act of perception, no seeing without thinking. We all interpret the flux of experience through means of interpretative schemata, initial expectations about the world, and priorities of interests. What we actually see is limited by where we look and what we focus on. This amounts to only a small proportion of what we could have seen. At each stage of interpretation more and more is lost. The brain receives only a small fraction of what initially was perceived and it stores even less.

Language comes into this process at a late stage, since it is involved in the storing of perceptions and thoughts. Whatever has a name can become familiar, and is easier to classify and remember. Only what has a name can be shared. Communicable perception has to be coded in language. So language, which is given by society, determines which perceptions are potentially social ones. These perceptions, fixed in language, become a kind of second nature. We inevitably impose our classifications on others, and on ourselves. Language plays a vital role in what has been called the 'social construction of reality' (Berger and Luckmann, 1967). Language fixes a world that is so much more stable and coherent than what we actually see that it takes its place in our consciousness and becomes what we think we have seen. And since normal perception works by constant feedback, the gap between the real world and the socially constructed world is constantly being reduced, so that what we do 'see' tends to become what we can say.

Languages are systems of categories and rules based on fundamental principles and assumptions about the world. These principles and assumptions are not related to or determined by thought: they *are* thought. Whorf called these fundamental organizing assumptions a 'science' and a 'metaphysic', that is, a systematic account of reality and the *a priori* assumptions on which that account rests. Such assumptions are embodied in language, learnt through language, and reinforced in

5

language use. According to Whorf, the main difference between these assumptions and those in the official science and metaphysics of a community is that the former act largely unconsciously. Institutional science and metaphysics require a professional class of scientists and metaphysicians to articulate their basic assumptions, but even these professional thinkers use a language, and through their prior use of its categories and processes these communal assumptions filter into their thinking. The interrelations between the two kinds of science and the two kinds of metaphysics make an important subject of study.

Whorf's terms 'science' and 'metaphysics' suggest interesting connections. But language, typically, is immersed in the ongoing life of a society, as the practical consciousness of that society. This consciousness is inevitably a partial and false consciousness. We can call it ideology, defining 'ideology' as a systematic body of ideas, organized from a particular point of view. Ideology is thus a subsuming category which includes sciences and metaphysics, as well as political ideologies of various kinds, without implying anything about their status and reliability as guides to reality.

Language is an instrument of control as well as of communication. Linguistic forms allow significance to be conveyed and to be distorted. In this way hearers can be both manipulated and informed, preferably manipulated while they suppose they are being informed. Language is ideological in another, more political, sense of that word: it involves systematic distortion in the service of class interest. Yet the two kinds of ideology are not entirely distinct, in theory or in practice. Science is a systematization from a point of view: so is a political ideology. Political ideology is liable to project fantasy versions of reality, but science deals in hypothetical constructs whose status is not always so very different.

The affinity between the two kinds of ideology can be seen from an interesting passage in Whorf. Comparing English and Hopi, a language of North America, he says:

> By comparison with many American languages, the formal systematization in English, German, French or Italian seems poor and jejune. Why, for instance, do we not, like the Hopi, use a different way of expressing the relation of channel of sensation (seeing) to result in consciousness, as between 'I see that it is red' and 'I see that it is new'? We fuse the two quite different types of relationship into a vague sort of connection expressed by 'that', whereas the Hopi indicates that in the first case seeing presents a sensation 'red', and in the second that seeing presents unspecified

evidence from which is drawn the inference of 'newness'.

(Whorf, 1956, p. 85)

Whorf's observation here is brilliantly acute, but his question is capable of more than one answer. He assumes that the English speaker would want to be able to make this distinction. But a nation of shopkeepers might positively wish to blur the distinction between direct perception and inference, and so might develop a form which seemed to claim a status for the second equivalent to the first. The lesson from this may be that we'd be safer buying a second-hand car from a Hopi than from an Englishman.

Interestingly, English speakers do in fact regard these judgements as different in kind, but this is shown in a different part of the grammar. We can say *a new red car* but not *a red new* car. Whorf himself noted that the order here is determined by a subcategorization of adjectives into 'external' and 'internal'. *Red* is more 'internal', a more reliable principle of classification, than *new*. English speakers really know this, whether or not they're conscious of knowing it, although they don't display this knowledge all the time.

Yet the lack of distinction shown by the use of *that* is also justifiable in terms of ideology in the first sense. The philosopher John Locke, for instance, not exactly a jejune thinker, argued that the idea of *red* is not different in kind from an idea like *justice*. One is simple, the other complex, but this is only a difference of degree. Sensory judgments are judgments, matters of opinion like other judgments. So in terms of this epistemology it is sensible to say *I think it is red*. The Hopi distinction between redness and newness is as much of a distortion as their conflation in English. In fact English allows both distinction and conflation, and it would not be surprising if Hopi did too, without Whorf having noticed it. English on this occasion reflects two epistemological theories, not one. Both of them are useful and 'true', the use and the truth inextricably entwined. This kind of tangle is the norm for language, not the exception, so that linguistic analysis of languages of developed countries will probably reveal, not a coherent metaphysic as Whorf assumed, but the opposite: confusions, contradictions, incoherence, traces of the schizoid universe of a class society.

MODELS AND TRANSFORMATIONS

The grammar of a language is its theory of reality. The most revealing theory of language will be one which follows the form of the grammar.

We regard language as consisting of a related set of categories and processes. The fundamental categories are a set of 'models' which describe the interrelation of objects and events. These models are basic schemata which derive in their turn from the visual perceptual processes of human beings. These schemata serve to classify events in the world, in simple but crucial ways. In their simplest form they tend to involve one or two objects in a specified relation to a verbal process. In the first model there are minimally two entities related by a process. One of the two is seen as causing the action, the other is affected by it. In a sentence it might be *The batsman struck the ball*. (Throughout the book we shall use the convention of italicizing linguistic examples.) So here the action is seen as passing from the *actor* across to the *affected*. We call this model the *transactive model*. In the second model there is minimally one entity related to a process. As there is only the one entity it is difficult to know whether it is actor or affected; in fact neither category really applies, since this model is vague about precise causal and affected status. An example would be *The batsman runs*. We call this model the *non-transactive model*. The third model type involves relations of a different type, not a relation of action or process, but of simple relation. This may be between two entities, *The sports master is an ex-football international*; or between an entity and a quality, *His footwork is superb*. We call this model, with the two subtypes, the *relational model*.

Quite clearly the transactive and the non-transactive are both about action, and in the book we refer to them jointly as *actional models*, or *actionals*. The other model we call the *relational model*, or *relationals*. Some confusion may arise for readers who are familiar with the terms *transitive* and *intransitive*, which might be thought to describe the same thing as our terms *transactive* and *non-transactive*. However, the two pairs of terms are distinct; ours is meant to indicate the real nature and meaning of the models, that is, action passing on from an actor to an affected, or action restricted to one entity. Some examples will illustrate that the terms transitive and intransitive are used much more loosely. Any *noun-verb-noun* construction is called transitive: thus *Bill resembles his father, the parcel weighs ten pounds, John plays tennis*, are all transitive. But it is clear that they are not transactive, that there is no action going from an actor to an affected. Transitive and intransitive are labels for structures with a particular form; transactive and non-transactive are labels for models with a particular meaning. A transitive may be transactive or it may not. Basically, the relation between the two is that while one is about meaning, semantics, the other is about surface form, order. The two are rarely in a one-for-one relation.

As far as relationals are concerned, they are about the classification system of the language. Those models which establish relations between nouns are frequently *equative*: *John is Lear*; those which establish relations between nouns and qualities are frequently *attributive*: *John's Lear is stunning*. Relationals may be transitive: *Young Billy seems the perfect gentleman*.

This gives the following scheme of basic models for English:

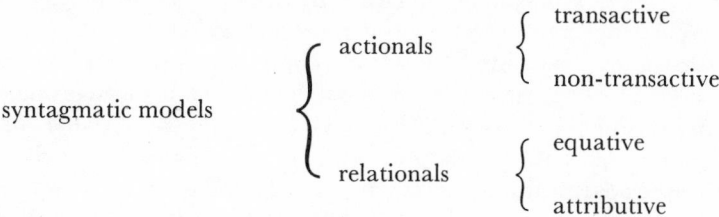

Further classifications lead to a larger set of submodels. English syntax distinguishes, for instance, between physical processes and mental processes; but this scheme shows the set of basic models in English. Actionals represent the relationships perceived in the physical world (and, by analogy, in the mental world of thought and perception); relationals display the results of the activity of the mind, making judgments, commenting, and so on.

The world is grasped through language. But in its use by a speaker language is more than that. It is a version of the world, offered to, imposed on, exacted by, someone else. The syntagmatic models offer the first classification of an event, in one or another of the meanings of the models. But no model can be offered directly from speaker to hearer. Every syntagm (the linear and structural form in which the models appear in actual language use) is classified many times over, as a whole and part by part. Some of these classificatory acts are obligatory. For example, each utterance in English must show tense; that is, speakers must indicate whether the utterance is true for now, true of the past or the future, or true in some other hypothetical way. Included here is what linguists call modality, that is, indications of the degree of likelihood, probability, weight, or authority the speaker attaches to the utterance. These classifications are relative, performed by the speaker in that context, for that audience. Although the classification process is prescribed by convention, it is the speaker who performs it and who chooses which classification to apply. So there are rules for indicating, for instance, whether a statement is new or second-hand, but speakers of English are no more to be trusted than sellers of cars.

There is another kind of operation which can be performed in language: transformations. The theory of transformations is Chomsky's major contribution to linguistic theory, though we use the term in a partly different sense from him. (For a formal discussion, see Hodge and Kress, 1974.) In our account, transformations are a set of operations on basic forms, deleting, substituting, combining, or reordering a syntagm or its elements. So *The car was wrecked* is transformed from (*someone or something*) *wrecked the car*, with the actor (someone or something) deleted and the elements of the syntagm reordered in the passive. In transformational theory it is assumed that transformations are always innocent (that is, they do not alter the meaning of the basic form) and can always be reversed. In actual discourse this is, sadly, not always the case. Transformations serve two functions, economy and distortion, often so inextricably mixed that even the speaker cannot separate them. Transformations and modal classifications perform opposed functions. Modal classifications are a service, provided by the speaker for the hearer. Transformations are more like permissible tamperings.

Both Whorf and Chomsky use the metaphor 'deep' to describe a level of organization below the surface of a language. It is an extremely useful metaphor for representing the total structure of an utterance. Below the surface of an utterance, in this view, are successive layers of structure, variously transformed or classified. A hearer or reader can attempt to recover these until the underlying set of basic forms is reached. Full decoding, then, is a journey into these depths, following in reverse the hypothesized genesis of the utterance: a description of the underlying forms, and a precise history of what has happened to them.

SPOKEN AND WRITTEN LANGUAGE

The Swiss linguist, Ferdinand de Saussure, often regarded as the father of modern linguistics, envisaged linguistics as part of a larger discipline, which he christened semiology, 'the life of signs in society'. In this view language is the most important social system of signs and well worthy of serious study in its own right, but ultimately to be explained by a more subsuming theory. Most linguists would agree that spoken language is primary, but the methodology of their discipline forces them to ignore all the specific resources of spoken communication. Linguistic science has developed precise ways of translating aspects of the system of sound signals into visual forms, which are then studied in that form. The precision is a gesture towards the oral form, which is then treated as a visual, written one. The distinctive resources of spoken communication which are not transcribed are eliminated from linguistic theory. So, in so far as spoken communication has resources which do not appear in written representations of it, it will seem impoverished compared with purely visual communication, expressed in writing. Quite unconsciously, a community which is defined by its mastery of the written medium disvalues the resources of oral and gestural language, and hence the culture of its users.

Some of these resources, like gestures, expressions, posture, etc., are beginning to be studied now, under the name 'paralinguistics'. These all greatly enrich and complicate the system of modality. Perhaps the most important feature of spoken language is intonation. Linguists working with languages like Chinese, Vietnamese, and some West African languages, where differences in pitch have decisive effects on the meanings of words and syntax, cannot ignore this dimension. Whorf also was aware of the syntactic functions performed by intonation; but of contemporary linguists, only Halliday has developed this insight in relation to English in any systematic way. Yet intonation patterns provide a rich source of systematic expressive devices for English. The voice of a speaker can turn statements into questions or commands, invert the meaning of any part or the whole, and join clauses in a variety of subtle relations. The written form of the language has to develop a variety of devices simply to be equal to the resources of the spoken language. The description of the syntax of a language must accordingly be able to record this large and important component of the grammar. Otherwise, the oral dimension of a culture will be undervalued simply because of the inadequacy of the linguistics. The gap between the text and the performance of a play illustrates vividly how much linguistic knowledge is involved here. The competence of the actor or director covers the large lacuna in most contemporary linguistic theories.

The syntactic resources of intonation in English consist of variations in pitch. Alterations of pitch are subtle and various. In combination they produce a number of significant intonation patterns, defining semantic fields with a precision that goes beyond what can be done in written forms. The stream of sound that passes between speaker and hearer is organized by the voice into fields, themselves ordered into units of focus and field, the basic form of all units of perception. The focus of a field is indicated by highly prominent pitch movement, its boundary by the end of a pitch-contour. The pitch-contour gives a precise indication of the shape of a field: rising pitch pointing forwards, falling pitch pointing backwards. So a falling pitch at the end of a unit indicates a closed field, a rising pitch an open one. If a speaker finishes on a rising note, this is a sign of an uncompleted field, usually a question, offering the hearer an open field to complete. A firmly closed field usually indicates certainty, reinforcing or counteracting other overt indications of modality, allowing a kind of counterpoint, or contradictory modality, in which, however, the intonation pattern usually is primary.

.By these means a speaker can indicate complex relationships between fields, building up larger compound fields. Using just a minimal notation of accents to indicate relative prominence and direction of pitch (′, ″, or ‴ for rising pitch and ‵, ‶, or ‷ for falling pitch), we can show some of the larger distinctions the voice can make. Take the sentence *He couldn't sleep, although he was tired.* The neutral reading of this would be

He cóuldn't sléep, althòugh he was tirèd.

This is a symmetrical paratactic ordering, with the two clauses leaning against each other. It could also be delivered as

He cóuldn't sléep, although he was tirèd.

Here the fields have floated further apart, so that the concessive clause, *although he was tired,* comes as an afterthought, almost fully independent. Or this whole sentence could be made partially dependent on an earlier utterance, by a contrastive reading:

He cóuldn't sléep, although he wäs tired.

This contradicts an earlier statement to the effect that he wasn't tired. That statement may never have been made, of course: in the state of covert war that is normal conversation, the speaker may be putting words into the hearer's mouth, pre-empting moves. A final pattern that is possible for this sentence would be

He couldn't sléep, although he was tirèd.

Here a single word is detached from the field of the sentence, becoming a self-contained unit, an embedded field or fragment of a field. This often has the effect of giving it a different modality, perhaps implying, for instance, that I call him 'tired' but really we both know that he was drunk.

Since intonation patterns are part of the grammar of the language, there are also ungrammatical patterns. For instance,

He couldn't sleep, although he was tired

could be produced by the voice but would be a meaningless ordering of the fields. Conversely, a staccato sequence of pitch movements indicates an ungrammatical or meaningless utterance, one which has broken down into its atomic fields, e.g.:

was sleep couldn't tired although.

The spoken language is commonly felt to be more vivid and direct, partly because information is ordered in gestalten or patterns whose form is natural to the human perceptual mechanisms, even if this codes a visual percept which might have been ordered otherwise. Spoken forms tend to be easier to remember. This can be a weakness as well as a strength for oral modes of transmitting a culture. A form can remain, encoding a pattern of relationships, while the content has changed utterly. So the wisdom transmitted by this mode can be contradictory without this seeming unacceptable. For instance, the proverb *The exception proves the rule* still has currency, although a semantic shift in 'proves' from 'tests' to 'proves (it is right)' has inverted the original meaning. Another quality of spoken discourse is its necessary tolerance of internal contradictions. Sentences are embedded in discourse, each sentence being a stage in a dialectic, implying a context characterized by antagonism and conflict. The advantage of written forms of language is that these contradictions can be controlled to a greater degree. Within the sphere of a written discourse the writer has time and freedom to manage contradictions on his own terms. He can notice and censor out overt signs of contradiction and incoherence. He can eliminate from his official text slips of the tongue and all such signs of momentary loss of control, or accidental revelations of private meaning. The contradictions will still be there, but displaced and made less accessible. Writing gives this kind of power. The linguistics that is to be a tool for study of a culture must be able to analyse both modes of language, spoken language, where contradiction and conflict lie on the surface, and written language, where contradictions are no less potent for being less easy to see.

LINGUISTICS AND SOCIETY

We return here to the Whorfian conception of the aim of linguistics, as a heuristic instrument for the study of a culture. 'Culture' in Whorf's use of the term suggests a homogeneous entity uniting a harmonious society. Our conception of social reality includes antagonisms and conflicts within and between groups in a class society. So language should be seen more properly as the medium of consciousness for a society, its forms of consciousness externalized. Linguistics, then, is an exceptionally subtle instrument for the analysis of consciousness and its ideological bases, 'the true shapes ... of invisible and bodiless thought'. It is ultimately, therefore, a branch of psychology, as Chomsky and Whorf both thought, a form of psychology for which social fact is primary. Without immediate and direct relations to the social context, the forms and functions of language are not fully explicable. And a fuller understanding of social and psychological reality is the real goal of linguistics as one of the social sciences concerned with the study of man. Such a linguistics has much to contribute to its sister disciplines, and much to learn.

What follows, then, is necessarily both an exposition of a linguistic theory and a partial account of a culture. The comparative approach has served linguistics well in the past, showing Whorf, among others, how arbitrary his own language and cultural assumptions were, distancing him from them and enabling him to see them with fresh eyes. In this book, however, we will stay with English, so that we can establish the nexus between language and culture, taking examples from the seventeenth century to the present. With the exception of a few illustrative sentences, we use samples of actual language which have been used by a writer or speaker in a context that we can establish independently. This can serve us as a basis for talking about what the language is doing, and how a linguistic analysis bears on an understanding of social and psychological processes.

We have tried to keep formalism and technical terms to a minimum, since this book is written for everyone who is interested in language, society, and mind, not just for linguists. The aim of our linguistics is to be heuristic. To use Whorf's words, linguistics should 'be an instrument of discovery, clarification and insight', to make language itself speak. And as language belongs to the community, heuristic linguistics should be available to all.

2

TRANSFORMATIONS AND TRUTH

TRANSFORMATIONS AND REALITY

Ideology involves a systematically organized presentation of reality. How then can ideology be defined without a prior description of the truth? All such descriptions involve language, and presenting anything in or through language involves selection. Newspaper reports are very good examples: a reporter may witness an event and then be faced with the choice of calling it a *demonstration* (or a *demo*), a *riot*, a *street battle*, *war on the streets*, a *confrontation*, or so on. As he writes his report in whole sentences he needs to make the further selections of verbs (representing the actions) and other attendant circumstances (other people involved, effect of the actions, place where it happened). So the reporter might choose *demonstrators confront police* or *police confront demonstrators*; *rioters attack police* or *police attack rioters*; *police disperse rioters* or *riot disperses*. As readers of newspapers we know the forms, and we know the choices. We also know which papers tend to make which choices, and generally we act on our knowledge by buying one paper rather than another, in most cases the paper that challenges our own assumptions least of all. These initial selections are crucial, for they set the limits within which any ensuing debate or thinking or reworking of 'reality' takes place. We will discuss this process of classification in much more detail in chapters 4, 5, and 6. For the moment we wish to focus on the processes of interpretation, reorganization, reworking, which we can and do perform on the 'reality' presented to us through a given linguistic form.

Let us assume a homely situation, familiar to some, if only at second hand. Imagine a situation where some job was to be done by someone, and someone else asks whether it has been done: it might be the emptying of the garbage can. The wife might ask *Has the garbage been emptied?* to which she gets the enraged response *You know bloody well I've been out all day, how could I have emptied the garbage can?* (or some version of this). We can ask: Why did the husband get angry? and how did he know that his wife had been aiming this at him? After all, he had not been mentioned. The answers lie in the fact that the wife had chosen to present reality in one way, but then 'transformed' that version of reality into one which differed from the original version. The original form was one in which the husband appeared as the person who was supposed to do the emptying: *Have you emptied the garbage?* In the 'transformed' version *you* had disappeared; it has been deleted by the wife, using the linguistic process of turning an active sentence into a passive one. We can show this in a slightly formal way in two stages, as follows:

   i. Have you emptied the garbage? ⇒ Has the garbage been emptied by you?

(where the double arrow means 'has been transformed into'); then by deleting the reference to *you* we get

   ii. Has the garbage been emptied by you? ⇒ Has the garbage been emptied?

In the first stage the order of *you* and *garbage* has been reversed, changing the theme of the sentence ('what the sentence is about') from *you* to *garbage*. The second process deletes reference to the actor of the action, *you*. If we put ourselves in the position of the husband trying to understand the wife's utterance, we see that he has to go through this process in reverse. If we reconstruct his process of interpretation, it might go something like: this question is about the garbage being emptied, though it doesn't say by whom. Who does she mean should have emptied the garbage – oh, me! This sentence is really about me emptying the garbage (or actually about me not emptying the garbage). Why didn't she come straight out and say so! This constant sly nagging really gets my goat: I'll tell her!

The wife, of course, might have seen things differently: I want him to empty the garbage, but I can't order him to do it, so I must do it indirectly, and if I mention him directly he'll fly off the handle, so I'll ask generally about the garbage without mentioning him, he'll get the message, and he can't get back at me.

The wife is partly correct, for had she not deleted reference to *you*, or turned the active into the passive, that is, had she said *Have you emptied the garbage?*, then the husband's strategy might well have been to pick on the theme of the sentence, *you*, and make that the focus of the clash:

16

why has it got to be me? Why can't you empty the . . . garbage? So the wife's transformations are well motivated. It is clear that her initial selections *did* set the ground on which the confrontation took place, did limit the scope of the interaction. It is equally clear that her transformation of the linguistic form served very specific and, as she felt, very necessary purposes.

In this chapter we look in close detail at some of the transformations which occur in various kinds of interaction, and speculate about the relation between linguistic processes and their ideological motivations. Like hearers and readers we start from the forms that are there, which, following linguistic terminology, we call surface structures. We attempt to recover the forms which were the starting point of the utterance. Again following linguistic terminology we call these the underlying structures. As in every speculative act, we may come up with the correct answer or we may not; and we assume that this is the situation we are all in as language users. In this approach we differ from most linguists, who assume that the underlying structures can always be clearly recovered. When we reach the underlying form we know that it is a hypothetical form. We also know that it is not the truth, for at that stage we have only reached that form in which the speaker or writer chose to present reality. Short of having been there ourselves and witnessed the 'same' event, we can get no nearer the truth than this.

As our first example for an extended analysis of transformations we have chosen an editorial from the *Guardian* of 20 December 1973. Here the writer has a more or less clear ideology, which provides the terms and structures in which he describes the situation to himself. An editorial is the place where the processes of selection and assimilation, of rewriting and transformation are most dense. It is here that the paper's ideology is clarified and re-established, reasserted in relation to troublesome events. It is also the place where the paper speaks most directly to its readership, presenting its perception of 'reality' in the form which it regards as most suitable for its readership. Ideologically, and therefore linguistically, we would expect editorials to be complex and revealing. Here is the text: its subject is the miners' overtime ban of the winter of 1972–73, in response to which the government led by Mr Heath introduced a three-day working week for industry.

A Necessary Measure
The three-day week for industry is extremely hurtful. A sudden blackout for a whole city the size of Leicester or Bradford is worse. It can kill people. Mr. Len Murray, speaking yesterday

for the TUC, said that the three-day week for industry is 'no solution'. He also called it 'a national lockout' and 'nonsense'. Truly it is no solution. That can come only through negotiations with the miners, rail drivers and power-engineers. But the three-day week is an inevitable precaution while coal stocks at the power stations are running down. The Government has been much criticized for not introducing petrol rationing sooner. Until the three-day week was announced last Thursday, Ministers were accused by the Opposition of being complacent and too slow to act. If the Government were to allow a situation in which power supplies to whole areas had to be cut off with minimum warning, it would be criminally irresponsible.

The figures given by the Prime Minister may or may not be the whole truth. He says that coal accounts for 70 per cent of electricity generation and oil for only 20 per cent. Deliveries of coal to power stations over the past four weeks have averaged less than two-thirds of what they were expecting. CEGB stocks stood at 18 million tons in October. They are now running down at the rate of about one million tons a week – three times the normal rundown. The three-day week and other electricity savings are expected to reduce coal consumption by about 400,000 tons a week. Painful though the savings must be, especially in January, they are common prudence, The Government knows that in early 1972 it was caught out by picketing of power stations which curtailed coal deliveries. The rail dispute is having a similar effect. The Government must take precautions now. It cannot wait to see what happens.

If normal working by rail drivers and engineers were to be resumed, the situation would be less difficult. But full working in industry – particularly in coal using industries such as steel-making – will be impossible until the miners lift their overtime ban. It should not be forgotten that, by mutual agreement, essential maintenance in the pits is done on overtime. All weekend maintenance is technically on overtime. The ban therefore at once cuts production in ordinary hours. To say 'pay the miners' is too simple, as was argued here yesterday. Their position ought to be improved, but that cannot be achieved at one step or without agreed restraint by other claimants. These are matters for negotiation.

This editorial presents a complex judgment on a complex process. In understanding any process, causality is of crucial importance. If the causal steps are clearly indicated – those who started an action are specified, the effects are shown, and those affected are mentioned – then our judgments can be made on reasonably secure grounds (unless we have been told outright lies, but no linguistic analysis can guard against that anyway). The two actional models mentioned in chapter 1 present distinct versions of causality. In the *transactive* model there is an *actor*, the *verbal process*, and an *affected* entity. Thus the source of the process (physical or other) is indicated in the *actor*, who is presented as the causer of the process; and the entity which is *affected* by the process is equally indicated, *actor* and *affected* being linked by the *verbal process*. In the example we discussed above the labels would apply in this way:

Have	you	emptied	the garbage?
	actor	*process*	*affected*

This is a rudimentary version of mechanical causation. The *non-transactive* model on the other hand presents only one entity directly involved in the process: it is not, typically, distinguished as either actor or affected. Here is a sentence from the editorial: *It [the Government] cannot wait to see what happens.* It contains three clauses (much contracted on the surface) joined in a structure: *It waits/it sees/what [i.e. something] happens.* Taking the last of these,

Something happens

it is clear that *something* is not an actor, it does not initiate or cause the process *happens*. Nor is it really affected; *something* is simply involved in the process, and it is not clear in what precise way. And the other two clauses, *it waits* and *it sees* (*it* being the Government) really are the same: there is no sense of the Government being actor in *it waits*, nor any clear sense of it being affected. In *it sees* it may be regarded as affected in a slightly stronger sense, but again it is not actor. The version of causation expressed in the non-transactive model is implicit or inherent causation, and spontaneous, sometimes self-caused action.

The editorial is about actions, and the absence of actions. So we might expect the predominant model to be the transactive. If the writer is concerned with clearly establishing causes and causal relations, then the transactive is the best model for the job. However, when we look at the language of the editorial, we find that there are just five occurrences of this model: *It can kill people*; *The three-day week . . . [is] expected to reduce coal consumption*; *picketing . . . curtailed coal deliveries*; *the miners lift their overtime ban*; *the ban . . . cuts production.* Closer inspection reveals that other forms that look like these are not transactives; many are verbal processes – *criticizing, announcing, accusing.* If a systematic theory, an ideology, is guiding the use of language here, then we would expect systematic use of linguistic forms to be evident. And some of these systematic uses are very quickly apparent. All the transactives concern events and actions by, or seen as the responsibility of, the miners. So the miners or circumstances brought about by them are shown here as the only potent actors: the Government is presented in the syntax as unable to act. A closer look at the actors reveals another fact: all, with the exception of *the miners,* are either abstract nouns – *the three-day week, a sudden blackout, the ban* – or the results of actions (that is, actions turned into objects, verbal processes turned into nouns), or both – *the ban, picketing, a blackout.* Following linguistic terminology, we call the latter nominalizations. These are sentences, or parts of sentences, descriptions of actions and the participants involved in them, turned into nouns, or nominals.

Two kinds of exclusion operate here. First, the predominant syntactic form is not the transactive, so that the model which is about actions with causes and effects is very much in the minority. Second, certain categories of actor are excluded from those transactives which do appear. The Government does not appear, on the surface, as an actor, so that only one party in the dispute seemingly has the power to act. All the actors which do appear on the surface are abstract entities, with one exception, *the miners.* Taken together, these facts do point to a system, an ideology and its expression in language. The miners presumably would have seen things somewhat differently. They might have seen their claim for higher wages very much in terms of causes and effects, and for them presumably the Government was in a position to act – that was their demand. From their point of view we would have expected a much more transactive syntax, with the Government appearing in the role of actor. As far as the nature of the actions and actors is concerned, again the miners might have seen some of the processes in more concrete terms, so that there would have been less use of abstract nouns as actors. (This hypothesis could be tested by performing the same type of analysis on the relevant texts from the journal of the miners' union.)

The fact that abstract entities appear as actors (abstract nouns in the language representing abstract entities) is a feature of the metaphysics and science of English, which any theory of language will have to deal with. We shall discuss the whole question of the presentation of reality in language in chapter 3, when we deal at length with the linguistic models which English has. Here we are particularly concerned to explain two things: first, how some abstract nouns come into existence, come into the language, and second, how speakers use and interpret them. We start by looking at a noun which may or may not be in a dictionary of the English language, that is, one whose status as a stable word is somewhat doubtful. Here it is in the sentence in which it occurs in the text:

Picketing . . . curtailed coal deliveries.

If we asked speakers of English what the meaning of *picketing* was, they would probably explain it by describing the kinds of things involved: strikers, the action, a factory, or, in this case, a coal-depot. The noun is a contraction of a significant kind. The single word necessarily implies a particular kind of actor and a particular object of action. We might represent the process in this way:

strikers picket a factory ⇒ picketing

Because we can interpret the nominal as being 'derived from' the full sentence, the deletion of actor and affected is not a complete elimination. However, there are two major effects associated with that transformation, which amount to a quite radical changing of the original form. First, although we know that there was an actor and an affected, the specific identities of both have been lost. We can guess about their identity, but we can never be certain. Second, in the resulting surface form the only thing that meets us is the verbal version of the action which was performed, and in this way our attention is directed to what is present and directed away from what is no longer there. So the focus of the expression has been altered by the speaker, our vision has been channelled and narrowed. A last effect, which is perhaps somewhat more subtle, lies in the change in nature of the concept from *verb* to *noun*, and all the attendant changes in meaning which that change entails. Verbs in English tend to be about actions or processes, and they have to be placed in time. Nouns in English tend to be about objects, abstract notions, and concepts. This is only a tendency, but it is sufficient to direct our first interpretation.

An activity which was initiated and performed by the miners, in a specific place and time, now seems to have autonomous existence, and can appear as the actor in a new construction,

Picketing curtailed coal deliveries

The affected entity in that sentence is yet another nominalization:

again we would not meet the noun *coal deliveries* in a dictionary of English. Its source seems to be a sentence of the form

Someone [rail drivers] delivers coal.

In this nominalization only the actor has been deleted, and the verbal process and the affected participant have been 'taken into' the noun. This nominal is more informative than *picketing*. The existence of the two types of nominalization indicates that the writer of the editorial has choice in this matter. In the one case he is interested in a general activity that unionists at times indulge in (*picketing*), in the other he wishes to be more precise, and so he brings more into the nominalization.

At any rate, the apparently simple sentence

Picketing curtailed coal deliveries

has, underlying it, a considerable complexity, a varied history of transformations. As readers of this editorial we should have to be alert and willing to engage in mental exercise to get beyond the seductive simplicity of the final form, with just three entities, and seemingly precise relations, where everything seems to be there on the surface. If we add to the real complexity of the sentence the fact that the verb *curtail* is a comparative, meaning roughly *provide not as much X as before*, we can see that few commuters on the 8.05 from Brighton would have the energy to perform the mental gymnastics required. Especially as they would have to perform them not once, but just about a dozen times on every full line of newsprint that they scan. After all, the crossword is there for mental exercise.

Having done the analysis, we could have this possible full version of the utterance: [Miners] *picket* [mines and coal-depots so that rail drivers do not] *deliver as much coal as before* [the start of the dispute to power stations] (where brackets indicate what has been deleted and italics indicate things present in the surface). This paraphrase contains so much more material than the concise actual surface form that readers would be forced to reflect on too many of the variables in the dispute. Reducing the complexity of an argument and limiting the terms which it can contain is a drastic intervention. Showing less means someone else seeing less. And seeing less means thinking less.

We can now readily fit two of the other nominalizations into this account: *It* [a blackout] *can kill people; The three-day week . . . [will] reduce coal consumption*. The former contains a noun derived from a sentence:

Something/someone blacks out a city ⇒ a blackout

Blackout is a word which we would expect to find in a dictionary. This points to one process which language uses to construct new words. If the contexts and the needs for a particular nominalization occur frequently enough, the nominalization will be taken into the vocabulary as a new and stable noun. *Picketing* is probably well on the way to that status, *coal deliveries* less so. In the next example, *coal consumption* is probably close to *coal deliveries* in its status as a stable noun. The *three-day week* has passed out of its position as a candidate for word status with the passing of that particular political dispute. It has a derivation which differs from the other two, and readers who are not familiar with that event in British history will have no way of recovering the underlying structure and the deletions. In the first place it is an abbreviation for *the three-day working week*; and this presumably derives from

Someone works for three days (out of the normal five).

The important point at this stage is that the process of nominalization is common to the examples discussed so far, and its functions are similar in all cases. In discussing the next two examples, *the miners lift their overtime ban*, and *the ban cuts production*, we begin to deal with words whose status as stable nouns is unquestionable. *Ban* and *production* will be found in any dictionary of English. Yet it is not difficult to see the affinities which these two words have with the ones we have discussed so far. Both are descriptions of actions which involve participants, both in fact are descriptions of transactive actions:

someone	bans	something	⇒ ban
someone	produces	something	⇒ production

In the case of *production* the *-ion* ending is an outward sign of its derivation, but *ban* has no such marking. There seems therefore a choice for a hearer as to how he or she might interpret these two words. First, we might assume that the speaker had in fact started from the full sentence form (as before), or at least was aware of the expanded form at some earlier stage in the production of the utterance. In this case it would be quite proper to regard these as nominalizations, though of a kind which have become so conventional as to be clichés. Second, we might assume that speakers use these words, and hearers understand them, as though they were like *apple* or *bench*, but referring to things which happen to be abstract, not concrete physical things. For this kind of speaker or hearer, the linguistic form creates a world of thinglike abstract beings or objects, which are capable of acting or being acted on. Here language determines perception in two ways, by creating an alternative world which can only be 'seen' in language and by imposing this alternative world, with its apparent solid reality, on the material world, so that we no longer see or believe in the world of physical events. This is perhaps the most powerful effect that stable words have on us.

There is a third possibility, which is probably very common in practice. Speakers or hearers may produce or interpret such phrases sometimes one way, and sometimes the other. One condition that is likely to affect this is the importance of the utterance, and the time spent producing or interpreting it. We choose our words carefully when something is at stake, and we need time for this. Clearly, for the writer of a *Guardian* editorial the composition of a leading article is a matter of importance. For the commuter it is something to be scanned quickly. Writers tend to create such shadowy worlds of abstract entities, and readers to live in them. Another condition that affects which kind of interpretation prevails is familiarity with the transformations involved. Obviously, someone who does not know the transformation will not be able to reverse it, to arrive at the underlying structure. Such transformational facility may be distributed unevenly, along class lines. That means that different groups within the one general language community will habitually 'read' the same words in radically different ways.

There is another quality that has been virtually removed by transformations from the surface of the language: negativity. We noted that *curtail* has an inherent negative. So does *ban*; its meaning might be paraphrased as *not do (something)*. When the miners decide to ban overtime, they decide not to work more than their 'normal' hours. But the form of the word does not show any negative, so that it seems that the negative has been completely absorbed into the new unit. All the other verbs in the sentences that we have discussed so far are like this: *kill* → *make not alive; reduce* → *not do as much as before; lift* (in the sense here used) → *no longer impose; cut* → *not* (produce) *as much*; and of course *curtail*. We may ask, as we did with the nouns, whether speakers and hearers are aware of the internal structure of these words, that is, whether they have an internal structure like that on the right of the arrow as their starting point, which is transformed into the single unit, or whether they have not. The effect of the single word which incorporates the negative invisibly so to speak (compare words like

24

*dis*miss, *un*do, *de*bunk, which have overt marks of the negative) is to present the not-doing – the refraining from action or the negation of it – as though it were a positive action.

If we wish to ask why these transformations have been used, the essential starting point is simply to describe the processes that have taken place, as we have done. To summarize, in these processes a series of complex actions are collapsed into surface forms which make them seem extremely simple, and refraining from action is portrayed as though it was taking positive action. We can be specific about the processes and about the effect, so that we are on firmer ground in hypothesizing about motives and functions in particular uses of these forms. The miners' withdrawal of their labour is presented as the only direct unqualified action in the editorial. Responsibility rests firmly on their shoulders. That is offered as the only uncomplicated fact in an otherwise complex situation. Note, however, that it is the syntactic form only which makes this claim. The writer is well aware of this, as we can see from the opening sentences:

1. The three-day week for industry is extremely hurtful.
3. It [a sudden blackout] can kill people.

There is a contrast between the relative damage resulting from the two actions, the government-imposed three-day week and the union-caused blackout. Though strictly and syntactically the unions do not appear as actors in relation to *kill*, we know that blackouts do not just happen but are caused. We are forced to search for the real causer of *kill*, the real antecedent of *it*. And here the deletion of actors in the nominalization *blackout* is useful, because while we can substitute *miners* the writer of the editorial is protected from involvement by the transformations he has applied. His position is not all that unlike the wife's strategy in the face of the husband's assumed anger.

Processes other than transactives concerned with physical processes occur in the editorial. We have mentioned verbs of saying, thinking, etc.: *Mr. Len Murray, speaking yesterday*; *He called it . . .* ; *The Government has been much criticized*; *the three-day week was announced*. Most of these are in the passive form. Instead of *Someone criticized the Government*, we have *The Government has been criticized*. The number of passives in the editorial is astonishingly high, and the majority of them are agentless passives (this is true for many texts in English). There is one common feature of nominalizations and agentless passives, namely the deletion of the actor. As with nominalizations, we realize in most cases that the actor has been deleted, but also as with nominalizations we cannot always be

Linguistic changes	Effects
1. *The passive transformation*	
(a) It inverts the order of *actor* and *affected*, e.g.:	The theme of the sentence (what it is about) changes from actor to affected.
The opposition accused the government.	
The government was accused by the opposition.	
(b) The *actor* is no longer directly attached to the verb, but instead is linked by a preposition, *by*.	The link between actor and process is weakened, that is, the causal connection is syntactically looser.
(c) The verb *to be* is introduced, and the main verb changed from an actual process to a finished process.	The process, because it is completed, becomes more like an adjective, a state.
(d) The *actor* may be deleted: *The government was accused by the opposition. The government was accused* ——	The cause of the process is deleted, and it may be difficult or impossible to recover.
(e) The surface structure now has a strong affinity with a *noun-'is'-adjective* construction. That is, from *transactive* it has changed to the surface form of *attributive*.	Causality is no longer the main concern, but instead attribution or classification is. The change from verbal process to quality or state is complete.
2. *The nominalization transformation*	
(a) It deletes one or more of the participants in the whole model: *Workers picket a factory.* ↓ —— *picketing* —— ↓ *Someone delivers coal.* *coal deliveries* ——	Interest shifts from the participants and causers of the process to the process (made nominal), and in some cases to the affected participant. Even where the deletion is noted, the specific identity of the participant may be irrecoverable.
(b) A new noun is formed.	The change from *verb* to *noun* entails a range of meanings: process → state; activity → object; specific → general; concrete → abstract.

Linguistic changes	Effects
(c) Nominalizations are not marked for tense, so they are outside indications of time or modality (see chapter 5).	Speakers can avoid some of the classificatory acts – indicating when, how likely, etc., which are obligatory with verbs.
(d) Complex relations are collapsed into single entities.	Simplicity can be asserted where in reality complexity is the case.
(e) The new nominals can function as participants in new constructions: *Picketing* curtailed *coal production*	This further increases the opacity of the nominals; once they function as actors, affected etc., we are less likely to attempt to interpret. Also, simple causes can be posited where complex causes are the case.
(f) The new nominals may become stable entities, new nouns in the dictionary.	The perceptual and cognitive inventory of the language and therefore of the language user has been altered.

3. *Negative incorporation*

(a) The negative particle is 'taken into' the form of the word, which is (becomes) a single unit.	The word is perceived as a single unit; the negation of an action is seen as the taking of positive action.
(b) The word can appear in active-passive transformations: *The miners ban overtime. Overtime is banned by the miners.* (Note that words with overt negation cannot appear in actives: *He was unknown* ⇐ *They unknew him.*)	As above; but note the restriction on verbs with overtly expressed negation. This shows that the refraining from action, when openly expressed, cannot appear as a positive action; though it can appear as an *attribute (in the passive form) of the* affected noun.

certain of the specific identity of the deleted actor. So in the sentence *It should not be forgotten . . .* we know well enough that this is an injunction to some psychological actor not to forget: but who is he or she? The reader of the *Guardian*? The Government? The leader writer? The miners? All of them? Presumably it makes some difference. If one is negotiating pay claims these are things to be very specific about. No doubt different readers supply the actor of their choice. In some passives the deleted actor seems very easily recoverable: *essential maintenance in the pits is done on overtime.* Here the deleted agents are obviously those people who do essential maintenance. But the effect of the deletion is to take these people entirely for granted and to eliminate them from the printed text. This is not a trivial omission, since one of the miners' main grievances was the fact that actual men have to do this work, going down the mines in unpleasant conditions, during weekends and outside normal hours. The 'economy' of not mentioning these agents has the further effect of suppressing their existence. It takes a stand on the issue being described. The construction *essential maintenance* allows us to point to another significant function of nominalizations – it provides a noun, to which a judgmental adjective can be attached. In the underlying form *essential* would have to be attached to a specific word, *essential machinery*, *essential safety checks*, or else the writer would have to reveal who judges this to be essential – *the Coal Board regards it as essential that* . . . But in this surface form the judge may remain anonymous, and a subjective assessment is presented as an integral part of the objective content. The affinities between this process and those so far discussed are not too difficult to see.

It is time to summarize some of the changes which are involved in the passive transformation (including one or two which we have not, so far, discussed) and point to the effects of these linguistic processes. Directly following this we summarize the processes involved in the other transformations and their effects.

All the processes mentioned here work to obscure the originally chosen models; deletion, simplification, collapsing of forms into single units, all act to alter the way in which a reader meets the material and tend to structure his interpretations in specific ways. He is continually coerced into taking the surface form as the real form; and that surface is a radically transformed version of the originally chosen linguistic form.

It should be stressed that what we have seen in this passage from the *Guardian* is not simply bias against the miners. There does seem to be that: but the prevailing syntactic forms are typical for leader articles in this paper. Relationals are the rule, and transformations tend to be into this preferred model. It is of the nature of this model that it allows only a limited realization of transparent causal processes. The result inevitably is mystification of these processes. There would be mystification even if the *Guardian* was crusading on behalf of the miners (or, more plausibly, arguing guardedly that their case was on the whole a strong one). The processes of classifying are carried on at a high level, with classifications weighed against each other in a complex, multifaceted judgment. This is a paper for top people. But the higher the level at which this activity is carried on, the greater is the mystification of real, physical processes, of large- or small-scale causal sequences. So a miner might not understand this judgement in all its complexity: but the reader of the *Guardian* wouldn't be helped by this editorial to understand mining, or the physical and economic context of the whole dispute.

SOME TRANSFORMATIONS OF NORMAL SCIENCE; OR, A BRIEF ESSAY IN THE SOCIOLOGY OF KNOWLEDGE

Perhaps it is not surprising to find ideological slanting in a newspaper editorial, even with so reputable and independent a paper as the *Guardian*. It's interesting, however, that the language used by scientists is also heavily transformed. To take an example that will be familiar to linguists, here is the opening of Chomsky's epoch-making *Syntactic Structures* (1957):

> Syntax is the study of the principles and processes by which sentences are constructed in particular languages. Syntactic investigation of a given language has as its goal the construction of a grammar that can be viewed as a device of some sort for producing the sentences of the language under analysis. (p. 11)

The language here is exemplarily 'scientific': neutral, objective, impersonal. It is also – a necessary price for these virtues – extremely vague about key elements in most of the processes at issue. Active transactives are the most transparent form in which to represent causal processes. In this passage there are no unmodified transactives. Only seven sentences later does Chomsky venture on his first active transactional. This is a paradox worth exploring further: an apparent contradiction between the linguistic forms of scientific objectivity and the natural form of scientific theories.

In this passage Chomsky uses three passives:

1 the principles and processes by which *sentences are constructed* in particular languages
2 syntactic investigation of *a given language*
3 *a grammar that can be viewed* as a device

In each case the actor has been deleted. In each case it is extremely difficult to recover the actor precisely, more difficult than was the case with the *Guardian*. Example (1) shows this clearly. There is a *by* form, as though these *principles and processes* are the actors. But these principles do not do the constructing. Their relationship to the process would be more precisely given by 'through' or 'in terms of', that is, the *by* phrase is more like an instrument than an actor. As it stands we might assume that (1) is derived from an underlying sentence such as

4 The principles and processes construct sentences in particular languages.

But this is a very peculiar sentence, probably so peculiar as to be ungrammatical. If we go back further in trying to interpret it we might suggest

Speakers construct sentences according to principles and processes

and

That speakers construct sentences according to principles is itself a process.

This would be prefaced by an analysis of *Syntax is the study* . . . which might be

Syntax is the name for how someone studies the principles according to which people construct sentences and the processes which result.

This may not be how others interpret the sentence. The point is that its interpretation is extremely difficult. If we regard sentence 4 as grammatical, then all human actors have been irrecoverably lost. If we try to account for human actors, we have to go to something like the extended paraphrase above, but it is difficult to see what trans-formations could change these back to the surface we have got. It ought to be impossible to conjoin *principles and processes* as subjects of *construct* (as in the active above), though they can be conjoined as objects of study.

In phrase 2, *given* derives from an underlying form X *gives* Y *to* Z. Here Y is the *language*, but who is understood to give this language to whom? Z presumably stands for the individual linguist who under-takes to investigate the language, but X, the giver, is unknown. This is an important omission in any sociology of knowledge. Who determines the subject matter for the investigation? Is it the person or group who determines the goals? *Given* here is moved into an attributive position, *a given language*, so that this question obtrudes less than it would if the fuller passive form was used: *a language that is given*. In phrase 3 there is a similar uncertainty about *can be viewed*. Who can view it like this? Others? Or the constructor of the theory? Again, substantial issues about the scope of theories and how that scope is defined, about the status of the investigator, and about objectivity, are involved.

But, as with the *Guardian* passage, nominalizations are more common, for instance,

> Syntax is *the study* of the principles and processes
> *syntactic investigation* of a given language
> *the construction* of a grammar

As often with nominalizations, the actor is deleted. In each of these cases the actor is the linguist, who studies principles, investigates language, and constructs a grammar. He is easily recoverable, though he is probably not the same linguist in each case, but a standard average linguist. Even so, the surface forms have slightly strange characteristics. In *syntax is the study* the object of an action is equated with the action itself. In the next example the action in its nominalized form 'has' a goal, strictly the goal of its actor, as we would presumably interpret it. We seem to have a rule here whereby the actor is deleted, and the nominalized action replaces him as subject of a clause which is about possession, *X has Y*. The effect is to displace the goal from the human actor onto the action itself, irrespective of who performs it. Although the utterance is interpreted as the result of a transformation, it also affects a reader through its surface form. The surface presents a world without people, where no one thinks or speaks but language is produced, where no one studies or investigates, but investigation proceeds unerringly to its goal. It may be that this language is harder to read if it is taken seriously, that is, if we attempt to relate it back to precise statements of processes in deep structure. It may well be that scientific language is not meant to be read other than superficially. Everyone who has tried to teach Chomsky to the uncommitted must know the sense of difficulty they experience. Perhaps facility in reading language of this sort comes from an agreement to read the surface as though it were an untransformed realization of the underlying structure – as we mentioned at the beginning of the chapter; and part of learning to be a scientist is precisely about this. It does involve accepting an unreal world where principles construct sentences, where investigations have goals, and sincerity might well play golf.

This phenomenon can be accounted for illuminatingly using Kuhn's (1962) influential account of how scientific theories relate to a particular community of scientists. During a period of what Kuhn calls 'normal science' scientists accept a 'paradigm', a common body of assumptions, methods, problems, and subject matter, which organizes their activities as members of the community, but remains implicit. He distinguishes periods of normal science from scientific revolutions, when radical innovations grow out of crisis, usually as the result of the achievement of one or two outstanding individuals. But revolutions are rare. Most scientific activity is 'normal science', in which a professional community is united by common assumptions, goals, and tasks, which would seem incomprehensible or trivial to the intelligent layman, who is excluded from the community by his incomprehension.

In some respects Chomsky seems to be writing the syntax of normal science. The language is opaque to laymen, setting up a barrier around the privileged knowledge of the community of specialists. The use of *given* shows exactly the vagueness to be expected of a normal scientist, who passively accepts definitions of goals and tasks from an ill-defined or unknown source, the community of scientists, or the 'paradigm'. The idea that the *investigation* can have a *goal* independent of the investigator also reflects the controlling assumptions of the paradigm in normal science. The elimination of the speaker could also be seen as a paradigm-assumption for linguistics at the time Chomsky was writing.

The interesting thing about all this is that Chomsky was not a 'normal scientist'. He was a radical innovator, and these sentences were the opening of his most innovative work. As students of the so-called Chomskyan revolution will know, in this passage the new orientation is already signalled in the second part of the second sentence:

> Syntactic investigation of a given language has as its goal the construction of a grammar that can be viewed as a device of some sort for producing the sentences of the language under analysis.

Chomsky in fact wanted to opt out of the contract implied by *given* and to take a universalist position, in terms of which he would in practice be able to work largely through an analysis of his own language. This exploits the vagueness of *given* because Chomsky can retain the same formulae, use apparently the same models for the structure of knowledge as his community, but reinterpret its key elements. Another Chomskyan departure was his notion of generative grammar. In this passage, the idea of a grammar as a 'device for producing sentences' was not at all what the normal linguist would have accepted as an account of grammars. The syntax of this is interesting in two ways. The proposition is prefaced by *can be viewed*. Here the modal *can* makes the deleted agent even more difficult to specify. The sentence is ambiguous between *the construction of a grammar that can then [if the linguist wants] be viewed as a device* (where *can = is possible*) and *the construction of a grammar whose property is that it can be viewed as a device* (where *can = is allowed*). In the first case, the viewer is not a 'normal' linguist, but would be tolerated by normal linguists, since he is carrying out a possible secondary task, reflecting on the task that normal linguists perform. In the second, the generative grammarian is also the constructor of the theory: the precise form of the goal of syntactic investigation is *his* goal. In the second interpretation, the Chomskyan revolution has already happened; in the first it is not a revolution, but a new way of looking at what linguists have always done. So the same sentence has two meanings in relation to successive paradigms. It has the form of the normal science of both stages (and it will be basically the same individuals who will subscribe to these different paradigms). The ambiguity is no doubt a consequence of Chomsky's uncertain position. He is appealing to his community for a hearing at least, while undermining the foundations of their paradigm. The mystification inherent in the passive transformation allows him to sustain this ambiguous role. He can exploit the mystification his community is habituated to for his own purposes; though this does not mean that he need be aware of what he is doing, a clear-sighted manipulator of his naive 'normal' colleagues. His use of the forms of language of his community (which exclude the 'intelligent layman' or any other source of popular support) shows his tacit acceptance of that community as sole arbitrator.

The phrase that most clearly contains Chomsky's new conception of the goals of grammar is *a device of some sort for producing the sentences of the language under analysis*. This is, significantly, close to a surface transactional. However, it too contains a crucial uncertainty. The form 'an X for —ing Y' has two alternative deep structures. For example, *a power saw for cutting wood* may be derived from either (a) *a power saw with which men cut wood* or (b) *a power saw which cuts wood*. Similarly, *a device for producing sentences* can derive from either (a) *a device by means of which speakers produce sentences* or (b) *a device which produces sentences*. The second seems to envisage a machine-grammar which produces sentences. In the first, the conception of the task unequivocally includes speakers. This is the same uncertainty as we noted in the opening *principles and processes*. The difference between the two structures is of the utmost importance, for this is a central proposition of the new paradigm; and a difference as large as this might be held to constitute a difference in paradigms. The transformation allows Chomsky to proceed without resolving his uncertainty, and without acknowledging it. The strategy is supported by non-transformational means too. We shall look at these later: for instance, the modal verb *can* and the vague *of some sort*, which add no cognitive content to the phrase but have a modal force, diffusing a convenient imprecision over the whole phrase. But transformations are the main means whereby Chomsky can render his meanings and uncertainties opaque to the normal linguist and perhaps even to the revolutionary linguist himself. Under this cover he can reshape his paradigm.

FUNCTIONS OF TRANSFORMATIONS

We can now present some observations arising out of these analyses in a more systematic and general form. Our use of the concept of transformation differs, in part, significantly and controversially from general transformational theory. Our departure from the generally accepted theory is shown in italics.

1 The interpretation of utterances entails reconstructing their deriva-tion. *The interpretation which a hearer makes may or may not coincide with the underlying structure which the speaker had in mind.*
2 Of the linguistic operations that occur in the derivation of an utterance, it is useful to distinguish a special set which char-acteristically do not add new material or new elements to the deep structure. We have been calling these operations 'transformations', taking over the term from Chomsky. Transformations in this sense delete, join, or reorder elements which are present in underlying structures.
3 *In our use, transformations may transform one model into the form of another, or collapse models into single syntactic elements.*
4 *The relation between transformed structures and their pre-transformed form is an equivocal one. The transformed structure differs in significant ways from the underlying structure* (though it may not be interpreted by a hearer as different), *yet it will be interpreted in part or whole as 'meaning' the same.* So the relationship is one of simultaneous identity and *disjunction.* Ideally the identity is prominent, and the underlying pre-transformed structure directly recoverable, as is the case with the expanded passive form. *But typically the surface form has a partly autonomous significance, and the full interpretation of transformed utterances is*

34

normally an unstable, perhaps idiosyncratic, resolution of the different levels of interpretation. That is, interpretation probably involves a kind of double vision, whereby the underlying structures are both seen and not seen, or 'seen' and not heard.

5 *Transformations always involve suppression and/or distortion,* but they are also normally reversible. *The standard that acts as the measure of what has been suppressed or distorted is given by the underlying structures uncovered by reversing transformations.* The 'relevant truth' which acts as a standard then is given by full propositions *in the form of basic models.*

6 *The typical function of transformations is distortion and mystification, through the characteristic disjunction between surface form and implicit meanings. Since it is usually a help in reversing transformations to know the content independently, transformations can act as a code, fully interpretable only by initiates safeguarding their privileged knowledge. But transformations can also create the illusion of such knowledge for both hearer and speaker, masking contradictions or confusions, and imposing an unexamined consensus.*

SOURCES AND CONTEXT

Our discussion draws substantially on general linguistic theory but departs from it in some fundamental ways. We wish to give a brief indication of reference points in the field with some context supplied. Our main concern here is to provide non-linguist readers with a minimal though helpful set of references which they might use both to place our theory in relation to current work and to read into the field at certain points. Some of the references we give are readily available. Others will require the reader to refer to a reasonably good linguistics library.

Our use of transformations derives initially from Chomsky. The important works here are *Syntactic Structures* (1957) and *Aspects of the Theory of Syntax* (1965). Chomsky wavered between adopting a 'realist' position on syntax (which assumes that linguistic processes and forms correspond to some psychological reality) and a non-realist position (that is, one which assumes that the constructs of a theory of language are merely formal and have no 'real' connection with the mind, but serve only to allow us to describe linguistic forms satisfactorily). We take a strongly realist position and regard all transformational analyses as hypothetical reconstructions of psychologically real processes. For a discussion of psycholinguistic experiments which took a similar line see Judith Greene's *Psycholinguistics* (1972). A more up-to-date and advanced book is Fodor, Bever and Garrett (1974). In a recent paper,

'Towards a realistic model of transformational grammar', Joan Bresnan (1977) argues that, while Chomsky's 1965 theory could not stand up to the demands of a realist interpretation, the current theory used by him and his co-workers, the lexicalist–interpretative theory, is adequate to such an interpretation. Our own position is somewhat more fully argued in Hodge and Kress (1974). Chomsky took the notion of transformations over from his teacher Zellig Harris. The latter had seen these as relations between sentences in actual disourse, so that, if the sentence *The police shot 200 Africans* occurred in one part of a text, it was transformationally related to *the shooting of the Africans* in the same text at another place. We accept Harris's use, which is compatible with the view that transformations are psychologically real. The background to the development of this key linguistic term is given in Kress and Trew (1978).

Three particular transformations we discuss have been extensively studied. On nominalizations there are two basic positions. One assumes that phrases such as *John's beliefs* come into existence as a result of transformations from full sentential forms, which is the position we adopt. This was first argued by R.B. Lees (1960). The other assumes that they are not derived in this way. A fairly full discussion of this issue can be found in Chomsky's 'Remarks on nominalization' (1970). In our discussion of verbs which contain negatives, we draw on work in semantics known as componential analysis. A ready initial reference to this can be found in J. Lyons's *New Horizons in Linguistics* (1970), in the essay by Manfred Bierwisch, 'Semantics'. This theory has been influential in a branch of transformational generative grammar known as 'generative semantics'. Some articles on this theory appear in *Readings in English Transformational Grammar* (Jacobs and Rosenbaum, 1970) (those by Lakoff, Ross, and McCawley). An easier introduction is George Lakoff's (1970) *Irregularity in Syntax*. The treatment of passives is discussed in Chomsky (1957 and 1965); for a more recent treatment see Akmajian and Heny (1975), which incidentally is a very good comprehensive introduction to recent transformational theory within the Chomskyan group. Halliday (1967/68) discusses the function of the passive in relation to the distribution of 'theme' and 'information focus' and actor and affected.

Our analysis of newspaper language in this chapter was necessarily brief and specific. A more extended discussion, bringing out the relation of language and ideology, can be found in Tony Trew's 'Theory at work' (1978) and in Fowler, Hodge, Kress and Trew (1979).

As far as our use of the concept of transformation goes, we do not draw on work in transformational theory after about 1969. Chomsky's (1971) paper 'Deep structure, surface structure and semantic interpretation' marked a departure from the *Aspects* theory towards a theory known as 'interpretive semantics'. From here Chomsky and his immediate group have moved towards a more surfacelike form of the grammar, with very few transformations, and anything that looks at all semantic banned from the grammar. Two journals represent this strand of transformational work, *Linguistic Inquiry* and *Linguistic Analysis*. Interestingly, in this work the questions of functional motivations for transformations and psychological reality are taken up again (see the reference to Joan Bresnan's paper above). The 'generative semantics' strand of transformational theory has moved into areas which are of interest to our theory, in particular an increasing concern with the pragmatics of language. We refer to these at the end of the relevant chapters. However, as far as the concept of transformation itself is concerned, we make no use of the changes within this work. One development from generative semantics, 'relational grammar', has in fact abandoned the concept of transformation. We refer to this briefly at the end of chapter 3. The publications of the *Chicago Linguistics Circle* contain much of the relevant work in this area. A recently published reader in relational grammar is edited by Cole and Sadock (1977), *Syntax and Semantics, vol. 8: Grammatical Relations.*

3

LANGUAGE AND PROCESSES: MODELS FOR THINGS THAT MOVE

SIMPLE SCIENCE

It is natural to be interested in things that move. Cats and dogs and birds as well as men will tend to focus on moving objects in a visual field. Even at the lowest level this predilection represents a vital concern with 'why things happen', which at a higher level we call science – 'knowledge of the causes of things' in Lucretius' definition. A language is the repository of the 'science' of a linguistic community, a set of models that make reality seem manageable. We can see this interaction of perception and models in the simplest sentence types in any language. When we look at a moving object we see a single whole, an entity moving, the movement inseparable from the entity. Languages typically break down this perceptual unit into entity and action, nominal and verb.

The simplest syntactic form available to speakers of English for the linguistic (re-)presentation of the event is in the form 'the boy moves'. Its simplicity seemingly mirrors an equivalently simple event. The event is presented as having the two-part structure of nominal participant + physical process. This division, as we have seen, corresponds to nothing in the percept itself. Thus, in the act of linguistic presentation a crucial change has been introduced, which is facilitated by the simplicity of the syntactic form. The linguistic form constitutes a model, which strongly influences the interpretation of such percepts, since it requires that the event be analysed into these two parts before it can be communicated. Such classification becomes so automatic that it seems to inhere in the percept itself.

There are several ways of talking about the model involved in this sentence type. The model represents a two-dimensional percept in the lateral plane of the cone of vision. From this we derive the term *lateral* model to talk about the percept at the visual end of the 'perceptual chain', which stretches from the physical/visual to the psychological/ linguistic. We may wish to discuss the semantic content of the linguistic form, focusing on the nature of the event and of the process, which in this case is one of (physical) action. This provides another label: the model is an *actional*. We may wish to be more specific and give more detailed indications of the kind of event it is, specifying the kind and number of entities involved in the process and their relation to each other and to the process. In the case of our first example there is one nominal entity and the process. The process therefore does not pass from one nominal entity to another: it is not *transactive*. It is a *non-transactive* model. *Transactive* and *non-transactive* are specific kinds of actionals. The terms we have used so far, and their relation, are

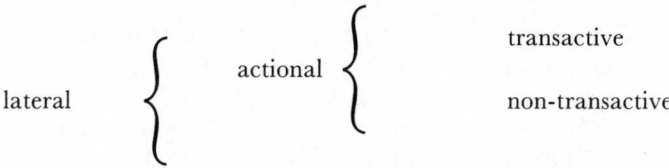

$$\text{lateral} \left\{ \text{actional} \left\{ \begin{array}{l} \text{transactive} \\ \\ \text{non-transactive} \end{array} \right. \right.$$

Lastly, we may wish to talk about the surface structure. There is a convenient and perfectly adequate label in traditional discussions for forms with one nominal process, the *intransitive*, and an adequate label for forms with two nominals directly associated with the process, the *transitive*. Thus when we speak of *intransitives* or *transitives* we are indicating the surface syntactic form of models. It is crucial to keep in mind that the four kinds of label – *lateral, actional, (non-)transactive, intransitive* – do not necessarily coincide, and by itself no one of the labels is a sufficient description of any linguistic form. Transactive does not equal transitive, nor does non-transactive equal intransitive. We shall discuss some forms later in this chapter in which a non-transactive is realized by a transitive; this non-matching is a common feature of English.

Most non-transactives are two-place models, in which the two places – nominal and verbal – in the syntagmatic chain seem to represent elements of the event. As we have shown, this dissociation of the process from the entity associated with it, and its sequential ordering – process following nominal – is a feature of the linguistic form, and not of the actual event. It has immense psychological, and hence semantic, import. Sequential priority comes to stand for temporal priority, and that which is temporally prior is perhaps not unnaturally seen as causally prior to that which is temporally subsequent. This is a hypothesis about English, though research may show that it has much wider validity. Thus the chain of translation from visual to linguistic entails a massive reinterpretation. The most significant effect or consequence of the reinterpretation is the introduction and imposition of a causal interpretation of events. Nevertheless the very simplicity of the non-transactive model gives little help in understanding causal processes. An action is related to an entity; the entity is presented as (sequentially and therefore) temporally prior. The nominal seems causally involved, perhaps as initiating the action, but the precise nature of the relationship is indeterminate.

The other seemingly simple sentence form for describing processes in English is

The boy hit the ball.

The crucial difference is that here there is a clear causal relationship between the two nominal entities and the process. The syntactic form gives a schematic representation of it. In English, the linear direction of the syntax, the word order, gives a conventional representation of the direction of the causal process, of what is acting on what. A relation of the two entities to the action is recorded. The subject is seen clearly as the initiator of the action, the first-mover as far as the action is concerned. (*The ball hit the boy* relates the same entities in a different causal sequence.) The surface form of this example is that of the transitive. The corresponding deep structure label is *transactive*, indicating the semantic content of the model, namely, the action passing from the cause to the second nominal entity.

If Lucretius was right, then transactives should be the preferred model for the 'science' embodied in a language, and non-transactives should go with a defective, imprecise, 'non-scientific' grasp of causality. Something like this is implicit in a brilliant article by Halliday (1971), analysing the language of William Golding's novel *The Inheritors*. In Golding's novel, Lok, from whose point of view the story is told for most of the work, is a Neanderthal man, whose primitive mind cannot grasp the significance of the actions of 'The People' (*Homo sapiens, Homo faber*), who are invading the territory of Lok's tribe. Lok's incomprehension is registered partly through Golding's use of non-transactives. These obscure the nature of complex processes, fragmenting causal sequences into meaningless units, loosely related by mere temporal contiguity. Lok can't understand the 'science' of The People, and he and his race are eliminated.

Halliday is clearly right about the function of intransitives, or, in our terms, the non-transactive model. But we must also note that, although

Neanderthal man may have been eliminated, non-transactives have not. The descendants of The People still use non-transactive models, without being run over by a bus every time they venture out of doors. The crucial difference between Lok and speakers of English is that non-transactive forms exist in English alongside transactives. This alters the place of that model in the conceptual world of the speaker of English. For Lok non-transactives constitute the total set of perceptual linguistic models; for speakers of English they are part of a larger set, and thus represent one possible choice among several. Lok necessarily perceives and expresses perceptions in terms of the one available model; hence his thought is narrowly determined by that form. To use a non-transactive model does not brand a speaker as a Neanderthal man, and someone who uses this form may well be able to see round it, to understand more complex causality. But it does reveal which kind of model the speaker is content to use at that particular point, how precisely he is conceiving processes, how 'scientific' he is being, or which kind of 'science' informs his thought.

Neanderthal Lok would have been in distinguished intellectual company. Here is Francis Bacon, often called the father of modern science, prophet and propagandist for the new science, whose major achievements, however, he seemed curiously unable to comprehend.

> Surely, like as many substances in nature which are solid do putrify and corrupt into worms; so it is the property of good and sound knowledge to putrify and dissolve into a number of subtle, idle, unwholesome, and (as I may term them) vermiculate questions, which have indeed a kind of quickness and life of spirit, but no soundness of matter or goodness of quality. This kind of degenerate learning did chiefly reign amongst the schoolmen: who having sharp and strong wits, and abundance of leisure, and small variety of reading, but their wits being shut up in the cells of a few authors (chiefly Aristotle their dictator) as their persons were shut up in the cells of monasteries and colleges, and knowing little history, either of nature or time, did out of no great quantity of matter and infinite agitation of wit spin out unto us those laborous webs of learning which are extant in their books. For the wit and mind of man, if it work upon matter, which is the contemplation of the creatures of God, worketh according to the stuff and is limited thereby; but if it work upon itself, as the spider worketh his web, then it is endless, and brings forth indeed cobwebs of learning, admirable for the fineness of thread and

work, but of no substance or profit.

(The Advancement of Learning, I, iv, 5)

There are a large number of intransitives in this passage: *putrify, corrupt, dissolve*. They realize non-transactive models, used for both physical and non-physical processes. We can see the vague account of participant roles in the causal process, characteristic of the non-transactive model, in the opening sentence:

many substances . . . do putrify and corrupt into worms.

Putrefy is invariably non-transactive in both Elizabethan and modern English, but *corrupt* can be used transactively. When it is used transactively, we automatically distinguish the agent from the object of the action:

X corrupts many substances.

In this form it is more obviously implausible that worms could emerge as a result of the corruption. The strange genesis could only seem plausible if it happens under cover of another non-transactive: by the addition of (*and*) *they turn into worms* (which may be an underlying phrase in Bacon's passage, represented by the single word *into*.

The intrinsic limitations of the non-transactive model in all this are clear. The direction of causality, who is doing what to whom, what is acting on what, is left uncertain. As a result, no causal chain can be envisaged, since in terms of the model there is no distinction between causer/actor and affected, the beginning and end of the causal unit. A whole set of questions about causality are unaskable, or receive only pseudo-answers, answers which essentially restate the vagueness of the model. For example: why do solids putrefy and corrupt into worms? The answer cannot be given in terms of causes and effects, unless the question is understood as a request for translation into a transactive model. Why did the door open? Because John opened it. If we stay within the non-transactive form, the answer can only be something like 'because it is the property of such substances to do so', i.e. 'because doors open'. (Parents will be familiar with this kind of situation, as question-answer sequences with three- to four-year-olds are frequently conducted across this conceptual divide. Interestingly, the children tend to be on the transactive side.)

This is not exactly non-scientific. The dialogue corresponds to a different kind of science, or a different level of science. In the early seventeenth century when Bacon was writing, it was still respectable to

42

believe that life might be generated spontaneously out of mud. The science that proceeds through non-transactive models will tend to be a large collection of particular facts about self-caused events which coexist. This is precisely the programme Bacon recommended for science in his writings. It is a kind of science. It may also be the only adequate science available at a particular stage. Non-transactive models may be used wherever and whenever a theory is required to account for data beyond the scope of the theory. However, the real question is which model serves as the paradigm for science as a whole at any given stage. For instance, we now know that the agents of *putrefy* are bacteria; but science before Pasteur would have been unable to supply a precise agent. So a science that dealt only with units of cause-and-effect would have either to use a dummy agent of some kind, perhaps a passive with a permanently irrecoverable agent, or not talk about the phenomenon at all. Either way, the phenomenon will seem to be devalued. Transformed utterances always appear derivative, since the fact that they are transformed enters into their interpretation for those readers who recognize them as transforms.

The indeterminacy of the non-transactive is an important property. It has the immediacy of a basic model without requiring an understanding on the part of speaker or hearer of the causality involved. It may even seem more immediate, more palpable, and hence unarguable, because of this. For instance, *dissolve*, which Bacon uses non-transactively, can be used in modern English both trans-actively and non-transactively: *The coffee dissolved the sugar, The sugar dissolved in the coffee*. The former represents the causal process trans-parently. The latter, which situates the act of dissolution in the coffee, expresses causation obliquely, through juxtaposition, but presents the focal elements in the percept (the grains of sugar fusing and disappearing) more vividly. To use terms that have been applied to Bacon, the non-transactive model is more empiricist, antitheoretical. Bacon was certainly more empiricist than scientist.

Another way of seeing the respective merits of transactive and non-transactive models is in terms of the traditional Aristotelian causes, material and effective causes. A science concerned only with material causes, with causes proceeding from the nature of the material, could account easily for energy, life, purposive movement. It would tend to animism, and tolerate the marvellous. A science concerned only with effective causes could deal with complex sequences of causation, but would have no account of energy or life, the source of motion. One would be a non-transactive science, the other a transactive science.

Transactive science is not clearly superior. It is only superior at explaining transactive processes. Bacon, for instance, with his general non-transactive models, was able to foreshadow the atomic theory of matter. He postulated underlying forms in matter, something like their atomic structure, which is a non-transactive conception.

Bacon also uses the non-transactive model to represent social relationships. A complex example is

This kind of degenerate learning did chiefly reign amongst the schoolmen.

The places in the model are the nominal *this kind of degenerate learning* and the process *did chiefly reign*. *Amongst the schoolmen* is not itself part of the model, but a (prepositional) extension of it. The nominal is considerably transformed, *learning* being the nominalization of a transactive model in which learners and teachers, actor and affected, would be fully specified. These nominal participants have been deleted in the nominalization transformation. The nominal *learning* is modified by *degenerate*, and *degenerate learning* is itself the result of a series of transformations, from the underlying structure *learning has degenerated* (or possibly *learning is degenerate*). However, in the first underlying form we have a non-transactive model, *learning has degenerated*, in which the abstract *learning* degenerates non-transactively, without any possibility of explaining how or why. In the second possible underlying form, we have a classificatory model, *learning is degenerate*, and the act of classification indicates the speaker's direct intervention in the speech event. This leads into the area of modality which we discuss in chapters 5 and 7.

The complex, abstract, and transformationally derived nominal *degenerate learning* fills the nominal place in the non-transactive model *degenerate learning did reign*. There it has the meaning of initiator/causer/actor/responsible entity, which is vaguely suggested by that place in the non-transactive model. The function of the transformational processes leading to *degenerate learning* can now be seen clearly. The non-transactive model obscures causal relations, but in this instance that obscurity is heightened by the presence of a transformationally highly complex nominal in the model. Yet, although the causal relations are vague and obscure in this model, the facts of power are presented in a direct and immediate form: *degenerate learning did reign*. Here the general semantic impact of the model is further augmented by the lexical meaning of the verbal process *reign*. The prepositional extension *amongst the schoolmen* has most immediately and obviously the function of delimiting the 'scope' of the model. In fact this extension is a favoured means by which the non-transactive model indicates a further (affected) participant, crucially, again without being precise about the (syntactic) relationship. The effect is akin to that of the transactive version *degenerate learning ruled the schoolmen*. The difference between the transactive and the non-transactive lies precisely in the diffuseness of the non-transactive version. The same thing happens in the British national anthem, where in *long to reign over us* the monarch reigns, and long will reign, but the relationship of dominance has to be reinforced by the spatial preposition *over*. In non-transactive models, spatial relationships – *amongst the schoolmen, in the coffee, over us* – replace a wide variety of causal relationships in the transactive model. In the case of *amongst the schoolmen*, the relationship between model and extension is roughly that of patient, goal, or object of action. In the case of *in the coffee*, the relationship seems more akin to that of agent: it is the coffee which dissolves the sugar. The effect of the prepositional extension in all these cases is to diffuse or obscure the nature of the relationship.

Bacon also uses passivization to mystify power relations, as with

> their wits being shut up in the cells of a few authors.

This is an example of a surface form which has just about achieved autonomy, in the sense that few readers perceive it to be the result of a transformation. *Shut up* has almost become an adjective, a quality attributed to *their wits*, and the actors who were responsible for the incarceration seem irrecoverable (*Artistotle their dictator* is mentioned but he is cell as well as jailor). *Shut up* is a complex form, subject to a number of interpretations. It seems to function as a single verb (a 'phrasal verb'), and in that interpretation it participates in a transactive model. Some of the problems derive from the complexities of phrasal verbs, which we discuss in some detail in the section 'Complex fields' later in this chapter.

There is another form which presents similar problems in this extract,

> the spider worketh his web.

From previous uses of *work* in the passage it is evident that Bacon conceives it as a non-transactive process (with the second nominal *his web* related to the model by means of a prepositional extension, in this case *upon*). We have here an instance of a non-transactive model which has a transitive surface form. We need a general label for this phenomenon, which for English takes a bewildering variety of forms, and the label *pseudo-transactive* seems appropriate. The advantage of this label is that it signals the apparent transactive nature, and some speakers may in fact interpret it as a real transactive. This sentence is not unlike such examples as *He sang a ballad, She danced the tango*, where one unit of meaning – singing and the song, dancing and the dance – is shown as general verb and specific noun. The equivalent sentence in this case would be *the spider spins his web*. In the next example Bacon, interestingly, uses the non-transactive intransitive: *the schoolmen . . . spin out unto us . . . webs of learning*, when he might have used the transitive *the schoolmen spin webs of learning*.

There are, however, a number of true transactives in the passage: *I may term them, knowing little history*. There is also the transformed phrase *the contemplation of the creatures of God*, which has one deep-structure transactive underlying it. These are *mental-process transactives*. Such transactives do not in fact establish causal relationships in the same way as physical-process transactives. To take one of these,

They knew history.

They are not acting on *history*. History is not changed by their knowing it. The reverse would be truer: they are changed by knowing history. This is generally true of mental-process transactives. The basic transactive model for such processes is *patientive*: the perceiver is passive, his action is a reaction. The basic transactive model for physical processes can be termed *agentive*, in which the subject is the prime mover in the action. English recognizes the differences between these two kinds of process in a number of ways. But by having the same surface form, the transitive, for both, it also presents them as though they were essentially the same.

As well as mental-process transactives there are also *mental-process non-transactives*, which have the effect of blurring the direction of causality, hence blurring the distinction between agentive and patientive. The effect of this on accounts of mental processes is to make them seem more active:

He saw the bird. (transactive)
He looked at the bird. (non-transactive)

With the first, the model presents perception as a passive process. The image of the bird impinged on his retina, so he inevitably saw it. With the second, the normal tendency of the non-transactive model works to focus on the fact of action, blurring causal processes, so that *look* is both active and passive, a self-caused action which is also a response. Perception represented through the non-transactive model is characteristically seen as a more active and purposeful process on the part of the perceiver than through the patientive transactive model. And whereas in the patientive transactive model the perceiver's reaction depends on the object of perception, in the non-transactive it does not. The following examples show the contrast.

non-transactive: He listened for the sound, but couldn't hear it (again).
transactive: He heard the sound, but couldn't hear it.

non-transactive: He looked for the recipe, but couldn't see it.
transactive: He saw the recipe, but couldn't see it.

Bacon's preference for the transactive for mental processes therefore becomes significant. It shows the perceiver in such acts as passive, and the act of perceiving as an automatic response. Here is another example: *X contemplates the creatures of God*. In terms of this example contemplation is dependent on its object. It is interesting to find Bacon using non-transactives for physical processes, and transactives for mental processes. We might suppose from this that Bacon saw natural processes as an unordered set of events with indeterminate causes, but mental processes as passive responses to external events. However, natural processes mediated through non-transactives provide a consistent parallel for mental processes as represented through patientive transactives. As a result of this persistent parallelism, mental processes can come to be seen in terms of both kinds of model. The non-transactive provides images of self-generated, irrational processes while the transactive provides statements about desirable forms of knowledge. The same split can be seen in Bacon's thought as a whole. On the one hand he believed in careful observation, on the other he had a deep distrust of what he called the 'idols' of the mind, the capacity of the mind and senses to distort experience. This second Bacon is the characteristic user of non-transactive models for mental processes. He is also the more interesting thinker: in terms of this kind of model it was natural to notice the autonomous power of language – 'Words, as a tartar's bow, do shoot back upon the understanding of the wisest, and mightily entangle and pervert the judgment' (*Advancement*, II, xiv, 11) – and the active role of the mind in interpreting experience.

TO THINK AS A CHILD

Bacon was not a child when he wrote *The Advancement of Learning*, nor was he a Neanderthal man. Yet the science that proceeds in terms of non-transactives is necessarily less explicit about causes, and hence more primitive as a science, even though it has other strengths. ('Primitive' does not mean inferior.) It is also worth looking more closely at the connections between non-transactives and the language and thought of a child, and at adult conceptions of children's language.

Here is the opening of *The Enormous Turnip*, a Ladybird 'Easy Reading' book for five-year-olds, written by Vera Southgate.

> Once upon a time, in the Spring, an old man sowed some rows of turnip seeds in his garden.
>
> As time went by, the rain fell on the seeds and the sun shone down on them, and the turnips began to grow.
>
> Every day, the turnips grew a little bigger. But one of them grew much faster than all the others.
>
> It grew large, then very large, then huge, until at last it was enormous. No-one had ever seen such an enormous turnip.
>
> One day, the old man fancied a plateful of turnip for his dinner. He took off his jacket, put on his big boots and went out into his garden.

The language here seems suitably simple, adapted to the level of a five-year-old child's vocabulary and comprehension. But there are a number of transactives, starting with the opening sentence:

> an old man sowed some rows of turnip seeds in his garden.

Superficially this seems a straightforward transactive, with a locative preposition, *in*, to fix the site of the action. However, in terms of physical processes this man is sowing seeds, not rows: *rows* refers to the place in which he sows them. so the underlying sentence is

> An old man sowed some seeds in rows in his garden
> or, more abstractly,
>
> A did B in C in D.

A number of transformations can operate on this model, whereby C or D can replace B as the surface subject of the action. The story has C as object; with D as object the sentence would be

> An old man sowed his garden with rows of seeds.

This series of transformations is not possible with all transactives. For instance:

> John threw some pebbles in holes in the ground.
> But not: John threw some holes of pebbles in the ground.
> Nor: John threw the ground with holes of pebbles.

So the model underlying our first example is clearly a powerful one, able to organize two extensions to the field. The reason for this seems to lie in the close syntactic relation of process and affected nominal, *sow* and *seed*. This is another instance of a pseudo-transactive, discussed above. *Seed, rows (of seeds)*, and *garden* are all treated in English as possible nominal realizations of the lexical content of *sow*. In fact all three nominals – *seeds, rows* or *garden* – may function as the single surface object: *The old man sowed some seeds; The old man sowed some rows; The old man sowed his garden.* We will return to this question later, in our discussion of 'complex fields', but at any rate it is clear that understanding the use of the verb *to sow* requires an understanding of this highly articulated model. Yet, in the story, this complex model is presented in a transformed, mystified form. The transformation reduces the number of elements apparently organized by the model, since *rows of seeds* seems like a single nominal. The X-of-Y form is apparently analogous to container-plus-material, like *a bag of seeds*. This surface simplicity in fact makes the nature of the process more obscure. Alongside this sentence, fortunately, is a picture of the old man dropping seeds into a shallow trench, with the shovel he has used to dig the trench stuck in the ground beside him. So an unmystified version of the model underlying the sentence is available to the child – so long as he or she attends to the picture, not to the words.

After this bewildering start, the story-teller switches to a straight-forward non-transactive model: *time went by; the rain fell; the sun shone; the turnips began to grow.* She is describing a single continuous biological process here, the maturation of plants such as turnips. The various phrases refer to factors relevant to the growth of turnips or other plants. However, the effect of using non-transactive forms typically destroys any clear sense of a continuous causal process. We have phrases referring to the rain, the sun and the turnips growing. Sequence can suggest a weak form of causality, and frequently does, as we pointed out above. It may also in fact be totally devoid of any causal implication. Here, in this sequence of non-transactives, the sun and the rain cause the turnips to grow; but does the sun shine as a result of the rain falling? The story-teller might have added *The birds sang.*

49

This would have made it seem even less likely that sequence was meant to suggest some kind of causal relationship between the events. A user of non-transactives can have varying degrees of interest in causal sequence without this affecting the grammaticality of the utterance.

It is likely that Miss Southgate has an adult, scientific understanding of the processes involved and specific assumptions about the knowledge and ability of five-year-olds, and that these have determined her selection and ordering of details. Her story can be reinterpreted through a complex transactive model. However, there is no transformational relationship between the two models, or the two versions. The transactive version is not implied by the non-transactive surface. If the story were retold in transactives, the resulting sentences would be different in important respects. Here are two non-transactive/transactive pairings:

> non-transactive: The rain fell on the seeds.
> transactive: The rain(water) moistened the seeds.
> non-transactive: The sun shone down on them
> transactive: The sun warmed the soil.

But telling the story through non-transactives helps to make it much more plausible, since what is happening is extraordinary, magical, and mysterious, quite inexplicable in terms of the transactive model for the process. One turnip grows to be enormous. There is nothing that makes this particular one enormous – no super-fertilizer, no special grade of seed. But because all the seeds just grow, non-transactively and hence outside any causal system, no reason needs to be given for this outsize growth. Non-transactives can make the inexplicable seem possible: like life generated in mud, monstrously large turnips, or energy from the nucleus of atoms.

This passage has two mental-process clauses, *no-one had ever seen* and *the old man fancied a plateful of turnip*. It also has a number of transactive physical actions, like

> He took off his jacket.

Took off is a phrasal verb, but the action here is conceived transactively. There is a deep structure,

> He took his jacket off his body.

with *his body* deleted but recoverable, as an 'inherent participant' (that is, 'understood' to be there) in the process expressed by the verb. As with the sowing of the seeds, we have a powerful transactive model here, capable of organizing a complex field, relating three entities to a single process. The user of this transformation takes for granted a complex grasp of the model, though there is no guarantee that five-year-olds understand and use the transformed form correctly. It may be that transactives of considerable complexity are part of the competence of fairly young children. Perhaps to mediate reality predominantly through non-transactives is to underestimate quite seriously a child's capacity to grasp transactive causality.

Adults talking to children naturally try to use 'simple' language which they feel will be within a child's comprehension. Inevitably the vague notion of simplicity covers innumerable particular assumptions about children's thought processes, assumptions which are no less potent for being unconscious and embodied in the forms of language used. To illustrate this, we will take an interesting experiment performed by Piaget, reported in his *The Moral Judgment of the Child* (1932). He is concerned with what he calls objective versus subjective responsibility: moral judgments which are exclusively concerned with material consequences as against judgments which take account of intention as well. From his observations, he concludes that the notion of subjective responsibility develops later than objective responsibility. His method is to tell a child a pair of stories about two accidents. In one, the material damage is considerable, but the intentions are innocent; in the other, it is the converse. The child is asked to retell each story, then to say which of the two central characters is the naughtier. Piaget is concerned to eliminate the language variable: 'In psychology one must speak to children in their own language, otherwise the experiment resolves itself into a trial of intelligence or of verbal understanding' (p. 116). In practice this proves difficult, and understanding how to 'speak to children in their own language' is not easily distinguishable from understanding their own and the experimenter's mental processes. (Our attention was first drawn to this example by Edward Condry, who conducted some undergraduate research involving Piaget's concepts and their relation to Bernstein's notion of codes.)

One pair of stories he uses deals with damage to cups. This is the English translation (p. 118):

A. A little boy who is called John is in his room. He is called to dinner. He goes into the dining room. But behind the door there was a chair, and on the chair there was a tray with fifteen cups on it. John couldn't have known that there was

51

all this behind the door. He goes in, the door knocks against the tray, bang go the fifteen cups and they all get broken!

B. Once there was a little boy whose name was Henry. One day when his mother was out he tried to get some jam out of the cupboard. He climbed up on to a chair and stretched out his arm. But the jam was too high up and he couldn't reach it and have any. But while he was trying to get it he knocked over a cup. The cup fell down and broke.

In comparing the use of models in these two tales we might start with transactives. In tale A there is a passive, *He is called to dinner*. The deleted actor here is presumably the mother. Behind the equative *there was a chair* lies a reality which could have been more faithfully presented through the transactive model: *Someone placed a chair behind the door, Someone put a tray on this chair*. What is important about these transactives is that they contain the real culprit: someone = Mother. (Male readers will be pleased to note that it is implausible to suspect Father of this crime.) The language is heavily ideological, concealing parental responsibility, concealing even the model in whose terms that responsibility can be most clearly seen. The child who refuses to blame John may have developed the notion of subjective responsibility, as Piaget assumes; he may also have gained facility in seeing through ideologically motivated selection of models of causality.

There is one mental-process clause, *John couldn't have known*, in terms of which John is less culpable. The modality of this, however, is formidably complex, in contrast to the surrounding language, which is in the simple present. The accident itself is recorded entirely through non-transactives. This partly rectifies the balance, because this series of non-transactives serves to reduce the child's sense of John's responsibility for the accident. The successive stages of the disaster are contained within adjacent self-contained events: his entrance, the door knocking, the cups going bang, and the cups getting broken. What the narrator took with one hand he gives with the other: he conceals the real culprit, but presents the events in a form which minimizes the fact that John directly, if unintentionally, began the fatal sequence of events.

In story B there are no passives. Mother is mentioned in this story, but she is innocent (except perhaps as the source of a prohibition about eating jam). There is a larger number of direct transactives: *get some jam, stretched out his arm* (taking *stretch out* as a single unit). More important, whereas the criminal action in A is presented through non-transactives, in B Henry's fatal action is in the transactive, where his agency becomes manifest: *he knocked over a cup*. There is no evil intent in this – he had no wish to break the cup. But he is clearly labelled as the, cause of the fatal action. So a child might pick Henry as the naughty child because the transparent transactive directly attributes the action to him. The child might also be responding accurately to a number of cues in the two passages. The first boy, for instance, *is called John*. The passive form has a vaguely defined deleted agent, probably not fully recoverable, but implying the social nature of the act of naming. The name links John to his society . It is also the way his mother summons him to the scene of the crime. With Henry the name is an attribute, outside the social process. As well as being greedy and acquisitive, he is a relatively autonomous individual. In English, *What is your name?* is more official, impersonal, in contrast to *What are you called?*, which is used only to newcomers, mainly young ones, in a group. This is a request for the name which the group can *call* the newcomer to control his behaviour. The effect of this stylistic difference in the case of these two stories is obscure. Perhaps it presents Henry as an autonomous individual who would be less blamed for an equivalent act than a member of the family group. Perhaps it presents him as a pariah, automatically culpable. The moral judgment that followed would depend on the child's attitudes to group membership and its contribution to assessment of blame.

Piaget records the interrogation of various children who listened to these stories. We decided to repeat the experiment, reading the English translation of the stories and asking his questions. Our aim was not to test his conclusions but to look at the role of language in the experiment and the relation of the language of the child to the language of the passages. Here is a direct transcript of one child's comments, a girl aged eight (italics represent emphasis in speech).

A. This boy called um John was called to *dinner* and – um – *behind* the ah living-room *door* there was a chair with fifteen *cups* on it . . . and he didn't know the cups were there so he opened the door and they all smashed on the *floor*.

G. Right um what happened in the second one?

A. This boy called Freddy um – when his Mum was out he wanted some *jam* . . . and when he got a chair to try and reach to it he found that he couldn't reach and he accidentally knocked a cup and it crashed on the *floor*.

G. This boy, how many cups did he break?

A. Fifteen.

G. Fifteen, and the second boy, how many cups did he break?

A. One.

G. One . . . But tell me who was the *naughtier* boy?

S. Who wanted the jam.

G. Why do *you* think, A?

A. Um because . . . um . . . he couldn't see them.

G. So therefore?

A. He broke fifteen *cups*.

G. But why did you think the one that broke the one cup was naughtier?

A. Because um because he wanted some jam and that was very naughty. (giggle)

This girl, to start with, eliminates the difference of address: both are 'called' by their name. She has filtered out that distinction of style as irrelevant to the judgment, the filtering itself being a significant act. In repeating the first story she uses one more transactive than the story did: John *opened the door*, the decisive act, which is obscured in the original. But she fails to translate the equative form into the transactive there, so she seems to accept that the chair with cups on it was innocently there.

With the second story, however, she does not accept the fortuitous placing of the chair under the jam shelf; she introduces a transactive, *he got a chair*, attributing the action to Henry (renamed Freddy). She is quite capable of seeing 'round' the devious selection of causal models, recreating the action in terms of transactives, and assigning agency appropriately. Why did she not do so in the case of the chair with cups on it? It is evidently wrong to suppose that intellectually she is incapable of doing so. One explanation might be that she is reluctant to do so. If the real culprit is Mother, she feels reluctant to assign blame there. Being an intelligent girl, she may well have worked out that there are no bon-bons for calling Mother 'naughty'. (This was confirmed on subsequent questioning:

'Why was the chair there?'
'I think the boy's mummy put it there.'
'Was she really the naughty one then?'
'Yes (giggle) but mummies don't get smacked.')

This girl regards Henry as more culpable, even though the interviewer tried to emphasize the material difference, the greater number of cups that John broke. She is not explicit about her reasons – there were long

54

pauses before she offered her explanations, yet she was not uncertain about the judgment itself. Her first reason reduced John's culpability to 'he couldn't see them'. But as far as intentionality is concerned, in her account of story B she had inserted *accidentally* into the transactive. Both mishaps were accidents in her view. Her stated reason for blaming Henry/Freddy was purely to do with motives, *he wanted some jam*, a subjective criterion. This is a translation of a purposive action, *he tried to get some jam*, into the motive for the action. She condemns that motive, but with a giggle, as though aware that this pseudo-reason is a fine coup, a nonsense that will silence the impertinent questioner, an elegant and subversive paradox (wanting jam is naughtier than breaking fifteen cups) that supports a judgment which she takes seriously, but whose grounds she is unwilling or unable to reveal. The analysis does not show what those grounds are, but it shows that her grasp of causality and capacity to see through ideological manipulation is well advanced. An investigating psychologist needs to be wary that what he takes for the child's limited intellectual capacity does not result from his own failure to understand language as ideology.

THE RIME OF THE ANCIENT CHILD

Transactive models are scientifically more adequate, essential to the conception of complex processes, and to developed notions of moral responsibility. Why then do non-transactives persist? Why does Lok live on? His reincarnation in Bacon provides part of the answer: so does his later metempsychosis, into the poet Coleridge. Here is the climactic moment of Coleridge's famous 'Rime of the Ancient Mariner' (Part IV).

> Beyond the shadow of the ship,
> I watched the water-snakes:
> They moved in tracks of shining white,
> And when they reared, the elfish light
> Fell off in hoary flakes.
>
> Within the shadow of the ship
> I watched their rich attire;
> Blue, glossy green, and velvet black,
> They coiled and swam; and every track
> Was a splash of golden fire.

O happy living things! no tongue
Their beauty might declare:
A spring of love gushed from my heart,
And I blessed them unaware:
Sure my kind saint took pity on me,
And I blessed them unaware.

The selfsame moment I could pray;
And from my neck so free
The Albatross fell off, and sank
Like lead into the sea.

The Mariner's guilt was due to a single, apparently slight, transactive action: he shot the Albatross. The result was a widespread alienation of the Mariner from all his fellows, and between nature and man. It is at this point in the poem that the link between man and nature is restored. It is interesting that the precondition for this seems to be that nature is conceived entirely through non-transactives, as a series of self-contained events, actions without external causes or consequences. The snakes *moved, coiled, swam*, and *reared*, and *light fell off*. The closest to a physical event with cause or result is the last-mentioned, *when they reared, the elfish light fell off*. The two non-transactives follow each other temporally. As is usually the case, this may indicate that one is the result of the other; but it need not.

The Mariner's response to this is all-important. But again this is presented through non-transactives: A *spring of love gushed*, not *it moved my heart*. *My kind saint* is mentioned, as the actor for a transactive account of the regenerative process. The two accounts coexist as possible different kinds of explanation. The decisive act he performs is to pray; the Albatross then *fell off* and *sank*. As with the cups in John's sad tale, the use of non-transactives blurs the attribution of responsibility. Consequently, the Mariner is not clear who is responsible for his no longer being responsible.

From here on the narrative again proceeds in non-transactive terms:

The helmsman steered, the ship moved on,
But never a breeze up blew.

In terms of this model, things become possible that a strictly scientific account would exclude: ships moving with incredible velocities, turnips growing to enormous size. Alienation of man from nature cannot exactly be overcome, since in the non-transactive model only one entity, man or nature, can be the focus. The other can at best be the locus of the activity. But an exploitative relationship between man and nature cannot be conceived clearly either, since the non-transactive cannot represent both within the same model. This must be a large part of the powerful attraction of the non-transactive model for Coleridge and many other artists. In its terms a whole series of distinctions become blurred, following from the primary indeterminacy about causality in the model. This can be called 'primitive' or 'childlike', in keeping with common myths about noble savages and the innocence of childhood. But these are sophisticated adult myths, which certainly misrepresent children, and are probably misunderstandings of so-called primitives as well.

COMPLEX FIELDS

Starting from visual perception, we conventionally interpret lateral models, actionals in particular, as presentations of one visual percept. This perceptual field is structured into perceptual focus and field. So far in our discussion we have concentrated on forms which present one perceptual field, that is, single models with the maximum number of constituting elements. But actual forms of language frequently depart from this simplicity, presenting instead forms that contain more than the two or three places of simple models. They present what are in fact 'complex fields'.

Two distinct linguistic mechanisms are involved in the presentation of complex fields. The first involves the *extension* of a model; the second involves the *conflation* of two (or more) models. Surfaces do not absolutely reliably indicate which of the processes is involved, but as an example of the first we can cite one which we used earlier:

The sugar dissolved in the coffee.

Here the extension depends on the presence of a preposition. In the next example it does not:

Mary knitted Bill a tie.

Here *Bill* is the extension of the basic transactive model *Mary knitted a tie*. The nature of the extension quite obviously depends on the relations within the model. Transactives with an unambiguous agentive nominal (i.e., a clear actor) always permit a *benefactive* nominal extension. That is, where there is a clear actor, clearly responsible for a transactive process, he may do this for someone who benefits from this action. Mental-process transactives (patientives), on the other hand, do not permit benefactive extensions. *He saw her the problem* is just not possible in English. Another possible non-prepositional extension with transactives is illustrated by

She knitted (him) a tie all night.

This *temporal* extension indicates the scope of the process in question. It does not distinguish mental- from physical-process transactives and it is equally permissible for both:

The problem worried him all night.

However, while benefactive extensions can clearly appear as subjects – *Bill was knitted a tie (by Mary)* or *Bill had a tie knitted (by Mary)* – temporal extensions cannot – *All night was knitted him a tie*. This tells us something about the very deep-seated interpretation of the position of the first noun in a sentence. Non-transactives can similarly support non-prepositional extensions. These tend to be interpreted as the scope or *range* (using Halliday's term) of the action expressed by the verb:

He swam the river.

The surface transitive form might suggest that this is a transactive. But the fact that it is difficult, awkward, or downright impossible to make them into passives (*The river was swum by him*) shows that they are not transactives.

All non-prepositional extensions can appear as prepositional extensions in surface structure:

She knitted him a tie. – She knitted a tie for him.
He swam the river. He swam across the river.

This is, incidentally, a good test for the kind of model involved. With a transactive the link between *verb* and *noun* is not disturbed,

She *knitted the tie* for him,

whereas with a non-transactive the preposition 'comes between' verb and noun,

He swam *in* the river.

The range of prepositional extensions is not exhausted by these examples. Two other types, for example, are instrumental, *She knitted the tie with no. 8 needles*, and locative, *She knitted the tie by the hearth*.

One difference between the non-prepositional extension to a model and the prepositional extension is a greater diffuseness, or vagueness, in the prepositional extension. Fillmore (1968) discussed one form of this, using pairs like *The garden is swarming with bees — Bees are swarming in the garden*. Our examples concern the extension to the model:

The coffee dissolved the sugar.	– The sugar dissolved *in* the coffee.
The disturbances killed ten people.	– Ten people were killed *in* the disturbances.
Chairman Mao swam the Yangtse.	– Chairman Mao swam *in* the Yangtse.

Superficially, 'phrasal verbs' appear to be like prepositional extensions of models. Closer analysis reveals a fundamental difference. It is possible to regard them as conflations of two models. Here is an example which we discussed above,

He knocked over a cup.

We regarded this as a transactive in our discussion, and the hypothetical underlying form could be

He knocked a cup./The cup goes over.

The term *phrasal verb* seems appropriate in this light. The surface form of the verb carries an indication of another phrase, or a whole clause. The preposition stands for the transformationally deleted second model. In this account phrasal verbs are surface realizations of model conflation rather than model extension. There are problems in this area. To mention one more (first discussed by G. Lakoff, 1970), prepositional extensions involving instrumentals can be realized in the form of conflated models:

He sliced the loaf with the new bread knife.
He used the new bread knife to slice the loaf.

which has the underlying form

He used the new bread knife./He sliced the loaf.

It may be that all prepositional extensions are instances of conflation of models; however, that remains a hypothesis.

The clearest cases of conflation occur in examples (first discussed in Halliday, 1967) such as

Reg grows tomatoes,

which may be analysed as

> Reg causes./Tomatoes grow.

No part of the surface structure signals the process of conflation. These forms are common in English, and the fact that they have a surface transitive form leads to their frequent interpretation as transactives. The simplicity of the surface, a structurally unambiguous transitive, makes it ideologically a most useful form. Simplicity is always convincing, and here it is used to subvert the real syntactic relations. To take another example discussed by Halliday,

> The warder marched the prisoners.

In the underlying form the models are

(A) The warder caused X.   (B) The prisoners marched.

(where X = B), that is, two non-transactive models. In the conflation, the actor/subject of B becomes the object of the verb, and the actor/subject of A becomes the subject of the verb. The resulting surface structure is interpreted, on casual reading, as a transactive with *warder* as actor and *prisoners* as affected. The actor role of *prisoners* has thus been taken by another nominal. But models like A have 'priority' over models like B for this transformation. The actor of A becomes the imputed actor for the new sentence. The assumption that underlies the process is that power can be regarded as direct agency.

The effect of this linguistic process is to reassign the actor roles in the two conflated models. The real actor of the process is denied credit and responsibility for the action he performs, and this credit is assigned to the syntactic participant who is regarded as more powerful. It is a thing not lightly done. The ideological function is clear.

SOURCES AND CONTEXT

Most linguistic theories assume that there is a limited number of basic sentence patterns or sentence types in a language, and that the vast variety of actual utterances are constructed around this basic set. Chomsky's *Syntactic Structures* (1957) used the concept of 'kernel sentence'. Though it had a technical definition (sentences derived by the application of obligatory transformations only), in fact this was a set of forms, between five and seven, which could not be analysed in more basic terms. Even one of the most recent developments arising out of transformational generative grammar, *relational grammar*, uses a similar approach: 'A clause consists of a network of grammatical relations. Among these relations are "subject of ", "direct object of ", and "indirect object of " ' (Perlmutter and Postal, 1977). However, the semantic interpretation of such underlying forms arose from work done' in the mid-1960s. The two important strands are the work of Halliday and of Fillmore. The relevant work by Halliday is in three articles, 'Notes on transitivity and theme in English', which appeared in 1967 and 1968; the relevant article by Fillmore is 'The case for case', which appeared in 1968. Both move from a structural description of basic sentence patterns to a consideration of the deep semantic and conceptual structure of clauses (in one case) and propositions (in the other) in English.

In considering this area – the grammar of transitivity – Halliday uses the notion of 'clause-types'. These types enshrine the possible syntactic and semantic presentations of the relations between objects and processes 'in the world'. For Halliday there are fundamental ways of presenting such relations, and they have specific surface forms. He sees clauses as structurally, semantically, and conceptually unified wholes, though they have an internal structure.

Fillmore's approach is in many ways similar, though he does not use the notion of clause-types. The relevant concept in his theory is that of 'case-frames'. Again he is concerned to discover fundamental semantic and conceptual relations which underlie the syntax of English. He regards the verb as central, and describes the kinds of relations which verbs enter into with nominals. These relations he labels 'cases'. The verb *give* typically appears with an *agent* (the giver), an *object* (which is transferred), and a *recipient* (which he calls *dative*) of the *object*. The 'case-frame' into which *give* fits is thus [object + dative + agent]. This is not totally dissimilar to Halliday's clause-type, though it differs in focusing on the internal structure and relations of the elements in the case-frame.

Our own approach is heavily influenced by these formulations. It differs in two respects:

1 We use the notion of 'model' (in a manner similar to Halliday), but more strictly than Halliday. In our view there are a very few models only. These models may have extensions, or may be conflated; they may be transformed into the surface form of another model; but their number is no greater than we have outlined.
2 We derive the form of the models from the process of visual perception, or, at the very least, attempt to relate the form of linguistic models very closely to visual perception.

4

CLASSIFICATION AND CONTROL

CLASSIFICATION AND REALITY

Human beings do not live in the objective world alone, nor alone in the world of social activity as ordinarily understood, but are very much at the mercy of the particular language which has become the medium of expression for their society. It is quite an illusion to imagine that one adjusts to reality essentially without the use of language and that language is merely an incidental means of solving specific problems of communication or reflection. The fact of the matter is that the 'real world' is to a large extent unconsciously built up on the language habits of the group.... We see and hear and otherwise experience very largely as we do because the language habits of our community predispose certain choices of interpretation.

(Sapir (1921) in Whorf, 1956, p. 134)

Classification is at the basis of language and thought. Without acts of classification no one could relate concepts or words to new concepts or messages, because words and concepts only exist through classification. As social beings we learn through classifications, and we learn classifications. These are always socially given. A child looking at a dog on a lawn may have an impression on his retina of brown and white shapes on green (even to convey this unprocessed image we have to classify its parts). Through experience, in which language plays a determining role, there is a progressive clarification, passing from the original image to words. The child may start by saying 'cat', because the only word for 'furry animal' he or she knew before referred to the family tom. The parents correct the child: 'No, it's not a "cat", it's a "dog".' In this way the child acquires a vocabulary through successive stages of negation and delimitation, learning in the process one major classificatory system of his society. During this important stage of development the child is learning about language and reality simultaneously: what a dog is, and what 'dog' means. So learning the language is learning the reality. Language becomes a second reality, the taken-for-granted basis of individual messages and thoughts.

Since language provides the major access for individuals into the classification system of their society, the analysis of language provides the easiest way into an analysis of that system. Different languages enshrine different classifications of reality specific to their particular societies. An example that is often used to illustrate this is a comparison between Eskimo, which has three words for *snow*, and English, which has only one, reflecting the importance of snow in the two cases. Conversely, Eskimo has only one word to cover the concepts of *insect*, *pilot*, and *aeroplane* (both examples are from Whorf).

But words are of the surface. Speakers of a language can always get round words by using other words. Whorf draws attention to principles of classification which are fundamental to the structure of the language itself. These are basic assumptions about reality which are built into the language at so deep a level that they act largely unconsciously. Whorf likens them to a science and metaphysics, or a world view. This theory of reality sometimes appears on the surface of language, in overt categories, like the division between nouns and verbs, entities and processes, in English. Sometimes it exists as the rationale – usually not stated, and learned entirely unconsciously – of the rules of grammar. An example of this is the system of tense in English, a classification of time into a number of categories. Sometimes these categories are what Whorf called 'covert categories'. These are categories with no outward signs, and essentially they involve prohibitions which are silent because they are always obeyed. For instance, in English we would never say *He shattered up the dog* though we could say *He cut up the dog*. We can say *a weak cup of tea* but not *a weak car*, and *a strong cup of tea* or *a powerful car* but not vice versa. Why? The prohibitions are difficult to explain, and almost certainly haven't been explained to people who use the correct forms automatically. Normally they are not even experienced as prohibitions, since we have all become so accustomed to avoiding that which is prohibited.

Classification imposes order on what is classified. So classification is an instrument of control in two directions: control over the flux of experience of physical and social reality, in a 'science'; and society's control over conceptions of that reality. But classification systems do not exist for a whole society; different groupings have different systems, though the differences may be slight. Furthermore, the contingencies of the situations in which individuals meet, and their at times divergent interests, place strains on these classification systems. In this way classification becomes the site of tension and struggle – on one level between individuals, as each tries to impose his or her system on others or gives way to superior power. On another level, the struggle goes on between social, ethnic, national, or racial groupings.

A classification system constrains thought, giving a basic unity to everything expressed within it, whatever its content, and making alternative systems of classification seem incommensurable. A common language has always been a powerful means of creating solidarity within a social group. It defines that group against other groups in ways that are felt to go deep into basic structures of thought and feeling. Nationalist political programmes normally have a language programme as a major component. Repression of minority cultures similarly acts through suppression of their language. Even within more homogeneous communities, groups who wish to set themselves off from society at large tend to evolve distinctive languages, with a special vocabulary which excludes outsiders and unites the group.

The basic system of classification is itself abstract, and isn't manifest until it is made actual by human agents engaged in social interaction. This abstract character is a source of strength and weakness: strength, in that the system itself is never scrutinized, so it is not usually open to criticism; weakness, because it is constantly being subtly renegotiated by individuals who are responding to forces outside the language system. Classification only exists in discourse, and in discourse it is always at risk. The social basis in discourse acts as a motor of change in the system over time. Two kinds of change seem to occur most often in the evolving system of a language. New materials and new interests are incorporated into the old system, leading to a different 'fit' between language and reality, and a different set of relations between existing categories. The result is that all categories have a slightly altered scope or function within the whole, which is essentially a new system disguised as the old one.

Change can occur more visibly, with the evolution of new categories. These have more far-reaching effects than is commonly realized. The new does not simply coexist with the old; it can have profound effects on the economy of the system as a whole. The dynamic of such changes comes from outside language, from changes in the material, social, political technological, or ideological environment. These present new problems or new goals to the classification system, which adapts accordingly.

Individuals are both active and passive in relation to the classificatory scheme, moving between the given system and the content to be classified. Classification is a living process, and language offers not only an existing set of classifications, but also a set of operations to enable the individual to further classify or reclassify his reality. The process of classification for an individual is never wholly free or wholly constrained. It typically ranges between these two poles, or the illusion of these poles. When it seems totally constrained it is susceptible to evasion or change, and when it seems neutral and free the terms of that freedom and the site of that neutrality are prescribed.

CLASSIFICATION AND CLASS

The ruling ideas in every epoch have always been the ideas of the ruling class.

(Marx and Engels, 1970, 1848)

It is not only capital, in the strict economic sense, which is subject to appropriation, manipulation and exploitation, but also *cultural* capital in the form of the symbolic systems through which man may extend and change the boundaries of his experience.

(Bernstein, 1972, p. 172)

Any argument about the relation between language and class arouses fierce controversy. When a writer claims, as Bernstein has seemed to do, that the possessing class has expropriated the working class of the means to thought as well as of the instruments of material production, working-class forms of language and thought seem to have been disvalued. Neither left nor right is happy with an argument that suggests that the middle class is oppressively, intellectually superior, while the working class is the stupefied victim of that oppression. But no one disputes the differences between working-class and middle-class language within one larger speech community. The only questions to decide concern the function of these differences and their role in a total economic and social order.

Here, as a sample of two kinds of language, is an extract from Rosen's *Language and Class Workshop* (1974, No. 2, p. 11):

What impresses me about the older women's talk is that it is purposeful while still being open. They also seem to me (subject to correction) to be more willing than most men to move between the personal and the impersonal, and they use careful indications of what is personal to generalize from, and what is individual and may be divergent from the general situation. They handle internal disagreement in a tolerant and constructive way. There is one superb organizer of the spoken paragraph – Frances; but her eloquence and Freda's confidence of status and dignity are not allowed to overrule the least assured speaker. The exchange defines a set of common problems without needing to be unanimous.

(Sue Shrapnel)

FREDA: From the time I left school I must have had about a hundred different jobs. I've done everything in the semi-skilled line – master of none, you know. Waitress, laundry worker, factory worker – you know; you name it, sort of thing – I've done it. In fact, I was five years as a welder, but would never be recognized as a skilled welder – bearing in mind I was only gas-welding; but nevertheless, the men who were doing exactly the same job were getting roughly about £7 a week more than me. But we did have a bit of a battle in the factory one time: they brought out a bonus scheme, and they were going to pay the men £1 extra for their skill. So we demanded the same – bearing in mind there was only three of us. We got it; and we just refused to work until they gave us the £1. And we knew that our particular job was essential to do the – finished product. So as I say, we won; we got the £1.

Sue Shrapnel's language is written, whereas Freda's is the transcript of speech, perhaps edited slightly. The two kinds of language are themselves classified by our culture, written language having higher prestige than spoken. The transcript of Freda's language retains distinctively oral forms, such as *you name it, sort of thing*, where *sort of thing* is a 'filler' which indicates caution by the speaker. Sue Shrapnel uses the phrase (*subject to correction*), which signals a similar kind of caution. However, it is a high-prestige form of cautious vacuity.

All utterances, and hence the utterers, are constantly subjected to classification by those who hear them. Such classifications or judgments tend to be mediated through expectations about class. They emerge as judgments about qualities of intelligence, character, etc., but they are almost invariably shaped by class assumptions. Transcribers of oral discourse have the choice between transmitting the oral forms as closely as they can, thereby exposing the discourse to the judgment 'oral, therefore inferior', or normalizing it in the direction of the written form. The person transcribing Freda's language could have emphasized its oral nature more, by attempting to approximate the sound of the utterance, writing *must of, yuh know, woz,* etc. The effect of this convention is to imply that the speaker is illiterate, and in doing so it introduces, covertly, a host of negative judgments about the speaker. The total judgment on the utterance would be correspondingly more negative even though Freda said and thought exactly the same things. With the language of middle-class speakers the normal convention is to transcribe it into the conventional written form. Whenever this convention is departed from, the effect is to imply a negative assessment of the speaker. The former Tory prime minister Edward Heath's vowels were subjected to this process by the satirist John Kent – 'Heow are you?'

In her introduction to the transcription of Freda's language Sue Shrapnel is very positive about the virtues of the working-class speech she is looking at. She clearly rejects the view, associated with Bernstein, that working-class speakers have deficient resources of language or thought. Bernstein assumes that the restricted code of working-class speakers has inherent difficulties with generalizations and abstractions, and cannot easily cope with shifts of role within the speech situation. Sue Shrapnel claims for the speakers she describes great readiness to *move between the personal and the impersonal,* and the ability to make careful distinctions between the general and the merely particular.

Sue Shrapnel's case clearly involves classification of the utterances of Freda and others, using terms like *purposeful, open, personal, impersonal.* Of these only *personally* occurs in the transcription (in a passage not quoted here). Either Sue Shrapnel is bringing the underlying categories of working-class speech to the surface, or else she is imposing an extraneous system of classification on this speech. Since her categories have wide currency in academic discussions of language and class, the second is more likely. There is an intrinsic problem here which confronts any enterprise such as this. To justify working-class language to middle-class (especially academic) readers, she has to translate the phenomena into terms they would understand, into their system of categories, their language. This inevitably eliminates the original system of categories. It has been transformed into an alternative language and appropriated into its terms. If she didn't do this, the strategy open to her would be simply to transcribe and 'let the language speak for itself'. But if she did that she would be leaving the language vulnerable, exposed to a ready-made negative judgment by middle-class speakers. They might well use similar categories to Sue Shrapnel's to dismiss such speech. An intervention like hers is caught between two conditions. Classification of utterances along class lines is a continuing process, and a dominant class will inevitably disvalue the modes of thought and language of a subordinate class. But so long as the language and values of the dominant class are automatically the dominant language and values in a society, justification of the values of an opposing class will tend to be in those terms, too. This will therefore reaffirm the values of the dominant group at the expense of what is significantly different in the subordinate class's system of categories and values.

Contrasting the two kinds of language, we find one major difference is the extent to which each is in itself concerned with classification and evaluation. In the written paragraph there are twenty-one adjectives, or transformationally derived adjectives. In the spoken extract, which is slightly longer, there are seven. As well as this large quantitative difference, there is a qualitative difference. The written form has a large number of attributives, the *noun-'is'-adjective* form – eight, against one for the spoken, *was essential*. The attributive model brings out the act of judgment, so Sue Shrapnel is being much more overtly judgmental. Her use of this form is also more productive. For instance, the talk of the older women is *purposeful while still being open*. Here she has categorized *the talk* twice, leading to a balanced judgment on it, for which there is no single word in the English language. *Personal* is balanced against *impersonal* and *individual* against *general* in a similar way. She also uses transformations more freely in this area. Sentences or parts of sentences are transformed into adjectives, so that they can be part of a judgment: *full of purpose ⇒ purposeful*; *X diverges from Y ⇒ be divergent from Y*; *someone speaks ⇒ spoken*; or they are transformed into nouns, so that they can be classified themselves: *they indicate something ⇒ indications (+ careful)*; *they disagree ⇒ disagreement (+ internal)*; *she organizes something ⇒ organizer (+ superb)*.

Freda, by contrast, never uses more than one adjective to qualify a noun. She uses one form of classification more than Sue Shrapnel does, the *noun-'is'-a-noun* form: *[I have been] a waitress, laundry worker, factory worker*. The phrases that follow this list are very revealing: *you know; you name it, sort of thing – I've done it. You know* invites the hearer to complete the list, suggesting a consensus of values between speaker and hearer. But the opposition between *you name it* and *I've done it* captures exactly the relationship between Freda and the system of classification which she uses here. These terms are all standard terms used by management to describe jobs. The *you* who names jobs is management: Freda is the one who *does* them. Similarly, the majority of adjectives that she uses are management terms. *Semi-skilled, skilled, bonus scheme, finished product,* the adjectives are linked to their nouns to form an almost indissoluble unit, given by management and accepted as the descriptive currency by Freda. The economic dimension of this process is clearly perceived by Freda. The difference between *skilled* and *semi-skilled* is £7 a week. The meaning of a *bonus scheme* included, initially, £1 a week extra for others, not the women. In this factory, behind the distinction between skilled and semi-skilled lies the distinction between male and female.

Freda understands the manipulative use of terms by managements, and as a militant she opposes some instances of such use. On one occasion in this passage she sets one set of categories, *essential to do the – finished product,* in opposition to another, *skilled/semi-skilled.* However, this strategy still leaves her accepting the basic system of terms of management, an alien set of terms and categories. This is an example of the clash of two classification systems, the management's and the workers'. And while speakers can be productive in using their own system, extending it, altering it, reshaping it, they do not have this productive capacity in relation to an alien system. The latter remains inert and unproductive for them. The world of work falls into the classificatory domain of management, and Freda therefore necessarily uses the terms from that system. Our brief sample does not show whether she has a set of terms from the point of view of her own class. At any rate, in an event as public as this interview she would feel constrained to use the 'appropriate' set of terms, which is management's.

The interviewer's language initially seems much more general and abstract. This impression comes largely from her use of nominalizations. As we have seen, they are the results of deletions of participants and contexts to create a world of reified entities, which on the surface of the utterance engage in a whole series of apparent activities. In the first extract *eloquence, confidence,* and *exchange* are actors, and *indications* and *disagreement* are quasi-objects which can be *handled* or used. In Freda's text, the only nouns which take the actor role are humans, *we, they, men, you.* Similarly, things that can be possessed in Sue Shrapnel's text include *talk, eloquence, confidence,* whereas in Freda's text they are nouns such as *job* or *skill.*

There are two levels on which we can describe this difference. We

69

can remain on the surface of the discourse. Here one would say that the category of *actor* and the category of *possession* have different scopes in the two languages. Sue Shrapnel's language has a whole class of actors and possessions which are not present in Freda's language (and may barely be possible in it – we haven't a large enough sample to make that claim more strongly, but it is possible in principle). This makes the former a richer language on the surface, and the latter seem correspondingly poorer, perhaps even 'linguistically deprived'. However, if we look at a deeper level, this greater richness can be seen to be transformationally created. The transformations which are used involve considerable deletion. The price of the surface richness of the one language is mystification of real processes. Freda's language retains a firmer grip on the processes in her world, as the necessary basis for practical activity.

There are two aspects which make the one language superior to the other. Although the transformational resources of the one may result only in mystifications, they do allow the speaker to produce a language commodity which is highly valued. The productivity and socially greater power of her classificatory system means that she can readily produce complex judgments and evaluations in favour of whatever cause she supports. She has the linguistic resouces and social position to be an effective advocate or judge. Her defence of Freda's language is publishable. Freda makes no defence of Sue Shrapnel's language, and if she did so, using the kind of language shown here, it would not conform to the norm of what is publishable. (This of course totally ignores the possibility that Freda might be an effective writer.) Sue Shrapnel's judgmental facility marks her as a member of the class of arbiters in our society. This qualifies her for a level of employment which is closely aligned with the rulers, whatever her personal political commitments may be. However, academics and teachers are not to be equated with the effective rulers in our society, for intellectual capital and the means of production of intellectual and linguistic commodities are not distributed in parallel to the distribution of material resources. But every system of distribution is based on a system of classification of the goods to be distributed and the classes to whom they are to be distributed. These goods include the systems and modes of classification. They in turn provide intellectual and linguistic access to the rationale of the social and economic order of the society as a whole.

ANTI-LANGUAGE AND ANTI-SOCIETY

A large and complex society will always contain subgroups within it. Such groups commonly evolve or create a kind of language which serves to reinforce a sense of identity within the group and to exclude outsiders. Halliday (1976) has called languages of this kind 'anti-languages'. He looked at three examples, Elizabethan underworld language, Polish prison argot, and Bengali underworld language. All these are languages of what could be called anti-societies, societies which are consciously oppositional to the dominant society but contained within it. Other such groups in English or American society would include teenage gangs and members of various cult groups. But a similar phenomenon can occur at the other end of the social scale. Marcuse, in *One-Dimensional Man*, describes what he calls 'the language of total administration'. This is the language which gives cohesion to total administrators, the functionaries of large bureaucracies, and mediates their reality. Chomsky (1973) has collected examples of such language. Here is an American pilot describing napalm bombs and their development:

> We sure are pleased with those backroom boys at Dow. The original product wasn't so hot – if the gooks were quick they could scrape it off. So the boys started adding polystyrene – now it sticks like shit to a blanket. But then if the gooks jumped under water it stopped burning, so they added Willie Peter [WP = white phosphorus] so's to make it burn better. It'll even burn under water now. And just one drop is enough, it'll keep on burning right down to the bone so they die anyway from phosphorus poisoning.
>
> (*The Backroom Boys*, p. 23)

This is only a rudimentary anti-language. Vietnamese and Viet Cong are renamed *gooks*, and *white phosphorus* is *Willie Peter*. There is a simple switch here: the Viet Cong are given a meaningless name to dehumanize them, and white phosphorus becomes meaningful and human, given a human name. There are two other features of this language which are slight shifts, though they are regular enough forms. The unknown adults at Dow Chemicals become *boys*, and the commodity they produce remains a *product* even when it is a weapon of war, thus eliminating the category difference between peace and war, which would restrict *product* to the sphere of peacetime commodity production.

71

This language is clearly very close to the dominant language, just as the society whose language it is feels itself very close to the dominant interests in the surrounding community. Even so, the function of such language is clear, that is, to transform what is troublesome and problematic in reality into something less disturbing, something homely and harmless: victims into *gooks*, bombs into *products*, destructive chemicals into *Willie Peter*, and men into *boys*. Precisely because the anti-language is so functional is it revealing about the ideology of the group. An anti-language is a device for managing reality, creating the necessary counter-reality.

With any anti-language, it should be possible to write a complete grammar, relating it systematically to the parent language. Such a grammar would be at one and the same time a set of ideological transformations and a precise and powerful diagnostic tool. The study of a sublanguage of this kind requires careful and extensive collection of language samples, but the methodology can be illustrated conveniently on the smaller, self-contained text of a single literary work. A poem can be regarded as the image of a world, and its language can be analysed as the language of this world. In so far as that world departs from the world outside the poem, and the language from the language of the poet's speech community, the grammar we establish will be an anti-grammar which gives the rules that constitute the poem's anti-world.

This is essentially the approach followed by Thorne (1965) in an analysis of a poem by the seventeenth-century English poet, John Donne. Here is Donne's poem, quoted in full.

A nocturnal upon St. Lucy's Day, being the shortest day

'Tis the year's midnight, and it is the day's,
Lucy's, who scarce seven hours herself unmasks,
   The sun is spent, and now his flasks
   Send forth light squibs, no constant rays;
     The world's whole sap is sunk:
The general balm th'hydroptic earth hath drunk,
Whither, as to the bed's-feet, life is shrunk,
Dead and interred; yet all these seem to laugh,
Compared with me, who am their epitaph.

Study me then, you who shall lovers be
At the next world, that is, at the next spring:
   For I am every dead thing,

In whom love wrought new alchemy.
  For his art did express
A quintessence even from nothingness,
From dull privations, and lean emptiness:
He ruined me, and I am re-begot
Of absence, darkness, death; things which are not.

All others, from all things, draw all that's good,
Life, soul, form, spirit, whence they being have;
  I, by love's limbec, am the grave
  Of all, that's nothing. Oft a flood
    Have we two wept, and so
Drowned the whole world, us two; oft did grow
To be two chaosses, when we did show
Care to aught else; and often absences
Withdrew our souls, and made us carcases.

But I am by her death (which word wrongs her)
Of the first nothing, the elixir grown;
  Were I a man, that I were one,
  I needs must know; I should prefer,
    If I were any beast,
Some ends, some means; yea plants, yea stones detest,
And love; all, all some properties invest;
If I an ordinary nothing were,
As shadow, a light, and body must be here.

But I am none; nor will my sun renew,
You lovers, for whose sake, the lesser sun
  At this time to the Goat is run
  To fetch new lust, and give it you.
    Enjoy your summer all;
Since she enjoys her long night's festival,
Let me prepare towards her, and let me call
This hour her vigil, and her eve, since this
Both the year's and the day's deep midnight is.

The linguistic form that expresses an anti-world most directly is negation. A poet or any other user of a natural language can create an anti-world by using just one component of a standard grammar, negation, simply denying or inverting statements about reality. In this poem, Donne uses a number of such forms; *not, none, no, nothing(ness)*, and the prefix *un-*. There are also partial negatives, like *scarce* and *light*, which carry a negative sense (*scarce* is *less than a norm, light* is contrasted with *constant* and so has the force of *not strong*).

A further linguistic resource is less obviously negative in its form. This is the system of tenses. Consider the sentence

Were I a man, that I were one,/I needs must know.

This is a hypothetical form, presenting an unfulfilled possibility: 'If I were a man, . . . but I'm not.' That is, the verb in a form indicating remote possibility has a negative force.

The same principle applies, in a weaker form, to other tenses. The simple past tense, as in *love wrought new alchemy* or *oft did grow/To be two chaosses*, is positive in form about the past. But this positive is contrasted with the present, in which love has no alchemy for the poet, and in which his lover is dead and no longer grows with him, into chaos or anything else. So the past tense conveys a meaning of 'not anymore so, not the case now'. The future and the imperative have similar implications. Only the present tense implies existence. The tenses therefore project four worlds: the present which exists positively alongside the poet's negative existence; the past, in which he was positive but which has now been negated; the future, from which he is excluded; and a negated hypothetical state, which could have existed now but doesn't.

There is another, less obvious, form of negation in the poem. Consider from the first line *it is the day's (midnight)*. Night and day are opposites in English, and this is part of the knowledge of a speaker of the language. We also know that *day* is the positive term and *night* is the negative. That is, *night* is *−day*. Similarly with some other pairs in the poem: *life* and *death, laugh* and *cry, full* and *empty, summer* and *winter, all* and *nothing*. In each of these, the first is the positive, the second the negative form, in a classification system that has remained constant since at least the seventeenth century.

In this poem Donne is aware of this underlying valency, but his response is seemingly to defy it. *Day's (midnight)*, once the deleted *midnight* is supplied, sounds odd. Midnight is the midpoint of a night, not a day. It exists on the boundary between two days, so it can hardly be called any one day's midnight. But this is the midnight of the shortest day, the day which is closest to being a night. So Donne's paradox half suggests the reclassification of *day* into its opposite, *night*. A similar process works with *life*. *Life* in the poem is not only *shrunk*, it is *dead*. Again, and more unmistakably this time, a positive term has turned into its opposite. Birth and death are yoked together in the second stanza with *I am re-begot . . . of death.* By a similar paradox, *all* becomes *nothing. I am . . . the grave/Of all, that's nothing.* Death is total negation, so that because he is nothing he must be the negation, or grave, of everything.

What Donne is doing here is to take the received classification of entities into positive and negative and reclassify them, so that the negative with which he identifies almost becomes the positive: *night* → *day, death* → *life, nothing* → *everything.* This is a common device in anti-languages. For instance, *Hell's angels* to describe an anti-group joins the negative *hell* with the positive *angel*, which reclassifies either *hell* as positive or *angels* as negative, incorporating the negative judgment of society and their own positive judgment on themselves into a single ambiguous unit.

Donne's process of reclassification goes one level deeper. Take the phrase *who am their epitaph.* In English, then as now, *who* is a pronoun that refers to an entity which is human and animate. Here it is linked to *epitaph*, which is non-human and non-animate. Similarly, *laugh* as a verb, according to the rules of English, which reflect an underlying common-sense version of the world, normally takes a human agent. Less odd-sounding but following the same principle, the *I* is only a *thing*, which is usually inanimate. Conversely, plants and stones *detest and love.* The effect is to create an eerie anti-world in which dead things laugh, and presumably living things do not, where humans are inanimate and stones and plants have feelings. The effect is achieved by a process of reclassification, whereby + human $\rightleftharpoons$ − human, + animate $\rightleftharpoons$ − animate (where $\rightleftharpoons$ means 'can be reclassified in either direction'). The process of reclassification is an act of negation carried out on fundamental categories in the science/grammar of the dominant language itself.

We can now attempt to set out the generalizations which seem to describe the distinctive qualities of this language and this world. Donne takes over the vocabulary and basic grammatical rules from English, but uses distinctive processes of negation. We need to specify the structures that negation works on, the forms that negation takes, and the constraints that apply to its use.

A. *Standard language.* Donne takes the following rules from the standard language:

Rule 1   Nouns, verbs and adjectives are classified in antonyms as either positive or negative.

Rule 2   (i) Actors (nouns) are classified as $\pm$ human, $\pm$ animate, $\pm$ self.

          (ii) Processes (verbs) are classified according to the agency they permit: $\pm$ human, $\pm$ animate.

Rule 3   Negation can be full or partial, realized through particles or by tense and modality:

          (i) By particles: full – *no, not, none, un-*

                              partial – *scarce, light*

          (ii) By tense and modality: full (unfulfilled hypothetical) – *were*

                              partial (past, future, imperative)

                              – *did express, shall be, enjoy*

B. *Anti-language.* The anti-language has all the processes for forming negatives to be found in the standard language, plus two others:

Anti-rule 1   The valency of antonyms may optionally be changed, from positive to negative ($+ \rightleftharpoons -$).

Anti-rule 2   The classification of agents may optionally be changed:

                    $+$ human $\rightleftharpoons$ $-$ human

                    $+$ animate $\rightleftharpoons$ $-$ animate

There are also two obligatory rules:

Anti-rule 3 $+ self$ must take a negative form.

Anti-rule 4 $+ self$ cannot be a transactive agent of physical-process verbs.

We put this in the form of a grammar because the rules are strictly observed, and because in this form the underlying logic is clearly revealed. However, though this grammar initially only reflects and realizes the poet's attitudes and beliefs, it, like any grammar, can come to create them. We can hypothesize, on the basis of this formalization, that in this language certain things are unsayable. For instance, *I love her* breaks anti-rules 3 and 4. *I did not kiss her* or *I will not touch her again* are double negatives in this grammar, and thus break anti-rule 3. But these things are not unsayable because they are ungrammatical. They are ungrammatical because they are unsayable. The function of the grammar is to hypothesize precisely what will be difficult or impossible to say. In this poem Donne conceives of a total disjunction between himself and others, corresponding to the distinction between animate and inanimate that these others would make. The thought of himself acting positively in the world, or feeling any emotion, is unendurable. Seeing himself as a total negativity, he attacks the basic classification system of his community, partly transforming it into a negative world in which he can feel at home.

This analysis suggests some generalizations about the form and function of anti-languages:

1 An anti-language is parasitic, taking its basic system of rules from the norm language.
2 An anti-language is defensive, protecting its community from direct grasp of problematic reality. It is not a language to think in, but a language in which to escape from thought. So it reveals, through its evasions, what parts of reality are problematic for that community.
3 An anti-language is oppositional, and expresses this opposition by an attack on the classification system of the norm language. The attack takes the form of full or partial inversion, exploiting and extending the negativity component of the norm grammar.

A final observation is necessary for a theory which attempts to account for the language of Donne's poem, prison language, and the jargon of US pilots in the Vietnam war. The social structure that gives rise to anti-languages can be highly various. The anti-society can consist of one member or many. It can be relatively high or relatively low on the social scale, and be more or less totally excluded by the society as a whole. None of this can be predicted from a study of the language alone. We can summarize this as follows:

4 An anti-language is inexplicable without reference to the anti-society and its place in a larger social structure.

Strictly we should relate this account of Donne's anti-language to its social basis. (For a fuller account of this see Aers and Kress, 1978.) Although the 'Nocturnal' seems a purely personal poem about the loss of a lover, it may also express Donne's sense of his general social relationships. In letters to friends written by Donne at this time, that is a constant theme.

STRUCTURES OF SOCIETY, STRUCTURES OF LANGUAGE

The distinctions in the grammar between animate and inanimate human and non-human, reflect major distinctions in the accredited science of our community, between the biological and physical sciences, and between the social and natural sciences. Language also reflects the social structure of the community in a variety of ways. A social structure is an ordering or distribution of power and social functions. At the largest level power is distributed asymmetrically between social classes or different national or racial groups. Such a distribution is normally reflected in and sustained by differences of language, class languages, and regional and social dialects of various forms. Power at the smallest level is also directly reflected in and mediated through language, as we show in chapter 5. But, cutting across divisions by class, nationality, or race in every society is a division in terms of sex. This division is not manifested in quite the same way as divisions of power. In some societies there are special languages, women's talk formalized to the extent of a discrete language. There are detectable differences between women's and men's talk in contemporary English-speaking societies, but the distinction is not nearly so overt as between class languages. The relations between the sexes are also mediated through specialized terms of address, and by women's use of forms of speech which are appropriate for use by an inferior.

But, as well as this differential distribution of the resources of language along sex lines, sexual differences can become a principle internal to a language, part of the structure of its 'science'. This is done primarily through systems of gender. Gender is grammatical sex. Many languages have overt systems of gender, whose characteristic it is to have markers for grammatical sex. Grammatical sex must be distinguished from biological sex in two ways. A gender system may assign a sex to inanimate objects which have no sex; thus the Latin *mensa*, table, is feminine in gender. It will also often assign a sex which contradicts the biological sex. Examples of this – often quoted – are, from German, *das Mädchen* (the girl) which is neuter, and, from French, a sentence like *Le professeur est enceinte* (The professor (masculine) is pregnant).

This all may seem irrelevant to English, which doesn't have an overt system of gender. However, as Whorf (1956) has pointed out, English does have gender, but it has gone underground and become what he calls a covert category. A study of covert gender in English shows the function of gender systems in general and the functionality of covert systems in particular.

Whorf used the pronoun test to reveal covert gender in English.

Take the word *ship*. In Latin this is *navis*, feminine. In French it is either *le navire* or *le bateau*, masculine. *Ship* can take the neuter pronoun, *it*, but it also frequently takes the feminine, *she*. *She's sailing tomorrow*, never *He's sailing tomorrow*. When a ship is launched, the ritual words are *May God bless her and all who sail in her*. It would be very difficult for an English speaker to say *Save him, and all who sail in him*, though for a French speaker it would be the required form. The pronoun test has also been used by feminist writers to reveal that words referring to positions of power have masculine gender even if their occupant is female. A *chairman, author, doctor* is *he*.

Another interesting case is the word *car*. The Latin *currus*, a chariot, is masculine. The French *la voiture* is feminine. The pronoun test, especially for males in our society, classes *car* as feminine. English and French, it seems, agree on its gender. Advertisers recognize and exploit covert gender. So car advertisements frequently include a woman draped over the body of the car, identifying the car with the woman. It would be unusual to show a man draped over the bonnet. Men tend to stand taller than their cars in advertisements, next to them, indicating a superior/inferior relationship between man/master and car/woman/servant.

Although the categories male/female are common and important to all societies, the way in which they are applied, especially in language, is clearly different. The French seem not to wish to order ships under the category feminine. The English do. The Germans regard them as neuter. French and English, however, agree in assigning feminine gender to *car*, while Germans regard it as neuter. There is no biological basis in either case. Why, then, is a car, for instance, regarded as feminine? The answer must lie in attitudes to cars, and attitudes to women; that is, there are conceptions of the relation between men, women, and cars which establish an analogy between them. Perhaps the basis of the analogy is possession or dominance (or perhaps the way cars respond so immediately to the action of a masculine actor, purring into life and action at the (male) touch of a switch!). Whatever the rationale, the basis is clearly ideological, a projection of social relationships onto a world of objects.

But the gender of *car* in English is not quite as simple as this account suggests. Women assign feminine gender to cars less often than do men. In particular, small cars are more likely to have masculine gender. The Walt Disney film about a Volkswagen which drove itself called the car 'Herbie', which is masculine, but diminutive. Perhaps this goes with the social fact that a small car like a Volkswagen tends to be the second

79

car in America. Because it is driven by the woman it assumes masculine gender but juvenile status, reflecting another of the stereotype roles for women. Whatever the explanation, this example suggests two advantages of a covert system of gender. It can evolve 'silently' in response to changing attitudes, and it can allow different versions of an ideology to coexist within the same language.

An overt gender system fixes a set of sexual associations for a culture. A covert gender system is simply the same kind of set, which is learned and displayed indirectly. But even in languages with overt gender, the set of gender associations is often wider than the overt gender system indicates. In Latin, for instance, *pulcher* (beautiful) or *castus* (chaste) are rarely used of adult males, though adjectives in Latin formally have masculine, feminine, and neuter markers. So we could say that Latin has covert gender classifying adjectives as well as overt gender classifying nouns. In practice there is a continuum. It ranges from gender systems which are grammatically fixed sexual associations, relatively pervasive in a culture, to networks of sexual associations which are relatively free and more localized in a culture. The difference is one of degree rather than kind, just as overt and covert systems are different in their means, not in their fundamental character and function.

The operation of culturally fixed sexual associations, or of a generalized covert gender system, can be seen clearly in advertisements aimed specifically at a sexually defined market, especially with products whose function is directly linked to sex roles. Perfume is one such product (French *le parfum*, Italian *il profumo*, both masculine). Take the following typical enough advertisement, for Cerisse by Charles Revlon. The picture shows a blonde woman seated, in a white dress, with a white cat in her lap. Behind her is a fountain, with water trickling out of the mouths of lion-heads. Beside the picture are the words: 'Very cool. Very fragrant. Very very exciting. Cerisse. By Charles Revlon.' Below this is a bottle of the product, in clear glass.

A woman, of course, has feminine gender. Fountains in French are feminine in gender. They seem to have feminine valency in English, too, as does water. Cats are less consistent. In French they are masculine, in Latin feminine. In English, the unmarked form seems to be feminine, with *tom* available to indicate masculine sex (dogs being the reverse). But lions are masculine, and the lions' heads behind this cool beauty are evidently slaves to her allure.

Adjectives can also have a covert gender. *Fragrant* describes women, not men, not even a man who wears scented after-shave. *Very very* is an interesting intrusion of 'women's language' into an otherwise neutrally presented gender system. *Very very* shows the emotional extravagance permitted to women, but not men, in the ideological version of sexual characteristics of our society.

In such advertisements, gender is often carried most potently in adjectives. An advertisement for Nulon handcream reads '*soft* and *silky smooth. Beautiful* to the touch. *Nourished* and protected by Nulon. A blend of *natural* ingredients which really work. With a *delicate fragrance* and a *light refreshing* feel.' Here all the italicized adjectives are sexually specific, with feminine valency. An advertisement for Boots Skin Balm starts: 'Our unique skin balm is made with buttermilk, clover honey, marigold, beeswax, olive oil, almond oil, maize oil, cocoa butter, juniper and orange flower water. Honest-to-goodness. Every one of these ingredients in our new Buttermilk and Clover honey unique skin balm is naturally good for dry skin.' The list of ingredients here is glossing 'natural' (*nature* is feminine in gender in Latin, French, and German; *Mother Nature* in English).

We can use these advertisements as an initial body of material to analyse. First we might set up a list of adjectives which have clear feminine valency: *soft, smooth, delicate, beautiful*. We could add *moist* to the list, as the opposite of *dry*, the main quality that women must avoid in hair, hands, face, and elsewhere. These adjectives project a set of nouns – *softness, delicacy, fragrance* – which will have the same grammatical sex. Some adjectives formed from nouns fall into this class: *silky, milky, natural*. The original nouns have feminine valency (for instance, *Mother Nature*). There is a further set of verbs formed from these adjectives: *soften, smooth, beautify*. These retain a feminine valence as actions especially appropriate to be performed to or by a woman. There is a larger, more open set of nouns which have the qualities of the feminine adjectives conventionally ascribed to them: *flowers* and *honey* (natural, sweet, delicate, beautiful), *silk* (natural, beautiful, soft).

Clearly, the over-all category *feminine* is mediated by a set of categories specifying femininity (or masculinity) for the language and culture. So we can set up the following abstract schema for femininity:

Defining categories	Typical qualities	Feminine nouns	Feminine verbs
− active + weak + obedient + pleasing + caring	Adjectives implying one or more defining categories	Nouns with preferred linkages with feminine adjectives	Verbs with preferred feminine agents

In this schema, the defining categories constitute the ideology. the qualities listed all define modes or potentialities for acting or being acted on. The ideological definitions act to prescribe the behaviours appropriate to the female role as established (usually by men) for that community. These prescriptive definitions can be realized directly in surface forms. A moralist, for instance, might say that a woman should obey her husband, please him, and care for him and for their children. This ideology may contain contradictions, which tend to obtrude in an explicit form. For instance, a woman should be passive not active, weak not strong, but she should not lie in bed all day. Direct presentation of ideology is also more obviously coercive, and hence more liable to be resisted. An indirect and implicit presentation of ideology, then, has clear advantages. It is widely pervasive, giving 'books in the running brooks, sermons in stones'. It acts unconsciously, at a level beneath critical awareness. This allows it to accommodate contradictions in the ideology more easily. Any explicit form of the ideology becomes a derived structure, an attempted reconstruction of what has been naturalized by a member of that culture. The utility of a covert gender system for nouns thus becomes clear. It consists of a heterogeneous set of objects which are marked to indicate sex roles. This set is learnt by speakers of a language at an early age, even before they have been fully socialized into these roles. The weakness of the implication is compensated for by massive redundancy. Sexist messages are transmitted continuously day after day and year after year, till they penetrate the unconscious, being stored there in the form of images. Freud (1900) has shown how these categorizations determine the associative significance of symbols in dreams. The major defect of an overt gender system is that it is relatively inflexible, especially in literate cultures where the history of the language remains visible in written texts and dictionaries. This makes it a conservative influence on ideology, perhaps introducing unwanted irrationalities into the system, as some nouns retain a gender classification which is increasingly inappropriate to the dominant ideology. But the absence of overt gender in a language like English doesn't mean that English culture is not sexist. On the contrary, it has evolved a language for transmitting sexist concepts which is equally widespread, more flexible, and arguably more efficient as an ideological instrument.

SOURCES AND CONTEXT

Although the topics which we discuss in this chapter, and in Chapters 5 and 6, have been and are the concerns of many linguistic theories, most frequently they have been discussed as matters within language alone. The notable exceptions to this are to be found in the work of Edward Sapir and Benjamin Lee Whorf. We have already referred to the latter's work; the former's book *Language*, published in 1921, remains one of the classic humanistic statements on that subject. The theory of classification has been a major concern in anthropology and sociology, and one very good collection of essays from that point of view is Mary Douglas's *Rules and Meanings: the Anthropology of Everyday Knowledge* (1973). An essay which is closer to a connection with language is Edmund Leach's 'Anthropological aspects of language: animal categories and verbal abuse' (1964). M.A.K. Halliday's *Grammar, Society and the Noun* (1967) is the best recent statement in the tradition of Sapir and Whorf; in it he makes concrete links between language and culture.

Within linguistics classification has been a covert concern: the statement of syntactic rules depends on prior statement of classes of categories. On the one hand, the classes have to be established; on the other they are established through the discovery of what category may appear in specific syntactic links with another category. In Chomsky's *Aspects of the Theory of Syntax* (1965) a major theoretical concern is to establish so-called 'selection-restriction rules'. These would predict that in 'normal' English utterances such as Donne's *I am every dead thing*, for instance, would be ruled out as ungrammatical (so that part of the poet's art consists in 'breaking the rules' of a language). However, in this work, as in related work (for instance, in the theory of case-grammar put forward by Charles Fillmore (1968) in 'The case for case' or by Wallace Chafe in *Meaning and the Structure of Language* (1970)), there is no attempt to link the linguistic categories with the cultural ones. This is less true of linguistic work on such topics as colour and gender, for instance. A most interesting book dealing with colour terminology is Berlin and Kay's *Basic Color Terms* (1969). Further work in this direction has been conducted by Eleanor Rosch; this is reported in 'Human categorization' (1975). One last area which should be mentioned here is that of kinship terminology. Although the work is predominantly anthropological, nevertheless the fact that it deals with linguistic entities (names for kinship relations) has meant that it is concerned with linguistic systems. The effect of this work on linguistics generally has been marked. The analyses tend to be highly formal; one such is Floyd G. Lounsbury's 'A semantic analysis of Pawnee kinship usage'.

The relation between social groupings and language has been much written about. There is a large literature on dialect, both geographical and social: the first three sections in Pride and Holmes's reader *Sociolinguistics* (1972) contain essays on this topic. Similarly, there is a large body of literature which subjects language differences of this kind to more politically aware interpretations. Here Bernstein's terms 'elaborated' and 'restricted code' figure very prominently. Essays by him and W. Labov, using American data, can be found in Giglioli's reader *Language and Social Context* (1972). This debate is focused on the notion of 'linguistic deprivation'. Nell Keddie's *Tinker, Tailor . . . The Myth of Cultural Deprivation* (1973) contains essays on this topic. Our own discussion owes much to this, but is set more closely within the theoretical terms provided in Halliday's (1976) essay 'Anti-languages'. Not only does Halliday's concept deal with these 'dialects' as coherent and fully systematic languages, but his account permits us to relate specific languages to the conditions and forces which give rise to social groupings. From here it is not too difficult to make the link with special languages of all kinds: secret languages (one example, a language associated with Australian Aboriginal rituals, is described in Kenneth Hale's (1971) 'A note on a Walbiri tradition of antonymy') and taboo languages which have been described in many societies. One such general type deals with special languages used by men and/ or women. R.M.W. Dixon's (1971) 'A method of semantic description' describes one such language, again in Australia, in the Dyirbal language of Northern Queensland. In this society there is an 'everyday language' and a 'mother-in-law language', which is used in the presence of sexually taboo persons. There is some evidence that English has systematic differences of this kind, used differentially by male and female speakers. The impact of the feminist movement has given rise to some serious research on sexism in language, and of particular interest here are Robin Lakoff's (1973) 'Language and woman's place' and also Barrie Thorne and Nancy Henley's collection of essays *Language and Sex: Difference and Dominance* (1975).

5

UTTERANCES IN DISCOURSE

MINIMAL CLASSIFICATION

The classification system of a language is prior to any individual utterance, providing the speaker with words, hierarchies of categories, models and structures, as the raw material of communication. However, some classification operations must be performed on every utterance by the speaker himself. These minimal obligatory classifications are the speaker's indication of generality, truth and validity, and range of applicability to the whole and to its individual parts. The term we use for this is *modality*. It indicates the mode within which an utterance is presented as true, reliable, and authoritative. Modality has traditionally been regarded as part of the verb system, where the term described the set of modal verbs. *He may come* has a different status from *he should come*: the first is about possibility in a general sense, the second about obligation. (The speaker of the second sentence may of course not be telling the truth. The auxiliary makes a *claim*, it is not a proof). However, modality pervades every part of an utterance; it is not restricted to the verb alone. If a speaker does not classify his utterance and its parts in the required ways, he will produce a sentence whose meaning is sufficiently clear, but which will seem glaringly ungrammatical and unacceptable. The speaker will be regarded as (intellectually) incompetent because he has not sufficiently classified his own utterance.

For instance, the direct realization of the transactive model would be a sentence of the form *Milkman bring cream*. This is ungrammatical in English. An acceptable form is

The milkman brings the cream.

Schematically we can represent this as follows:

Nominal			Process		Nominal	
determiner + noun + number			verb + tense		determiner + noun	
the	milkman	ø	bring	s	the	cream

(Here the first line labels the 'places' in the model, the second gives the linguistic labels, and the last shows the actual classificatory entities. The symbol ø indicates that a classification has taken place, but that it is not represented by an actual item in the surface. Nouns in English have to be classified as either singular or plural. Plural is most frequently indicated by -s, singular by the absence of a mark.)

The difference between the unclassified transactive model, consisting of nominals and process, and the classified surface form is that each place in the model has been further specified. These specifications act through what can be thought of as slots in the model, predetermined places which must be 'filled' at least once. Using our example to establish provisional categories for each slot, we have

determiners:	definite, indefinite
number:	singular, plural
tense:	present, past

We noted in the earlier discussion of models and their realization in surface structure (in chapter 3) that there is not a one-to-one relationship between, say, transactive and transitive. This non-matching of semantic category and surface form is the rule in language. Here it means that, while generally speaking *plural* is realized by -s and *past tense* by -*ed*, there are many exceptions. Some examples of 'irregular plurals' are: *man – men, knife – knives, sheep – sheep, ox – oxen.* Some 'irregular past' forms: *choose – chose, run – ran, hit – hit, lay – laid.* These are fossils from the various evolutionary periods of the English classification system.

The classificatory óperations are interdependent. For instance, *a* is impossible with a plural noun; there is agreement in number between subject and verb; and tenses agree with other indicators of time in an utterance. This interdependence is not only formal. To see the modal effect of determiners consider the following:

> Man is rational
> The man is rational
> A man is rational

All three are in the present tense. The first is offered as absolutely general and universal, true of all men (indeed, of all men and women) at all times. The universality follows from the absence of an overtly present determiner. Paradoxically, this sentence form, which would be regarded as defective and proof of incompetence if produced by a child or a foreigner, is the most universally applicable and certain of utterances if produced by someone who is regarded as a competent 'classifier'. In the first case, we assume that the slot is empty because the speaker didn't know how to fill it. In the second case, we assume that the slot has been filled, but by a ø. It signals the absence of a specifier, and this in turn is interpreted as meaning that the application of *man* is universal, applied to every entity which is properly classified as *man*. We interpret the absence of the determiner according to a prior classification made by us of the speaker. If we have classified him as a child, foreigner, or imbecile, we regard the absence of the classifier as a sign of a missing classificatory act. If we have classified him as competent, we regard the absence of the classifier as the sign of a philosophical mind at work.

The second sentence is also in the present, so it too implies a general truth, but the effect of *the* is to limit this claim to one instance. About this one man, the statement is offered as universally true. The determiner also implies certainty about the identity of this man, who is by this classification assumed to be known to both speaker and hearer. *The* therefore introduces limits as well as certainty into the basic utterance. *A*, as in *A man is rational*, however, has two interpretations. One is universal, making it equivalent to *Man is rational*. Here *a* stands for *any man at all*, and hence *all*. In sentences with a different modal classification of the verb, such as *A man has come, a* would more likely imply a single man whose identity is not known. It is thus as particular as *the*, but less certain, or certain of less, than the definite article. This second interpretation might just be possible with *A man is rational*, but we can see the strong bond which exists between modal operations on different parts of the model, in this case between the form of the verb and the interpretation of the determiner. We can also see the parsimony of the system of determiners in English, where both *a* and ø have at least two contradictory meanings each. The same is true of *the*, as we shall show.

The basic models seem to be at their simplest when their verb is in what is often called the 'simple present' tense. However, this form of the verb is neither simple nor confined in its meaning to present time. The illusion of simplicity comes from the fact that only a single surface marker is involved, -*s* for the third person singular, and apparently nothing for all plurals and for first and second person singulars. But this is extreme economy, not simplicity. One surface element (taking ø as an element) serves to guarantee that a large number of important operations have taken place, and that the status of the utterance has been checked in a number of ways. The -s form acts as a rough-and-ready certificate of reliability, stamped on so automatically that the criteria aren't displayed. Such a procedure has its obvious dangers. Modal classification of the verb is the speaker's classification of the reliability of his utterance. A form which seems to guarantee the reliability of the utterance without specifying the tests that have been carried out is clearly a powerful and suspicious linguistic form.

It is persuasive partly because it seems so transparent, so automatic a reflection of reality. A verb is in the present, we might suppose, because it is about the present. It is singular because the actor is a single entity. It may well seem that all these decisions are taken by reality, not by the speaker, so that the form can be utterly trusted. But reality is never as fixed as this. To adapt Disraeli, there are lies, damned lies, and classifications. The real world doesn't exist in discourse without being classified. The classification of reality, and the classification of that classification, is never to be wholly trusted.

Take the following sentence, a headline from the *Sun* newspaper in 1974:

Shirley fights the three-bob loaf.

It is a transactive of winning simplicity, introducing an account of Shirley Williams, then Labour Minister for Prices, and her plans to subsidize bread prices. The -s of *fights* signals a number of things. It indicates, for instance, that the subject is singular. We might ask, why should this be registered in the verb as well as in the noun? It is common to find agreement between subject and verb in languages other than English. One reason that is often suggested is that agreement between subject and verb helps to organize these elements of the sentence. But English does that unmistakably by word order. Dialects which do not use the -s singular form seem clear enough about which noun is the subject of which verb. An inflected language like Latin has agreement between subject and verb, while also distinguishing the subject from other nouns through case-endings.

Part of the reason may be the modal function of the distinction between singular and plural. This distinction affects the status of the utterance, primarily what can be termed its sharpness of focus. In the *Sun* headline we have two singulars, neither of which is in fact determined by reality. Another version of this sentence would read, equally or more accurately.

Shirley and a department including many civil servants and secretaries fight the three-bob loaf.

The effect of this is to make the statement seem less precise, less focused, less reliable. Now there are innumerable hand-to-hand fights going on with this fearsome loaf. Plurals have a kind of imprecision which singulars do not. Take

> Bugner fights Ellis tonight.
> Bugner and Ellis fight tonight.

In the first there must be a single action (the singular imposing unity on what could otherwise be regarded as many related actions). In the second they may be fighting each other, at the same time, or they may be fighting different opponents, in different bouts, at different times, perhaps even in different continents. Similarly, a plural object affects the status of the statement:

> Shirley fights seventeen three-bob loaves.

Here Shirley may be fighting seventeen loaves at once, or she may be fighting them separately. But the doubt is less in this case than with *Bugner and Ellis fight tonight.* A plural subject affects the status of the utterance more drastically than a plural object. So there are reasonable grounds for having agreement between subject and verb rather than between verb and object, though the latter is a possible decision.

The same is true for relationals. Consider

> The ball is red.
> The balls are red.
> A cricket ball is red.

With the first, the statement seems to be immediately checkable, by direct perception. With the second, it would be possible to ask 'are they *all* red?' The reliability of the statement is less. The third is as general as the second but not as focused.

The general effect of a plural is to indicate a compound field. A sentence in which everything is in the plural will feel more diffused and complex than a sentence which uses only singulars, even if the reality described is the same. As the proverb has it: 'You can't see the wood for the trees.' A singular, like *wood*, makes the percept/concept seem manageable. There are a variety of strategies for achieving such focus. The headline we looked at uses a definite article; the use of determiners and of singular/plural are related operations. The sentence could have been *Shirley fights three-bob loaves*. Really, of course, there were lots and lots of loaves (some of which already cost more than three bob, or 15p). If the 'wood' had been shown, on the one side there would have been Shirley and a small army of bureaucrats paying subsidies to various people in bakeries throughout the country, to try to peg the price charged for millions of loaves of a certain kind. The enterprise would be revealed as a piecemeal operation which could not be easily visualized as a heroine grappling with a singular villainous loaf. The choice of singular or plural is not simply dictated by reality. This example shows that speakers have considerable freedom to define things as 'single', with all the advantages that entails. A popular newspaper like the *Sun* typically uses singulars where possible, in articles as well as headlines, in its attempt to present and 'familiarize' political reality especially, as 'homely', concrete, definite, and hence easy to manage for those who manage it. Conversely, there can be advantages in using plurals. For instance, *The fact is* . . . may sometimes be less useful than *The facts are these*. . . . With the second the complexity of the situation and the multiplicity of considerations begin to assert themselves as something that only older, wiser heads can deal with. One is simplistic, the other can be mystificatory.

Fights, in the example we have looked at, is conventionally called the present tense. But in this sentence, which is typical enough, it is not clear that Shirley is actually fighting at the moment. The *-s* present is vague on that point. It can mean that she habitually fights loaves, that such is her job. It can also mean that she will certainly fight these loaves. (*Bugner fights Ellis* could be a headline announcing that a fight has definitely been arranged.) It could be used if she is fighting these loaves at the moment, but in English the present continuous (*is fighting*) is the form used to signal present action.

Corresponding to the 'simple present' is the 'simple past', whose marker is usually *-ed*. Frequently it indicates that the event described occurred in the past. However, we saw in Donne's 'Nocturnal' that it could also signify a kind of negation, meaning *not now*. This implication is part of its general significance in current English. Consider the two questions

> I wonder if you can see me?
> I wondered if you could see me, (Sir)?

The two differ in tense, the second being the past form of the first. But in actual use they both refer to the same time. What is different is the relationship between the *I* and the *you*. The second is more polite and deferential. The effect of the past form is to make the statement more tentative. That is, its modality changes from more to less certain. This effect is more marked when the *past* classification is attached to a modal verb or to a verb which has a modal function, as is the case with *wonder* and *can* in the examples. But even when the straightforward -*ed* past is applied to an ordinary lexical verb it has a modal effect as well as indicating tense. *Shirley fought the three-bob loaf* not only locates the action in the past, it limits its scope in a way similar to the effect of a determiner. It marks it as a particular event, and not as a general truth. The distinction is subtle in its effect. In the conventions followed by English newspapers, as well as distinguishing headlines from text, the past-present form can distinguish institutional from private utterances. In the *Sun* of 16 December 1977, Mr Callaghan *denounced* and *accused*, Mr Foot *declared*, but a letter of intent to the International Monetary Fund *says*.

What we seem to have here is a functional shift. Features which originally coded time now code general modality as well. The inner logic of this shift seems to be as follows: tense served initially to place an event in a chronological relation with the utterance, *close* or *distant* from the *now* of the utterance. Whatever is happening now can be vouched for by the speaker. He or she is experiencing it as actuality. An event which is not now cannot, because of its distance from the speech event, be vouched for so strongly. It is not experienced as being as real as an event *now*. By an inversion, what feels certain, or what the speaker claims is certain, is classified by the present form, even if it is not in present time. Conversely, what feels less certain, less actual, is coded as 'past', even when it refers to an event that is occurring in present time. Similarly, a speaker's wish to express conceptual or social distance from propositions or persons can be coded in the -*ed* form.

It may be significant that English now does not distinguish between singular and plural in the simple -*ed* past, though the past forms with the auxiliary verb *to be* (*was* and *were*) still maintain the distinction. If it is the case that the -*ed* past has a modal function akin to that of the plural, then the distinction between blurred and focused, added to the distinction between close and remote, might seem nearly redundant.

MODELS OF SPEECH AND POWER

The hard-working -*s* of the present tense ending signals two other meanings. It indicates that the subject is in the third person, that it is some person or thing other than the speaker or the hearer. This, too, has a modal function which we can see if we contrast it with the other persons (in English, first person *I* or *we* and second person *you*). Take the following three forms:

> Shirley fights.
> I fight.
> You fight.

With *I* as subject the utterance has all the reliability of a first-hand claim (though with the potential unreliability of a claim about oneself). Its source or authority is absolutely clear, and if it seems less than certain that is because of doubts about the honesty of the speaker. With *you* as subject, the speaker is setting himself up as an authority on another person's actions. Again, the modality is dependent on particular judgments about the participant's reliability. If the action is a mental-process one, there is a more marked shift in the modal effect of the two persons. If I say *I feel well* I am usually presumed to be an expert on how I feel. A counter-statement would usually be not *You feel ill/well* but *You look ill/well*. You can be an authority on how I look, but not on how or what I feel. Only someone with considerable social power can override this. A sergeant-major might tell a suspected malingerer *You feel perfectly well, get on the —— parade-ground*. A psychiatrist can have me committed to a mental hospital despite or because of my protestations of sanity. Power can become knowledge.

With the third-person form, these considerations do not apply. A sentence in the third person has been detached from any particular speaker. Its modality can no longer depend on an assessment of the reliability of its source. It no longer carries obligatory indications of who is the authority for the utterance, or how close it is to that source (although that would be possible: *Fred said that Bill told him that Joe heard Shirley say she fought the three-bob loaf*). This uncertainty ought to make the third-person form seem unreliable. The contrary seems to be the case, however. The detachment from a particular person gives the utterance an impersonal force. First- and second-person forms, like determiners, limit the scope of the utterance. The third-person form implies a neutral transmitter and it is the form in which to present a statement as authoritative.

This is true even for God. Milton failed to understand this in his dramatization of God in *Paradise Lost* and made the mistake of having God say in the first person what his prophets have said about him.

Such I created all th' Ethereal Powers
And spirits, both them who stood and them who failed;
Freely they stood who stood, and fell who fell
Not free, what proof could they have given sincere
Of true allegiance, constant faith or love,
Where only what they needs must do, appeared;
Not what they would? What praise could they receive?
What pleasure I from such obedience paid.

(Paradise Lost, III, 109)

This is orthodox Christian doctrine when said in the third person about God, but when it is said in the first person by him, it inevitably sounds less impressive, the words of an egotist whose words we would judge warily in real life.

There is a systematic classificatory relationship between the three grammatical persons:

I fought	(A speaking to B)
you fought	(B speaking to A)
he fought	(B speaking to C about A)

The relationship between the first two persons is organized by speech roles in what we can call the transactive speech model, since it conceives of the speech exchange as dynamic and interactional. We see the transactive speech model as closely analogous to the syntagmatic transactive model. The latter has two participants, one active and one affected, related by a process. The transactive speech model similarly has two participants, one active (the speaker) and one affected (the hearer) related by a process (the message).

Syntagmatic transactive model:
actor   process   affected

Transactive speech model:
speaker   message   hearer

In this model the speaker is always *I* and the hearer *you*. Hence the model is

I   message   you

The role of the speaker can normally be taken by either participant, and either can be active. Just as in a given event I may classify myself as actor or affected (*I saw the accident, Bill showed me the accident*), so in the speech model I may assume the role of either speaker or hearer. Of course there are restrictions in specific situations: where I am very much inferior to the other participant I have to wait for 'permission to speak'; just as in a similar situation it may be unwise for me to choose the syntactic role of actor for myself. Otherwise speakers switch persons easily in an exchange (*I did – You didn't – I did but you didn't – Of course I did, it was you who didn't* . . .). Both pronouns code a place in the speech model as well as an identification of the participants.

Statements in the third person do not depend in the same way on the transactive speech model. Whereas the identity of *I* and *you* is recovered from the speech situation, that of *he/she/it* is recovered from outside the speech situation. The speech model has an ambiguous place with these forms, since any utterance could have originated as a first- or second-person utterance or could have been a neutral third-person statement from the beginning. The third-person form, then, either involves a deletion of parts of the full transactional speech model or it is organized by a different model, a non-transactional speech model which (like the non-transactional syntagmatic model) consists of only two terms, statement plus speech-participant.

The speech model also organizes another aspect of modality. The speech model occurs in three forms: question, statement, and command. As we have noted before, there is a non-matching relation between the model and the surface form. The neutral form of a statement is a declarative; the neutral form of a command is an imperative; and the neutral form of a question is an interrogative. We can show this in simple tabular form:

Semantic category	*Surface form*
Statement	declarative
Command	imperative
Question	interrogative

As we shall show, any semantic category may be realized by any one of the surface forms on the right. Each one of the three forms involves a specific role-relation between speaker and hearer. In the statement, the speaker is giver of information, the hearer is recipient of information. In the question, the speaker is seeker of information, the hearer the possible provider of the information. In the command, the speaker is commander, the hearer is the commanded.

As we pointed out, there is no one-to-one relation between the underlying models and their surface forms. We will therefore explore the relation between the surface forms and the underlying models that organize them, in some detail.

To start with the imperative, take a command like *Jump*. This is understood as a deleted form of *You will jump* (the deleted items come out if the speaker adds *Jump, won't you?*). That is, the speech model organizes the relation between the speaker and the hearer, but it is a form of the speech model which has been further classified. Instead of a symmetrical relationship between speaker and hearer, there is here an asymmetrical power relationship between commander and commanded. Commander is speaker (+ power), commanded is hearer (− power).

As we showed, there are a number of forms that a question may take, though again organized by the transactive speech model. One form is a yes/no question (so called because the only possible answers are either *yes* or *no*). *Is Joe fighting tonight?* clearly involves a specific modality. This question indicates uncertainty about whether the statement is true or not. But it differs from *Joe may be fighting tonight* in that the former assumes that there is someone listening who may know whether he is or not. There is an asymmetrical relationship posited between speaker and hearer. Speaker is classified as (− knowledge), the hearer as (+ knowledge). The reply, accordingly, has the speaker classified as (+ knowledge). This classification is transitory and localized. The same speaker who asked *Is Joe fighting tonight?* may be an answerer of questions on who has the better knock-out record. And, as well as the transitory classification (+ knowledge), there is also a more stable classification, arising from social context and interaction, as (+ expert). That is, the speaker may be a habitual occupier of the position (+ knowledge), a position of relative authority. Such stable classifications normally invert the transitory classification made for the duration of a speech event. If the questioner is (+ expert), the question *Is Joe fighting tonight?* is interpreted as *He knows whether Joe is fighting tonight, but wants to test us.* A question where the questioner is (+ expert) is interpreted as catechistic, aimed at eliciting obedience (an attempt at producing the right answer) rather than information.

In actual discourse, the three forms of the speech model and their surface realizations interact in a complex way. As we noted, the interrogative can be used to give commands and an imperative structure can be used to ask a question. This complexity is rule-governed and well motivated. Take as an example an interrogative used as a command:

Can you get the meal ready?

The surface form classifies the speaker as (− knowledge). In some situations (− knowledge) implies (− power), so that the asker of a question may be classifying himself as (− power). But a question requires an answer, so the questioner is also controlling the behaviour of the hearer. In this respect the questioner's classification is (+ power). This makes questions ambiguous about the distribution of power between the participants. It is therefore a highly convenient form for mystifying power relationships. In the example above, spoken by a typical male chauvinist husband, there is an initial stable classification of the speaker as (+ power) and a temporary classification as (− knowledge), which partially cancels out (+ power). If the wife immediately goes to get the meal ready, we can deduce that the stable classification (+ power) has proved dominant. If, on the other hand, she quickly says *yes* or *no*, we can deduce equally that the temporary classification (− knowledge) has proved relevant and dominant. Of course, these things point to well-established relations between the two. Further complexities can be introduced with effortless ease by experienced players. For instance, yes/no questions are also realized by rising intonation, indicating an open field, whereas commands have a falling intonation, a closed field. So the husband's interrogative could be said with a falling intonation:

Can you get the mèal rèady?

This gives an utterance which is syntactically an interrogative, but has the intonation pattern of a command. The self-classification in this case would be speaker (permanently + power) (temporarily − knowledge, + power), so that the utterance has an 'overbalance' of power. But he could use a rising intonation:

Can you get the méal réady?

This gives speaker (permanently + power) (temporarily − knowledge, − power), which seems to cancel out the claim to power. The effect of this in actual use seems to be to allow the hearer to either accept or reject the command. Although a question by a speaker who is classified as (permanently + power) about the hearer's ability to perform an action (especially one of which the speaker may be a beneficiary!) is normally interpreted as a command, the openness of the field here seems to signal to the hearer that he or she may avoid this command. Of course, social relations are so finely nuanced that in specific situations this may still be interpreted invariably as either command or question.

Other devices may be used to further complicate the mediation of power relations. In the three examples the husband could have added *please* or *darling*, which could neutralize the power relation, unless said with falling intonation as the rest of the command. He could add *woman* or *wife*, in some of these, not in others.

In many conversations, the most important content concerns power relationships communicated through classifications which operate on the basic speech models. Skilful dramatists in the realist mode exploit this form to communicate general messages about relationships through exchanges which seem on the surface to be totally trivial. As an example, here is the opening of John Osborne's famous play of the 1950s, *Look back in Anger*:

> *Jimmy*: Why do I do this every Sunday? Even the book reviews seem to be the same as last week's. Different books – same reviews. Have you finished that one yet?
>
> *Cliff*: Not yet.
>
> *Jimmy*: I've just read three whole columns on the English Novel. Half of it's in French. Do the Sunday papers make *you* feel ignorant?
>
> *Cliff*: Not 'arf.
>
> *Jimmy*: Well, you *are* ignorant. You're just a peasant. (To Alison) What about you? You're not a peasant are you?
>
> *Alison*: (absently) What's that?
>
> *Jimmy*: I said do the papers make you feel you're not so brilliant after all?
>
> *Alison*: Oh – I haven't read them yet.
>
> *Jimmy*: I didn't ask you that. I said . . .
>
> *Cliff*: Leave the poor girlie alone. She's busy.
>
> *Jimmy*: Well, she can talk, can't she? You can talk, can't you? You can express an opinion.

Jimmy starts with an interrogative, but it's an odd interrogative, making curious use of the speech model. It is transactive in form, but reflexive. He is asking himself a question, so that he occupies both places of the model. A reflexive speech model like this communicates non-transactively. This interrogative may act as a command. *Why*-questions are concerned with causality. Directed to an expert (+ knowledge) they confirm his status as expert. Directed to a non-expert (− knowledge) they have the force of a prohibition: *Why do you do that?* (for *You shouldn't do that*).

The speaker is either (+ expert) or (− expert) and (+ power) or (− power), with the hearer correspondingly classified in the opposite manner. With the hearer classified as (−power, −knowledge), this would be a command: *Don't do it!* But all this is directed against himself. Speaker or hearer, he is both expert and non-expert, powerful and non-powerful: in a word, confused. The next interrogative is to be taken as a command:

Have you finished that one yet?

Out of any specific context, the speaker can be classified as either (+knowledge) or (−knowledge). Since Jimmy can see Cliff reading, (−knowledge) is ruled out. Hence, the interrogative must be interpreted as a command.

The correct response to this interrogative when it is taken as a command is in fact untrue: it would be *yes*, though Cliff hasn't finished. Cliff would then have to hand the paper over to Jimmy. In this form of the exchange, the utterance is a test of whether Cliff accepts a / subordinate role, though Jimmy does not have to reveal that a test has been carried out. But Cliff doesn't answer *yes*. He treats the interrogative as a true question, answering *Not yet*. This simultaneously rejects Jimmy's classification of him as inferior and classifies Jimmy as (−knowledge), using Jimmy's surface self-classification against him.

Jimmy then asks:

Do the Sunday papers make you feel ignorant?

This cannot readily be the realization of a command. Commands are requests for action, and actions must have an underlying transactional, in which the hearer is the actor of the requested action. The available classifications for the questioner are (±expert). If he is (+expert) then the question becomes catechistic. The stress on *you* establishes a contrast with *me*, revealing an antecedent and implied *The Sunday papers make me feel ignorant*. The required answer is clearly *yes*. Had Cliff answered *no* he would have challenged Jimmy's status as (+expert) in two ways, by refusing to be catechized and, more overtly, by saying that he feels less ignorant than Jimmy about Sunday papers. On this occasion Cliff answers *Not 'arf*. So where he subverted Jimmy's claims to power, he tacitly accepts Jimmy's claims to be an expert.

Jimmy then turns to his wife Alison with

You're not a peasant are you?

This is a compound structure. The first part is a yes/no question (if it is spoken with a rising intonation), the second part is a so-called tag-question. The answer has already been given – *no*. As a question its

98

function seems to be to get agreement from the hearer, so as to confirm the status of the questioner. But Jimmy has just established with Cliff that the correct answer is *I am a peasant (like you)*. The 'correct' answer is both *yes* and *no*, which makes the question an impossible one to answer. Whichever Alison said would be both right and wrong. Such a question usually leads to people feeling uneasy and uncertain how to respond. That is part of their function. Alison, however, isn't embarrassed. She responds with her own question, which functions as a request that he repeat his question purely for her. She classifies herself as a privileged hearer. Only someone classed as dominant can do that. Jimmy obeys the command, necessarily going back to a version of the question he asked Cliff, *I said do the papers make you feel you're not so brilliant after all?* To this Alison replies with the answer to another kind of question, *Oh – I haven't read them yet*, as though Jimmy had asked the 'simple' question. *What do you feel?* This challenges not simply his particular proposition but his status in the speech situation. She refuses to admit that he could be asking a question reserved for the dominant. Some relationships to knowledge are signs of power. The right to define the answer to a question comes from social power. But the question form is ambiguous, seemingly concerned only with knowledge. Commands, or assertions of power issued as seeming questions, can always be taken at their face value by those with relatively greater power. There is a systematic ambiguity at issue here which is manifested in many forms. The truth is either what the dominant say it is or what it is. The ambiguity allows a power relationship to appear as a matter of knowledge, but this necessarily makes it possible that the surface form will be taken at its face value, and a command of some kind will be treated as a question. When this happens, the power classifications and their realizations have broken down. The mystification doesn't work, either because the hearer doesn't see the covert power relationships or because he (or she, in Alison's case) classifies the participants differently. In this play, Alison is from a rich middle-class family, Jimmy of obscure working-class origins. The kind of certainty this gives her is something that Jimmy tries unsuccessfully to destroy throughout the play.

We can summarize the nature and function of 'authority' models as follows:

1 The power model is constituted by classification of the basic transactional speech model into an asymmetrical relationship. There can be two versions of this model, or two criteria of power:

social power and intellectual power. The relationship between these criteria can be complex and variable, even within one society. In the world of education, for instance, intellectual power is the ostensible basis for the social power of teachers over the taught. In commerce or industry, intellectual power may be a commodity that has been bought and is under the control of those with social power. Generally, the socially powerful do not like to feel ignorant, and the intellectually powerful do not like to feel impotent, so there is a tendency for the two criteria of power to be fused, each category of the powerful appropriating the other's criteria.

2 The classifications involved are relatively stable or relatively negotiable. If the criteria of power are fixed, and the power relation is unproblematic, then power can be realized through commands, often in the imperative form. In the imperative, the actor is deleted from the surface of the utterance. This relies on the actor being recoverable directly from the context through the fact that he or she is always the one addressed. Participants need to be aware of the markers of power or inferiority. Uniforms in many social groups, or adulthood within a family, all signal stable power classifications within the relevant sphere. Where the power relationship is fixed but covert, or in some way problematic (as within a 'liberal' family, classroom, or firm), complex processes of reclassification are undertaken by the participants. But, as the situation is stable, the processes will be rule-governed and so will not in fact obscure the underlying power relationship. Yet in most cases there will be legitimate ways of temporarily reversing the power relationship, and precise ways of challenging the basis of the classification will be laid down.

3 The complexities and the kinds of operations performed will reflect precisely the complexities of the relations between the individuals in the communicative event.

SOURCES AND CONTEXT

Our account of determiners – *the*, *a*, and also singular and plural – relates to the discussion of generic features in language. An interesting treatment is Wallace Chafe's in *Meaning and the Structure of Language* (1970). Writers such as Whorf (in 'Science and linguistics' (1956), the caption to one table says, 'What are to English differences of time are to Hopi differences in the kind of validity') and W.E. Bull (*Time, Tense and the Verb*, 1960) have been most influential on our own approach to tense. M.A.K. Halliday's (1970b) definition of modality, in 'Functional diversity in language, as seen from a consideration of modality and mood in English', is wider ranging than other accounts. Within it he deals with modal verbs, modal adverbs and adjectives, the combinations of these, intonation and its contribution to modality, as well as the choices of words which a speaker makes.

A major strand of linguistic work over the last decade or so has been concerned with speech acts, that is, with the fact that some utterances perform the function of acts which cannot be performed otherwise. The approach goes back to J.L. Austin's *How to Do Things with Words* (1962), which was taken up particularly by the American philosopher J.R. Searle, for instance, in 'What is a speech act?' (1972) and *Speech Acts* (1969). Transformational linguists have made wide use of the concept; one example is J.R. Ross's (1970) 'On declarative sentences'. A recent discussion of syntactic and pragmatic accounts in relation to one such act (commands) is W.J. Downes's (1977) 'The imperative and pragmatics'. The extension of linguistic work into the study of conversation, discourse, extended texts in general, is an important development in the field of pragmatics. Philosophers, linguists, and sociologists have all played a part in this. We have mentioned Austin and Searle in connection with speech acts. The 'act' which a speaker intends to perform with any given utterance is not usually on the surface, as we have shown. In speech-act theory this has been handled by assigning two kinds of 'force' to a speech act: *illocutionary force*, which describes what the utterance is about 'on the face of it', and *perlocutionary force*, which describes what a speaker actually intended to do with it. For instance, as a husband and wife are walking along a street, she might say, 'Isn't that a beautifully set-out window?', the illocutionary force being *question*, the perlocutionary one being *command* ('Have a look at that dress!'). In other words, there is a massive amount of indirection in utterances which a linguistic theory needs to deal with. The philosopher H.P. Grice has worked on conversational implications (for instance, in his (1968) 'Utterer's meaning and intentions' and (1975) 'Logic and conversation') and on other aspects of the semantics of conversations. On the sociology side there are a number of important strands: there is the work of Michael Argyle on social interaction, represented by articles such as 'The communication of inferior and superior attitudes by verbal and non-verbal signals' (1970) and his book *Social Interaction* (1969). Wootton's *Dilemmas of Discourse* (1975) looks at some of these issues in a detailed and helpfully concrete and specific way. One major influence has been the work of the ethnomethodological school in sociology. Their detailed analyses of all types of human behaviour have focused attention on aspects of meaning in non-verbal and verbal interactions which had not been focal in previous research. From the point of view of language perhaps the work of Harvey Sacks, for instance, his (1974) 'An analysis of a joke's telling in conversation' or (1972) 'On the analyzability of stories by children', is most important. The whole enterprise of moving the concerns of linguistics from the study of syntax alone to the study of discourse owes a tremendous amount to the anthropologist and linguist Dell Hymes. His work is immensely wide-ranging; from our point of view the most important part of it is in the area of the ethnography of language and centres on his concept of 'communicative competence'. This concept was important as a contrast to Chomsky's much narrower and theoretically different use of 'competence', and in focusing the attention of linguists on the search for those kinds of knowledge that are displayed by speakers in all uses of language. His (1972b) 'Models of the interaction of language and social life' and (1972a) 'On communicative competence' will give an outline of his approach. Lastly, readers might be interested to compare our approach, and that of the writers mentioned so far, with an attempt by R.D. Laing to provide a model for the analysis of the layerings and indirections of conversational interaction, in an appendix 'A notation for dyadic perspectives' to his *Self and Others* (1971).

6

CLASSIFICATION AS PROCESS

OPERATIONS

Every language provides its users with a powerful set of devices for classifying their world. Classification is a constant and continuing process, not a once-for-all state of affairs given by society and its language.

One simple but productive device is the relational model in its two basic forms: *noun* + *'is'* + *noun* and *noun* + *'is'* + *adjective*. The first allows the speaker to establish relationships between various categories: *The chairman is a woman.* The second allows attributes to be linked to any entity: *The building is big/old/rambling/convenient.* The activity at issue with each of the two types is rather different. With the first type, the activity is essentially the articulation of the logic of an existing system. With the second, the options are more open, and the activity is one of judgment, specifying qualities of whatever it is that is being judged or commented on.

Relational models represent the act of classification explicitly. Classification can also take place within a basic model. In both actionals and relationals, any noun can be qualified. The basic form of the nominal group in English can provisionally be given as *modifiers (of many kinds)* + *noun*:

$$\text{modifier} \quad + \quad \text{noun}$$

Some modifiers are adjectives. Some of these can take the second place in an attributive model:

$$\text{The girl} \quad \text{is} \quad \text{beautiful.}$$

A transformational relation exists between this model and the form where the adjective precedes the noun, as in *the beautiful girl*. A nominal such as *the beautiful girl* is itself part of some other model, for instance,

The beautiful girl was a foreign agent. The transformational relation is thus between two models:

transactive: The girl was a foreign agent.
attributive: The girl is beautiful.

The attributive model is 'absorbed' into the transactive model, and the adjective is placed in front of the common noun. The act of judgment expressed in the attributive model thus becomes a part of the actor/ nominal in the transactive model.

Another set of attributive adjectives, as in *normal work*, are derived in a different way. Their source is an actional model, *They work normally.* When this sentence is nominalized, *normally* becomes an adjective prefixed to the nominal *work*. The relation is as follows:

They work normally. ⇒ normal work

There is, however, one large class of adjectives which can come before a noun, but which cannot be explained transformationally in the same way. Take, for example, *the main meal*. There is no grammatical form *The meal is main* or *They meal mainly* from which to derive this. Both of these are ungrammatical in English. Nor does *a great deal* in the phrase *a great deal of money* seem to come from *a deal is great* or *It deals greatly*. These words seem to enter the modifier place directly and not as a result of transformational processes. We considered the simple sentence as consisting of a set of places. Each place has further 'slots' which function to define or further classify these main places. We have so far described the places and 'slots' in the models in the following way (taking the transactional model as illustration):

transactional: actor/noun process/verb affected/noun
place 1 place 2 place 3

Each place has a number of slots; the only one we have discussed so far is the modifier slot:

modifier + noun verb modifier + noun

In addition, all nominals carry an indication of specificness (as we discussed in chapter 5) and we call this – in accordance with linguistic tradition – the determiner, and the slot the determiner slot. The picture we have now is as follows:

determiner + modifier + noun verb determiner + modifier + noun

Quite clearly, those attributive adjectives which derive from underlying relationals are distinct from determiners. But those which do not derive from underlying relationals (like *a great deal*) have more in common with determiners. For instance, just as *the meal* does not come from any hypothetical *meal is the* or *it meals thely*, so *the main meal* does not come from *the meal mains* or *it meals mainly*. Both types of 'slot-filler' act to limit the scope of the noun. The difference between *a meal* and *the meal* is that *a* allows any member of that class, while *the* limits it to one specific, identified member. But the principle of selection which is involved here, the reason why this meal was identified from among the whole set of meals, is left implicit. In a similar way, *main* selects one kind of meal from the total set of meals, but it identifies the criterion of selection. *The main meal* is more specific than *a meal*, and more explicit about the criteria of selection than *the meal*, though less limited in reference. Words like *main* act as fine-tuners in the determiner system. They apply directly to the noun and by modification they delimit its range of reference. There are thus two slots before the noun, a determiner slot and an attributive slot. As we have seen several times now, there is no one-for-one relation between underlying meaning and surface form. So a determiner like *main* may appear in the attributive slot, looking, on the surface, very much like an attributive adjective. Furthermore, any one slot may be 'filled' more than once. In our example, *the main meal*, there are two determiners; in *the lovely white cottage* we have one determiner, *the*, and two attributive adjectives, two modifiers, *lovely* and *white*. The singular/plural classification closely interacts with the determiner system, since plural number allows the absence of a determiner — *Meals taste good*, but not *Meal tastes good*. As we pointed out in chapter 5, nominals have to be minimally classified for singular and plural. As it turns out, this classification interacts with the determiner system, and the necessary and obligatory presence of a singular/plural classification can be extended and generalized to the obligatory presence of a determiner. In applying these classifications, speakers seem to rely on rules which draw on groupings of determiners. So if the speaker uses the plural classification, he need not use *the* or *a*; if not, he must use an article, *the*, *a*, and (optionally) further determiners.

This linguistic process, and the resulting forms, are the reflection in language of a particular habit of mind, which inclines to categorize and subcategorize an object of enquiry, dividing and subdividing it in a neat and orderly fashion. Such a cast of mind is often associated with bureaucracies, and we find the form strongly represented in the language produced by administrators. Here is part of an information sheet put out by the administration of the University of East Anglia during a dispute about food prices:

The facts about catering prices
During the last two weeks there has been a great deal of discussion about the level of catering prices at U.E.A. Apart from anything else, this has caused a great deal of disquiet amongst the staff concerned who may be forgiven for thinking that their work is being criticized in some way. . . .

Professor X said that the University was prepared to take the following steps:
1 The average price of a main meal in the Refectory would be reduced to 35p.
2 The price of a filled roll would be reduced from $8\frac{1}{2}$p to 8p.

There are a large number of determiners in this passage which cannot be derived from an underlying equative. The title contains one definite article and one determiner, *catering*. *The facts* here clearly functions as equivalent to *the real and relevant facts*; that is, since the word *facts* in itself means 'untampered-with reality', the additional classification by *the* can therefore only mean *real, relevant*. One other possibility is that *facts* has a contrastive intonational prominence. In that case it would mean *the facts* rather than *the lies*. *Catering prices* is more interesting. If we try to derive it transformationally, we might suggest *The prices are catering* or *The prices cater*. Both these are ungrammatical and are evidently not plausible derivations. The underlying sentences would have to be something like *X caters [and] X or Y prices the food*. The uncertainty of this derivation suggests that it has no psychological reality. It is more likely that *prices* have been directly classified as *catering prices*. This is not the most obvious way of classifying them. Students would have classified them as *food prices*. The process by which this classification arose might be something like this. Food prices depend on catering costs; so the whole issue, including these prices, can be filed under the heading of *catering*. Since the administration saw the issue from their point of view as a catering problem, they defined the prices with that label. The student union in this dispute, incidentally, also used the term *catering prices*, accepting the classification system of the dominant party in the dispute even though its terms and point of view were at another level seen as antagonistic.

Catering here is nounlike, and this is a common form for determiners. This example shows how any term which could be the label of a file can act as a determiner. This makes the operation an extremely productive one, and an *ad hoc* one: systematic in terms of the classificatory system of one group, but incomprehensible to outsiders. There is no generally valid rule-governed relationship between the two entities linked. Transformations may be involved in the stage prior to the classification operation, as has occurred with *catering*, which is a nominalization from *X caters for Y*. The effect of using a transformed actional as a determiner is to make the underlying form especially difficult to recover, since, in order to reach it, the hearer/reader has to get to know or understand the *ad hoc* classificatory system before beginning to reverse the regular nominalization transformation. The consequence is that processes can be used as principles of classification, yet virtually all sense of their nature as processes is lost. This is the reflection in language of a quality of administrators that many have noted: the primacy of the filing system over what is being filed.

The determiner slot can be filled a number of times. For instance, *facts about catering prices* could have been presented as *catering prices facts*. Here *facts* would have been the main 'heading', this being sub-categorized as facts about prices, and subcategorized further as prices in the catering section. It is an orderly system, which can be represented diagrammatically as follows:

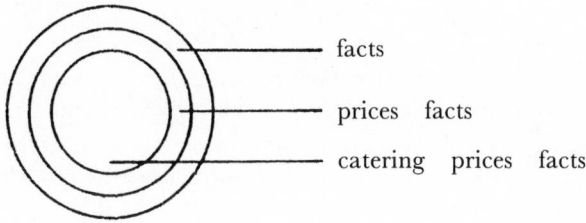

The process of subcategorization could continue further. We could have *refectory catering prices facts*, or *university refectory catering prices facts*. But a noun phrase as long as that would be difficult to process. Compared with the relative anarchy of *great big juicy fat steaks*, where attributes just pile on the noun, the determiners have to be interpreted in relation to a fixed hierarchy of terms, representing a complex and ordered system. The order of the determiners is more fixed than the order of attributives, since the former codes the classificatory system.

Determiners in English are ordered from the smallest to the largest category. Hence we can recreate the logical order of the classification operations directly from the surface order. This is a useful fact to bear in mind for anyone who wishes to use linguistic forms diagnostically, to understand implicit systems of classification.

This kind of classification is an intellectual strategy which is guided by the classification system of a specific ideology, and which also acts to project the picture of a world ordered in its terms. For instance, in this passage we have *The average price of a main meal in the Refectory*, where *in* gives the place in which these meals are eaten. But it also acts as a classificatory phrase. *In the refectory* limits *meals* in the same way as *main* does. The physical location is treated as though it was a category, not a place. Physical reality is thus interpreted and coded in the classificatory system to correspond to the categories of the administrative mind.

As an intellectual strategy classification is an instrument of control. With *catering prices facts* the effect is to make fewer and fewer *facts* seem relevant as the largest category is categorized and subcategorized. An extreme example, such as *refectory catering prices facts*, is classified so many times and seemingly so precisely that it makes a concern with prices in general appear clumsy and irrelevant. As another instance of this process limiting and controlling the range of meaning in the passage quoted, we have the apparently innocuous *during the last two weeks*. This seems innocent, absolutely precise, much more so than *recently* would have been. *Weeks* is classified twice, by *last two*. (*The weeks are last* is impossible, as is *The weeks are two*, so that these are determiners.) But the effect of this precision is to cut down the relevant timespan to manageable proportions. In fact there had been *a great deal of discussion* about the price of food for months, even years. The precision of *last two weeks* makes those earlier discussions irrelevant to the present controversy.

This text is virtually without any evaluative terms. We find *the average price of a main meal* but not *the extortionate/generous price of a repulsive/delicious meal*. It is clear that determiners and attributives represent two distinct kinds of intellectual/linguistic operation; though, as we pointed out, they can act through the same part of the syntagmatic model. To see a passage which is richer in attributives, we will turn to a different kind of text. The following is an extract from *Fanny's Double Feature* (1969), a piece of soft pornography by Norman Jackson.

Yes, you won a few and you lost a few, the drowsy darling ruminated philosophically as she lay there on the deck lounge at

108

the edge of the Twinkle swimming pool reminiscing. But Vance Towers – virile cinematic romancer, sex-king of the silver screen – had represented easily the most frustrating failure of her two-year career at Simone's . . . ah well, c'est la vie.

But what a waste of good man-material, she reflected once again as she conjured up the image of the perverted performer's stallion-like private part. Golly, wouldn't some deserving girl, or girls, be delighted to have the use of such an implement of joy? If only she'd been able to push Towers over the hump as it were, to persuade him of the proper function of his king-sized natural endowment. Why, he was almost as well-built, sexually, as Fanny's precious Virgil back home in New York.

Her luscious lower regions suddenly turned to hot, flowing jelly as the sleepy sweetheart drew naughty mental pictures of her beau's beloved love-lance. Lord, how she'd have loved to have that mighty oak planted deep inside her at this moment. If only Virgil could be here right now, making mad love to her beneath this sexy California sun.

On the heels of this passionate wish, her amorous hunchback did indeed seem to join the cuddly captivator, even as she drifted off into a sound sleep.

The style of this work is highly mannered, with an almost obsessive use of adjectives in the attributive position. Generalizations about this sample would apply closely to the rest of the novel; a linguistic analysis of it should be diagnostic of the mind of the author in writing the novel. Or, from another point of view, it should enable us to establish the specific grammar of the text so precisely that we could programme a computer to write as many sequels to *Fanny's Double Feature* as the market would bear.

The most striking characteristic of the style can be illustrated by looking at the labels used to describe Fanny, the heroine: *drowsy darling*, *sleepy sweetheart*, and *cuddly captivator*. On the previous page she is *dainty doxie*, *stacked sweetie*, *flaxen-haired favorite*, and *precious prostie*. The principle is clear. She is referred to by a *the + adjective + noun* construction, in which the adjective and the noun have the same first letter. All the adjectives are attributives and can be seen as transformations of underlying relationals:

The darling is drowsy.	⇒	The drowsy darling
The sweetheart is sleepy.	⇒	The sleepy sweetheart
The captivator is cuddly.	⇒	The cuddly captivator

Some of these contain mini-narratives. For instance, *the cuddly captivator* contains the nominalization *captivator*. The underlying form is *Someone (Fanny) captivates someone (a male) (and) Fanny is cuddly*. The heroine is the focus of these mini-narratives, which exist outside real time. But the major activity is the piling-up of modifying attributes around the focus, Fanny. Not here the order of the hierarchically arranged determiners; the classificatory principle now is simply that the attribute be a suitable 'feminine' quality and that it should alliterate with the word which stands for Fanny. The effect is somewhat like the garish wrapping of a commodity.

What occurs here is that in all these descriptions the single individual Fanny is related to one of a large set of nouns, either words for particular kinds of female (*prostie, sweetie, darling, doxie*) or transformed nominals which could categorize a female (*captivator, favorite*). There seems no end to the list of terms that Norman Jackson can produce. As a system of categories, it has the serious defect of massive redundancy and total overlap. In contrast to the tidy-mindedness of the administrators' classification system, this one is nearly chaotic. The analogy would be a filing system in which every file contained the same entry: Fanny.

In this pervasive process of reclassification the constant term, *Fanny*, disappears. The individual is removed from the text. Any one of the large set of words for describing a woman – *prostie, doxie, cutie, sweetie, captivator, darling* – can be used to stand for Fanny. Thus every one of the classifying terms is Fanny; the terms signal absolutely no distinction of a significant kind. They would describe any other female individual (in that age range) equally well. The same goes for the modifiers – *precious, cuddly, stacked, flaxen-haired, dainty*; each one applies quite indifferently to any one of the words used for Fanny. The modifiers and the nouns together are labels saying 'commodity female'. In this way they apply to Fanny as well as to any other female. The set of terms, modifiers and nouns, describes a range of attributes seen as characteristically, desirably, and relevantly female – from one point of view. Any individual female once identified, as Fanny, or Billie, or Janey, or Lucy, is described and seen in those terms, quite indifferently. In this way the process, while similar to the administrator's urge to classify, differs in its total promiscuity.

On the surface constructions such as *precious prostie* may be read as though they were *determiner + noun* forms. Read in this way they would distinguish a *precious prostie* from a *cheap wife*, or even distinguish a *cuddly captivator* from a *curvy captivator*: the attribute would distinguish one individual from another, a *drowsy darling* from an *alert darling*. In a novel which is concerned with characterization the definitional use of adjectives should be at least as prominent as their attributive use. But the process is ambiguous, automatic, and promiscuous (and guided by principles such as rhyme and alliteration – *precious prostie, dainty doxie* – and rhythmic pattern – précious próstie, fláxen-haired fávorite – which have little to do with meaning) so that the phrases can only be read as disembodied collections of attributes. These could be attached to any female image, convenient for a rote pornographic fantasy which is not particularly strong on characterization.

The same process occurs with the other main entities involved in erotic events in this kind of soft pornography. Take for instance *mighty oak*. We can suggest the following derivation at some time in the past:

His penis is like an oak.   →   His penis is an oak.

Thus *oak* becomes a term in the set of terms which can replace *penis*. *Oak* is then either related to *mighty* by a relational, which is transformed to an attributive adjective, or alternatively it is classified directly by *mighty* acting through the determiner slot, to give *mighty oak* again, this time definitionally.

The process which leads from *His penis is like an oak* to *oak* becoming one of the set of terms meaning penis, is highly productive. It is encouraged by the wish for euphemism on one side, and the enjoyment of word-play on the other; the latter draws on great resources of ingenuity and imagination, especially in areas such as sexuality. The number of nouns which can be substitutes for *penis* is thus very large, and can be constantly increased. The same applies to the other parts of the body which interest the pornographer. The result is an extremely productive device, which allows the pornographer to refer to the few but potent objects in his world by as many words as he wants. The surface richness and multiplicity of terms is illusory, though, as *penis = oak = lance = sword = tool = member = prick = shaft = pole =* . . . In this style, the major activity is classification, not erotic performance. The classification system operating here is the *reductio ad absurdum* of classification systems, near-arbitrary, irrational, ambiguous, repetitive, and redundant. Like all classification systems, it is organized by and encodes an ideology. Some of the main features of this ideology are revealed by an analysis of its linguistic forms and processes.

MODELS AND JUDGMENTS

Whorf (1956) suggested that the order of adjectives in front of a noun in English is governed by a rule which states that the adjectives referring to more intrinsic qualities come closer to the head noun. From our study of determiners and attributive adjectives we can make this intuition more precise. All the modifiers are strictly ordered, determined by the process of categorization which in itself implements the classificatory system. If Whorf's intuition was correct, then those attributives which are regarded by a culture as intrinsically part of a noun will commonly be found closer to the noun. Thus most speakers will say *a large red ball*, not *a red large ball*. In turn, the order of adjectives can indicate the judgments which a culture makes about intrinsic and extrinsic attributes and qualities. Furthermore, some attributives will be felt by speakers to be so extrinsic as to be too unstable to use in the prenominal position. *The meal is ready* is regarded as so transitory that it is not possible to say *the ready meal*.

Hence, the order of words before the noun is extremely revealing about principles of classification used by speakers and cultures. Most speakers of English will say *a beautiful black girl*, not *a black beautiful girl*. The colour is felt to be the defining characteristic. If someone produced the utterance *a black beautiful girl*, he would clearly be classifying beauty and colour quite differently from the norm. Sex seems more intrinsic than colour for most English speakers: we usually say *a black female doctor* not *a female black doctor*. These preferences reflect a particular classification system, which enshrines ideologically determined assumptions intermixed with some that have their source in popular science or 'commonsense' notions.

According to this science, colour seems more stable and intrinsic than size, and qualities attributed to something by someone are the least stable: *the beautiful large red box*, not *the red large beautiful box*. When variation is possible within what is permitted, or departures from the norm for the society are allowed, this is an equally precise record of the processes of classification and a clear guide to the principles of classification which have been at work.

Complex value judgments are to be found especially prominently in the utterances of arbiters of taste, like art connoisseurs, gourmets, and literary critics. Here is a typical passage, from F.R. Leavis (1963), one of the most influential literary critics in England this century, writing about Yeats:

> The resulting poetry has a fresh unliterary spontaneity comparable to that of Shelley's, but a spontaneity that has behind it Victorian literary sophistication instead of Wordsworth and the French Revolution, and so is the more remarkable an achieve-

ment. Yet everywhere there is a recognition, implicit in the shifting cloudy unseizableness of the imagery, that this 'reality' must be illusory, and that even if it could be reached it would leave human longing unslaked. And this recognition is subtly turned into a strength: it validates, as it were, the idealizing fanaticism of the poetry and counterpoises the obsession with the transcendental, just as the exultations and despairs of love are counterpoised by the sense that

> ... time and the world are ever in flight;
> And love is less kind than the grey twilights
> And hope is less dear than the dew of the morn.

The poetry of *The Wind among the Reeds*, then, is a very remarkable achievement: it is, though a poetry of withdrawal, both more subtle and more vital than any pure product of Victorian Romanticism.

(New Bearings in English Poetry, p. 37)

The most straightforward model for presenting a comment or judgment is the relational. Leavis's text has many examples which show the complexities which it is capable of expressing. Take the last sentence.

The poetry of TWAR, then, is a very remarkable achievement.

This is a judgment on the quality of the poetry contained in a particular volume of poems by Yeats. The nominal *achievement* is derived by a nominalization transformation from *X (Yeats) has achieved something*. *Achieve* contains an evaluation as part of its meaning. *To achieve* differs from *to complete* or *to do* in that it implies *success* and a positive evaluation of the action. So here is a complex judgment whose stages are:

> The poetry of TWAR is an achievement.
> The poetry of TWAR is a remarkable achievement.
> The poetry of TWAR is a very remarkable achievement.

Each stage essentially repeats the same positive evaluation. It gains weight not only from the fact that the content of the judgment is repeated, but also because the act of judgment has been repeated, with the same result each time. Leavis could have had second thoughts at each stage, and called it *an unexciting achievement, a modest achievement,* or *a fairly remarkable achievement, a fairly modest achievement.*

The second part of this sentence shows more complicated processes at work:

> It is, though a poetry of withdrawal, both more subtle and more vital than any pure product of Victorian Romanticism.

Analysing this in stages, we note the classifiers *pure* and *Victorian*. The *of*-form functions similarly to define which kind of poetry (*of withdrawal*) and which kind of product (*of Victorian Romanticism*). In this way the object which is to be evaluated has first been carefully specified.

The first relational is *It is a poetry of withdrawal*. This is a classification of such poetry. However, Leavis has inserted *though*, indicating an element of negation. Purely from this, we recover two further implicit judgments: *Poetry of withdrawal is not usually subtle; Poetry of withdrawal is not usually vital*. *Though* acts to suspend these judgments in the present case. The comparative in the next clause also contains a judgment to this effect. The comparative is a determiner-like operation which, however, acts on two syntagms. A reconstruction in this case would be:

1 This poetry is subtle. That poetry is subtle.
2 This poetry is *more* subtle *than* that poetry is subtle.
3 This poetry is more subtle (than that).

A comparison is a double judgment, which comes to a relative positive judgment on one part and a relative negative judgment on the other.

Both serves a similar function to *though*, indicating a potential negation. The difference between *subtle and vital* and *both subtle and vital* is that in the first case *subtle* and *vital* are presented as compatible, whereas in the second case they are seen as usually incompatible, but coinciding in the present instance. So *both* indicates the cancellation of an unstated relational *subtle is not vital*.

The core of the judgment which Leavis is making is *It is a poetry of withdrawal which is subtle and vital*. What he actually wrote sounds much more complex and controlled than this core judgment. This impression has four main sources.

1 His precision about the object of study, what it is not, shown in his use of classifiers.
2 The density of judgments, deriving from his combination of overt judgments with allusions to judgments he is not making or is cancelling out.

3 The scope of the judgments which he does make, which act comparatively on two judgments simultaneously.
4 The judgments he makes on traditional or expected judgments, by' conjunctions and negations of judgments.

This last is the most important in making someone an arbiter of taste. It is an act of judgment directed at the received system of judgments itself, and hence it is the act of a higher order of judge. It is, after all, easy to fill out a syntagm which has a single entity as its topic: *Yeats's poetry is subtle, vital, dreamy, spontaneous,* etc. What Leavis is doing is challenging habitual assumptions, in this case the supposition that subtlety and vitality are incompatible. This is more important than a particular judgment on Yeats's early poetry would be. There might be many people, even students of literature, who had not read the early Yeats and would not greatly care whether it was more subtle, or more anything, than pure Victorian Romanticism. What does matter is that assumptions about the necessary relationship between subtlety and vitality have been revised, or so Leavis claims. The early Yeats becomes important because he forces this revision, or more exactly, because he is the example chosen by Leavis in making the revision.

Similar comments apply to the rest of the complex judgments quoted. To take just part of the first,

> The resulting poetry has a fresh unliterary spontaneity comparable to that of Shelley's, . . .

This involves a change from *is* to *has*, that is, the use of a differing form of a relational model. It allows Leavis to treat the judgment *spontaneous* as a noun, which he then classifies directly. From the double modification of *spontaneity* as a noun, we recover the following sequence of judgments;

> The poetry has an unliterary spontaneity.

Unliterary here acts as a classifier, establishing the two subcategories of *spontaneity, literary spontaneity* and *unliterary spontaneity*. The latter is further modified by the evaluative attributive *fresh*:

> The poetry has fresh unliterary spontaneity.

We can see how much more intrinsic and criterial *unliterary* is than *fresh* by trying to change the order: *unliterary fresh spontaneity*. This sounds odd. *Fresh* is more strongly a comment than a principle of classification, but *unliterary* is predominantly a classification here.

On the surface Leavis seems to be repeating himself three times, since *fresh*, *unliterary*, and *spontaneous* have similar meanings in this context. But by recovering the precise process we see that a much more complex judgment is at issue. The category *unliterary* defines one kind of spontaneity as against *literary spontaneity*. This second phrase is an apparent contradiction in terms, similar in structure to Leavis's own *vital subtlety* (or *subtle vitality*). Leavis has evoked the contradiction, to cancel it in the case of Yeats and Shelley; though on what grounds is not clear, since the poetry of both is written and is therefore literary by definition.

With Leavis as with Norman Jackson – though with a different degree of seriousness – the primary activity in the discourse is concerned with a classificatory scheme. In general, a society's most prestigious evaluators transmit exemplary operations on a received system of (value-laden) classifications. This activity is more important than whatever is being classified. The particular poem, painting, or wine being judged is simply the material which provides the occasion of the judgment and which then becomes the symbol for a particular ideological message. In the present case, Leavis's criticism has as its major content messages about the reconciliation of an opposition between subtlety (the intellect, intricacy, precision) and vitality (life, energy, spontaneity); but this message is implicit in his text and is transferred onto the object of the judgment, Yeats's poetry. A particular reading of Yeats's poetry then becomes a kind of validation of the critic's ideological solution, proof that this solution has been achieved somewhere by someone other than the critic and is something admirable which deserves to be imitated.

CLASSIFICATION, LOCATION, AND POSSESSION

Two surface forms common in English, examples of which occur in the Leavis text, are first, *Poetry has spontaneity*, and second, *the unseizableness of the imagery*. An apparently equivalent construction in English is the *'s* possessive, as in *Shelley's poetry*. It is plausible to regard all three as examples of the possessive. The *has* form shows the model in its full form and the constructions with *of* and *'s* transformationally derived from the full model. Possessive forms behave curiously and code meanings that do not seem entirely explicable in terms of possession. For instance, *John has a chair* could mean that John owns a chair, or simply that he is sitting on one. These could be regarded as different kinds of possession, legal ownership in one case, ownership by proximity in the other. The *'s* form, *John's chair*, and the pronominal form *his/your/my chair* have a similar ambiguity. There are some clear benefits to this ambiguity. In the case of chairs, a host can say to a guest *that's your chair* and rely on the guest to sit on it, not carry it away. Too overt an insistence on ownership and property relations could be a source of awkwardness in social relationships, though people are expected to know who really owns what.

There is another *has* form which does not seem obviously possessive. In *The wall has a curve*, the *curve* is a part of *the wall* rather than a possession. However, the part-whole relationship can be seen as another kind of relationship akin to the first two, called inalienable possession. Alienable possession indicates a relation where the possessed item is not an integral part of the possessing entity: *John's chair*. Inalienable possession, on the other hand, indicates a relation where the two entities are regarded as integrally and essentially part of each other.

The possessive *'s* has meanings like those discussed above and a range of additional meanings. *John's chair* can refer to a chair made by John, even if it is now owned by someone else. We can see this as another example of inalienable possession, where the act of making the object is the basis of the claim. Another common use of the *'s* form is in constructions such as *John's school/firm*. By analogy with other uses of the form it ought to be suggesting that the *school* or *firm* belongs to or is part of *John*. In reality the apparently possessed term is the larger, and the apparent possessor is a part of it. However, we tend to interpret it in the usual way, as though the school or firm is somehow a part of John. This makes it interesting for an analyst of our culture. For one thing, the possession model is used for a relationship between an individual and an institution. For another, the terms of the model are inverted in interpretation so that the possessed part seems like the whole, and the possession like a possessor.

The *of* form also indicates relations in the same general semantic area as the others. Some instances are *a glass of milk, a pound of potatoes*. The general relationship involved is a version of the part-whole relationship, with *milk* and *potatoes* conceived as an undifferentiated mass. In general, the *of* form codes intrinsic relationships of various kinds: *the city of Newcastle; the capital of Spain; the name of the game*.

Lastly, we need to mention the verb *to own*, which unlike *to have* expresses possession directly, overtly, and unambiguously. *John owns a chair/beach/car* allows no ambiguity about whether he is in a 'possessive relation' with a *chair/beach/car* temporarily, or permanently and legally. *John owns a car* is a transitive, which looks seductively like a transactive, as though *John/actor* caused the action of *owning*, which affected the car. We prefer to regard *own* as a word which exists to make conventional classification seem like physical/natural action. The fact that passives are difficult (*the owned car* is probably not a possible nominal in English) lends substance to our suspicion.

There are two simplifying observations we can make on this complicated picture:

1 The various uses seem explicable in terms of two models, one capturing a relation of contiguity and the other, one of inclusion.
2 The surface forms systematically obscure the distinctions coded in the basic models.

We can now consider some of the implications of an initial classification in terms of one or other of the models. Take the example from Leavis that we have looked at:

> attributive: *This poetry is spontaneous.*
> possessive: *This poetry has spontaneity.*

One function of the possessive model is to establish a relation with another nominal entity, which can then in its turn be easily classified. It has another effect, however: it interprets the relationship involved through a model of possession rather than attribution or equation. The initial noun, *poetry*, is classified as a possessor, rather than as the bearer, of an attribute. Interestingly, there seems to be a highly idiosyncratic constraint on this model. The noun in the possessed relation must refer to 'good' or neutral qualities. We find *Mary has great beauty*, but not *Mary has great ugliness*; *Poetry has spontaneity* but not *Poetry has dreadfulness*. The 'logic' seems to be that a negative quality cannot be a commodity, and therefore is not to be represented as a possession.

Actionals are regularly transformed into the *of* form (though not commonly by Leavis). An example from Chomsky is *the construction of a grammar*. This is derived from *X constructs a grammar*. The relation between an action and the result of the action is coded by *of*. We could talk of *Chomsky's construction of a grammar*, where the relationship between actor and action is represented as another type of possessive relation. It is a significant fact about English culture that the relationship between an actor and the action initiated and carried out by him (in a nominalized form) is frequently realized as a possessive one: *Chomsky's construction*. It is syntactically distinct from that between action and affected: *the construction of a grammar*. Moreover, the actor-action relation, $X's$ Y, is syntactically closer than the action-affected relation, Y of Z, at least in this surface form.

Transforming one model into a different surface form is significant, an act of choice, however habitual and unconscious the transformational process may be. The importance of the range of possession models lies in the fact that they reflect a society's understanding of the nexus of relations involved in possession. Specific uses of any one model by individuals are revealing, and in being part of normal language use they have general symptomatic value. The *has* relationship reinterprets a world of qualities as a set of quasi-commodity relationships. The ideological force of this use lies in the fact that it systematically reinterprets one scheme into another. Like a gender system, it acts as a constant training in the use of the primary categories of the ideology. The *of* relationship, which habitually links nominalized activities with the 'products' of these activities rather than with the actors, repeats in a transposed form the ideology of an alienated commodity-oriented society. The rules for the use of these models and their transformations correspond closely to Marx's (1970) description of the fetishism of commodities in capitalist society:

> A commodity is therefore a mysterious thing, simply because in it the social character of men's labour appears to them as an objective character stamped upon the product of that labour; because the relation of the producers to the sum total of their own labour is presented to them as a social relation, existing not between themselves, but between the products of their labour. This is the reason why the products of labour become commodities, social things whose qualities are at the same time perceptible and imperceptible by the senses. In the same way the light from an object is perceived by us not as the subjective excitation of our optic nerve, but as the objective form of something outside the eye itself. But, in the act of seeing, there is, at all events, an actual passage of light from one thing to another, from the external object to the eye. There is a physical relation between physical things. But it is different with commodities. There, the existence of the things qua commodities, and the value-relation between the products of labour which stamps them as commodities, have absolutely no connexion with their physical properties and with the material relations arising therefrom. There it is a definite social relation between men, that assumes, in their eyes, the fantastic form of a relation between

things. In order, therefore, to find an analogy, we must have recourse to the mist-enveloped regions of the religious world. In that world the productions of the human brain appear as independent beings endowed with life, and entering into relations both with one another and the human race. So it is in the world of commodities with the products of men's hands. This I call the Fetishism which attaches itself to the products of labour, so soon as they are produced as commodities, and which is therefore inseparable from the production of commodities.

(*Capital*, p. 72)

Here is the full set of models which we have discussed so far, with an example illustrating each one:

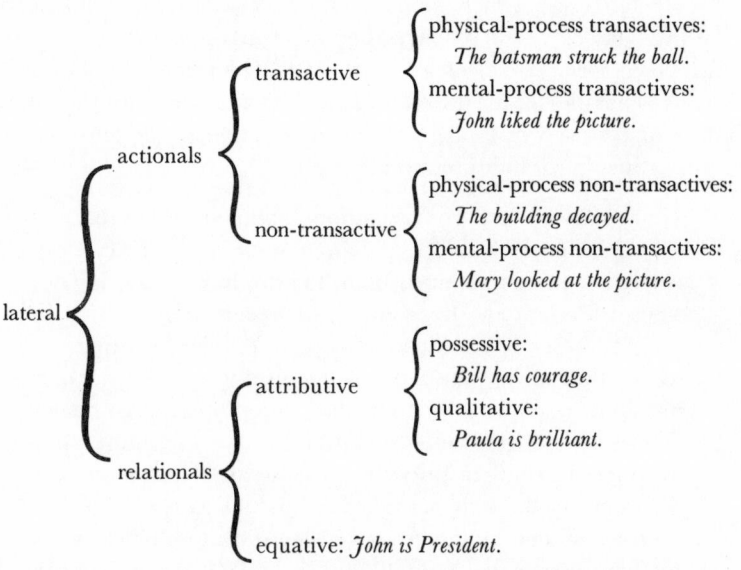

SOURCES AND CONTEXT

The components of our analysis here draw on a number of theoretically disparate sources. Our use of 'slots' is very similar to so-called structuralist treatments in the fifties and early sixties, when linguists attempted to construct taxonomies of linguistic items partly by their typical environments and partly by their place in a structured sequence. We connect this with Whorf's assumption that such ordered sequences had their motivation in aspects of meaning at a rather deep level. This assumption has given rise to some work in linguistics. Another major source for our discussion is the transformationalist treatment of prenominal adjectives as derived from underlying structures with embedded sentences with predicative adjectives. The first statement of this was in C. Smith's (1961) 'A class of complex modifiers in English'. A critique of this approach, pointing out that not all adjectives can be so derived, is Dwight Bolinger's (1967) 'Adjectives in English: attribution and predication'. There is an analogous debate in philosophy, concerned with the distinction between categorization and classification. Chapter 7 of J. Passmore's *Philosophical Reasoning* (1961), 'Allocation to categories', deals with this. Lastly, the problem of possessive forms in English has a long history in linguistics. Fillmore's (1968) 'The case for case' contains some discussion of possessive constructions, in particular of the notions of alienable and inalienable possession. John Lyons's (1967) 'A note on possessive, existential, and locative sentences' links, as we attempt to do, these various surface forms to an underlying shared semantic notion.

7

REALITY, POWER, AND TIME

MODALITY AND POWER

'Knowledge is power', wrote Francis Bacon, the ideologue of science. Marx and Engels held the opposite view, in their equally famous dictum from the *Manifesto of the communist Party*: 'The ruling ideas of an age have always been the ideas of the ruling class'. Behind the contradiction between the two statements lies a problematic relation between knowledge and power. What the powerful say can often be 'right' because it is said by the powerful. But this cannot be the sole basis for their claim to be right. There may be occasions when the powerful are in fact right, and they need to distinguish between the two kinds of claim, based on knowledge or power. Similarly the less powerful may wish to conceal the grounds of their assent, separating the superior reason of their masters from their superior power.

This ambiguous attitude to the relation between knowledge and power is reflected in the system of modal auxiliaries in English. Modality in general establishes the degree of authority of an utterance. The modal auxiliaries (*may, must, can*, etc.) perform this function, but they contain a systematic ambiguity about the nature of authority – whether it is based primarily on knowledge or on power. *She can talk* means either *She is able to talk* (representing the speaker's knowledge about her capacities) or *She is allowed to talk* (indicating the speaker's permission). Similarly, *She must talk* indicates either the speaker's prediction or an expression of compulsion. *She may talk* either gives permission or suggests a possibility.

Sometimes the context of an utterance makes the modality unambiguous; but in practice unambigious uses are the exception. This is precisely what we would expect if the ambiguity of the form is highly functional. A common occasion of modal auxiliary use is in interactional discourse, where coercion is masked by the surface forms of rationality. Jimmy Porter uses them in a typical way, in the extract we quoted from *Look back in Anger*. *She can talk, can't she?* he says to Cliff about Alison. The superficial meaning here seems to be that Alison has normal lungs, vocal cords, and knowledge of the language. However, Jimmy wants her to talk. The tag question *can't she?* is addressed to Cliff, but its meaning is unclear. Is Jimmy inviting him to confirm the statement as true, or is he ironically asking Cliff, as one relevant authority (Jimmy being the other one), whether Alison has permission? The first may seem more likely on this occasion, but the second would have its motivation. It would be a way of blaming Cliff, implying that Cliff is usurping authority over Alison and is responsible for her silence – which he may be, since he has just told Jimmy to shut up.

In English, modal auxiliaries precede the main verb. They do not take *-s* in the third person singular (there is no *He cans run*) and the verb following them has no tense marker (there is no *He can runs*). They 'absorb' the tense marker, so that the 'past' of *He can run* is *He could run*, not *He can ran*. This strongly suggests an interdependence between the *-s*, in particular its tense function, and the modal auxiliary, such that they are similar in function. Since modal auxiliaries replace or absorb the *-s*, we might expect that they code time reference as well as modality, just as conventional tense markers do. *You must be the thief* is either an inference made in the present or a command which will be realized in the future. *You may fly* is either permission given in the present or a reference to a possibility in the future. Modal auxiliaries thus do have indications of time reference, but they are less precise in this respect even than the conventional tense markers.

The ambiguity about authority – power or knowledge – varies according to which speech model the auxiliary appears in. In the transactive speech model they are least ambiguous. In an imperative, such as *Come!*, speaker and hearer, addresser and addressee, commander and commanded, are so clearly known that the question of authority is least problematic. Hence an imperative is nearly always a command, where the authority clearly comes from the power of the speaker. The deleted and understood modal *will* functions unambigiously. *You must come*, as a command, implies that the speaker is able to give orders in his/her own right, though the authority may have been delegated. If the speaker's own power is low, relative to that of the addressee, he or she may be forced to declare the source of his or her authority: *Mummy says you must come*. Interestingly, children are fully aware at an early age (from five or six years on) of the mechanics of these utterances, and they often start with the authority undeclared: *You've got to come – I won't – Mummy says you've got to.* With the non-transactive speech model, the authority relation of the speaker is at its least clear. *He must come*, as a command, makes no claim that the speaker is the source of the command. The command is depersonalized and given an impersonal authority which is not specified and therefore is more difficult to challenge. The third-person non-transactive, then, has clear advantages for an ideologue, who wishes to mystify the basis of his authority and the fact that authority rather than reason is being appealed to. Here is a passage from Edmund Burke, the influential counter-revolutionary ideologue, writing in the immediate aftermath of the French Revolution.

> Good order is the foundation of all good things. To be enabled to acquire, the people, without being servile, must be tractable and obedient. The magistrate must have his reverence, the laws their authority. The body of the people must not find the principles of natural subordination by art rooted out of their minds. They must respect that property of which they cannot partake. They must labour to obtain what by labour can be obtained: and when they find, as they commonly do, the success disproportioned to the endeavour, they must be taught their consolation in the final proportions of eternal justice.
>
> (*Reflections on the Revolution in France*, p. 271)

The *musts* here do not all have the same force, but all are to some degree ambiguous, ranging between the first, *must be tractable*, and the last, *must be taught their consolation*. The sentence *the people . . . must be tractable and obedient* is offered as a deduction or necessary consequence. If they want to acquire, then they must be tractable. But though there is a reason or motive given for this tractability, an obligation is involved. The context for an 'inference' interpretation of the sentence would be something like: 'Look, the people are lying on the ground to let the magistrate's coach roll over them. They must be tractable and obedient.' I deduce from this expression of devotion that they are tractable.

However, as the *musts* continue, the obligational/coercive sense becomes increasingly prominent, until we reach *they must be taught their consolation*. This is a passive, which has an underlying *X must teach them their consolation*. Exactly who this X is, is unclear. It is also unclear whether Burke is commanding, advising, or, just possibly, deducing. He may simply be drawing X's attention to the need to *teach the people their consolation* if X is to avoid bloody revolution. The non-transactive speech model conceals the force of the utterance. Combined with the passive all signs are removed from the surface of the utterance that Burke has shifted the target of this command – if it is a command. Burke exploits the indeterminacies of the form to negotiate the contradictions in his role as ideologue, both instructing the people in their duties and reminding his masters of their responsibilities.

Burke uses *can* twice in this passage, each time ambiguously; *that property of which they cannot partake* and *what by labour can be obtained.* The first use of *cannot* probably has *are not allowed to* as its most prominent meaning, but the other meaning, *are not able to*, is also possible, implying some unspecified reason not associated with a legal system, although in a text such as this, and often quite generally, there is an implication that the *not permitted* reading derives from an initial *not possible, not able to*, reading. For instance, *You cannot swim here*, 'because it is so dangerous/difficult that you are not able to', becomes 'It is forbidden (for your own good)'. In Burke's text there may be an initial 'Some are naturally fit and hence able, others not, to partake of property' which becomes a general prohibition, 'for the good of the whole society'. Conversely, *can be obtained* seems most prominently to imply *are able to obtain*, but the other interpretation remains available, *are allowed to obtain.*

Modal auxiliaries are vague about temporality, and Burke makes use of this feature. A clause like *the people must be tractable* in its 'obligation' reading refers to the future, when the people will be made tractable. But it can also be interpreted as a general law which applies now, in the past, and in the future. All the modal auxiliaries used in the passage share this quality, giving Burke's exhortation an indeterminate temporality. It is partly a description of the present state of affairs and its rationale, partly an exhortation to action. The indeterminacy is convenient for a conservative ideologue whose contradictory task was to portray a specific counter-revolutionary programme as the continuation of a social and political system sanctioned by tradition and convention from time immemorial.

This ambiguity and vagueness is clearly functional. We can hypothesize and suggest that, since language functions to deceive as well as to inform, every component of the grammar will contain one set of forms which allow the speaker to avoid making distinctions which are primary and another set where these distinctions have to be made sharply and with precision. We shall call the set of vague forms the simple forms, or the simple models, and the set of precise forms the articulated forms, or the articulated models. Thus transactives on the one hand distinguish absolutely between causer and affected, whereas non-transactives blur precisely this distinction. Similarly, the causer-process relation is coded precisely in the transactive and blurred in the prepositional variant of that model: *The coffee dissolved the sugar – The sugar dissolved in the coffee.*

Modal auxiliaries encode probabilities and hearer-speaker relations, but blur precise distinctions of past, present and future, knowledge and power, *is* and *ought*. From our hypothesis we would expect that English also contains a set of articulated forms which make these distinctions in a clear and precise form, to represent differences of time, knowledge, and power unambiguously. One way of indicating modal status is through modal adverbs, *possibly*, *probably*, *certainly*, etc. Although the modal auxiliaries conflate tense and modality, they can be 'translated' into unambigious forms. *He may come* becomes *He will possibly come*. This rules out the permission meaning of *may*. The adverbial *possibly* applied to *may* disambiguates it. In *He may possibly come*, *may* cannot have the meaning *is allowed to*. The sentence is equivalent to *He possibly will possibly come.*

There is a large class of verbs which have modal function. All transactive verbs referring to speech processes or mental processes can be used modally, to indicate the authority of an utterance or the relation of the speaker to the utterance. As transactives they express the relations involved in an explicit form. Take *Oh, I think that would be difficult*. Without any modal operations it is *That be difficult*. The speaker has applied modal operations on this three times, to indicate his relation to the utterance. First *will* is introduced. *Will* is then changed to *would*, with the introduction of *-ed*. We noted in chapter 5 that the *-ed* form suggests the modality *not now* and has a somewhat negative force. With modal auxiliaries this effect is very marked and consistent. The 'past' forms of the modal auxiliaries (*may – might, can – could, shall – should, will – would*) are all less certain or more tentative in meaning. The speaker then gives the proposition a new main clause *I think*. Syntactically, the clause *that would be difficult* is thus subordinated, or embedded, to the new main clause. Conceptually, it now seems that the utterance is first and foremost about the new mental-process main clause. However, the function of this, in English, is not to draw attention to intellectual processes or powers, but to indicate that what follows is the 'opinion' of the speaker. This typically introduces an element of tentativeness and uncertainty.

Verbs like *think* have a non-modal as well as a modal use. They behave differently in the two cases. Like the modal auxiliaries, they are interrelated with the -*s* present. They take this form in their modal use, even when they refer to present time, and not the present continuous (*is thinking*), which is the form for action in 'time now' in English. We say *John feels he is wrong*, not *John is feeling he is wrong* (where *he is wrong* is subjectively true in John's judgment). But, when the mental-process verb is not used as modality, we can have *John is feeling the effects of his drinking*. This follows from the fact that modality is outside temporal classifications in English.

These modal markers give a precise record of the sequence of operations which the speaker has performed on the utterance. An analysis of this part of an utterance is therefore sensitively diagnostic about a speaker's attitude to the utterance. An accurate transcript of speech will typically pick up many modal indications which neither speaker nor hearer was conscious of in speaking. Take the following brief extract from an admissions interview at a university, between a member of the teaching staff and a prospective student:

Interviewer: Do you find the system, er, makes sense?
Interviewee: Yes, I think I'm, er, beginning to understand it better now, and I must say, I'm quite sort of impressed. . . . I, I quite like the idea of, er, sort of flexibility, I think is the key word, isn't it? – in the sort of prospectus.

If the bare transcript was not already cruelly revealing, we could add either a video-tape or some notation to indicate the interviewee's movements forwards and back, his shifts in position, facial expressions, and so on, all of which have a modal function. (For a fuller analysis in context, see Fowler *et al.*, 1979.) We can summarize the following points, which have general applicability to materials of this kind.

1 The major content of an utterance is often to be found in the modal operations, rather than in the ostensible content. Here the core of the utterance is *Yes, I like the flexibility*.
2 There are a large number of ways of realizing modality: non-verbal and verbal, through non-deliberate features (hesitations, *ums*, *ers*, etc.) and deliberate systematic features which include fillers (*sort of*), adverbs (*probably, quite, better*), modal auxiliaries (*can, must*), and mental-process verbs (*think, understand, feel*), and intonation, which we have not discussed here.
3 The speaker translates uncertainty about status in the power situation into uncertainty about the status of his utterances. We see

vividly in this instance the relationship between power and knowledge, or claims to knowledge and claims to power. A speaker uses modalities to protect his utterances from criticism. A large number of modalizers indicates considerable fear on the speaker's part and vulnerability, rather than intellectual uncertainty. In this case the interviewee signals anxiety even when he may well be certain: *the sort of prospectus*.

4 Although pauses, stuttering, hesitation, and shifting in one's seat all have modal significance very similar to something like *Well, on the whole I really would like to say that in so far as I understand it from what little I've so far been able to read, I'm rather impressed by the concept of flexibility*, this latter verbalized version has prestige in our culture. The capacity to translate modality into regular verbal operations carries the further message (itself a component of modality): 'The person who is in control of such complex modalities, and doesn't have to stammer and scratch his chin, must be a member of an intellectually powerful class with a proper awareness nevertheless of his social position.' Such people rightly do well in interviews.

TIME, TENSE, AND HISTORY

According to Whorf, speakers of Standard Average European (that is, of languages like English) see time as a scroll which unrolls from the future to the past. We spatialize time, Whorf claims, and impose a sense of linearity and progression on what is experienced as more like a flux. For Whorf this conception of time, enshrined in our tense system and elsewhere in the grammar, is fundamental to Western thought. The categories of the tense system provide basic premises for conceptions of history and science, affecting notions of causality, sequence, identity, and truth.

The situation in English, however, is more complex than Whorf suggests. English has two systems for indicating temporality. First, the simple tense system: the *-s* and *-ed* forms which, as we have pointed out earlier, carry modal as well as temporal meanings. Second, a system composed of those forms usually described as aspect: the *have -en, is -ing* and *to infinitive* forms, which we regard as dealing predominantly with the sequence of events reported within one sentence, and their relation to a given reference point. The *-s* and *-ed* forms make up a single dichotomy of now/valid against past/non-valid. Future, with these forms, is realized by the *-s* with an indicator of temporality, such as a temporal adverb, *I fly tomorrow*, or the *-ed* if there is unlikelihood, *If I flew tomorrow*.

Our study of noun modalizers (determiners, attributives) and modal auxiliaries suggests two hypotheses. (1) Temporality and modality are significantly related though distinguishable. There is semantic justification for the fact that they act through the same place in the verbal structure in syntagmatic models. (2) Complex strings of tense and modality items are constructed as the result of successive operations. The order of these operations is coded and gives the significance of the complex structure.

Discussions of tense in English and other languages usually distinguish tense, which is said to be about time, from aspect, which indicates distinct meanings concerned with the manner in which the verb's action is perceived and presented. The *-ing* (as in *He is swimming*) is called the continuous or progressive aspect, because it describes the event as *continuous with* a specified period or as *in progress* at a specific period, emphasizing the ongoing aspect of the event. As the *-ing* never appears without a preceding *is* or *was*, the full aspectual form is in fact *be -ing*. The *has*, as an auxiliary, as in *He has forbidden it*, is called the perfective aspect. This presents the action of the verb as *perfected*, or *completed*. Again, this perception is made from a specific reference point; and with reference to that point the action is presented as *just completed*. I might be walking off a squash court and someone else might ask, *Have you (just) been playing squash?* The verb is always in its *past participle* form. In most cases this is the same form as the *-ed* past: *He had delighted the audience with his playing*. In some cases the past participle has an *-en* ending. The full aspectual form is *have -en* (where *-en* symbolizes the past participle ending). The *-ed* or *-en* ending seems to signal 'pastness' for the verb, completed action: hence it becomes more 'statelike' than 'processlike' and functions easily as an adjective.

The mysteries of the English tense, aspect, and modality system turn out to be entirely explicable in the light of our two hypotheses. Constructions involving them are formed by the application of a limited set of operators. One set can be called *sequencers*. There are three of these; they indicate sequence in relation to a specified point. They indicate whether an event is before, after, or at the same time as the specified point. They therefore act exactly as Whorf intuited, to cut up any stretch of time as though it was a scroll, to be divided into relative present, relative past, and relative future.

The suffix *-ing* signals simultaneity with a specified period of time. This is, of course, indicated in the traditional term 'continuous'. Shifts

129

in this reference period account for some of the puzzling features of the form. *She is talking* usually refers to a period which is contemporaneous with the utterance. In *She is talking there tomorrow*, *tomorrow* (or some part of it) acts as the reference period. In *She was talking when he went out*, the second clause provides the reference period (in the past). This codes simultaneity between the two actions, but it also implies that her action preceded and followed his, and hence suggests simultaneity of her action with at least the whole of his action. Her action therefore lasts as long as his, and possibly longer.

The *to* form, as in *He stopped to eat*, is the sign of *action after a specified point*, of *posteriority*. In *She tried to talk*, the effort precedes the process of talking, which is at that point only potential action; hence it allows for the possibility of failure. There is a systematic difference along these lines between *to* forms and *-ing* forms, where both are possible. *She tried talking* represents the action of the two verbs as simultaneous. *She stopped talking*, where the *stopping* is simultaneous with the *talking*, can be compared with *She stopped to talk,* where the cessation of some activity (not *talking*) is followed by *talking*. Some modal auxiliaries, such as *ought*, are obligatorily followed by *to*. This signals the temporal gap between *present* obligation and *subsequent* action. This link is so close that one might think of these as a new set of auxiliaries – *ought to, used to, was to, needs to*, etc. – which signal sequence, in addition to the meaning carried by the verb.

Both *-ing* and *-en* never appear without the verbal auxiliaries *be* and *have* respectively. Although the auxiliaries *be* and *have* look exactly like the 'full' verbs *be* and *have*, they are not normally regarded as having the same meaning. We want to suggest that the auxiliaries do in fact have very much the same meaning, and that their function cannot be carefully understood unless they are regarded in that way.

The meaning of the auxiliary *be*, like that of the main verb *be*, asserts existence, identity, attribution. That is, it acts like the linking *be* in the relational model. Where it appears as the only auxiliary verb, it carries the *-s* or *-ed* marker of tense/validity. The *-ing* aspect marker never appears on the same word as the *-s* or *-ed*. This is an interesting phenomenon, for it seems to point to a fundamental incompatibility of *-s* and *-ed* on the one hand and *-ing* on the other. We assume the *-s* and *-ed* are the tense and validity markers and that they are attached to that word which in any one utterance is regarded as the real verb. In the utterance *He is writing a letter* the *-s* is attached to the 'auxiliary' *be*, which is therefore marked as the actual verb; by the same token *writing* takes on some of the syntactic status of an attribute. This is a matter of degree, of course: generally the major meaning of the *be* is the aspectual one, though sometimes the relational meaning becomes more prominent – for instance, in this sentence from a *Guardian* editorial of 31 August 1977, *It wasn't a riot, and the Tiber is not foaming with blood.* (It may be that with non-transactives the *-ing* form tends to have the attributive meaning more readily.)

The order in which the operations are applied can be recovered by using the fact that the *-s* or *-ed* markers are attached to the verbal item (the *be*) which is introduced as part of the continuous aspect. In *He is running* the first step is the selection of the actional/non-transactive model: *He run.* Assuming that *be* and *-ing* are introduced jointly (as *-ing* always occurs in verbal structures with the auxiliary *be*), we then have *he be running.* Interestingly, some English dialects permit this as a surface form; that is, they permit an utterance marked for aspect but not for the minimal modality of validity. Lastly, the *-s* or *-ed* form is selected, giving in this case *He is running.*

The passive operates similarly. The auxiliary verb *be* is introduced as an automatic consequence of this transformation. In the passive, however, especially when the actor has been deleted, the relational interpretation is much more likely. In many examples it is difficult to interpret these as derived from transactives: *The car is (completely) smashed up; She was (most) delighted; The barn was situated close to the main road.* There is a marked difference between passives with *-s* and *-ed.* The *-s* passive is nearly indistinguishable from a relational model, predictably. Its meaning is composed of: *-en*, action completed before a specified point (thus not at the moment a *process*); *be*, a relation (of attribution) between noun and past participle; and *-s*, valid now. In other words, it is a relation involving a completed process (a state) valid now. (With the *-ed*, the lack of validity draws attention to the possible impermanence of the state; hence, the possibility of its derivation from a process is raised.) When the past participle is modified, the relational interpretation is complete. *She is most delighted* would hardly be interpreted as a transformed structure. In one particular case, passives with negatives, this relational interpretation is so strong that there is no plausible transformational source. *He was (completely) unknown* has no underlying *Someone unknew him completely.*

All of this draws attention to the fact that the event or process nature of a verb is not an absolute matter, but a rather delicate and finely balanced one. An action which is over, either because it happened 'in the past' or because it is talked about as 'just completed', is like a frozen action, a state. In a language such as English the difference is given grammatical status through the distinction between adjectives and verbs; and once the distinction exists it exercises a persuasive influence on our perceptions. It is, however, a conventionally established and maintained distinction, as our discussion shows.

There is an interesting parallel between the passive and a nominalization that we mentioned in chapter 2. In the passive (with the actor deleted) the process becomes an attribute of the affected participant: *He smashed the car up – The car was smashed up*. In nominalizations of actionals, the process caused by the actor becomes a possession of the actor: *The miners ban overtime – the miners' ban*.

Just as we interpret the auxiliary *be*, whether related to the progressive aspect or the passive transformation, by reference to the relational model *be*, so too we interpret the *have* which is introduced as part of the perfective aspect. This *have* signals its connection with the possessive model in English, and that model is the key to the understanding of the 'auxiliary' *have*. Of itself this is a most remarkable fact about English. Whorf claimed that English speakers spatialized time. The pervasiveness of the 'auxiliary' *have* shows that they habitually treat completed actions as quasi-possessions: *He finishes his job – He has finished his job* (or, *He has finished*). As this form is about temporality as well, placing events in relation to specified points in time, it shows that temporal relations are partially understood in terms of possession. The possessive interpretation of *have* depends to some extent on the model in which it occurs. With non-transactives the perfective meaning is more prominent: *The drought has broken; He has arrived*. With transactives (especially when the actor is human) the possessive meaning becomes stronger: *I have seen the Mona Lisa; I have completed the task*. Here it seems that the relation between *now* and a distant past is mediated through a possession-like model. It may well be that the possessive interpretation is stronger depending on the plausibility and even desirability of the completed event as a quasi-possession. *I have run in the Olympic Games* or *I have run a four-minute mile* would qualify for the possessive interpretation, as might *I have been to Florence*, whereas *I have run round the block* and *I have been to bed* would not.

Chomsky (1970) discusses some curious features of the perfective aspect. In talking about the sentence *Einstein has visited Princeton* he claims that this can only be said while Einstein is alive. With some exceptions, which we will look at, this is so. When we look at the components of the form we see why: *visited* places the event at some time previous to the utterance; *has* establishes a link between the two events, either through contiguity or the quasi-possession we have discussed. The -*s* establishes the statement as valid now, that is, *Einstein has visited Princeton* is currently a valid statement. But, as Chomsky observes, in our culture we would not say this. This prohibition seems to reflect a reluctance to regard the possessive relationship as continuing after death. A similar taboo would make us say of the deceased, 'He *had* great wealth/charm', not 'he *has*', unless by an agreed fiction he is reclassified as alive: 'He *has* eternal riches in the bosom of his fathers.'

But the passive version of the Einstein sentence is possible even after he is dead: *Princeton has been visited by Einstein*. The logic of this is that the quasi-possessive relationship now exists between Princeton and Einstein's visit, and is marked as valid by the -*s* in *has*. This will be a source of pride to Princeton as long as Princeton stands. It is not dependent on Einstein being alive, because it is now a possession of Princeton's, a valid statement about the situation now.

The grammatical rules in this case clearly reflect cultural assumptions. The exceptions are similarly sensitive and revealing about these assumptions. For instance, *Einstein has worked in this room* would be possible in certain circumstances, where a culture-hero is treated as having effective life in the present. Or *Einstein has influenced the course of modern physics*, where the -*s* form indicates the present validity of this claim, rather than the continuing existence of Einstein, except in so far as the validity of the utterance concerns Einstein's immortality.

Any account of aspect and tense in English has to include the so-called future tense. In practice it is a complex modality rather than an indication of straightforward temporality. Events which are expected to occur in the future can be expressed by using the -*s* with temporal adverbs, as in *He leaves tomorrow*, as well as by a whole range of modal verbs or aspectual/temporal sequences, indicating varying degrees of certainty: *We win tomorrow*; *We will win tomorrow*; *We must win tomorrow*; *We may win tomorrow*; *We intend to win tomorrow*. The future, in English, is not so much a category of time as a sphere of judgment about which English allows speakers to be more or less definite and certain, depending on their authority as predictors.

If the so-called tense system in English is in fact a complex of judgment, sequencing, and translation into possessive and attributive models, it should be revealing to analyse the use of this complex in texts which are essentially concerned with such processes. We have already analysed a piece of scientific text in chapter 2; now we will look closely at historical discourse. Here is the influential academic historian, G.R. Elton (1962):

Down to the end of Richard II's reign the history of English administration is, generally speaking, well known and fully studied; thereafter, we grope in the jungle, with few and indistinct paths blazed through it. No doubt there are gaps even in the high middle ages – questions yet unasked, doubts yet unresolved – but all is sweetness and light compared with the grim fifteenth century whose ever scantier records reflect the decay of good government at the centre. Yet if the significance of Tudor reforms is to be seen, it is necessary to arrive at least at a tentative view of what happened to England's institutions between the fall of Richard II and the fall of Thomas Wolsey. Those hundred and thirty years do, in a manner, form a unit; their discussion in this chapter is not abitrarily determined.

(*The Tudor Revolution in Government*, p. 10)

This is the opening of Elton's first chapter; it is standard language for an English academic historian writing this century. Some of the typical forms he uses are:

1 Passives, especially to refer to acts of decision or judgment by the historian: *(it) is well known, fully studied.*
2 Frequent use of the *-s* form: *records reflect, 130 years do form a unit.*
3 Infrequent use of *-ing* forms (only *generally speaking* in this passage), frequent use of *-en* (in passives), and use of *to* forms prior to acts of judgment by the writer.

All the passives here are agentless, which has the effect of effacing the historian from the surface of the text. This has a number of other functions. With *(it) is well known*, for instance, we can ask 'Who knows it well?' – all adult Englishmen? all historians? specialists in medieval history? G.R. Elton? The passive with a deleted actor is typical of academic and scientific discourse in general. It creates an impression of objectivity through the impersonality of the language. The temporal structure of the passives is relevant here. *(It) is well known* presents two temporal moments and modalities. *(It) is* has the *-s* marker, indicating the certainty about its validity which the speaker has at the moment of speaking. *Known* has the *-en* marker, indicating anterior time. The mental process involving knowledge precedes the speaker's present certainty. In this instance, the knowledge appealed to might go back for centuries. This utterance therefore has two components, present subjective certainty and past object of certainty. The two are asymmetrically combined so that the subjective certainty assimilates

134

the object of that certainty, the subjective present incorporating the past into its confident sphere. We are not encouraged to wonder how many people *know* these facts, or how Elton can know that they know them.

There are two instances of the *-s* form, which similarly conflate subjectivity and objectivity, present and past. *[The] records reflect the decay* and *Those hundred and thirty years do form a unit.* In content these seem about the past, yet they are in the *-s* 'present'. On closer inspection we see the subjective component of both verbs. The records reflect decay for the consciousness of the historian and this is true of the present, irrespective of the pastness of the events. In the same way, the years form a unit, again in the historian's mind; and that is a fact of the present. The *-s* here and throughout the passage signals Elton's certainty; and what he is certain about is his own judgments, his own consciousness.

The most complex temporal structure which he creates is *if the significance of Tudor reforms is to be seen.* Reconstructing the successive operations by working backwards, we have: *-s* (true for the *now* of the utterance); *to* (sequentially later than this *now*); the passive *be* (giving the surface of a relational model); *seen* (perception which is portrayed as completed and hence adjective-like prior to the relation being established). That is, the writer is certain about the conditions which will lead at some future point to a state of perception which is presented as by then already completed and statelike. He has situated the *seeing* precisely, in a complex temporal structure.

Seen, however, is a mental-process event, in which the historian or his reader is involved. Those events which are part of the subject matter of this history are handled differently. For instance, *between the fall of Richard II and the fall of Thomas Wolsey* sets up a chronological relation, but without using any of the devices so far mentioned. *Fall* may be derived (bearing in mind our comments in chapter 2) from an underlying *Richard II/Thomas Wolsey fell.* Had Elton used these forms, the *-ed* form would have indicated only that both events were in the past. The nominalization allows him to do without specifying any indications of pastness and to assimilate the events into the confident present of his scheme. He indicates the relationships between events by using a spatial metaphor: *between* one fall and another there is a temporal gap. He is spatializing time, as Whorf claimed English speakers in general do, but he detaches events from the temporal-modal system to do it.

The basic categories of Elton's discourse, then, are the present and the past, subjectivity and objectivity, historian and history. Although passive transformations and the deletion of actors have largely removed the historian-writer from the surface of the text, his consciousness is all-pervasive. Every -*s* present signals its confident presence. The temporal-modal acts of judgment are complex and precise. Subjective time is many-layered and carefully ordered. The events of history itself are detached from their actual contexts. In this language the writer's subjective present rules the past, subjectivity guarantees objectivity, and the historian creates history.

SOURCES AND CONTEXT

Our discussion in this chapter is again set firmly within a general Whorfian framework. The particular references that we use here are those to Halliday (1970b) on modality and Bull (1960) on tense, which we mentioned in chapter 5. Additionally, our treatment of modal verbs draws indirectly on a discussion by Boyd and Thorne (1969) in their article 'The semantics of modal verbs'. In that they take the speech-act approach of J.L. Austin (1962) and apply it to an analysis of English modal verbs. The major point to be made about this treatment is that it regards modal verbs as pointing to a specific utterer; this seems to us a necessary assumption. Modal verbs derive their force from the judgments of utterers, and are made as assertions about specific actors. A very similar point is made by Seiler (1971), who in his article 'Abstract structures for moods in Greek' says: 'The problem of "will" and "wish" in modal expressions will never be solved as long as one takes these notions as unanalyzed primitives. . . . In the semantics of "will" we must ask who is the person who wants something, from whom does he want it, and what is it that he wants.' An interesting connection between transitivity and modality is made in Josef Calbert's *Modality and Case Grammar* (1971). Lakoff's (1966) distinction between stative and non-stative adjectives and verbs remains an important way of seeing this whole area. Other writers who have regarded auxiliaries as having some (or all) of the force of main verbs are J.R. Ross (1969) in 'Auxiliaries as main verbs' and R.D. Huddleston (1969) in 'Some observations on tense and deixis in English'.

8

NEGATION

VISIBLE DIALECTIC

Every modal operation leaves a trace in the surface form. Where there has been a succession of modal operations, there is some indication of the order in which they have been applied. The unmodified base proposition is the key to the interpretation of modalized utterances. Modal operations are, of their nature, dependent processes, given significance through the model or the elements which they modify. In this respect they differ from transformations; and the result of the modal operation is a different relation between deep and surface structure. Transformations give rise to an alternative surface form which is more or less autotomous and through which the underlying form is more or less clearly visible. Modal operations leave the underlying form unchanged and represented directly on the surface.

This can be seen particularly clearly with negation. Even with a simple negative the positive form must be understood so that the hearer knows what is being denied. That is, both speaker and hearer must entertain the positive form in order to understand the negative. When further negation or another modal operation is applied, the interpretation consists of reversing the successive operations, so that the hearer recreates the original process and reaches the original proposition in its positive form. Take as an example *You possibly don't stink*. This is roughly equivalent to *I think you stink, but I'm giving you the benefit of the doubt.* The evolution of this meaning proceeds through reversal, first of *possibly*, then of the negative, to give successive stages *You stink* → *You don't stink* (that's what you want me to say) → *You possibly don't stink* (your defence is at best possible, but my original proposition still remains more convincing). The modality of this last form, then, is complex. It is the result of half-cancelling a cancellation, and the successive acts record a significant process of judgment in the form of a debate, which may of course only be internal. The surface form allows the order of the moves in this particular case to be recovered with certainty. The alternative order would have been

You stink. → You possibly stink. → You possibly don't stink.

But *possibly* clearly modifies the whole unit *don't stink*. Another way of representing its structure would be through parentheses: *You (possibly (don't (stink)))*.

Intonation patterns are important clues to modal processes. Contrastive intonation acts as a kind of negative. *You dò stink* is the end result of a see-saw process:

You stink. → I don't stink. → You dò stink.

This seems equivalent to the original proposition, but it has a subtly different modality. The surface records that the statement has been denied and reaffirmed (that is, the surface gives it this history, though the history may be an unreal one). We can continue the process. The apparently synonymous *Honestly, you dò stink* registers a second denial and a further reaffirmation of the original proposition. This establishes that the proposition is highly contentious, and in general we would be wise to doubt the self-evident truth of statements prefaced by *honestly* or *really*.

Not is only one modal operator, and surface forms can register a complex series of operations. Here are two sentences which appeared in an advertisement for a cough-mixture, one meant to be spoken by a less than loving husband, the other by an ideal husband:

1　Can't you stop coughing, dear? It's keeping me awake.
2　Poor dear, you must feel rotten – can't I get you anything?
　　(and he reaches for Brand X)

The underlying utterance is clearly visible. In its premodalized form it is *You cough*. To reach it we have to reverse the intervening modal operations. First we have the question form. Questions, like imperatives, result from transformational operations with a modal effect. A question has the effect of introducing uncertainty. That makes it a partial negative. The question *Can't you?* partly negates *You can't*. That is, it acknowledges *You can't*, but hopes that this is not final. *You can't* in turn directly negates a deeper *You can stop coughing*, which is either a statement giving permission, or a statement that the wife is able to stop. Actions which are under the control of an individual can be made the subject of a command. There is no imperative in the utterance, or at any of the successive stages. The wife is left to perform the final act of interpretation herself: He says I am able to stop; not stopping keeps him awake; hence, as he says I'm able to stop, I must stop.

Stop here is itself a kind of negative. *Stop* and *start* act not unlike auxiliary verbs and indicate a change in the state of the verb that follows. Thus *Start eating* presupposes that no one has been eating, *Stop slurping* that someone has been. This presupposition of the truth of what follows is extremely strong, whatever action follows, as in the famous 'Have you stopped beating your wife?' *Stop coughing*, therefore, necessarily implies that the person is coughing now. *Don't cough* might be used of a person coughing at the moment or it might be used to prohibit coughing at some future stage.

We have now reached the underlying proposition, the irritant, as it were: *You are coughing*. The modal processes which have been performed on this are, in order:

(i)	affirmed now	You are coughing.
(ii)	negated for the future	Stop coughing.
(iii)	the negation established as a command (by the wife, for herself)	I must stop coughing.
(iv)	the command made possible by the assertion of the cougher's responsibility for stopping	You can stop coughing.
(v)	this negated	You can't stop coughing.
(vi)	the command and the negation half-cancelled by the question	Can't you stop coughing?
(vii)	this 'softened' by a term of endearment	Can't you stop coughing, dear?

The meaning of the resultant surface form carries traces of the meanings of all these stages, hence its peculiar mixture of part accusation, part ineffectual covert command, ill-concealed irritation, and claims to dominance.

Another way to see this sequence is as one half of a dialogue:

	Husband	*Wife*
(i)	You are coughing.	So what?
(ii)	Stop coughing.	There's nothing you can do about a cough.

(iii)	You can stop coughing.	Alright, I must stop coughing, but really it's not that easy.
(iv)	(I'd better not come straight out with it.) You can't stop coughing.	I'm trying my best.
(v)	Can't you stop coughing?	A bit of consideration wouldn't go amiss.
(vi)	(Better try to keep things reasonably cool.) Can't you stop coughing, dear?	

The motivation for each successive modal operation on the husband's part is either an expressed or assumed negative response from the wife. The husband's responses show some of the strategies for dealing with negation or unwillingness. The function of these modalizers is to counter opposition or objections. Multiple modality may therefore be a sign of a complex and antagonistic relationship which has been completely internalized. The series of moves in this husband's modal operations will be interpreted as a typical defining exchange, a fair sample of many nights of inconclusive marital warfare. The history of its modality is the compressed history of a relationship. The advertisers who chose the sentence to illustrate the 'bad' husband evidently knew that the modal operations could be easily reversed by other experienced combatants, for all their complexity. Shrewd judges would see that this husband's badness is in fact the quality of the relationship. So Brand X perhaps will save a marriage as well as curing coughs.

The 'good' husband's enquiry is less intricate:

> You must feel rotten.
> You feel rotten.

Here *must* establishes the observation as a deduction (*I see you're coughing so you must feel rotten*). *Must* has a slightly weakening modal force, equivalent to *very probably*. He might have said, *You feel rotten*. But she is clearly the authority on how *she* feels. *You feel rotten* on its own would be unlikely, almost ungrammatical, since it would imply that he knew how she felt better than she did. The husband has used the modal auxiliary which conflates knowledge and power, and hence allows him the illusion of power even if it is only the power of making solicitous deductions about his wife's state of health. He then asks *Can't I get you anything?* He too negates the *can* question, but the implication this time is entirely different. In the previous example the *can* was about the hearer/wife's ability, and her husband was the one who had the relevant knowledge about that. Here the *can* is about the speaker/ husband himself, and about not ability but permission. And here it is the wife who is in a position to permit or not.

Can I? → No, you can't → Can't I?

This sequence suggests a self-sacrificing wife, racked with tubercular coughs, still refusing to put her husband to any trouble. However,this mouse-husband has slipped a negative into his wife's mouth. She can yield to his insistence, and allow him to bring her a little of Brand X, but she will have to relinquish the role of patient Griselda — 'Well, if it's not too much trouble. . . . 'Again, the sentence is interpreted as though it recorded a dialogue, even if the dialogue it records, and the relationship it sums up, is a mere fiction, imposed by the wife in a marital struggle that differs from the first only in being more covert.

The dialectic can be more clearly internal. Here is a famous passage from Milton's *Areopagitica* of 1644 (1955):

> I cannot praise a fugitive and cloistered virtue, unexercised and unbreathed, that never sallies out and sees her adversary, but slinks out of the race, where the immortal garland is to be run for, not without dust and heat. Assuredly we bring not innocence into the world, we bring impurity much rather; that which purifies us is trial, and trial is by what is contrary. That virtue therefore which is but a youngling in the contemplation of evil, and knows not the utmost that vice promises to her followers, and rejects it, is but a blank virtue, not a pure; her whiteness is but an excremental whiteness. Which was the reason why our sage and serious poet Spenser, whom I dare be known to think a better teacher than Scotus or Aquinas, describing true temperance under the person of Guion, brings him in with his palmer through the cave of Mammon, and the bower of earthly bliss, that he might see and know, and yet abstain.
>
> Since therefore the knowledge and survey of vice is in this world so necessary to the constituting of human virtue, and the scanning of error to the confirmation of truth, how can we more safely, and with less danger, scout into the regions of sin and falsity than by reading all manner of tractates and hearing all manner of reason? And this is the benefit which may be had of books promiscuously read. (pp. 13–14)

The passage contains a large number of negatives of various kinds, which typically cancel one another out. Take the following, from the opening sentence: *I cannot praise a . . . virtue [that is] unexercised and unbreathed*. This is a double negative, equivalent in meaning to *I can praise a virtue that is exercised and breathed*. Part of the interpretation, however, is deciding the order in which the negatives were applied, and hence the course of Milton's dialectic. Either *praise* or *exercised* or *breathed* must have been negated first. In this case it is clearly *exercised* and *breathed* which derive from underlying sentences: *Virtue has exercised/been exercised*. The negative has been assimilated into the transformed actional. This whole unit is the object of Milton's praise, which is first modified by the modal auxiliary *can*, then negated. Its history is

1 Virtue is exercised (by someone).
2 Virtue is not exercised.
3 I praise a virtue that is unexercised.
4 I can praise a virtue that is unexercised.
5 I cannot praise a virtue that is unexercised.

Sentences 3 and 4 are the problematic stages in the dialectic. At this stage Milton seems to be praising precisely what he condemns in the final version. Sentence 4 is moving in this direction. Although *can* is positive, indicating that Milton is able or allowed to praise virtue, it also has some negative force. As in our previous examples it may be the denial of an expressed doubt, or it might indicate possibility but unlikelihood. If modality is regarded as placement on a continuum from certain existence to non-existence, certain authority to absence of authority, then *can* represents a point more towards negative modality. As so often, this *can* is ambiguous about the kind of modal principle involved: whether Milton is physically able to praise such virtue, or whether some authority allows it. The negative *not* then cancels that permission or ability. Milton is back where he started, with an *exercised* virtue, though *cannot praise* is less definitely negative than *do not praise*.

Milton is aware of the principle of thought involved here. In fact it is his main point: *trial is by what is contrary*. Virtue must know *the utmost that vice promises to her followers*. At one stage in his thought the ascetic puritan can praise a dangerously slack form of virtue, confident that a final negative will restore original virtue. Double negatives proliferate in the rest of the passage, all allowing him at some stage of his dialectic to entertain contraries. *Not without dust and heat*, for instance, proceeds like this:

with dust and heat → without dust and heat → not without
dust and heat

Again the dialectic passes through a moment of effortless, transcendent virtue, *without dust or heat*, before returning to insist on the necessity for effort that he started with. As well as these straightforward negatives, there are many covert negatives, for instance,

How can we scout more safely, and with less danger?

This question is probably a pseudo-question, to which the required answer is *we can't*. The question plus the *can* form add up to a full negative. That is, questioning ability or permission is another form of negating. *Can you (really) run that fast?* → *You can't run that fast.* Rhetorically, in speech, intonation would reinforce this with the pattern for a closed field. So the meaning is close to *We cannot scout more safely*. Its syntactic form shows that it has a different 'history' from the other form, a different place in the dialogue, and different effects. The phrases *more safely*, and *with less danger* are also interesting. Strictly these are synonyms, formed by complementary pairs of opposites: *more/less* and *safety/danger*. But again, though they finish up in the same place, Milton has got there by significantly different routes. He seems to have started with *safely* and intensified it with *more*. But that contradicts his main line of argument, which insists on the necessity of risk. So *safety* is cancelled by its opposite, *danger*. But *danger* invites the risk of real failure, which is not what he wants, so *danger* is cancelled out by *less*. In this process, *less* clearly acts as a negative. Less obviously, *more* also creates a negative, since *more safely* leaves what was previously *safely* as *less safely*.

This little structure is part of a larger whole, which we saw was a kind of negative. Underlying it is the following sequence: *We can scout more safely* → *We scout more safely*. The basic proposition, the starting point of the process, is safe scouting, which in terms of Milton's opening argument is a blank virtue, a youngling. *Can*, then, has weakened its force, putting it into the future as something possible or permitted. The *how* question effectively negates the modality. This leads to a surface question, however, which, if taken at its face value, would constitute a request for further safety. Such a request sees the present as too dangerous, and therefore to be avoided. *How can we?*, as a question, repudiates danger and the present, for safety in the future. That question is effectively answered in the act of being asked with a negative, *we can't*; but the motives and judgment implicit in the original question still remain. Milton has wished for a safer future and judged the present as too dangerous. The negative rejects any other way out. Milton at this point seems to be contradicting the position he was arguing earlier, but the contradiction is hard to detect, owing to the complexities of the dialectic. Dialectic of this kind allows double-think, where underlying a surface form is its negation; and below that perhaps a further negation of the negation, so that to understand the surface the hearer must be able to interpret it in the light of a double process of negation. If the author at a slightly later stage says the opposite in a doubly negated form again, it is not surprising that the contradiction is harder to see, since this antithetical relationship between the different propositions is also present in the deep structure of each. Self-contradiction is internal to a syntagm as well as to relationships between syntagms. Milton is able to have things both ways, without himself being aware of it.

We can summarize what we have shown about negation and modality in the following form, to make clear the implications for analysis.

1 Simple negation is the exemplary form of modal operation. All modals except the -*s* present contain an element of negation which is the key to their meaning.
2 Even simple negation can be applied several times to an utterance or its parts. The difference between an open double negative (*e.g., I'm not unhappy*) and a fused double negative (*e.g., I àm happy*) is that in the first the process is brought out, in the second it is suppressed.
3 The history of the modal operations that have occurred in an individual utterance is the history of the social processing of that utterance. The underlying pre-modalized form either has its source in the speaker or comes from outside and is regarded by the speaker as an 'alien' meaning. Full negation can be the suppression of one's own meanings or the meanings of others, and hence may be aggression directed against the self or others. Partial negation works similarly.
4 The pre-modalized form of an utterance has no marks of its origins, since these are provided through modality. The same linguistic operations apply to one's own meanings and to those of others. The resulting surface forms will not reveal whose meaning was the starting point of the utterance. An analysis of modal processing will uncover the precise stages of a dialogue, but will not necessarily reveal who is on which side. Nor will it reveal how far the process has

been internalized and become self-regulatory, or how closely it corresponds to the reality of social relationships and the conditions of actual discourse. Linguistic analysis, here as elsewhere, provides an analysis of consciousness and its unconscious bases; it does not provide direct access to social reality.

DOUBLE-THINK

Negative forms must be interpreted in terms of an underlying positive form. This need not mean that the user of a negative form really believes the opposite to what he seems to be saying. For instance, if someone said *there isn't a tiger in that room*, we would not suppose that there probably was one there. However, that room immediately becomes one where a tiger might reasonably be. In order to deny the statement the speaker must have conceived it in its positive form. That is, he (and we as hearers) must have thought of a tiger being there first, before the proposition has been understood in its negative form. The negative form does not guarantee the reality of the tiger, but it does guarantee the reality of the thought.

This means that there is a close relationship between negatives and hypothetical statements: 1. *There isn't a tiger in that room*; 2. *There might be a tiger in that room*. The second is the result of several modal-temporal processes, yet is closely related to the first. The point is not an exact equivalence, but the affinity of negatives with hypothetical modalities. One important difference between the two is that in the first the surface form is that of a confident assertion, so that the converse hypothetical form exists in the underlying structure, as a subordinate meaning. With the second, the opposite is true. Here the negative does not exist in the surface, and the surface draws attention to the possibility, not its non-fulfilment. The modal status of this surface form is indeterminate. It is either a hope or a deduction. The same is true of the sentence underlying the negative. The proposition might have been a statement by someone else which proved false, or it might have been a hope or fear, but its principle of validity is entirely lost.

As a result of this, negatives allow the covert expression of wishes or beliefs. The corresponding modalized form displays the wish or belief, and only implies negation. A negative is a convenient way of expressing forbidden meanings, evading a censor by the vehemence of the denial. It is also a way of planting ideas without any responsibility for them. A negative like 1, for instance, is an excellent way of creating anxieties about tigers. Or to one's wife: *You don't look a bit drab this morning, dear.*

The negative here would conceal – probably not well enough – the positive insult, which the husband could continue to deny, driving it in deeper with every denial. Negatives can create a universe of alternative meanings, which the speaker formally renounces but which exist as a result of his renunciation. His relationship to his meaning is peculiarly ambivalent. Hence the surprising frequency of what we observed in the case of Milton: a speaker believing both the negative and the positive form, the statement and its opposite. The negative statement corresponds to his public belief (since this is the form he presents to the world), while the underlying form contains a more private belief which the negative acknowledges as illicit in some way. Negatives can allow an extreme form of double-think, mediating a total contradiction by distributing its elements between the deep and the surface structure.

We can describe what is happening here in Freudian terms, if we see negation as the suppression of deep-structure meanings in accordance with the reality principle, reality here being either physical or social reality, determining what is untrue or what is forbidden (or, of course, both). Negation can resolve a number of kinds of opposition: between proposition and refutation, expectation and outcome, desire and reality, private and public belief. All these oppositions proceed from some kind of antagonism: between speaker and hearer, or between the speaker and his world, a world which fails to conform to the principles of his world, or a society which suppresses his knowledge and beliefs. With any negative we need to know who is suppressing what, and why. We must also realize that we cannot always tell how successful the suppression has been, or how far the suppressed positive survives. Freud talks of 'the return of the repressed'. Negated positives also return.

Freud (1901, 1905) locates the suppressed in the individual's own unconscious; he always deals with patients as victims. However, a negation can be endorsed by a speaker against his subject. Here is Edmund Burke again:

> Good order is the foundation of all good things. To be enabled to acquire, the people, without being servile, must be tractable and obedient. The magistrate must have his reverence, the laws their authority. The body of the people must not find the principles of natural subordination by art rooted out of their minds. They must respect that property of which they cannot partake. They must labour to obtain what by labour can be obtained; and when they find, as they commonly do, the success

146

disproportioned to the endeavour, they must be taught their consolation in the final proportions of eternal justice. Of this consolation, whoever deprives them, deadens their industry, and strikes at the root of all acquisition as of all conservation. He that does this is the cruel oppressor, the merciless enemy of the poor and wretched; at the same time that by his wicked speculations he exposes the fruits of successful industry, and the accumulations of fortune, to the plunder of the negligent, the disappointed, and the unprosperous.

(*Reflections on the Revolution in France*, p. 271)

Consider the negative in the utterance

> that property of which they cannot partake.

Burke, as the ideologue of the landed classes, endorses that negative, rejecting the aspirations of 'the people'. But, even here, the underlying proposition *they can partake (of that property)* must have been apprehended by Burke. He must have made it his own meaning, prior to its rejection. In one of the two senses of *can* it is obviously true, even for Burke. The lower classes were distressingly able to partake of the landed gentry's property, as the French Revolution had just shown. It was to prevent precisely that from happening in England that Burke was writing. The other meaning, which is the one most prominent in the final form, envisages a permission which might have been given. In order to declare against this aspiration, Burke must know what it's like to hold it, though it is the aspiration or political programme of others, not of himself. The negation is a suppression of the meanings of others, not himself. Yet even so it recreates what it is renouncing. Burke could, after all, have conveyed his meaning without a negative: *that property which belongs to others*. The revolutionary aspirations of 'the people' would have been less clearly visible beneath that surface form.

Negation realizes an irreconcilable antagonism. It attempts total suppression, making this act of suppression overt and unmistakable, even if it thereby allows the suppressed a strange kind of continued, if invalidated, existence. But antagonism and suppression can be less irreconcilable and overt. There are many forms of partial negation, which often seem to show a desire for precision, not antagonism. The Burke passage contains a typical example:

> the people, without being servile, must be tractable. . . .

Here a precise and subtle distinction seems to have been established,

147

between servility and tractability, or two related forms of political behaviour. If we present the propositions in a common form, we have: *The people must not be servile*; *The people must be tractable*. *Servile* and *tractable* a near-synonyms. It's quite likely that the same action could be regarded as *servile* by one person and as *tractable* by another. One might regard a doffing of the cap and tugging of the forelock as a sign of tractability, the other might call it servile. The distinction is not a precise and subtle one between related but distinct kinds of action, it is a strong contrast, probably neither precise nor subtle, between two different judgments of what may be the same behaviour. What Burke has done is to acknowledge that a totally opposed judgment is possible about the behaviour he admires. He then neutralizes that judgment, first with a negative, then with a transformational displacement to shift it out of focus. But this contrary judgment is still there, and Burke gives no indication of how the contradiction is to be resolved. He has gestured at an egalitarian judgment, then endorsed its opposite. A member of the lower classes who wished to please Burke would be unwise to suppose that there is a precisely calculated force to be exerted on his forelock, registering tractability but not servility. There is not a middle course to be steered, but a contradiction to be resolved.

But has proliferated in the preceding discussion. Adversatives (*but, yet, however*) are another way of presenting contradictions as though the process involved was refinement of meaning in the interests of greater precision. Here is an example contemporary with Burke, from the judgment of Mr Justice Hardinge against three men convicted of stealing $1\frac{1}{2}$ guineas during food riots in 1801:

Heated by your passions, and by liquor,

   (i) you were more and more inflamed, at every new step, against the peaceful neighbours, till the whole Town was at the mercy of undisciplined violence.

  (ii) It is true that no acts of *personal cruelty* appear to have taken place.

 (iii) But alas! at a moment like this, and with a reference to some very important features of your conduct, in a political view, I am deeply concerned at the intelligence which I must impart, that I see no ground of hope for your exemption from capital punishment; tho' I shall rather give my *opinion* to the King, who is the fountain of mercy, than determine your fate myself.

(iv) I lament (and so must every observer who looks at the *moral* difference of guilt) that many of your incendiaries and ring leaders, are to escape from *your* punishment.

(v) Yet the warning of this very difference is not without its use. . . .

[The judge continues to progress through *yets* and *buts* to his conclusion:]

(vi) I have suspected as long as I could, the sentence of the law, Oh! that I could suspend it for years and for ages! – It must, however, be delivered, and I fear that it *must be executed*.

[The Judge then delivered the sentence of death.]

(from the Appendix to Jones, 1973)

This is clearly a strange performance, reminiscent of Lewis Carroll's Walrus, who had a similar quality of concern for the ill-fated oysters. The general lines of the contradiction are between pretended concern and judicial violence, ostensibly between personal feelings and public necessity, which is only finally resolved in favour of necessity by Mr Justice Hardinge donning his black cap.

The relation between (i) and (ii) is a contrast, which could have been indicated by an adversative like *however*. *It is true* has an equivalent function, conceding part of the opposing case, indicating a dialectic process, recording someone else's negative, *there were no acts*. The concession here seems a large one. At one moment we have *the whole Town at the mercy of undisciplined violence*, the next we have *no acts of personal cruelty*. Yet we are not told how this contradiction is to be resolved. The judge's seemingly scrupulous fairness is in practice a toleration of self-contradiction: a capacity to restate the opposite case, acknowledge its force, and then proceed to ignore it.

A concessive *it is true* normally promises a contrary *but*, cancelling this truth out. This particular *but*, when it comes, introduces a new topic, which cancels out a different proposition, which exists only through this negation of it. This is a general function of adversatives. For instance, take: 1. *He is clever and evil*; 2. *He is clever but evil*. The difference between these two is that 2, through the *but*, invokes an otherwise invisible judgment that has been negated. Here it might be *He is clever (that's good), but evil (that's not good)*; that is, he is clever and evil, good and not-good. *But* is the only trace of what might be termed the deleted contradiction.

In Judge Hardinge's case, the most likely proposition he is opposing is in fact given in his speech, in negated form: *I see no ground of*

149

hope. . . . After he had registered a huge self-contradiction, he, or the defendants, might have seen some grounds for hope. What he is negating is not the statement but this inference, which has no other mode of existence. This *but*, however, is doing more work than that. It is juxtaposed with *alas!*, an expression of distress, contrasting with the delight he thereby pretends to have felt at the *ground of hope* offered by his previous sentence. Again this delight exists only as the negation of his proclaimed dismay. The *tho'* that introduces the final sequence of this sentence works similarly to the opening *but*, counteracting a possible, but otherwise unstated, judgment on what he has just said. The sentence that follows shows another form by which a kind of contradiction can seem like a careful judgment:

I shall rather give my *opinion* to the King, who is the fountain of mercy, than determine your fate myself.

There are two processes of negation in this. One is the use of contrastive stress, which implies a negation, whose base form may not be easily recoverable, *my opinion* (not *my judgment? verdict?*). He is evidently wishing to displace responsibility for the execution onto the King (*who is the fountain of mercy*). So a cluster of alternatives may simultaneously be negated through contrastive stress: he is giving an opinion only, and is not judging, condemning, and causing the execution of three men for stealing $1\frac{1}{2}$ guineas.

The *rather/than* contrast has a similar effect, probably establishing which of the contrasts he wishes to be uppermost. This has the effect of negating the second part: *[I do not] determine your fate myself.* This is hard to explain from a judge passing sentence, unless *myself* is meant to contrast his individual person with his legal status, as mere instrument of state justice. However the sophistry is achieved, this is a fine piece of double-think, a judge responsible and not responsible, determining and not determining the fate of the accused. The nature of the contradiction is manifest, even though its precise motivation may not be.

In his final summing up he is ostensibly poised between humane reluctance to deliver the death sentence and his obedience to the reality principle, the necessity that the sentence must be delivered. *Oh! that I could suspend it for years and for ages*! This is a hypothetical statement, the simple past with *can* having the effect of a negative, equivalent to *I cannot suspend it for years and for ages*! He pretends to wish that he had permission, or power, to suspend the sentence for ever. The negative which signifies that it is an impossible wish is implicit, not overt. The effect is as though a compassionate wish has come up against inexorable reality, lapsing rather than being negated.

In societies characterized by conflict and contradictions, forms of double-think will be a condition of survival, and languages will show a wide variety of strategies for achieving and interpreting it. Sarcasm is one simple way of achieving negation, using intonation as a cue, instead of negative modals. The literary analogue is irony, where cues other than intonation have to be developed. Judge Hardinge might have been ironic here. Had he been the creation of a novelist, the blatancy of his self-contradicton might have been meant to have the force of a negative. Irony, even sarcasm, is hard to interpret because of the characteristically ambiguous modality of a negatived statement. Laughter also affects modality in a similar fashion, and hence is part of syntax. 'I only meant it as a joke' has the force of a negative, usually invoked when other modal cues have been mis-interpreted (or when the speaker feels he needs to rewrite the modality of his utterance). Inability to interpret double-think is a form of social incompetence, a severe handicap if double-think is endemic to that society. A large part of the resources of language are designed to allow people not only to say what they mean but to mean the opposite as well, without ruffling the smooth surface of life or discourse. The system of modality reflects social relations precisely and sensitively, translating kinds of conflict and contradiction into forms of negation. By these means and others, the structures of society are internalized and become part of the individual's consciousness. His competence as a speaker then becomes his ability to produce and understand utterances out of this consciousness, as out of a second nature which has become his own.

SOURCES AND CONTEXT

In this chapter we have drawn more substantially on non-linguistic than on linguistic work. Discussions of negation in linguistics tend to confine themselves to structural description of negative items and particles on the one hand, and to an analysis of the scope of negation on the other. In *Syntactic Structures* (1957) Chomsky uses negation as part of an argument for establishing the simplifying force of transformations; in the course of that argument he discusses successive stages in the development of a complex negative surface form. The range of phenomena drawn into this include questions and sentences with contrastive stress. Chomsky does not, however, assert any cognitive connection or relation in meaning between these. The most extensive transformational treatment of negation is Klima's (1964), in his article 'Negation in English'. Our approach draws extensively, though indirectly, on the work of Marcuse, particularly his *Negations* (1968) (and through him on the Marxist and Hegelian tradition), and on that of Freud. Underlying our whole approach to language is the assumption that linguistic items and processes do not occur in the grammar simply as unconnected items, but as parts of ordered systems. In our view this is the case for all linguistic items: words, syntactic categories, syntactic processes. To take a simple example, the word *demo* occurs as part of a class which also includes *riot, demonstration, assembly, march*, etc. This is not the only class it belongs to; it also belongs to the syntactic class *noun*, and to specific subclasses within that. 'Word associations and linguistic theory' by Herbert Clark (1970) is a very helpful account of the classificatory systems in which linguistic items are multiply referenced. Given this assumption, then the selection of one item out of an ordered and finite system amounts to partial negation of the other items.

9

READING POWER

LANGUAGE AND THE WAR IN THE ARABIAN GULF

This book has been concerned with 'reading power' in a double sense. We try to read the traces and effects of power in language and discourse, in text and syntax, and in the process we seek to develop a way of reading that is powerful and enabling, part of an effective critical strategy. The earlier chapters of this book have described some major features of English, along with ideological meanings and functions that they typically can and do have. Our descriptions are embedded in particular analyses, because these meanings only exist in concrete instances of language in use, but so far we have not done full justice to the analytic strategy that requires and makes best use of descriptions of this kind. This analytic strategy rests on assumptions about language and society which we have not developed. This last chapter will try to do something towards filling these two gaps.

In a provocative statement Michel Foucault rejected language as a model for the study of discourse:

> I believe one's point of reference should not be to the great model of language (*langue*) and signs, but to that of war and battle. The history which bears and determines us has the form of a war rather than that of a language: relations of power, not relations of meaning.
>
> (Foucault, 1980, p. 114)

Our book acknowledges the force of Foucault's critique, but then attempts to propose a theory of language that denies his dichotomy. Having recognized the role of power in determining meaning, we do not have to accept that power and history are meaningless. On the contrary, the critique itself specifies the requisite form for a new theory of language, one that is not trapped in the massive and static structures of the Saussurean *langue* but rather takes for granted the interdependence of language and power, meaning and social process.

In developing such a theory we need to question the received notions of power and the ways it operates in social life and in the social production of meaning. Foucault has argued persuasively against a simplistic notion of power that identifies it only with oppression operating from above:

> What makes power hold good, what makes it accepted, is simply the fact that it doesn't only weigh on us as a force that says no, but that it traverses and produces things, it induces pleasure, forms knowledge, produces discourse. It needs to be considered as a productive network which runs through the whole social body, much more than as a negative instance whose function is repression.
>
> (Foucault, 1980, p. 119)

This polymorphous and perverse notion of power discovers it everywhere in a social formation, linking and crossing the public and the private spheres, constructing every interaction as in some sense 'political'. This leaves the organized power of the State as only the game of the biggest player in the political sphere, with society defined as a stable state of war. From this Hobbesian point of view Foucault asks: 'Isn't power simply a form of warlike domination?' (1980, p. 125).

We have a number of reasons for wanting to follow Foucault's lead here, using texts taken from a war as the basis for exploring issues of method, and examining the fundamental assumptions about language and society on which they rest. First we wish to separate the Saussurean *langue* from the concept of 'language', in particular denying two of Saussure's most firmly held assumptions. For Saussure, *langue* was a static and unitary system. In the discursive processes which surround war unity does indeed exist, but not as the automatic effect of a definition of language. On the contrary, unity is an achievement that has to be won and maintained in and through language, in order for domination to be effective and resistance to be mobilized. In a war this process of constructing alliances and oppositions is more visible, taking place at a faster rate, with a greater investment of social energies. So it is useful to look at the deformations of language in a state of war in order to understand how language operates 'normally', in the shifts and negotiations of a state of 'peace'.

It is no accident that Orwell's seminal work on language and politics grew directly out of his reflections on language and war. *1984* was based on the continuity between World War Two and the post-war period, drawing also on Orwell's experience of other wars as a journalist in the Spanish Civil War, and the undeclared civil war of Stalinist Russia, which Orwell knew about at second hand. This short list brings out a crucial point for a theory of language and power which uses the premise that peace and war are aspects of a single system. There are wars and wars, peaces and peaces, and they exist in sequences, syntagms of events that constitute versions of history. Ideological battles take place against the background of these versions of history at the same time as they seek to transform them, for immediate tactical reasons as well as for longer-term advantages, for use in times of peace as well as war.

The Spanish Civil War, for instance, was an experience that briefly radicalized a generation in Britain in their opposition to the fascism of Franco. World War Two mapped this structure onto a different kind of war, negating the memory of 'the Great War' by turning it into 'World War One', incorporating the idealism of the war against the fascism of the Spanish Civil War and mobilizing it into the construction of the last Just War. In this form it operated as part of the set of Grand Narratives that justified the role of the major powers in the international order for the following decades.

Since 1945 there have been many outbreaks of conflict that could be called wars, but in Britain and America a unique place is occupied by the Vietnam War. This was one of many wars whose origins were to be found in the tensions of post-colonialism. What made it significant was its effect on the construction of the imperialist Grand Narrative. Vietnam came to signify the Unjust War, the war that should not have been fought, where technological superiority on the part of a colonizing power went along with 'moral' inferiority and military defeat. One crucial factor in this ideological event was the role of the technology of information. Media coverage of the war exposed the discursive strategies of governments and militiary bureaucracies in all European countries, rendering them obsolete at a stroke.

It is in this context that we are interested in the 'Gulf War' which was formally declared on 15 January 1991, and lasted only a few one-sided weeks before the immense superiority of the American-led coalition achieved a crushing victory over the armies of Iraq that had occupied Kuwait six months earlier. Militarily it may not be the most interesting of wars, but ideologically speaking it is an exemplary instance. President George Bush proclaimed the ideological triumph of the American forces in his speech of 18 March to a group of soldiers returned from the Gulf:

> You know, you all not only helped liberate Kuwait, you helped this country liberate itself from old ghosts and doubts. When you left it was still fashionable to question America's decency, America's courage, America's resolve, and no-one, no-one in the world doubts us any more.
>
> (CNN 18 March 1991)

This speech is a typical enough instance of President Bush's rhetorical strategy for us to make some more general observations. The President draws attention to the double aim of the war, and the two levels at which it needed to be waged. The military war in the Gulf, waged with immensely superior technology and a better trained army, needed the support of an ideological offensive that had to be equally superior, oriented to a range of audiences in a number of coalitions, inside America and outside. The two levels were inter-dependent, since a measure of ideological success was necessary for the war to be undertaken in the first place, and conversely, military failure would have been difficult (but not impossible) to recuperate by ideological stratagems. But to some extent the levels operate sep-arately, since not all forms of military victory would be equally useful ideologically.

Some of the factors that constrained Bush's performance can be seen from a comparison of the two words 'decency' and 'courage'. What is interesting here is not whether using earthmoving equipment to bury alive thousands of soldiers who could not escape can be properly described as either 'decent' or 'courageous'. It is that the qualities at issue are such different kinds of virtue, one signifying the virtues of peace, the other the virtues appropriate to war, with 'decency', the virtues of peace, being given the priority. There are good reasons for this mild contradiction. President Bush is addressing returning soldiers, in a broadcast that would be heard across America and would be beamed into the homes of citizens of his allies, an audience containing considerably more civilians than soldiers, who needed to be reassured that this was a just war now that its success was no longer in doubt. There is a risk, in this speech, that the emphasis on 'America's' decency, courage and resolve might alienate the world audience which was also listening to this broadcast, but Bush chose to take this risk, aware that only American citizens vote in American elections.

We will leave aside judgments on the success of this particular speech, and concentrate on the considerations that lay behind it, for it is these considerations that are of general application. Bush's rhetorical strategy was not contradictory by accident. On the contrary, its whole point was to manage the contradictions that came from the competing interests that he was trying to satisfy. Anyone trying to persuade others to a common action that is not obviously in everyone's interests will need both to acknowledge and to resolve difference. For representatives of a political organization the requirement is especially acute. The power of a political agent necessarily rests on the consent and support of many individuals, their sense of solidarity with the aims and methods of the leading group.

This solidarity or acceptance can only be created through forms of discourse (language in its broadest sense, taken to include all semiotic systems). The basis for this acceptance (able to coexist with resentment, resistance and other hostile or antagonistic attitudes and actions) is found in a repertoire of representations of the social which we call ideological forms. But there is one characteristic of these forms that President Bush's performance leads us to emphasize. Far from an ideology being a single consistent but biassed version of reality, it normally comes complete with its own negation, in a deeply contradictory set of versions of reality whose contradictions are intrinsic to their function. We will call such a set an *ideological complex*.

There are two components that contribute to the contradictory character of ideological complexes. One component represents the world in a way that blurs differences, antagonisms, conflicts of interest. We will call this the *solidarity* function, or the S-form. The other expresses the interests of the group against its others, so that it exacerbates difference, hostility, superiority. We will call this the *power* function, or the P-form. The two forms mingle with complex promiscuity in most rhetorical performances, but the distinction between the two is useful as an aid to tracking the process of fusion that is typical of ideology in use.

This speech summarises the narrative of the war the President wished to endorse, and at the same time it indicates its place and function in a narrative sequence that was also a competing set of texts in an unstable relationship of intertextuality. The Gulf War is proclaimed as the definitive exorcism of the 'ghosts' of the Vietnam War, ghosts whose force was intensified by the failures of American policy in Iran and Nicaragua, and insufficiently negated by the triumph of the invasions of Grenada and Panama. This narrative is inflected differently for different nations. France's withdrawal from Algeria is not part of the American Grand Narrative, and for the British, the Falklands War made the Gulf War redundant, as the new Prime Minister John Major found to his distress in the first opinion polls after the Iraqi surrender.

In three years' time, the Gulf War will probably not seem either important or successful as a new Grand Narrative of war. But the events and the discursive processes that surround them are still likely to be typical enough. All the examples that we use to illustrate our argument will come from this situation. We do this in order to make a methodological point that our exposition elsewhere in the book obscures or misrepresents. In 1979 it was an innovation to analyse examples of language in use, structures embedded in texts, texts deployed in specific situations by specific agents for specific but not always obvious purposes. Above all it was an innovation to treat linguistic *form* as the product of social, political, ideological processes. But we still did not adequately acknowledge the scale and complexity of textual and discursive processes that are the proper object of the analysis of language and politics. In order for the book now to be as useful for analytic purposes as we would like, we need to put our account of discursive processes into a wider frame.

For analysts interested in this hybrid dual object, language in politics or politics in discourse, it is necessary to insist that meaning does not exist outside discursive and semiosic processes. It is constructed by various participants in texts that circulate in some material form in various social spaces, each situation and text a site where countless histories intersect. Meanings are realized in linguistic forms of all kinds. They also exist, for various discursive agents, in gaps and linkages, across and between texts and contexts, contexts that are themselves only another mode of existence of textuality, in a process that is constrained by sets of rules and practices (genres, discursive regimes) and disrupted by other rules and practices, held in place by the weight of innumerable repetitions and sanctions.

In this view power (social power as analysed by sociologists and political scientists) is a relation between people, not a relation between texts or meanings. But it is always a mediated relationship, and cannot exist without the signifying systems that constitute it. So it is also possible to say that power is only an effect of discourse, if 'discourse' has a general sense equivalent to 'semiosis' (the process of construction and circulation of signs). For this reason, the operations of power can only be studied via texts, which are scrutinized for the various traces and clues and claims they contain; either secondary texts whose narrative seems to guarantee an object, power, that exists outside of its own textual frame, or texts which carry traces of the processes themselves by which power is or was mediated and constructed.

Political scientists normally rely exclusively on what we have called secondary texts, treating their 'content' as more or less transparent. Our method of analysis typically has sought out the other kind of text, scanning them for enigmatic traces of process frozen in text, fossils of power preserved in linguistic amber. The critical linguistics method is difficult and valuable, but it is also too strenuous to be the only hermeneutic method applied to all kinds of texts for all purposes. If political scientists typically treat their evidential texts as too transparent, our own method only avoided the trap of obscurantism and triviality by making large and unsubstantiated (or at least undeclared) assumptions about the political context at issue. The two approaches, then, are complementary.

Similarly there is a complementary relationship between the three main phases of the analytic traditions concerned with the study of political meanings. *Language as Ideology* was a handbook for what has come to be called 'critical linguistics'. Critical Linguistics has tended to merge with 'critical discourse analysis', which subsumes the account of linguistic forms of CL into a broader account of discursive processes. Social semiotics then emerged to subsume CDA into a broader study of all semiotic systems involved in the construction and circulation of meaning. But the successive stages have not rendered the previous stages obsolete. On the contrary, CDA requires an even stronger account of linguistic forms in order to carry out its primary activity of tracing the dialectic between text and process, linguistic form and social and semiotic process. The project of social semiotics likewise would be impoverished if it neglected to study discourse, and the role of verbal language in the semiotic repertoire.

In the discussion that follows, then, we will attempt to clarify issues and concepts that contribute to the analytic value of the account of language in the rest of the book. This usefulness is no less, we believe, because its approach seems to combine myopia and hyperopia, paranoia and naivety, empiricism and speculation in proportions that are not predetermined, directed towards a profoundly fissured object of indeterminate nature and scale. But the contradictions in the approach exactly match contradictions in the object: language as site and stake in political struggles, politics as condition and product of systems of meaning.

HUNTING 'TRUTH'

Language as Ideology presents an approach to reading, a hermeneutic strategy, and in important respects its theory of language arises out of that strategy, as precondition and discovery. The strategy seems characterized by endemic suspicion, a critical doubt that texts mean what they seem to, an apparent certainty that somewhere a very different 'real' meaning lies hidden. As one criticism of our approach has put it, 'one of the stock techniques employed by Kress and his colleagues is to look in the wrong place for something, then complain that they can't find it, and suggest that it is being concealed from them' (Sharrock and Anderson, 1981, p. 289).

In terms of this robust common sense, the whole strategy does look perverse and wilful. It seems to combine excessive scepticism about the meanings of others with an unsubstantiated faith in the certainty of our own interpretations. Such an unlimited scepticism is not much use even in those situations where it would seem justified, as in a state of war. It is a truism about war that 'truth is the first casualty', but journalists like Phillip Knightley, who used this in the title of a book, believe strongly that there is something that can be called 'the truth' which dedicated journalists can dig up or establish, and which scrupulous journalists will try to write. It is because Knightley believes in the possibility of truth that he can castigate his colleagues for making a travesty of it. Total trust and total scepticism in their different ways lead to questions of truth coming off the agenda, leading to either uncritical or cynical reporting.

Our own enterprise has an equivocal relationship to this notion of 'truth'. In the war in the Gulf, for instance, it is not in doubt that bombs were dropped, and people including women and children suffered hardship, mutilation and death. But in the barrage of claims and counter-claims of wartime reporting it becomes impossible to have even a good guess as to how much damage was done to whom and why. It is likely that with this war as with others, narratives will be excavated with more or less difficulty for many more years after the war has finished, and there may be many more that are never brought into the public domain. The efforts of investigative journalists and historians, political and military commentators and others who attempt to settle at least some of these accounts are instances of a critical stance that are easy to justify.

What *we* do may seem in contrast to be ludicrously or culpably irrelevant, ignoring the reality of human suffering in our concern with language. But the nature of our concern with language is inseparable from a concern with the wider issues that are raised by the war, including the vexed issues of 'truth' and 'what really happened'. The strategists who planned and managed the war on both sides knew the importance of controlling the flow of 'information'. In this process, developments in information technologies played an important role, constructing and circulating texts and versions of reality that won the 'battle for minds' which shadowed the war on the ground, without which the war on the ground could not be won, or would not have been worth the winning.

It is common for linguistically-oriented critics to attend too much to language, and to overvalue the importance of what is contained in words, especially words in written texts; but the opposite can also be the case. All the major ideological struggles will necessarily be waged in words, through texts that circulate in various ways by virtue of various technologies, in forms of language that bear the traces of these struggles in innumerable ways. The forms of analysis, the ways of reading that we seek to develop are neither unitary nor self-contained, but operate as components of a broader set of strategies of interpretation deployed on a diverse and unstable set of objects.

Propaganda typically operates with two broad strategies: manipulation of reality (lies, half-truths, exaggerations, omissions etc.), and manipulation of the orientation to reality. It is possible for propaganda to be fully successful without needing to resort to actual or demonstrable lies, so a form of analysis is necessary that can isolate these processes and mechanisms, irrespective of claims to truth. At the same time, propagandists cannot be assumed to play fair, so that it is necessary to draw on a complementary form of analysis concerned with 'truth', established from outside the texts at issue, though not outside all textual processes.

To illustrate one approach to the study of language and the media we will take the following list of vocabulary used in British media, taken from a fuller list published by the *Guardian* newspaper.

Mad dogs and Englishmen

We have	**They have**
Army, Navy and Air Force	A war machine
Reporting guidelines	Censorship
Press briefings	Propaganda
We	**They**
Take out	Destroy
Suppress	Destroy
Neutralise or decapitate	Kill
Decapitate	Kill
Our boys are ...	**Theirs are ...**
Professional	Brainwashed
Lion-hearts	Paper Tigers
Cautious	Cowardly
Confident	Desperate
Heroes	Cornered
Dare-devils	Cannon-fodder
Young knights of the skies	Bastards of Baghdad
Loyal	Blindly obedient
Desert rats	Mad dogs
Resolute	Ruthless
Brave	Fanatical
Our missiles cause ...	**Their missiles cause ...**
Collateral damage	Civilian casualties
George Bush is ...	**Saddam Hussein is ...**
At peace with himself	Demented
Resolute	Defiant
Statesmanlike	An evil tyrant
Assured	A crackpot monster

All the expressions above have been used by the British press in covering the war so far.

This was presented as a vocabulary list, and as such it builds up a convincing impression of crude bias. Even if it did no more it would have been useful. It could have been no surprise that the media coverage in Britain was biassed, but this text establishes that bias in a public form as itself a text. A content analysis carried out by an academic researcher might have drawn on a more carefully demarcated corpus, but the outcome would have been similar.

Truth as such does not seem to be an issue in this list. Many of the matching terms are virtual synonyms, and the difference between our 'press briefings' and their 'propaganda' would be difficult to demonstrate by mere appeal to 'the facts'. It would be easy to suppose that the difference is created by use of 'emotive words', positively and negatively charged items of vocabulary, but on closer inspection this does not seem adequate to all the instances here. For instance, 'kill' and 'destroy' are not necessarily negative in their connotations (and in fact the word 'kill' was used freely with allied soldiers as the agent, as in phrases like 'We've killed x number of tanks, artillery etc.'). What the list allows us to do is to recreate syntactic patterns, and it is these patterns rather than just the individual words that do the ideological work.

There are two main syntactic patterns that we can observe. One is the set of relational syntagms, 'our boys/theirs are' 'George Bush is/ Saddam Hussein is'. These syntagms contain the most overtly biassed descriptions, and seem to be the most obvious site where bias can be located and demonstrated. There is a smaller set of actionals: 'we take out / they destroy', etc. In the full list there were 23 relationals and 7 actionals. The actionals mostly function in a quite different way, contrasting euphemisms (about 'us') with direct statements (about 'them'). The recurring feature of the relationals is the sharp contrast that they make between 'us' and 'them'. This is the typical form of a P-ideology, emphasising difference and relations of superiority –inferiority. But in each column there are a number of contradictions. For instance, our boys are both 'cautious' and 'dare-devils', 'professional' and 'desert rats', while 'they' are 'cowardly' and yet 'ruthless' and 'fanatical'. Of course, these differences may have come from different stories in different newspapers, but in any case the contradictions do not strike a discordant note. The ideological complex can easily absorb them.

The actionals, as we have seen, are mainly euphemisms in the 'we' column, and direct statements in the 'they' column. The members of these pairs are not syntactic transformations. Rather, they are alternative choices from a number of paradigmatic sets, for instance 'we take out' – 'they destroy'; 'we neutralize' – 'they kill'. Here choice has similar effects to a syntactic transformation. With these actionals, the term under the 'they' column is the unmarked choice, a translation of the euphemisms that are used about 'us' into language that 'we' can understand. That is, what 'they' are doing reveals the truth of what 'we' too are doing, but the fact that 'we' are doing it is displaced from the text, understood but not to be said.

The effect of the euphemisms is to conceal both what we are doing, and the fact that it is a destructive act against other people. Blurring the nature of the act also blurs the crucial categories of ally and enemy, us and them. The effect of the euphemisms is the typical effect of an S-ideology, representing the enemy as not really the enemy, and war as not quite war, so that 'we' can appear as almost benign. This image is, of course, the opposite of the image of overt hostility constructed through the P-ideology forms in the relationals, more contradictory than the contradictions that we noted within the set of relationals. But this is how ideological complexes function. In this case, the contradiction is resolved because it also exists within each type. The euphemisms of the S-form are understood to encode a P-form underlying meaning ('we' know what 'take out' really means, and it isn't the garbage) while amongst the predominantly P-form relationals there is an S-form potential for compassion (e.g. 'desperate', 'cornered', 'cannon fodder').

The two basic models also represent two different kinds of discursive trace. Relationals represent acts of classification and judgment, whereas actionals represent events. For this reason, the actionals have a role to play in constructing a version of reality that is out of proportion to the number of times they occur in the text. The large number of relationals signals an intense activity of reclassifying an under-developed, problematic but largely uncontested model of reality, recuperating it for ideological purposes. But the strategy that is implied by this list is an over-stated hostility towards the enemy, and an under-statement about the amount of destruction that is being done to them.

This activity of classification, we have seen, constructs a world divided sharply into 'us' and 'them', but this serves to reinforce the bonds within the group that 'we' form, for those who accept and endorse these classifications of the other. However, the P-form representation of a world divided starkly into us and them tends to polarize readers/receivers into a similarly divided community, since those who can't quite endorse the full set of classifications are left outside the solidary community which does. If Hussein, for instance, is seen as more complex than a demented, defiant, evil tyrant and crackpot monster, then there is no clear place for the person making this judgment in the highly cohesive, all-or-nothing community of the P-form. The *Guardian* writer and readers are presumably outside this community, and in fact the effect of the P-form on such readers is to increase their sense of exclusion. This supposition takes us outside the text, since it is a hypothesis about how readers might respond to the structure that we have analysed, not a fact that is inscribed in the text itself. However, the hypothesis takes the form that it does because the forms contained in the text do appear to be traces of specific ideological and discursive processes in the community itself.

The text that we have been analysing is an article in the *Guardian*, not the full set of texts of the British press over the period. That full set, or a suitably designed sample, would be one appropriate place to test the hypotheses that we have suggested. But that does not mean that the *Guardian* text is only worth looking at if it is a faithful record of the full set of texts. Whatever its editors may think of the company they have to keep, this paper is part of the 'British press', and it would be interesting to know if any of the examples that they give came from the *Guardian*. The complete article consists almost entirely of fragments from other sources. In this way it is typical of newspaper articles, whose form is normally a pastiche of quotations from many sources, more or less worked over, retaining more or less reliable traces from their earlier contexts. The processes of 'quotation' in practice consist of a range of transformational procedures, which have a variety of effects.

For instance, in a straightforward content analysis of the chosen phrases taken without reference to their context, the *Guardian* examples would simply add to the list, yet it is clear that their appearance in this form is intended to be critical of that bias. So it is clear that it is neither the content of the phrases nor their quantity alone that constructs the ideological effect. We presume that the way this process works is through a combination of repetition and unobtrusiveness, and that this mode of working is crucial to the ideological effects that occur through language and through analogous means. In language a small number of elements are endlessly repeated, both grammatical items such as 'the', 'a', '-ing', and patterns such as transactives, relationals, intonation patterns, genres. These occur so commonly in texts that they play a substantial role in giving them their distinctive quality, yet they are also unobtrusive on each occasion that they are used, so that they come to be taken for granted as the precondition for language and thought.

The phenomenon has been described in various ways by a number of theorists. Halliday (1985), for instance, makes the distinction between 'Given' and 'New' as the crucial way that information is organized in speech. In the unmarked form, the first part of an utterance is assumed to be 'Given', the taken-for-granted shared assumptions that link speaker and hearer, and the second part gives the 'New', the information which is foregrounded as the part of the utterance that has value for the hearer or is open to most doubt. However it is that a component of communication successfully achieves the label 'Given', what is included in this category is ideologically the most potent part of the communication, since it has the status of not-in-dispute knowledge which unites participants in the communication act.

To show the complex and not-fully-understood ways in which this works in practice, we need only consider the effects that it is reasonable to attribute to the items listed by the *Guardian* in their original sources. A reader would accumulate items listed there somewhat randomly over a period of time, developing and reinforcing a rule that is never, however, stated to exist as such (e.g. 'Hussein is . . . X' where X represents a distinct paradigm containing negative terms). For this reason, a phrase like 'Hussein is a demented tyrant' would have a more potent ideological effect if it is almost totally ignored as predictable, rather than being treated as 'new information'. As predictable and nearly empty statement, its meaning becomes the rule itself, whose content is in some way the matching of a binary political universe to a particular instance.

The *Guardian* list no doubt has fewer items repeated than occurred in the original sources, but by listing them in this fashion it foregrounds the rule-system itself. There is no need for the rules to be spelled out. Such rules are known in advance, or the point of the article will not be clear. For these readers the nearly explicit statement is sufficient to imply a critique, even though the critique only takes the form of restatement under different conditions. The same principle applies to the kind of transformational analysis we do elsewhere, where the reconstruction and restatement of what is taken for granted by readers/ hearers is presumed to have a different, more critical effect precisely by being foregrounded. For this reason it is important to recognize the effects of new information technologies on the ideological effects of language. These technologies do more than recycle a content so that it reaches more people. They also continually alter the form of the texts that they transmit, and the ways in which they impinge on receivers.

It is necessary to summarize tendencies of kinds of text as the *Guardian* article attempted, but as we have seen it is also necessary to analyse whole texts that are the context for particular features at issue, since it is texts and clusters of texts that contain and condition the ideological meanings that are consumed in discursive practice. So we will look now at a typical enough text that came at the end of the war, headlined 'The fleeing army that died of shame'. It appeared in the *Sydney Morning Herald* of 4 March 1991.

We have chosen to analyse a text because a text seems so convenient a unit for purposes of analysis, but it is important to recognize how arbitrary that unit is. The decision to declare something a text depends

166

to a greater or lesser degree on particular motives of the reader or analyst. In this case we chose as our text initially a unit consisting of a photograph (the famous 'Road from Kuwait' photo, showing the scattered and burned out shells of cars, trucks, and other vehicles) plus the accompanying story headed 'The army that died of shame'. The picture plus the story can be taken as a unit, but the picture is itself a separate text, produced independently of the story. The headline/caption is another element, probably not authored by Robert Fisk under whose byline the story appeared; and the story itself straggles on from the front page to page 24 where it is completed. So the 'complete text' does not have a single author, and it is not certain that it has or is expected to have a single reader, who would begin at the beginning and continue diligently to the end.

In some respects the dominant component of the 'complete text' is the picture, in terms of size and position (above the printed text, the most striking element). Its dominance raises the issue of the relation between visual and verbal codes in the representation of war and the reproduction of ideology. Many commentators have remarked on the role of television in general and the CNN network in particular in establishing a dominant version of the 'reality' of the war. This dominance as an accepted background assumption (irrespective of its truth) becomes part of the way the present text is read. The picture, if read first, occupies the position of 'given', taken-for-granted reality, *not* 'new' or news. It works intertextually, referring to the bank of images already presented on TV in order to validate the story that follows, which does not illustrate the picture but draws on the modality value that it creates.

In this structure, a key role is therefore played by the phrase 'The fleeing army that died of shame', which is both caption to the picture and headline to the story. Formally speaking it is repeated once, on page 24, but it has already been repeated by virtue of its double position, read as both caption and headline, and as it unrolls like a scroll above each of the five columns on page 1 it is arguable that it is repeated on each of those five occasions, big enough to fill the reader's peripheral vision, assuming in relation to the story itself the status of 'given', taken-for-granted background. The transition of this piece of text from 'new(s)' to background assumption is part of the ideological work of the text.

This headline sounds 'poetic', an impression that would be reinforced for those who remember the title of a well-known novel, 'The ship that died of shame'. But the low modality that is associated with 'poetic' discourse is counteracted by the high modality that comes from its status and syntax as caption: '(This is) the fleeing army. . .' Here the high modality s-present has an even higher modality because it is not stated, and this high modality value affects the rest of the sentence. The overall modality value, then, is contradictory, a high value coming from its status as caption, and a lower value coming from its 'poetic' quality.

The 'poetic' quality comes from the relationship to the dominant classification scheme which distinguishes between animate and inanimate as agents of a verb like 'die'. In these terms an army cannot die: only persons can die. The picture shows not an army but a large number of abandoned vehicles, which can be said to have 'died' by a common figure of speech which is like a well-grooved metaphor. The effect of this, in the present context, is interesting. By using this form about the taboo category of death, the key elements are reclassified, so that death is not really death as we understand it, and the idea that life is something pertaining to humans and not to trucks or organizations becomes less clear cut.

The phrase contains the elements of flight, death, and shame attached to the head noun 'army', but the syntactic organization of the phrase both orientates the reader and is itself a form of meaning. The main clause is a non-transactive, 'died', which has the usual effect of constructing the action as self-caused, as opposed to '(was killed)'. In this case it allows the two possible agents to be proposed, in alternative readings of the text: the Iraqis died because they felt so ashamed, the Iraqis died because American pilots bombed them. As the subsequent text makes clear, the second is what 'really' happened. But the syntactic form invites the first reading at the same time it labels it in advance as not to be believed. It is a complex S-form, since it leaves the Iraqis seeming responsible for their own death and destruction, possible objects of both sympathy (because they have died) and righteous vindication (they were ashamed, and so they ought to have been). The contradictory modality that we have noted is functional, allowing complex and contradictory meanings to coexist in a part of the text that is prominent though not closely scrutinized.

Just as it is appropriate to separate out the headline/caption from the rest of the text when we count up the various syntactic forms, so also we need to distinguish different parts and aspects of the main text before we trust too much to counting. In the text (as *we* have analysed it, for *our* purposes) as a whole there are 104 clauses (in 39 sentences in 29 paragraphs); of these 31 are transactives (tr), 49 are non-transactives (ntr), and 24 are relationals (r). This gives an impression of an emphasis on the representation of action rather than classification. This impression is correct as far as it goes, though in this form the description is not ideologically illuminating, because these forms do not have a fixed, precise social meaning, distinct from the social meanings of the people, objects and events that they are attached to. What matters is how these forms become a part of the meaning of elements of the represented world, more ideologically potent for being part of the taken-for-granted background of the description. We therefore need a more specific analysis.

But before we provide that, we need to say a word about our analysis: it is a very 'light' analysis, relatively at the syntactic surface. For instance we have counted as clauses only those constructions where the verb is relatively free – for instance relative clauses 9, 10 for example, or embedded non-finite clauses 15, 55, 56, but not the pre-nominal adjectivalized verb derived from passives such as 51 'two carbonized soldiers', for instance. Or to take another syntactic feature, passives: we have counted relatively clear passives, but not instances such as 9. The 'lightness' or 'heaviness' of the analysis has to be derived from the purposes of the person performing the analysis: ours, here, is mainly illustrative, to get a sense of the deployment of certain syntactic features for particular political ends, but not to establish finely nuanced variations over the text, for instance.

However, even our light analysis reveals interesting patterns: only 31 out of 104 clauses in a text about extremely violent actions performed by one group of people against another, actually represent actions as involving 'doers' and 'done to', agency directed towards specific goals. Of the 31 transactive clauses only 5 do not involve mention of the Iraqis in some form or other, either as subject agents of the clause (s/i) or as direct objects of the action of the processes (o/i), or in passives (p), either as subjects or objects (p;s/i, and p;o/i). Here is the text, showing our clauses-analysis:

> The fleeing army that died of shame

1 tr;a	Although the sweet scent of women's perfume fills the air over the highway here,
2 tr;a;o/i	it cannot mask the overwhelming stench of death.
3 tr;a;s/i	The carcasses of more than 1000 vehicles
4 tr;p;s/i	which had been headed west toward Baghdad jam all six west-bound and east-bound lanes
5 ntr;s/i	and spill several hundred metres off the shoulders

6	ntr;s/i	stuck helplessly in the desert sand.
7	r	There were tanks and stolen police cars, artillery and fire engines and looted limousines, amphibious vehicles, bulldozers and trucks.
8	ntr	I lost count of the Iraqi corpses
9	r	crammed into the smouldering wreckage
10	ntr	or slumped face down in the sand.
11	r	In scale and humiliation it was
12	ntr	I suppose a little like Napoleon's retreat from Moscow.
13	tr;a;s/i	Napoleon's army burnt Moscow
14	ntr;s/i	and the Iraqis tried
15	tr;a;s/i	to burn Kuwait
16	tr;a;s/i	but the French did not carry back this much loot.
17	ntr	Amid the guns and armour I found heaps of embroidered carpets, strings of beads, pearl necklaces, a truck-load of air conditioners, men's shirts, women's shoes, cushions, children's games and casette tapes of Arab singers and such American performers as Lionel Ritchie and Funkadelic.
18	ntr	I found one truck
19	trp;s/i	that had been loaded with suitcases of matches, rugs, foodmixers, lipstick and the broken bottles of perfume
20	tr;a	that added to the area a pungent odour.
21	ntr	A child's music box lay in the sand
22	ntr	still playing 'and a happy new year'.
23	ntr;s/i	Saddam Hussein's road to ruin stretches for 160 kilometres up the highway from Kuwait City to the Iraqi border at Safwan.
24	r	It is a road of horror, destruction and shame.
25	r	Horror because of the hundreds of mutilated bodies
26	tr;a;s/i	lining its route
27	r	destruction because of the thousands of Iraqi tanks and armoured vehicles
28	ntr;s/i	that lie charred
29	ntr;s/i	or abandoned;
30	r	shame because in retreat Saddam's soldiery
31	tr;a;s/i	piled their armour with plunder.
32	r	The dead are strewn across the road only 13 kilometres out of Kuwait City

33	tr;a;o/i	and you see them still
34	ntr	as you approach the Iraqi frontier
35	ntr	where 52 of the Rumeilah oilfield wells are squirting fire into the sky.
36	ntr	At one point on the highway yesterday, I saw wild dogs
37	tr;a;o/i	tearing to pieces the remains of Iraqi soldiers.
38	r	It is, of course, the horror
39	tr;a	that strikes you first.
40	ntr;s/i	Scarcely 40 kilometres north of Kuwait City, the body of an Iraqi general lies half out of his stolen limousine,
41	r	his lips apart
42	tr;p;o/i	his hands suspended above the roadway.
43	ntr;s/i	He had driven into the back of an armoured vehicle in the great rout on Monday night.
44	ntr;s/i	Further on, corpses lay across the highway beside tanks and army trucks.
45	ntr;s/i	One Iraqi had collapsed over the carriageway
46	r	curled up like a foetus,
47	r	his arm beside his face,
48	r	a neat moustache beside a heavy head
49	tr;p;o/i	the back of which had been blown away.
50	ntr;s/i	In a lorry
51	tr;p;o/i	which had received a heavy hit from the air two carbonised soldiers still sat in the cab
52	ntr;s/i	their skulls staring up the road towards the country
53	ntr;s/i	they never reached
54	ntr	Kuwaiti civilians stood over the bodies
55	ntr	laughing and
56	ntr	taking pictures.
57	r	The wholesale destruction begins 40 kilometres further on beneath a freeway bridge
58	r	which stands at the bottom of a low hill
59	ntr	called Mutla
60	r	It was here
61	tr;p;o/i	trapped by allied bombing of the road at the top of the hill
62	ntr;s/i	that the Iraqis perished in their hundreds, probably in their thousands.

63	r	Panic-stricken
64	tr;a;s/i	they had jammed themselves in their six kilometre convoy, 20 vehicles abreast,
65	tr;p;o/i	and had been picked off by the US and British bombers.
66	r	'This is probably the worst carnage
67	ntr	you'll find in the Kuwaiti theatre of operations'
68	ntr	said Captain Drew O'Donnell of the US Army.
69	r	It was the result of a devastating combination of US aerial bombardment and artillery and tank fire.
70	r	The destruction began Monday night
71	tr;a;o/i	when A-10 close air support warplanes attacked the head and the tail of the column
72	ntr;s/i	as it moved slowly north.
73	tr;p	On Tuesday, while the convoy was paralysed
74	ntr;s/i	and unable to move in either direction
75	tr;a;o/i	aircraft
76	tr;p	launched from the carrier USS *Ranger* attacked again.
77	tr;a;o/i	Later on Tuesday, the Tiger brigade of the 2nd Armoured Division,
78	ntr	which had moved up through Kuwait with the 2nd Marines, attacked with 45 M1-A1 tanks and supporting infantry.
79	ntr	From the track marks and the position of the wrecks, it appeared
80	ntr	that when F16 fighter-bombers came in
81	tr;a;o/i	to strafe the column
82	ntr;s/i	some of the drivers of the 1500 vehicles tried
83	ntr;s/i	to turn around
84	ntr;s/i	and push back to Kuwait against the oncoming traffic.
85	r	Others
86	tr;p;o/i	forced off the road onto the desert sand became sitting ducks.
87	ntr	Our car bumped over the barrels of rifles and live grenades.
88	ntr	On top of one armoured vehicle
89	ntr	its engine idling

		I found the helmets of Lieutenant Rabah Homeida and Private Jannal Abdululah.
90	r	They had stood no chance
91	ntr	because in front of their vehicle lay another three kilometres of clogged Iraqi military traffic
92	ntr	at the end of which stood a squad of US soldiers from the 2nd Armoured Division
93	ntr	whose motto, Hell on Wheels, summed up the fate of the thousands in the ghoulish traffic jam below them.
94	r	Lieutenant Andrew Nye and Lieutenant Ray Monk of C Company, 1st Battalion, Staffordshire regiment, had spent part of the morning
95	tr;a;o/i	burying the dead.
96	ntr	Lieutenant Nye lost one of his own men in the fighting.
97	tr;p	'He was hit in the chest by a rocket-propelled grenade
98	tr;a;s/i	after some Iraqis had raised the white flag'
99	ntr	he said.
100	tr;a;s/i	'The Iraqis
101	ntr;s/i	who died on this road were stripping Kuwait City.
102	ntr	But I shudder
103	ntr	to think
104	r	what it would have been like in their position.'

The Iraqis are the subject/agents of 11 transactive clauses, either active (a) or passive (p), and of 19 non-transactive clauses. The non-transactives carry the same ideological meaning as the headline: these troops die and suffer of their own volition, without need for American military intervention. Of the 11 transactives with Iraqis as agents, 7 concern acts of treachery, robbery or pillage (13, 15, 16, 19, 31, 98, 100). That is, about three quarters of the time when they are constructed as acting on the world it is as robbers and looters, not as soldiers: active only, it is implied, as criminals not as an army. The category oppositions between peace and war, military and civilian are both mobilized and transgressed.

The Iraqis are constructed as objects in transactives, always with the American military as agents, in 15 clauses. There is one particularly significant pattern to note in the distribution of these forms in the text.

Six of the fourteen transactives with Iraqis as objects occur in the back page part of the story, from clause 68 on, on page 24, five of them in the active form (71, 75, 77, 81, 95), although this last section is only 22% of the whole text in column inches. Of the eight transactive clauses with Iraqis as objects in the first section (2, 33, 37, 42, 49, 51, 61, 65) five are passive (42, 49, 51, 61, 65) and three (2, 33, 37) are active. The active clauses do not have 'Americans' as agents but *women's perfume* in 2, *you* in 33, and *wild dogs* in 37. This indicates the importance of the position within the text as a whole, for these purposes. The last section, roughly a quarter of the text, contains the most direct representation of the events that the article gives. This is the P-form at last, representing the Americans as aggressors against the now-defenceless Iraqis, where the previous text intermingled P-forms (Iraqis as common criminals) and S-forms (Iraqis as casualties of uncaused or self-caused violence). We do not wish to over-emphasize the distinction, because there are still S-forms in the final section, and the earlier section contains both forms too, but there is a recognizable shift in the strategy of the article, which means that it contains one kind of contradiction for those who read the whole thing, and another for those who stop reading after the headline, or after the front page. This is not simply a difference in the ideological content of the same text, for different readers or different ways of reading. It will also contribute to a different ideological effect overall, since different components will be encoded as taken-for-granted under the different readings.

In the examples that we have looked at, the media did not seriously misrepresent 'what really happened', because this was not problematic on this occasion (in a war that was being won as convincingly as was being claimed). What the language does is to position readers in relation to this information. Readers are not only informed (to some degree) about what is happening now, they are reminded of what they must have thought before they began to read. Where one article alone may be seen as propaganda, our analysis has been concerned with this process of reconstruction as an instance of ideology in action, laying down traces of a prosthetic memory that is better, stronger and much more useful than the real thing.

READING READINGS

Meaning does not exist unless there are people who make it happen, in a process where those who receive texts (readers, listeners, viewers) engage in an activity which produces its own distinctive kinds of meaning, without which no text would have any social effect. This elementary proposition about social meaning and language in process has important consequences for hermeneutic strategies, including our own. Whose meanings do we suppose that we are explicating, and how do we claim to know? Kay Richardson (1987) has proposed that critical linguistics should or does assume a 'lay reader' whose strategies and meanings are what is recovered by this method of analysis. This is an interesting and powerful suggestion. It would serve to link this tradition of analysis with ethnomethodology and its concerns with the knowledges and routines by which sense is made by members of a community. It exists as one possible and important use or point of reference for a critical linguistic analysis. However, there are other uses or points of reference which are equally valid, in terms of a model of the social process that constitutes the minimal discursive act, as this is inscribed and preserved in material texts.

Most models of the communication process have privileged the source of messages, whether this is the sender in the sender–receiver model of communications theory, the author in literary criticism, the patient in psychoanalysis, or God in biblical hermeneutics. Over the past few decades many approaches have turned their attention towards the meanings constructed by the reader, and we see this move as indispensable to any adequate social hermeneutics. But it remains just as important not to forget about senders of messages as it is not to ignore the receivers. At every level, every element in the communication process has a double orientation towards production and reception, in a social production of meaning that is always co-authored by many participants, and is 'read' (monitored, inflected towards actual and imagined readers) by many more.

At the moment of uttering a piece of text, the utterer is also a reader of various components of a prior intertextual complex, while projecting and pre-empting the ways in which this new text will itself be read by its proposed readers. But those who read it may or may not be the same as those who were invented by the original act of discourse, and they may be more or less obedient. The meanings that they construct are therefore not precisely 'in' the text. But nor are they precisely 'out' of the text, or 'in' any other text. These meanings are realized in other texts which readers produce, which may or may not emerge in speech or in writing, and which are never transparent, never produced in social isolation. For this reason the apparent opposition between readers and writers disappears. The meanings of readers are only known through the texts that they construct, in specific conditions and contexts, in response to a designated text (among others). The meanings of writers are the traces and effects of innumerable prior acts of reading, realized only through text, again produced in specific contexts and conditions. Readers and writers are antagonistic and interdependent to different degrees, and no analysis can afford to forget either dimension. However, it is also proper for analysts to have strategic reasons for being more interested in one direction rather than another, tracking backwards down the chain of intertextual connections or forwards along the series of textual effects that flow from a chosen text or discursive moment.

In this section we will look at some of the different strategies that are useful in reading reception-texts, in recovering some of the meanings that come into play as texts circulate in various social arenas, in writing readings. As focus for the discussion we will use a set of 27 texts which were 'readings' of the 'army that died of shame' article. In the course of the discussion we aim to show the double face of the kinds of meaning that our original analysis brought out, and the need at every point in such an analysis to be aware of the kind of instability and indeterminacy that characterizes language in social use, and the continuities and regularities that nonetheless make it possible to generalize about and predict ideological effects.

The 27 texts were produced in an MA class in TESOL (Teaching English as a Second or Other Language), in a class exercise in which students, who were informed about the purposes of this exercise, were asked to summarize the article in no more than 80 words. These texts were constrained by various generic and discursive conventions: they are not unmediated readings. But in this respect they are like all readings, and like all readings they themselves can be read, in different ways.

One way of reading them is to transform them into the results of a poll, of the kind that was common throughout the war to gauge public opinion on the war. From this point of view, the texts could be assigned with remarkable ease and symmetry to one of three categories: pro-war (marked by repetition and/or elaboration of pro-war themes with none of the opposite); anti-war (marked by explicit critique of the pro-war stance of the article); and neutral (summary not marked by intrusions of explicit judgment for or against the war). The numbers in each category were exactly a third. In our case, this pseudo-poll (with an unrespectable size of sample) is a transformation of our texts into the forms of another genre. The official polls, however, were themselves transformations of fuller texts, in a number of genres, into the poll genre. Neither is more 'objective' than the other.

This first reading of our set of texts is, however, commensurable with the results of polls taken during this period. The pro-war vote during most of the war varied between just under 50% and about 70%. If our 'neutral' group divided evenly in a poll, the group as a whole would produce the balanced result. If the neutrals all went with the pro-war argument, then the pro-war group would aggregate to 70%. Our point here is not to claim that our sample perfectly represented the divisions of opinion in the Australian populace, that they are an average sample, but rather to anchor our linguistic analysis in terms of these broad categories of response. We will try to show the linguistic markers of each kind of position as a reasonably regular way of appropriating meanings from the original text, with characteristic modes of processing that predispose towards specific readings and uses of the common text. This kind of analysis, then, does not aim to repeat the findings of a poll: rather, it establishes an explanatory context for interpreting wide variations that may be found by different polls at different times.

The readings in the 'critical' category had a number of characteristics in common. In all of them, there were elaborate relationals, giving the judgments (on the war, on the article) that made the point of view of the writer unmistakable. But even more distinctive a characteristic of this position was an elaboration of the modality component, realized in the summary by use of words like 'seems', 'implies', and quotation marks (with discussion of the doubtful status of what was quoted). In many cases this was supplemented by a critical account of the media processes behind the construction of the war.

In these critical texts, there were very few instances of an appeal to another source as the 'truth' of what really happened. This strategy mainly relied on an access to a model of media processes, which was expanded and described in their texts, complete with various agents and actions ('the reporter links petty robbery with violent death', 'What's it about? It's about lurid copy in the final days of conflict'). In this case, contests over modality, in the broadest sense, were the most decisive site for resistant readings.

The pro-war texts had the opposite characteristics. Although they used relationals to contain their negative judgments, the use of relationals in these texts was not as elaborated as in the critical texts. But their judgments were more usually conveyed through adjectives attached to nouns, so that the fact of a judgment having been made was not displayed so directly in the text. These texts mostly employed a minimal form of modality, using the past tense to repeat the basic narrative in an unproblematic form. A typical instance is the following:

> Hundreds of Iraquis perished as they were trapped by the allied bombing of the road that stretched from Kuwait City to Safwan. The scene was one of horror, destruction and shame. Horror because of the hundreds of mutilated bodies on the road; destruction because of the thousands of Iraqui tanks and vehicles that lie charred or abandoned; shame because Saddam's soldiers had plundered.

This text reveals another property shown by many others in our corpus: the extent to which a text-within-the-text from the article was strongly represented in the corpus, linked around some key words: 'horror', 'destruction' and especially 'shame'. This part of the response text incorporated the part of the article that was most closely linked to the headline, and the headline, in this and other transformational variations, was present in almost every response. Most of the responses began by repeating this headline as the heading of the response itself. Those that didn't, still used the key word 'shame'. This shows that the article was read by most readers as though it was, for good or ill, in effect just an expansion of the headline, from which the whole article could be derived in some regular, rule-governed way. The processes linking headline to main text are not systematic or regular, not part of any recognized grammar of English, yet this is an important and common phenomenon, which we can formally describe as follows: article $\Rightarrow$ headline $\Rightarrow$ key word ('shame'). It operates in a powerful way like a parody of a correct transformation, deleting large chunks of discourse, leaving a final form which is then understood as implying the full content of the article as a whole.

There is another pattern in the responses which we could describe either quantitatively or as a kind of transformation. Of the 27 responses, only 5 referred in any way to the content of the final section, which represented the one-sided American assault and used more transactives in the active voice. If we describe the structure of the text as Headline + Shame text + Destruction text, then the dominant transformation was H + Sh + D $\Rightarrow$ H + Sh. Those who departed from this pattern were evenly divided between pro-war and anti-war responses. The numbers here are too small to base a generalization on, but this pattern makes sense, since the P-form of itself is not specifically pro-war or anti-war, and those who are committed, on one side or the other, will find it easy to use the demystifying P-forms rather than the S-forms. In this case, however, there was one difference between the pro-war and anti-war groups in their predominant syntactic patternings. The anti-war group consistently used more transactives in their summaries of the shame-text, bringing out the agency structures even though they did not refer much to the content of the final section. That is, they resituated its S-ideology in a P-ideology framework. We can summarize this activity in formal terms as: $H (S) + Sh (S) + D (P) \Rightarrow H (S) + S (S \Rightarrow P)$.

Readers and writers are constituted as gendered subjects, and the theme of war is itself marked for gender, a masculine domain which plays a central role in ideologies of masculinity. So it is important to investigate how gender plays a role in different refractions of this common text, written as it is by a man (Robert Fisk) about men doing things (in the main) to men. In our small sample, there was not a clear difference between women and men in terms of the three basic categories, pro-, anti- and neutral. However, there was one pattern of differences that recurred often enough to seem significant. On the one hand, the women's responses were more 'emotional', using more affective syntagms (relationals with emotive adjectives or nouns like 'carnage', 'horror' etc.). This seems to confirm the gender stereotype of women as responding 'emotionally', in this case highlighting the suffering of the Iraqis. Against this, there was a significant difference in the use of the first person pronoun, 'I'. Twenty per cent of the men used this form, confidently giving their personal judgment. No woman in the sample used this form. That is, the women could be more subjective in one way, inserting their personal feelings more systematically into their text, but they could only do so in a displaced form, effacing the self that was making these judgments.

There was another pattern that carried a similar contradiction. Eighty per cent of the men described the agent of the text as 'the article' ('the article says' etc.), whereas only 40% of the women used this form. Instead, 40% of the women personalized it, attributing it to the individual journalist ('Robert Fisk writes', etc.). Only 20% of the men used this form. That is, the men were more likely to propose the text itself as the abstract author of its own meanings, whereas the women were more likely to propose a specific human agent. But 20% of the women referred to no agent of the writing process, giving a summary of its content without reference to its generic status or supposed authorship. None of the men did this. In this small sample, then, the women tended either to emphasize or eliminate the specific author, whereas the men tended to mention authorship in an abstract form.

We can see from this how there can be gendered readings which turn out to be self-cancelling from other points of view, leading on this occasion to a set of overall judgments where women were not markedly different from men. However, although gender cannot be predictably tied to a pro-war or anti-war stance with this group, on this occasion, the differences are sufficiently marked to show why gender differences should always be taken into account.

This brief reading of the readings of the original text shows a number of important points about the strategies of a critical linguistic analysis. Our initial reading was not intended as an ideal reading, fully comprehensive and exemplary. Nor was it *the* lay reading, since there is not a singular reading that analysis must discover and formalize. On the contrary, our analysis laid down a number of tracks along which different 'lay' readings might run, tracks which constrain but do not determine readings. These form a repertoire which is not a convergent set (so that most readings can be expected to cluster around a common core, the 'basic interpretation', with a penumbra of subjective differences) but rather a set which has its own structural principles, corresponding to the basic positions that are available from the struggle itself.

Our analysis does not produce the same reading as the 'critical' stance, although it has some things in common with that stance, and a critical linguistic analysis can be expected to provide (among other things) a powerful support to the critical stance. We aim to produce an account of how different meanings can be distributed amongst different reading positions, in an account of textuality that insists on systematic (but not unlimited) multiplicity of readings and reading positions. But we do not propose just a form of pluralism. Our analysis not only shows the different readings that are possible, it also shows the routes that link them. Texts about the war were refracted by different structures of reception. The triumph of the war rhetoric wasn't and isn't inevitable, but resistance will only take place along the lines of cleavage of the structures of reception.

With this in mind, we could hope to indicate the kinds of intervention that would impinge most directly on the discursive structures of the 'neutrals', that might swing them over to the anti-war position. Or we could point out the gap in the anti-war position: that there was no alternative text about the war that these readers had which they could draw on to override the text that they had in front of them. An attack on the modality structures of the article was effective, as far as it went, but it might not be enough. Or we could point to the taken-for-grantedness of the basic narrative in the pro-war group, as an ideological structure that would not be easy to counter.

All these options are choices that could be taken by those who wish to make use of a critical linguistic form of analysis, but these options come from prior positions in a struggle, not from anything inherent in the nature of critical linguistics, or in the nature of language itself. And clearly, texts of this kind would not be a sufficient basis for tracking the range of discursive situations in which the meanings of the original article circulate, along with other texts in other media. A critical linguistic approach would have to be applied to all these classes of text, to be sure of what ideological themes survived in which contexts. Such a series of analyses might force us to revise what we had supposed was the most potent ideological effect of a given text or a given strategy. This fact is important to stress, in order to avoid giving the impression that a critical linguistic analysis can or should aim to give *the* meaning of a text or a form, in a comprehensive and exhaustive form. From this fact there follows not an anarchic proliferation of interpretations but a principle of analysis. The basic object in the analysis of social meaning is a *process* not a *product*. So the minimal unit for analysis is not a single form or text in isolation, but a reading of a sequence in context, containing prior or later forms or texts. A single instance on its own is not enough.

FISSURED TEXTS

Texts are constantly recycled, appearing in an endless succession of texts-about-texts, readings of readings of readings of readings . In order to understand this process we need to be able to see it in reverse, and read texts as writings of writings of writing of writings in a similarly open series of transactions, developing an archaeology of each text that links, however uneasily, with the histories of its future. In reading texts from this diachronic perspective it is no longer possible to sustain two of the most fundamental unities on which most strategies of reading are based. The text (any given text) ceases to be a self-evident unity, but appears as a relatively accidental site that marks where a series of discursive processes have briefly collided. Producers (authors, speakers) likewise lose the semblance of unity, and become channels through which various authors and agencies speak and act: the fissured authors of fissured texts.

It is useful to set the methods of *Language as Ideology* against these notions of text and author, because there is a danger that our methods as applied to polemical texts may seem to imply a more fixed and simplistic model, one in which hidden meanings of a single devious enemy are relentlessly uncovered and exposed. In this section, we wish to demonstrate how these methods are able to show the opposite, tracing the dispersed meanings and multiple sources that construct fissured texts and their fissured authors in a complex stratigraphy. By a seeming paradox, our intense interest in agency (Whose meanings are these? Where do they come from?) leads inevitably to a continual but productive deferral of a simple, final answer to these questions, and a recognition of the complicated networks through which power and discourse typically operate.

In the rest of the section we will look at the two aspects of language in use that are usually the most rewarding for CDA as a diagnostic method: transformations and classifications. With both, we need to stress the difference between the histories that are reconstructed from traces and signs in a text, and those that are reconstructed by other means, from other texts and other sources. Although the material history of the processes at issue is always important, if it can be known, the other histories are themselves social facts that should not be ignored, precisely because they are indeed constructs.

We will begin our discussion by looking at a brief item lasting 38 seconds that was broadcast on Australian national radio on 7 February, 1991:

> *Announcer*: The allied forces say the bombing of Iraq and Kuwait is now in a new phase.
> Initially the emphasis was on specific targets, such as bridges and oil installations.
> Now a US squadron commander has spoken of attacks against what he describes as targets of opportunity, or, as he put it, taking out anything that moves.
> One of the squadron's pilots – Major Thomas Galwraith – describes the change in emphasis.
> *Galwraith*: We pretty much go out there, we work a certain area, ah, at night, and we prosecute any of the targets that we might within that area. We attack the targets we observe on the ground, targets of opportunity, movers.

This item would be regarded as a typical instance of the genre 'radio: (war) bulletin'. Its brevity and its place late in the programme would have been enough to label it as not very important, one way or the other. A listener might find it difficult to classify it as pro-war or anti-war, partly because of the uncertainty about what made it 'news'. Its ostensible point is a 'new phase' of the war, but it seems equally interested in a new way of talking about the war, with Major Thomas Galwraith and his squadron commander setting new standards of circumlocution to describe what they do.

The text as broadcast clearly has two voices, Galwraith's and the announcer's. These are stitched together into an almost seamless text, linked by parallels of meaning. In fact, most of the introduction is a paraphrase of the Galwraith text, a frame or introduction that is also a reading of Galwraith's words, pre-empting the 'authentic' text that is to follow. In our efforts to attribute meanings to sources, we need to recognize at least this double agency in the construction of the text, while always being ready to find that that doubleness itself is further divided.

As an instance of transformational analysis, we will take the word 'movers' used by Galwraith. If this occurred on its own in the original speech, we could treat it as a nominalization that followed the normal pattern for English. We would then reconstitute it hypothetically as either the transactive sequence: (X) moves (Y) $\Rightarrow$ anything that moves something $\Rightarrow$ movers; or the non-transactive sequence: (X) moves $\Rightarrow$ movers. The bare outlines of these sequences are given to us by features of the text plus something that could be called 'knowledge of the language'. In this form it raises typical questions about the unspecified and deleted 'X' and/or 'Y' (Why did Galwraith leave it/them unnamed and outside his discourse?). Galwraith here is using a normal syntactic process to create a new word, and the fact that he has done this is itself significant. Lexicalisations – making a lexical item from a prior clause or a part of a clause – naturalize a transformational sequence. They distract attention from its constructedness and its prior sequences, and make them relatively unconscious. And finally, they indicate that this transformation is accepted by a group, no longer the product of an individual, no longer to be understood solely as Galwraith's meaning.

But we can draw on another part of our 'knowledge of the language' to note that this is a new word as far as most speakers of English are concerned. The novelty in this case is the ambiguity as to whether the 'mover' is the agent or the object of the action. 'Mover' is a regular noun where it refers to the agent (as in 'movers and shakers', a 'mover' on the charts etc.). This word seems to refer to what is moved (trucks etc.) by some human driver, and its oddness comes from its equivocation with the primary category distinctions between agent and object, human and non-human. This novelty is enough to signal the existence of an anti-language, spoken by Galwraith and we presume by others like him.

Usually this is as far as we could get with a transformational analysis of a single text. But on this occasion, it seems that the broadcasters have provided a do-it-yourself kit for all those critical linguists out there in radio-land. 'Anything that moves' is given as the prior text, a non-transactive that confirms one of our hypotheses but not the other. This is an admirably materialist form of critical linguistics, presenting actual prior texts, not projecting hypothetical and hidden 'deep structures'. Even so, two things should be pointed out. The fact that one of the hypothetical structures is attested does not imply that the other isn't: multiple originating structures are the rule, not the exception. Second, the non-transactive in itself does most of the work that could also be done by the two, since this form conflates agent and object, and in so doing equivocates between human and machine, animate and inanimate. The methodological lesson is clear if disconcerting: an initial ambiguity is likely to be systemic, so that more texts are better, but they cannot close off all ambiguity, because there could always be other texts that might support alternative conclusions.

The other aspect of texts that is always diagnostically revealing from a critical linguistic point of view is the trace of classification processes. In this instance, the word 'targets' is the focus of an extensive classification process. The word occurs five times in the short text, and serves to give the text something of its cohesion, since it is used in three different discursive contexts (preamble, indirect quotation, full quotation). It is semantically crucial, since it is the point of entry into language of the main activity of war that is being described. The word illustrates nicely how language operates to manage versions of reality. It is a noun which effortlessly turns hospitals, munitions stores, civilians moving in the open and anything else into the legitimate and desired object of an attack, part of a powerful binary system that divides the world into two classes of object: targets and non-targets. The word in this expanded sense had a wider circulation in the media, including such evocative phrases as 'a target-rich environment'.

But classification processes also operate on 'target' itself. 'Targets' is first classified by 'specific', which implies a minimal binary system with 'unspecific' as its other term. These targets are then glossed in terms that seem to imply another system, such as fixed (versus moving) or material (versus human). There is then the over-arching opposition between 'initially' (the past) and 'now' (the present), with the present being marked by a new classification system.

In fact what we have seems more like two systems. Both the squadron commander and the pilot use two alternative descriptors, 'targets of opportunity' and 'anything that moves/movers'. The first of these is difficult to relate either to a system of classification (its minimal opposite must be something like 'plan', which is not the opposite of 'opportunity') or to a transformational derivation. We might suggest 'a target which you see an opportunity to strike' or 'an opportunity to make X a target' but neither is finally convincing.

The 'movers'-system, as we have seen, can be transformationally derived. It may also be related to the more well-known term 'moving' (versus 'stationary') target. So the 'movers' system, in spite of being a neologism, is open in two respects: it can be related to the object or event that is being described, and it is part of a stable and symmetrical system of classification. 'Target of opportunity', in contrast, is part of an irrational system in two respects: it cannot easily be part of a well-ordered system of classification, and it cannot be derived readily from prior actional forms with a comprehensible reference to reality. It is opaque (an outsider would find it hard to guess what it meant, and what it applied to). Its opacity makes it more euphemistic than 'mover', with an opacity that is likely to apply to normal users of the form as well as to outsiders (though 'movers' is opaque and euphemistic to some degree). It is language devised to make it difficult to think about what is being referred to, or what system of classifications would make sense of it: language used to evade reality and rationality at a single stroke. From a diagnostic point of view all these things hang together, and the sense that they make points to unmanageable contradictions in the experience of the users. The analysis does not say precisely who is having these problems or why, but the problems have left enough traces to point the enquiry in fruitful directions.

In fact Galwraith uses not two but three forms to describe the targets:

1 'the targets we observe on the ground'
2 'targets of opportunity'
3 'movers'.

This gives three classification systems, not two, although the first seems so neutral that it is invisible. Each of these is an equivalent, in a different classification system. The first system can be termed every-day English (though to be precise it may be a military inflection of a variety of everyday language). The second two forms are variants within the same anti-language. But both of them have the same function, compared to the first, as the 'opportunity' system has compared to the 'movers' system. We can represent them diagrammatically as follows:

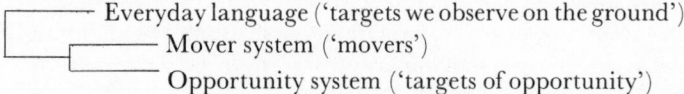

Everyday language ('targets we observe on the ground')
Mover system ('movers')
Opportunity system ('targets of opportunity')

Relatively speaking, the everyday language is more transparent than the anti-language and less oriented to solidarity, just as the mover system is more transparent and less solidary than the opportunity system within the anti-language. But the mover-system achieves its own kind of solidarity by emphasizing the hostile relations between the group and its enemies, whereas the opportunity system blurs this hostility, representing their death as just an 'opportunity' for the group. One is oriented to express power, part of what we have called the P-form, the other maintaining solidarity, part of the S-form.

It is easy to see the need for two such different systems if we consider the discursive constraints on Major Thomas Galwraith and his companions, because they are the same constraints as we saw operating on President Bush. In order to intensify the morale of the group as a killing team the enemy needs to be represented as entirely distinct, contemptible and easy to defeat. In order to represent the group as admirable to others outside it, the naked hostility needs to be blurred and disguised, especially so the more diverse the outside groups are. But in order to function effectively, the group also needs access to a relatively accurate representation of themselves and their enemy. And insofar as the boundaries around a particular occasion of discourse are likely to be leaky, these three functions need to be satisfied nearly simultaneously, though since this is impossible, the synthesis will always be only partial and the joins will always show, to a greater or lesser extent according to the perceived needs of the discursive situation. A private meeting in the squadron mess will have very different constraints from a press conference.

In studying this short text, the Galwraith speech, we have uncovered a series of rudimentary systems of classification, whose consistency with one another remains obscure. It would be possible to propose that the inconsistencies come from the different sources of the various discourses, but this is not a sufficient explanation. For both the squadron commander and the pilot, the greatest contradiction exists between the two anti-language systems that they juxtapose as

almost obligatory collocations. So we cannot say that the contradictions arise from differences between two different discursive
locations of their speakers. On the contrary, the contradictions seem to
be inherent in a single speaking position. Or to put it slightly
differently, each speaking position is discursively constructed as a
fissured entity, one that deploys competing and incompatible schemes
to make sense of the objects of their world. Our earlier discussion of
anti-languages implied that they are logically consistent in their own
terms, but this anti-language is divided within itself, and this is a
systemic and functional contradiction, not an accident or aberration.

If we wanted to examine the anti-language of the US troops we
would need to collect many more examples than this, using an
ethnographic approach to this community. This short speech is just a
fragment, torn out of its context so drastically that the context is hard
to reconstruct (both the interview in which it first occurred, and the
contexts in which that language form developed). Simply inserting it
into the framing media discourse transforms it into something
different, and foregrounds a more critical reading of it – just as the
sample of Vietnam anti-language that we analysed in our earlier
chapter was transformed by Chomsky merely by quoting it in his book.
Recontextualization is a powerful kind of transformation, since it
attacks the discursive framework itself, not just the representational
content.

But the media item itself contains other transformations that are not
foregrounded in the same way. The opening sentence has 'The allied
forces say', using regular processes whereby a single statement is cast in
a form that implies a single utterer or spokesperson, and attributed to
'the allied forces'. This linguistic–ideological move is one of the
foundational acts in the discursive construction of the war. It
establishes the essential unity of the 'allied forces', a unity which is
validated by their ability to produce such seemingly uncontentious
utterances. 'Bombing' is a nominalization which is close to the
underlying transactive that encodes the destructive events of the war.
But in this form, occurring where it does in the sentence and the
text, the transformational work that constitutes it is effectively de-
emphasized. As spoken by the announcer, this sentence would consist
of five information units: // The allied *forces* // say the *bombing* // of *Iraq* //
and *Kuwait* // is now in a new *phase* //. The new information in each unit
is italicized. Of these, none is remarkable. At this stage in the war it was
not news that there were *forces*; that there was *bombing*; that *Iraq* and
Kuwait were being bombed; and that the war was in a *phase*. What is

presented as new is not news; and what is truly new, the *new* phase, is presented as given, established, uncontentious information, slipped in as unremarkable, beyond comment, as what we all know (and accept). The emphasis is on the 'phase'. That is *new*, and 'news'.

The fact that 'bombing' is a nominalization in a relational sentence orients us to classifications and judgments rather than events. This in turn prepares the listener not to notice the slide from the realities of the bombing to strategic innovations (a new kind of target) and thence to new ways of talking about the war. This slide contributes to the ambiguous attitude to war of this item that we noted at the beginning. The item has a critical attitude to language which mystifies the reality of war as spoken by the American Major, but it does not have a similarly critical attitude to the surrounding 'normal' language which overwhelmingly naturalizes the assumptions that legitimate the war. The interest in language could come to overlay an interest in the reality of the war itself. This is in spite of the apparent critical intention of the item, which is part of the trend that we have already noted and celebrated, by which commentators have focussed on the mystifying, sanitizing language used in the reporting of this war. It is paradoxical that a critical intent could be co-opted in this way by features of context to serve some of the purposes of the information-management strategies of the Coalition. The analysis, we see, does not settle the question of whether the programme is pro-war or anti-war, in intention or effect. On the contrary, in this case it complicates it.

The same linguistic feature, in this case nominalization, has different meanings and effects even within the same short text. The differences arise because even within a short piece of text there are traces of other texts and other contexts, so that the text itself is radically heterogeneous, even in its own immediate context. The conventions of the genre carefully construct the appearance of unity, but the radical heterogeneity of discourse breaks open these apparent unities. The broadcaster quotes and requotes, recycling the discourse of others in more or less transformed ways which are more or less authorized by the broadcaster (the presenter, the writer, the ABC (Australian Broadcasting Corporation) as an institution, the American military information, the resources of the Western media) to degrees that are more or less likely or intended to be recognized by listeners. A content analysis adding up the total number of types of nominalizations used in a text or a body of texts or a set of discourses would miss the social meaning of the text or of its discursive form, by attributing regularities of a text or discourse to a presumed unitary 'position' (the ABC, the US military, US pilots, Major Galwraith and his squadron etc.) or unitary type (e.g. discourse of war, media discourse, radio, news etc.). But that is not to say that no generalization is possible. On the contrary, generalization is indispensable as part of the analysis of any individual instance. But what is generalized must be understood as a *structure of contradictions and a system of inflections with multiple points of origin*.

Our analysis thus far has concentrated on this one text, and tried to reconstruct the discursive processes that constituted it by examining traces in the text itself. In order to prevent misunderstanding, we need to stress that such an analysis is inherently incomplete, and needs to be complemented by analyses of other texts that provide evidence about the material processes at issue. The traces within a text are always incomplete, always dubious and open to different interpretations. To illustrate the point we will look at the following text, a fax that was made available to us by an ABC employee who felt that it would be useful material for a radio broadcast, to be given by one of us (GK) on the theme of language and the Iraq war. For this individual, a proto-critical linguistic mole inside the ABC, the item implied a critical view of the forms of language, but we will not analyse her views or judgments. The fax itself is full of features that repay a diagnostic reading of the traces of media processes.

We reproduce the fax to make the point that it is the materiality of text that is its greatest asset from the point of view of analysis. It is that materiality that allows traces of process to be transmitted long after the process is no longer available to be studied. For this reason the kind of linguistic analysis that we do can be likened to archaeology, which scans the material traces of the past where written records are scarce or unreliable. These traces can be lost or preserved in the course of their reproduction, and others can be added from later stages in a palimpsest of traces. For this reason text typically carries contradictory traces from different occasions, an erratic and sometimes unreliable record of its discursive history. The traces inscribed in the words of a text function in exactly the same way, so that it is useful to illustrate the method of reading by looking first at the material text itself, the fax (or the reproduction of the fax in the present book).

First of all there is the form of the fax itself, with its ink smudges and blurred type-face (see Appendix). They appear to be the result of a form of communication which is indifferent to qualities of presentation, concerned only with speed and efficiency in getting a message across, and these markers signify the ephemerality of the message itself. The full text gives the text as broadcast, with difference in type-face and

other signifiers indicating the very different status of the embedded
Galwraith text from the surrounding commentary, capitalized to
indicate its higher status in the economy of the overall text.

SLUG	TALENT	SUBBED	DATE	COPY	CART	TOTAL	CUM
targets opportunity 2	galwrait	howard	Thu Feb 7 07:25	0:23	.15		0:38
Dest: NOSE		NR:	Writer: alward			Lines:23	

History:

EX-RN-SYD
TARGETS opportunity
bbc alward

The allied forces say the bombing of Iraq and Kuwait is now in a
new phase.

Initially the emphasis was on specific targets . . . such as bridges
and oil installations.

Now a US squadron commander has spoken of attacks against
what he describes as targets of opportunity – or, as he put it –
taking out . . . anything that moves.
One of the squadron's pilots – Major Thomas Galwraith –
describes the change in emphasis.

CART:
BEGINS: WE PRETTY MUCH GO OUT THERE   WE
WORK A CERTAIN AREA   AH AT NIGHT AND   WE
PROESCUTE ANY OF THE TARGETS THAT WE MIGHT
WITHIN THAT AREA   WE ATTACK THE TARGETS
WE OBSERVE ON THE GROUND TARGETS OF
OPPORTUNITY, <u>MOVERS</u>.
ENDS:

In addition, there is the heading, full of information that we can use
to reconstruct a precise chain of recontextualizations of the original
Galwraith text. We can set out the sequence as follows:

Interview → extract → story → item → text → fax(→ lecture notes)
(T.G. +?)   (tape) (written)(recorded)(typed)(sent)(distributed)

There are of course many more links and chains that further
investigation might identify. Even so, this chain lists more stages in the
process than would have been easy to reconstruct from the text as

heard on the radio, a more extensive series of recontextualizations, each of which involves different participants in different relationships. The interviewer in the original interview has gone, as has most of whatever he or she and Major Galwraith said. The original editor or editors have also gone, and there is a gap between these processes and the broadcast on the ABC on 7 February. The BBC is acknowledged as a stage in the process, with the ABC in this instance only acting as a point of redistribution, though this is not obvious in the segment as broadcast. The employees of the ABC, however, are routinely supplied with this further information, which does not appear to be strictly tied to their performance of their function as broadcasters. The dense text, available only to the professionals and not to the public, seems to provide essential information that would demystify or at least problematize the processes of mediation of the news.

But although this supplementary text (the header) is full of information which we have treated as reliable, that does not mean that it is ideologically neutral. It would be possible, given good reason, to doubt its reliability. For instance, it states that there are '23 lines' whereas a count reveals only 22. If this kind of enquiry revealed that all the numbers were fictions (it was not broadcast on the 7th but was back-dated, it lasted more than 38 seconds etc.) that would be interesting, not because it obviously matters whether it was broadcast on that date (though it might) or because there is something magical about 38 seconds that is not possessed by 41 seconds, but because the reassuring precision of all these numbers seems so strongly to guarantee a meticulous professionalism that would never make mistakes about numbers. This is the ideological meaning of the form even if the numbers are correct, no less ideological for being translated impeccably into a professional practice.

We have treated this piece of text as a sample of a language, picking out some of the regularities that characterize it. In this respect it is like an anti-language, and signifies the ideology of the media professionals in the same way as the anti-language of Galwraith's pilots. Like all anti-languages it allows the world to be elided and reconstructed. In this case the brief headings can be justified in functional terms – the heading needs to contain a lot of information – but they are all achieved by sweeping deletion-transformations that compress the text more extensively than is permitted in the dominant language. However, these are recognizably derived from normal transformations, with the effect consistently of turning events into components of a classification process. As well as signifying professionalism

191

this replaces the complex and confusing world that is presented through the media with a sanitized set of classifications. The message and effect is: whoever is killed in the Gulf War, right or wrong, we are professionals with a job to do, as efficiently as we can.

The language of the heading, however, is not all of the same kind. The first heading, 'slug', is colloquial and 'human', as is 'talent', the normal almost flippant word used by these professionals to describe other speakers on the media. It is interesting how this story has been classified: by 'targets of opportunity', not 'movers'. It supports the view that it was the discursive event not the military action that gave this story its news value, and suggests that the journalists concerned were more intrigued by the more incomprehensible S-ideology form than by the more shocking P-ideology form: Major Galwraith as quaint rather than dangerous. But it is not our intention to argue for a single interpretation of this text, and especially not for a single ideological stance and purpose amongst its speakers. On the contrary it is worth noticing the sheer heterogeneity of the authorship that is concealed under the bland word 'writer'. The brief text as broadcast has as authors at least a combination of Galwraith and his interviewer; the squadron commander; the allied spokesperson; Alward; and Howard, the sub-editor, and no doubt more. Hovering above these is a set of generic requirements that is in many respects a meta-author of the text. The person who actually wrote down the words that we have before us is not obviously the most important link in the construction and transmission of this text, though it is he/she who is accorded the status of 'writer'.

This text lasted only 38 seconds as originally broadcast, and no one would argue that it changed the course of the war. But the processes that briefly intersected in this text were of great importance, acting on two distinct sites where the ideological struggle had to be waged and won. The armed forces needed to be formed as a cohesive unit, able to deliver death and destruction without guilt or pride. Media professionals had to be able to deliver the image of independent judgment, with criticism both expressed and contained. The necessary ideological apparatus encompassed different agents with different and incompatible interests which needed to be accommodated and over-written. Each of these sites was a potential point of weakness. A disaffected or uncontrolled media or army would both be damaging to the Coalition cause, during the war and even more so afterwards.

The lessons of the Vietnam War hung heavy in the minds of the Coalition strategists. But this war was indeed different. Technological superiority allowed a victory so swift that anti-languages had little time or need to form, and the military control over the best news sources remained formidable. The informal 'critical linguistics' tradition that the Vietnam War encouraged within the media, as part of its professional self-image, did appear on various occasions, but not in a potent or damaging form. Our brief illustrative analysis was intended to show one representative moment when that strategy emerged fleetingly but was contained, and how that event was reflected and mediated through language. It was a battle that was not quite fought, in a non-battle that was itself a significant feature of the war as an ideological event. But these transactions and negotiations always take place in discourse, in endless interactions which leave their traces in such texts as survive. We have compared critical discourse analysis to archaeology, but perhaps it is more like palaeontology, which scrutinizes fossils and reconstructs vanished forms of life from their traces left in stone.

LANGUAGE, SYSTEM, MEANING

'Language is one of man's most remarkable attributes', we wrote as the first sentence of chapter 1, as though whatever was to be said about its attributes, the existence of language as a coherent and knowable object is not in doubt. This assumption, however, is far from neutral or innocent. It has served as the foundational premise for the discipline, linguistics, which purports to study this object, so that the self-evidence of the category of language gives a similar natural legitimacy to the discipline. But the word 'discourse' refers to some of the same phenomena in a way that allows different possibilities for the study of the field. Forms of discourse analysis deal with current social institutions, not respecting the boundaries of 'language', or national languages such as English, French etc. The doublet language–linguistics, then, does not refer to an elemental fact, 'language', associated naturally and inevitably with the discipline that takes it as its object. On the contrary, it functions as a powerful ideological device, one which makes some forms of analysis seem natural and central, and excludes or marginalizes others.

We do not want to say that 'language' is a useless or invalid concept. On the contrary, the word refers to a body of knowledge that is an essential component of the enabling knowledges of everyday social life. Everyone has to be some kind of folk linguist, with theories about their own language and that of others. Our case is only that 'language' in

this sense displays massive regularities but also systematic contradictions, and its forms are widely distributed but not equally shared
throughout a community of users. There is indeed an object, language,
that needs to be understood, and there should be a theory that tries to
explain it. The questions that we want to address are: what kind of
object is it, and how should the theory be organized? We have come to
feel that the traditional answers to these questions are seriously
inadequate. In this section we wish to explore the terms of the new
theory of language that we believe is required.

Instead of setting out this knowledge in the form of a logical system,
the 'rules of grammar', we will begin with another way in which this
knowledge circulates in social life: through a set of well-known
instances which carry, implicitly and variably, a set of understandings
of how language works in social practice. To illustrate the process, we
will take three phrases that achieved a wide circulation during the war,
in the process becoming the focus for innumerable commentaries as
topics in an everyday practice of linguistics. The phrases we will look at
are: 'collateral damage'; 'smart bomb'; and 'mother of all battles'. All
three appeared in many different contexts, as jokes that explored and
extended particular understandings of language in use. These phrases
together with the commentaries that they evoked are parts of a popular
metalinguistic tradition that is itself an ideological force of no small
importance.

'Collateral damage' was selected out, by some collective process,
from many other instances of the kind that we analysed in the first
section of this chapter. It was used to illustrate the mechanisms of
euphemistic language, linking these mechanisms (nominalizations,
irrational classification schemes, low modality) to a particular kind of
user, context and use. The phrase is a shorthand for the knowledge that
Orwell's work has given currency to, a kind of folk critical linguistics.

'Smart bomb' works rather differently. The collocation comes from
popular discourse, and its meaning is the transgression of the categories
animate–inanimate. People are smart: bombs are only machines. This
opposition has been theorized by Chomsky and others (in a sixties
version of the grammar) through the category of 'selection restriction
rule' in the grammar of English. But the transgression is equally well
known and understood by speakers of English as regular and
significant, in terms of the ideological functions that it serves. We have
noted other instances of the aberrant form, in the 'carcasses' of tanks, in
the 'movers' that Major Thomas Galwraith took out. Popular genres
such as science fiction carry the same meaning in their obsession with

robots, cyborgs and prosthetic forms of life. And the phrase 'smart bomb' encodes one of the most spectacular experiences of the TV coverage of the war, the view from the bomb cam as it located its target and homed in, a prosthetic eye that linked the bodies of audiences with the events in the Middle East, helpless viewers controlled by the 'intelligence' of the plummeting bomb.

The phrase 'smart bomb' works because it encodes a contradiction, that the opposition between animate and inanimate is both absolute and can be transgressed. The two phrases, CD and SB, also carry different kinds of knowledge, from different parts of the language. 'Collateral damage' signifies a mystificatory use of language from an elaborate register, whereas 'smart bomb' uses colloquial language to signify popular pleasure with transgressive forms. Both phrases are instances of S-ideological forms, but where CD is commonly used as an exemplary instance of the failure of S-ideology, SB enacts the success of an S-ideological strategy, although for some, this phrase could be used, like CD, to exemplify the perversions of language and thought brought about by the modern marriage of war and technology. The point to insist on is that although both phrases are well known and fully comprehensible, the ideological content that they carry, the theories of language as ideology that they mediate, are complex and likely to vary throughout the society. Our own theory of language, then, faces a double task: first to explicate the inchoate, fragmentary and ideo-logically-freighted theories of language that circulate in a community in various ways, and second to propose a theory of these kinds of theories, a critique that can take account of the gaps and in-consistencies between the component fragments.

For this reason we want to look in somewhat greater detail at the third of our three phrases, tracing its life cycle during the period of the Gulf War. The phrase 'omm alma'arik' as spoken by President Hussein was immediately translated and circulated as 'the mother of all battles' in the English-speaking press. As a phrase in English, this was extremely effective as a propaganda device. It was quoted and parodied endlessly, always understood as a quotation that typified and signified Hussein, and behind Hussein the Iraqi people, as the Enemy, as a species of the Other. Where our other two phrases encoded a theory of distinct types of language use within English, this one encodes a theory of the language of an alien group, a folk theory of Arabic language, culture and thought.

There is something paradoxical about this ideological achievement. It could do the work that it did because as a phrase in English it is both strange (signifying otherness, readily identifiable as the speech of someone who does not speak English) yet also fully comprehensible, fully grammatical, so that its strangeness is something that is fully accounted for within the linguistic (and therefore ideological) systems familiar to English-speaking peoples.

To illustrate the way in which the phrase circulated, we will take two later uses of it:

1 'Hands up for the mother of all surrenders'
(*Sunday Times* Perth, 3 March, 1991: caption to front page photo of a large column of Iraqi prisoners with arms above their heads.)
2 'Abdul's white flag emporium – celebrate the mother of all surrenders.'
(*Playboy* July 1991, placard in a cartoon showing an Arab trader in front of a small booth in the desert.)

Both sources of these two texts explicitly declared their pro-war stance. Alongside this headline the *Sunday Times* carried another Gulf story headlined 'Medals for all Aussie forces in Gulf', and the feature article of this issue of *Playboy* was a celebration of 'our' returning heroes.

Clearly both phrases operate as quotations of the original phrase, and part of their meaning is this intertextual relationship. This relationship is a double transformation which we can represent as follows:

President Hussein → Iraqi people: 'the mother of all battles'
⇓ ⇓
(a) ST/US army → Iraqi troops: 'the mother of all surrenders'
(b) 'Abdul' → Iraqi troops: 'the mother of all surrenders'

The two phrases (a) and (b) transform the same word in the original phrase, substituting 'surrenders' for 'battles', but they have different transformations of the participants in the original exchange. Neither of these is a transformation in the classic Chomskyan sense, which referred only to syntactic transformations. Substituting 'surrenders' for 'battles' is a lexical transformation, a type of paradigmatic transformation, while the change in speakers and hearers is a discursive transformation. In most forms of linguistics, these three kinds of transformation are regarded as so distinct that the same word, 'transformation', should not be used for them all, and in deference to Chomsky it is the syntactic type that is canonical, the only 'proper' use of the term in linguistics. But all three forms take place in language, and they all seem to be rule-governed yet variable in similar ways. The assumption that these three forms of transformation are fundamentally different comes from a foundational premise in linguistics itself, the premise that syntax, lexis and discourse are essentially distinct. From this example as in innumerable other cases we can say that this premise not only appears to be unjustified, it is a major inconvenience for anyone proposing to analyse language as social practice, language in use.

In the discursive transformation of (a) (the newspaper article) President Hussein is transformed into and replaced by the new supreme commander of these defeated troops. In (b) (the *Playboy* cartoon) Hussein the military commander is replaced by 'Abdul' the opportunistic trader. These two options seem exactly opposed to each other (powerful/ American/ political–military establishment versus ordinary/Iraqi/ commercial) but in practice there are tight constraints on the choices possible here which function very like what are otherwise called grammatical rules. Stating it as a kind of rule we could propose the following: the phrase can only be attributed to someone who can be temporarily classified as an Iraqi, because part of the social meaning of the phrase itself is its status as a signifier of Iraqiness. This 'rule' or understanding allows the phrase to perform its primary ideological function, using the otherness of the enemy effortlessly against him, making Americans of high and low degree instantly fluent in Media-Iraqi, the language of the enemy.

This trick, by which the phrase was able to signify both otherness and familiarity, was partly achieved by mere weight of circulation, but it was aided by another very different property of the phrase: the fact that it encodes forms of language and ideology that are familiar to all English-speaking people. For although it is a marked form in English, it is also similar to a set of colloquial phrases, such as 'the father and mother of a hiding', and 'the daddy of them all', in which father and/or mother signifies size by reference to the ideology of the patriarchal family. 'The father and mother of a hiding' means 'a big or severe hiding', the connection between size and importance being nicely fused in this well-motivated sign. This is a severe hiding which is administered by the legitimate authority, the father of course, as the proper one to do so on behalf of his wife and himself. In relation to this intertextual reference, Hussein's phrase is fully comprehensible, as an aberrant version of patriarchal authority. 'Mother' should not be a signifier of power, presiding over such masculine things as battles.

Hussein has not only invaded Kuwait, he threatens the ideology of the family itself.

One way of grasping the aberration of the phrase would be to treat it as a collocation that combines incompatible categories. 'Mother' is human, female, positive (nurturant) whereas 'battle' is abstract, masculine and negative (destructive). Used in this sense, 'mother' (meaning 'big') is the transform of an adjective to a noun, whereas 'battle' is the transformation of a series of actions, organized around verbs, into a noun. Analysed in this way we can see that the phrase attempts to manage a large number of oppositions, and this helps to account for how and why it decomposes into its discordant components in this case.

However, this is only true up to a point. This phrase, precisely because of its contradictions, might in other circumstances have been an ideological triumph, linking abstract and concrete, nurturance and destruction, feminine and masculine into a single seamless contradictory whole. This is how S-ideology forms are typically constructed, and every language is full of forms and rules that allow S-ideological forms. And in practice, the 'mother of all battles' is neither alien nor 'ungrammatical' in English. It is simply an S-form inserted into a P-context that reverses its fusions and destabilizes its over-elaborate syntheses. The inversion is similar to what TV exposure did to another Hussein ideological gesture, when he stroked the hair of an English child hostage to 'instantly become a devious pederast' to British TV viewers (in the words of an Australian commentator).

From a syntactic point of view this phrase is a species of collocation. It has the common form 'x of y' that we have already discussed as part of an ideological grammar of English. This syntactic form, we have argued, is understood as the trace of a discursive process, an act of classification. 'Mother of all battles' is roughly equivalent to 'very very big battle', where the sequence of two 'verys' encodes a succession of intensifiers of 'big battle'. 'Big' is the first classifier, so that the phrase is interpreted as the trace of something built up recursively as 'battle → big battle → very big battle → very very big battle' etc. But the order of words in 'mother of all battles' (like 'the biggest of all battles') does not signify the classification sequence in such a transparent way. The sequence of classification operations here seems to go something like this: 'battle → big battle → the mother of battles → the mother of all battles'. The plural -s attached to battle is inserted after the noun, and 'all' is inserted before it, at a later stage of the process. As a result the sequence of traces is not entirely obscured, but it is made less available, less transparent, and at the same time the phrase becomes more cohesive, since the lines of cleavage are less marked. In the phrase 'very very big' it is easier to see how to decompose the phrase into its component parts. For this reason, both complexity and cohesion are part of the meaning of the phrase 'mother of all battles'. It is pre-adapted to becoming a cliché, in which the association of the elements (and the meanings that they signify) seems to be inseparable and inevitable, and therefore true but meaningless.

This phrase is, among other things, a translation which implies a theory of translatability, the MOAB theory of language and difference. This has some interesting parallels with what is called the Whorfian hypothesis. The Whorfian position has two strands: linguistic determinism (language provides the categories of mind and thought, and provides the categories which code culture) and cultural relativism (difference is absolute). The MOAB theory adopts a form of the first (a single phrase encapsulates the essence of Iraqi cultural difference) but equivocates with the second (Iraqi difference is totally comprehensible and familiar, an absolute limitation on 'them' but not on 'us').

We accept, of course, that there are many differences between languages but these differences are not part of a single, coherent system that is fully knowable for all speakers of the language but incomprehensible to all others. The translation that we have looked at is a transformation, an appropriation of a phrase in Arabic, and in order to understand the work that the translation is doing, we must be able to say something about this prior text. In analysing the Arabic form of the phrase we have to work at second hand, accepting the judgments of others who are expert in the language, stopping well short of any claims that we can grasp 'the' meaning of the phrase, or the meaning potential of the language itself. But these limitations are methodological virtues which should be applied to all analyses.

The phrase 'omm al ma'arak' is literally 'mother the battles', and it indicates a big or important battle. 'Omm', 'mother', is the centre of the ideological meaning of the phrase in Arabic as in the English translation. Our informants agreed that this phrase is new in Arabic as in English, a coinage by Hussein, though the use of 'omm' to signify a superlative is not itself new. A phrase that is literal but had we were told an intertextual relationship to Hussein's coinage is 'omm al shuhada', mother of martyrs. This referred in the first place to a historical woman whose sons all died on the battlefield in the heroic days of Islamic expansion, but is also used of other women who lose their sons on the battlefield. In a more metaphoric mode, 'omm al footooh', 'mother of opening' refers to Andalusia when the Arabs 'opened up' that country in the era of the second Umayyed caliphate.

But these intertextual connections are subordinate to the same process as in English whereby an ideology of gender relations overdetermines and is expressed through intertextual associations. The dominant ideology of Islamic countries is strongly patriarchal, and although there are distinct forms and contradictions within different parts of the Islamic world, these differences are not such as to make the ideological complex itself incomprehensible to people from Anglo-Saxon cultures, whose own gender ideologies are similarly contradictory, distributed asymmetrically throughout the society. The crucial point of similarity is the functional co-existence of S-forms and P-forms: an ideology that both gives a high value to women and also differentiates and subordinates them.

Syntactically the phrase is perfectly regular for Arabic, a construction noun plus article plus noun to indicate a relationship that can be described as a 'genitive' construction, which would normally be translated as 'x of y' in English. In this form, in modern vernacular Arabic, word order alone signifies the relationship. Use of word order as a major syntactic resource is of course frequent in English, as in the construction of noun head phrases. In Arabic as in English, there is a cluster of meanings signified by this form. In this case the relationship between 'mother' and 'battles' is not strictly one of possession but (in a way that is similar to the possession-model in English) a form of classification which is analogous to a relationship of possession.

But there is something curious about the form of this particular phrase, as we can see if we compare it with the more straightforward 'omm al shuhada', mother of martyrs. In Arabic, the first word is normally the head-noun, and the second is the classifier, so that in this case the woman is classified as a mother who is distinguished by having given birth to martyrs. With 'omm al ma'arik', although the phrase is about battles, the head noun is the element 'mother', not the element 'battles', which classifies this mother. So the phrase records a complex transformational process, whereby 'battle' is transformed to 'mother', and then the element 'battle' reappears to classify the 'mother', and is then pluralized, to signify size or importance. Compared to the English translation, the phrase displaces the focus more strongly away from 'battle', or more precisely, it equivocates with a strategy of displacement, so that the syntactic form of the phrase carries a meaning which contradicts the literal meaning of the phrase, understood as referring to battles not to mothers. Compared to the English, it invokes an ideology of motherhood more strongly, and mystifies the fact that this is a battle, not a woman, to a greater degree.

This discussion has not been exhaustive, about either version of the phrase, but some things are sufficiently clear. The phrase does not have 'the same meaning' in the two languages. There are strings of different meanings, coming from different histories, different intertextual connections, different systems of circulation. The two versions have a similar basic ideological structure, encoded in the syntactic form, but this is inserted in discourse in very different ways, to different effect. The English translation implies a critique of the Iraqi version, treating it as an insidious instance of an S-form, but it displaces this critique (which could be applied equally strongly to American instances) onto Hussein, as though only Hussein could appeal so cynically to motherhood. In this respect it has some of the critical linguistic meanings that we saw in the 'collateral damage' phrase, but the strategy of displacement neutralizes the critical force, giving it a similar effect to the 'smart bomb' phrase.

Evidently there is no single ideological meaning inherent in this phrase, nor in the two languages themselves. The English phrase implies that all Iraqis as Iraqis must be taken in by the ideology, as though to use the language is to be spoken by the ideology. The Arabic-speaking Australian Palestinians who elucidated the meanings of this phrase for us had no difficulty describing how the ideology worked. English speakers who are taken in by the phrase are trapped by the ideological cunning of what they only imagine to be Arabic. But not all English speakers are so entrapped.

BEYOND CRITICAL DISCOURSE ANALYSIS: A PROSPECTIVE THEORY OF LANGUAGE

Some general points arise out of our discussion. What can be called facts of discourse (e.g. positioning of speakers and topics, circulation of meanings and texts) are inseparable from what have been called facts of language (e.g. phonology, syntax, semantics, grammar), and both together are indispensable in tracing ideological forms and processes. So a form of linguistics must play a basic role in the study of social meaning, but it must be a very different kind of linguistics from most current forms, built around a different understanding of language as social fact. In particular we need to retheorize the key concepts around which the field of linguistics is currently constituted: 'grammar', 'syntax', and 'semantics'. Without this effort at redefinition, the phenomena colonized by linguistics through those terms will be unavailable to all forms of discourse analysis.

This theoretical problem has important practical dimensions. Currently, most forms of discourse analysis do not provide discussions of grammar and syntax. Critical discourse analysis uses syntactic analysis as part of its interpretative strategy; but this raises fresh problems for others who wish to use a critical linguistic form of analysis. Where does an aspiring critical linguist go for usable descriptions of syntactic forms, and patterns of sound and meaning? Will any linguistic theory or grammar do? Are some grammars better than others for these purposes? Are there ways of recognizing and/or using these grammars that can avoid some or most of the problems? Unless these problems are addressed and resolved, at least to some extent, then the entry into critical linguistic analysis is severely restricted, confined to those who already know, by some mysterious means, what is usable from which grammar.

There are two ways we could go about this task of redefinition: by identifying the key premises in contemporary linguistics which need to be challenged and changed, or by outlining the shape of the new theory of language which must accommodate the old. We identify the following as key premises to be challenged: that the study of language is distinct from the study of society (social structures, processes, agencies); that structure is independent of function, process, use; that syntax is independent of meaning; and that rules in language are independent of the operations of power in social life acting through the agency of particular language users as social subjects. By negating these premises we could project some premises of the new theory. However we should also proceed in a positive fashion, and sketch out this theory in its own terms.

Here we want to focus on two premises that are of fundamental importance. The first premise defines the essential difference of our approach compared with mainstream linguistics: our definition of language as irreducibly a *social practice*. The second premise provides the basis for the reorganization of the objects of linguistic analysis that is needed in order to develop a social theory of syntax and grammar that can be used in textual analysis. This premise is a new account of *the nature of the linguistic sign*. We will deal with these two premises in turn.

The first premise states that language is a social practice which is one amongst many *social practices of representation and signification*. From this it follows that the study of language is irreducibly dual, drawing on social and semiotic theories, theories of social forces and relationships, and theories of systems of representation and signification. Explanation in the study of language, then, will *normally* have this double reference. Instances where a fact of language can be usefully explained as either a 'purely' semiotic ('linguistic') fact or as a 'purely' social fact will be the exception rather than the rule, and they will owe this apparent characteristic to the fact that the other aspect is, for purposes of the analysis, assumed to be fully known and can be discounted.

Since language is a material social practice, it consists of both behaviours and texts, texts that are the traces of semiotic and social action, and behaviours that are not only known through texts but are themselves a species of text. From this primary data are inferred (by analysts as by participants) the sets of rules, systems and meanings which are produced by participants. This directly opposes the founding assumption of traditional linguistics, that there is an object, 'language', which is identified especially with the phonological and syntactic regularities of a language, which is a social fact that exists, in its unity and coherence, outside and prior to any particular linguistic act which instantiates it. In contrast, we suppose that the regularities are always contingent and provisional, not a higher order of fact but a second order of inference.

Text (a record of language in use) is always the product of socially situated participants, operating with relative degrees of choice in situations where discursive behaviour is constrained to different degrees by specific structurings of power and domination, ranging from equality (the dimension of solidarity) to inequality (the dimension of power). Different users of language have different orientations and degrees of access to a given set of meanings that constitute a 'language', and different positionings within a given situation can also give rise to differences of orientation and access. That is, language users as socially located individuals do not have access to the 'language system' as such, but have partial and selective access to particular configurations that together make up an open set corresponding to what is called, as itself a social act, a 'language'. The set of choices available differs markedly for different kinds of participant and relationship, and so the relevant system also differs from case to case, since the system is nothing other than the organization of a set of choices.

For these reasons, it is not possible to accept in an unproblematic way the notion of a 'language system', presumed to consist of a coherent 'core' of common features plus a peripheral set of permissible variants. In the same way, it becomes difficult to accept the notion of a linguistic rule as a constraint whose force comes not from society but from the language itself, as a mere condition of entry into the language itself. On the contrary, all the rules and norms that govern linguistic behaviour have a social function, origin and meaning.

We now turn to the second of our two premises, which is the key to its effectiveness as a theory of grammar and syntax: a redefinition of the nature of the linguistic sign, as simultaneously a semiotic phenomenon and a social fact. Without this redefinition, we would argue, it is not possible to have a comprehensive social theory of language with a usable theory of grammar and syntax. However, this redefinition is currently not on the agenda for most other theorists who see language as social process, and most of them would not agree with everything that we propose. Indeed, linguistics as a discipline has been pretty well uninterested in the concept of the sign; and this comment can be extended to include most work in critical linguistics and critical discourse analysis. We believe that this silence is highly revealing. Nevertheless, the task of redefinition needs to proceed with some care.

Our redefinition starts from Saussure's influential proposition about the nature of the linguistic sign: that there is one typical kind of relationship in all 'natural languages' between signifiers ('forms') and signifieds ('meanings'), and that this relationship is one of 'arbitrariness'. It is not our purpose here to do justice to Saussure about what he might have intended by 'arbitrary', though we wish to insist that for us the notion of 'conventionality' is not synonymous or even parallel with 'arbitrariness', as it was for Saussure. The two terms address entirely different aspects of the character of signs; although they have a superficial similarity of appearance. The point is to see what follows from this assumption. In the first place, it allows the separation of any form from the study of meanings. In the case of phonology, for instance, since the sound shape of words is presumed to be meaningless and unmotivated, it constructs the sounds of a language as without social meaning or function, since these sounds are presumed to be both arbitrary codings of meanings and common to all members of the social group concerned. It then requires the separation of prosody, intonation and expressive style from the study of phonology, since these appear to be composed of motivated signs, which vary significantly in different social contexts. As such, they then seem less 'language-like', given the definition of the linguistic sign as unmotivated and independent of social contexts, and their study is marginalized within linguistics.

Second, syntax comes to seem to be a set of rules for combining meaningful elements (words and morphemes) using elements that do not necessarily have meaning themselves (e.g. word order, word classes). However, the phenomena covered by 'syntax' consist of signs which are well-motivated. An instance of this is word order, in which 'firstness' and 'lastness' both have a motivated meaning (importance, in some generalized sense) which underlies the rules for the x of y form in English, and noun-article-noun in Arabic. So, to use a constructed example, the three utterances *Mary and Bill married; Bill and Mary married; Mary married Bill;* carry specifiably different meanings which rest on the use of word order.

Instead of supposing that the linguistic sign is always an 'un-motivated sign', we start from the observation that language consists of many different kinds of signs, all of them responding to social forces and semiotic considerations, always 'motivated' though in different ways and to different degrees. As a basic premise for critical discourse analysis, and for all forms of analysis of language and discourse that are concerned with the social functions of language, we propose that *linguistic signs are always motivated conjuncts of form and meaning.*

In most ordinary linguistic practice signs are not obviously newly made, and it is therefore instructive to look at language users who do make signs newly, children for instance, or learners of another language. Take, as an example, a 3-year-old child's characterization of a very steep hill he is attempting to climb as 'a heavy hill'. Clearly, the child does not know the word/sign 'steep', but wishes to communicate his experience of climbing this hill. He has to fashion a new sign. The signified is, for him as for all makers of a sign, a salient or criterial aspect of the 'object' or 'event' to be represented, in this case it might be 'extreme effort'. He needs an appropriate signifier to express this signified, and he has 'heavy' accessible to him in his vocabulary. This association of signified with a signifier is in no way arbitrary; it is entirely motivated.

It may be useful to focus on the characteristics of the motivating link. Aspects of the child's experience – significant expenditure of physical effort – which derive, literally, from the child's position and 'interest' in the world – in relation to his size and his physical strength: this is a significant effort – make him select that set of characteristics as the criterial characteristics of the object/event to be represented. At the same time, aspects of the object, namely the steepness of the hill and its height relative to the child's size, also enter into the selection of the criterial elements to be signified. In other words, that which becomes the signified represents aspects of the position and interest of the producer of the sign in relation to the object at a particular time, *and* aspects of the object to be represented. These criterial features then dispose the producer to search for an apt signifier of this signified. Other apt signifiers are imaginable; but the one chosen can be regarded as the most apt, and therefore the one which is most revealing about the producer of the sign, at the point and time of the production of the sign. The process rests on analogy, and is a metaphoric process. Signs are thus always the results of the action of metaphoric processes.

We wish to use this example to characterize the production of all linguistic, and indeed all humanly produced signs. It provides a means for examining the two terms 'arbitrary' and 'conventional'. In the child's family – as often happens for quite considerable periods of time, decades often – this childish sign might be used again later by a parent or a sibling, as a 'joke' or as a cute childish saying; after a while the 'joke' ceases to be a joke, hills are talked about as 'heavy', and the use of that sign in that family has become one of its conventions. Over time, the instance of the first production of this sign might get forgotten; it might get used by others, outside the family, and so the conventionality is strengthened. This sign is probably transparent enough not to take on the appearance of an arbitrary relation between signifier and signified, even after a considerable time. In many other instances the initial motivation will recede from the knowledge of those who use the form, and the sign can take on the appearance of arbitrariness.

The appearance of arbitrariness is therefore an effect of history. While the original receiver of the sign may have more or less understood the motivation, from a knowledge of the producer and of the contingent circumstances of production, later receivers, in different contexts of reading/reception are less likely to have knowledge of that kind, so that the motivation of the sign becomes less reliably perceived. Hence arbitrariness becomes a more plausible account.

But the effect of arbitrariness is also an effect of power. In a communicative situation with the least power-difference, the producer of the sign attempts to attend to the needs of the receiver in the construction of the sign; so in that situation he or she will look for the most transparently apt signifiers for the signifieds. As power difference increases, producers can – and may wish to – attend less and less to the communicative needs of the recipients of signs so that both the initial selection of the most salient and criterial feature of the object to be represented as well as the choice of signifier may be influenced by 'willfulness' on the part of the producer. This can be so in the case of the creative artist, or the powerful politician, or academic, or, entirely commonly in quite private interactions. With these signs as with all signs, history brings about increasing loss of understanding of the motivation, increasing loss of the transparency of the signifier–signified relation, hence increasing opacity. This again produces the effect of arbitrariness.

Conventionality, as we have said, is an entirely distinct matter. The maintenance of a particular reading of a sign over time requires the agreement – however that may have been achieved – of a community of users of the sign. This situation is generally glossed by the term 'conventionality' – whether it applies to matters of meaning in language or in other semiotic modes. Here too, the exercise of power over time to maintain a particular reading will lead to a loss of knowledge of the conditions of production of the sign, an increasing opacity of the relation of signifier–signified. In such conditions conventionality has very similar appearances and effects to arbitrariness; hence the use of the two terms as (near) synonymous.

To sum up: there is thus a continuum between 'conventional' and 'motivated' signs, or as we prefer to describe it, between relatively opaque and relatively transparent signs. All linguistic signs (features, syntactic forms, etc.) are the result of social processes, and hence are motivated conjunctions of signifieds and signifiers. These processes necessarily take place in time, which (from the point of view of users) can be long or short, so that the linkage always is affected by history (as ideologically/politically inflected time) whether this be the micro-history of an interaction or the larger histories of various institutions. The distinction that we make between 'diachronic' and 'synchronic' is therefore relative. We use 'diachronic' to refer to instances where it is the length of the chain which poses problems of interpretation (as in long etymologies which are not widely known) and 'synchronic' of instances where the deformation is more directly produced out of a specific situation, designed to exclude potential participants, as in various forms of anti-language.

Opacity of signs is a pervasive phenomenon in language, but the degree of opacity is not an intrinsic fact about the sign concerned, but a relationship with a kind of user, who will have a specific orientation and access to the opacifying tendencies of history and power (or more precisely, to the history of the effects of power on meaning). Opacity and transparency, then, are not qualities that inhere to an equal degree in all the signs of every language. If that were so then opacity (for instance) would not be a significant property of any specific instance of language use. On the contrary, the opacity of signs and texts is continually varying, so that this aspect becomes a highly significant social meaning of every moment of linguistic production.

In terms of this scheme, syntax occupies an important but not a privileged place amongst the set of signs that make up language. Syntax is neither a homogenous set of signs, nor is it logically prior (or posterior) to any other set of signs. The signs of syntax are always ideologically inflected social meanings, with a common core which is common for a specified group, and a spectrum of differences, again, mobilized by different groups or for different purposes. These meanings are ideological in two senses: as representations of social existence, and as traces or mobilizations of discursive positionings and activities. In this perspective there are sets of signs that are part of a larger semiotic repertoire, including words, sounds, graphic forms, and many other signifying elements and practices, and sets of rules, constraints and obligations that are realized in patterns of repetition or avoidance amongst any set of signifying elements, in any code. In thinking of how to package the signs of a language most conveniently for use by critical linguists, or critical discourse analysts, the more appropriate model may be a lexicon rather than a grammar. A semiotic lexicon would include syntactic signs along with other kinds of sign (intonation patterns, sound patterns etc.). Like a conventional lexicon it could have multiple points of entry, allowing for multiple systems of linkage between the constituent elements, rather than the single logical scheme that is the ideal form of a conventional grammar. If syntax is treated in this way as part of the repertoire of meanings of a language, it leaves the way open for a theory of grammar to be a general and fully historical theory of the social origins and functions of all the forms and processes of language, and of all the rules and regularities of discourse.

In saying this we are pointing ahead to further work, not describing an already accomplished task. Most forms of critical discourse analysis do not normally analyse all aspects of verbal and other texts to trace semiotic processes and social meanings, within a common framework. Our own form of CDA differs from other forms of discourse analysis in its attention to syntax as a carrier of ideological meanings, but it has only just begun to devote equally systematic attention to sound as meaning, and to the function of words and other semantic systems. Clearly, discourse analysis of all kinds needs to be able to analyse all aspects of the material forms of language – as sets of signifying practices, as social and semiotic facts. What is required is a form of close linguistic description that is at the same time a precise account of the transactions that constitute social meanings. Our own work is only a step along the way.

There is one further, last point. Language, linguistic forms and processes, seen in this way as the product of social practices, is just one of the many semiotic modes through which social meanings are coded. It becomes essential therefore at long last for linguists and for linguistics to see language as one of these many modes, and attempt to understand the social and cultural place of language in amongst the other modes of production of meaning in a specific instance, in a culture, and in a society as a whole, as well as beginning to assess and describe the interdependencies among them. The view, which is entirely implicit and therefore beyond question, that when I communicate I 'use language' as though I made a decision for this means of communication rather than another seems to be at odds with the practice of communicators. They no more make a decision to 'use language' than they make a decision to 'use gesture' or facial expression, or proxemic modes, or any other. The oddness of that assumption comes to light if I say that when I communicate I 'use gesture' – and as a kind of incidental effect there are also other means of communication brought into play, such as proxemic or verbal ones. It is this kind of realization which has given rise to work in Social Semiotics, an attempt to begin to describe other communicative modes, and their interrelations and interdependencies.

CRITICAL DISCOURSE ANALYSIS

We want to conclude this chapter with a summary of some principles that we hope will make the theory contained in this book easier to apply in practice.

Language is a set of partial systems of choices and rules

There are many regularities to be found in language phenomena, sets of systems organizing or constraining choice, and these choices are part of social meaning. But the sets of choices do not make up a single, comprehensive and coherent system that is equivalent to 'the language', and the meaning of particular components or subsystems is always relative to specific kinds of user, on specific occasions. Analysis that identifies a particular rule or regularity also needs always to specify who uses (or is used by) the rule or regularity and under what circumstances (context, position, genre).

Background meanings are both inside and outside a text

People produce meaning against a background of taken-for-granted knowledges (knowledge about the social and physical world and forms of textuality, 'common sense', linguistic and generic conventions etc.) which are part of the meaning of every text, a constraint in every discursive act. Because they are taken for granted, they are not normally fully declared in a given text, but if they are effective in a text they will normally leave their traces. Such background knowledge is usually widely distributed, so that it does not require a large sample to demonstrate that it exists, but it is inchoate and unclear, so that its specific forms are often difficult to articulate. Analysis of background meanings always needs to go outside a given text to other locations of the relevant knowledge, but it also needs to identify the sites where the set of background meanings can be seen.

Ideology has a double face

Ideology mediates and naturalizes contradictions, and normally it appears as a complex, as a set of contradictory elements or versions of physical and social reality. Ideological analysis is incomplete until it has located the structural contradictions that operate in practice, on behalf of a given set of interests.

Ideology is inscribed in social practice

Ideological forms are structures of meaning (versions of social relationships) that are inseparable from a set of practices that are themselves kinds of meaning. Ideological analysis of discourse must take full account of the ideologies inscribed in discursive practices.

'Context' is structured like a text

The various dimensions of context (participants, relationships, themes, the discursive actions that occur) can be analysed as a series of actionals and relationships that carry important social meanings, the ideological meanings of the discourse itself. Analysis must always take account of discursive events as social action, which are an indispensable part of the social meaning of every text.

Interpretation is struggle

Readers, hearers, viewers have different relationships to each other and to producers of a given text so the meanings that they produce are not fully predictable from a given reading of the text, or from the intentions of the authors where these can be excavated. Analysis must take account of both the radical indeterminacy of meanings in principle, and also the specific meanings produced by given discursive agents (readers, writers, hearers, speakers and others) in the processes of circulation surrounding a given discursive event.

History is meaning

Multiple histories, of different scales and from different locations and origins, typically intersect in particular texts and discursive events. These histories involve different systems of intertextuality, different politics, different technologies. It is these histories, and the processes that they record, that constitute the effective social meaning of a given form or text. Although these histories are too various for all of them to be included in an analysis, some framework of the relevant histories should be part of every analysis.

Truth is always at risk

Truth is constructed and reconstructed in every discourse, but no discourse contains full guarantees of its own truth. Analysis must note the various claims to truth (the modality markers diffused through every part of every utterance) and also look outside the text, outside the discourse, for other texts and other discourses which carry other versions of the truth that is in dispute. For CDA, 'truth' always matters, and is always open to dispute.

Syntax is meaning

Syntax carries meanings in the same kind of way as other signifiers of language. So the meanings of syntax are social and ideological, dependent on the factors that constrain other signifiers: different codes, different situations, different participants, different histories. The meanings carried by syntax are pervasive and important in every kind of text, communicating background assumptions and traces of the discursive process in an unusually full form. So some level and degree of syntactic analysis is indispensable in CDA, always allied to the analysis of other dimensions of meaning.

SOURCES AND CONTEXTS

We have indicated in the preface the thinkers whose works we have more consciously drawn on in our development of this theory since the writing of the first edition in the early 1970s. Perhaps one major influence on our work which is not mentioned there was the fact that both of us moved our academic locations: Bob Hodge to a School of Human Communication, and Gunther Kress to two successive institutions, in both of which Communication/Cultural/Media Studies were the main concerns. And then of course the mid-seventies to mid-eighties saw the full effect of the various forms of post-structuralism and postmodernism in the Humanities broadly speaking. The, for us, positive effects of that broad movement, including particularly forms of feminism, will be entirely evident in this chapter. At the same time it will also be evident that we kept very strong resistances to many aspects of that movement: we have kept strong notions of reference, of the social, and of individual agency – we think not naively – and of a strong anchorage of the semiotic project in a larger social and political project. We have taken from post-structuralism (as the methodological/descriptive wing of postmodernism) the possibility of a much more complex, a much more dynamic and historical and therefore more plausible model of the social, and of semiosis, including semiosis in language. We have rejected the notion of a theory which is – in our view – merely a description of currently dominant ideologies of fragmentation, of dispersion, of the appearance and the surface. We continue to believe in the absolute necessity for anyone wishing to understand and resist current social and political tendencies of broadly integrative theoretical accounts which always attend to the minutest specificities.

In terms of social theories we have continued to draw on Bateson, Bernstein, on Bourdieu in particular, on Habermas, on Foucault, Ricoeur, and on those who have provided influential interpretations of these thinkers for us, Norman Fairclough, Ian Hunter, John Thompson. Many of those whose interpretations have been most important for us were close colleagues, or good friends, or both. Their published works are in the bibliography, but as their conversations with us can't be listed in the same way, we do wish to mention here Bill Cope, John Frow, Mary Kalantzis, Allan Luke, Alec McHoul,

Stephen Muecke, Terry Threadgold, Theo van Leeuwen. Above all we have learned from all those who have continued the development of the broad-ranging work of Critical Linguistics, and Critical Discourse Analysis, even where they might not use that label themselves. Here we mention the work of Paul Chilton, Romy Clark, Teun van Dijk, Norman Fairclough, Roger Fowler, Colin Good, Jacob Mey, Kay Richardson.

APPENDIX

SLUG	TALENT	SUBBED	DATE		COPY	CART	TOTAL CUM
targets opportunity 2 galwrait howard			Thu Feb	7 07:25	0:23	.15	0:38

Dest: NOSE   NR: Writer:alward   Lines: 23

History:

    EX-RN-SYD

    TARGETS opportunity

    bbc alward

The allied forces say the bombing of Iraq and Kuwait is now in a new phase.

Initially the emphasis was on specific targets... such as bridges and oil installations.

Now a US squadron commander has spoken of attacks against what he describes as targets of opportunity — ' or, as he put it -- taking out...anything that moves.

One of the squadron's pilots -- Major Thomas Galwraith -- describes the change in emphasis.

CART:

BEGINS: WE PRETTY MUCH GO OUT THERE WE WORK A CERTAIN AREA AH AT NIGHT AND WE PROESCUTE ANY OF THE TARGETS THAT WE MIGHT WITHIN THAT AREA WE ATTACK THE TARGETS WE OBSERVE ON THE GROUND TARGETS OF OPPORTUNITY , MOVERS.

ENDS:...

                          MOVER

Facsimile of fax which appears on p. 190.

BIBLIOGRAPHY

This bibliography is intended to provide a useful selection of writings in Critical Linguistics, Critical Discourse Analysis, and Social Semiotics.

Aers, D.R. and Kress, G.R. (1978) 'Dark texts need notes', *Literature and History*, 8, 138–58.

Aers, D.R., Hodge, R. and Kress, G.R. (1982) *Literature, Language and Society in England 1580–1680*, Dublin, Gill & Macmillan.

Akmajian, A. and Heny, F. (1975) *An Introduction to the Principles of Transformational Syntax*, Cambridge, Mass. and London, MIT Press.

Argyle, M. (1969) *Social Interaction*, London, Methuen.

Argyle, M., Salter, V., Nicholson, H., Williams, H. and Burgess, P. (1970) 'The communication of inferior and superior attitudes by verbal and non-verbal signals', *British Journal of Social and Clinical Psychology*, 9, 222–31.

Austin, J.L. (1962) *How to Do Things with Words*, Cambridge, Mass., Harvard University Press.

Bach, E. and Harms, T. (eds) (1968) *Universals in Linguistic Theory*, New York, Holt, Rinehart & Winston.

Bacon, F. (1969) *The Advancement of Learning*, London, Oxford University Press.

Bateson, G. (1971) *Steps to an Ecology of Mind*, London, Paladin.

Baudrillard, J. (1981) *For a Critique of the Political Economy of the Sign*, trans. C. Levin, St Louis, Miss., Telos Press.

Berger, P.L. and Luckmann, T. (1967) *The Social Construction of Reality*, Harmondsworth, Penguin.

Berlin, B. and Kay, P. (1969) *Basic Color Terms*, Berkeley, University of California Press.

Bernstein, B. (1968) 'Some sociological determinants of perception. An inquiry into sub-cultural differences', in J.A. Fishman (ed.) *Readings in the Sociology of Language*, The Hague, Mouton, 223–39.

Bernstein, B. (1971) *Class, Codes and Control*, London, Routledge & Kegan Paul; St Albans, Paladin.

Bernstein, B. (1972) 'Social class, language and socialization', in P.P. Giglioli (ed.) *Language and Social Context*, Harmondsworth, Penguin.

Bernstein, B. (1990) *The Structuring of Pedagogic Discourse*, London, Routledge.

Bierwisch, M. (1970) 'Semantics', in J. Lyons (ed.) *New Horizons in Linguistics*, Harmondsworth, Penguin.

Bigsby, C.W.E. (ed.) (1976) *Approaches to Popular Culture*, London, Arnold.

Birch, D. and O'Toole, M. (eds) (1988) *Functions of Style*, London, Frances Pinter.

Bolinger, D.L. (1967) 'Adjectives in English: attribution and predication', *Lingua*, 18, 1–34.

Bourdieu, P. (1984) *Distinction: A Social Critique of the Judgement of Taste*, trans. R. Nice, London, Routledge & Kegan Paul.

Bourdieu, P. (1991) *Language and Symbolic Power*, Cambridge, Polity Press.

Boyd, J. and Thorne, J.P. (1969) 'The semantics of modal verbs', *Journal of Linguistics*, 1, 57–74.

Bresnan, J. (1977) 'Towards a realistic model of transformational grammar', mimeo.

Bull, W.E. (1960) *Time, Tense and the Verb*, Berkeley, University of California Press.

Burke, E. (1958) *Reflections on the Revolution in France*, London, Oxford University Press.

Calbert, J.P. (1971) *Modality and Case Grammar*, in C. Fillmore (ed.) *Working Papers in Linguistics*, Columbus, Ohio State University Press.

Carroll, J.B. (ed.) (1956) *Language, Thought and Reality. Selected Writings of Benjamin Lee Whorf*, New York, Wiley.

Chafe, W.L. (1970) *Meaning and the Structure of Language*, Chicago and London, University of Chicago Press.

Chilton, P. (ed.) (1985) *Language and the Nuclear Arms Debate*, London, Frances Pinter.

Chilton, P. (1988) *Orwellian Language and the Media*, London, Pluto Press.

Chomsky, N.A. (1957) *Syntactic Structures*, The Hague, Mouton.

Chomsky, N.A. (1965) *Aspects of the Theory of Syntax*, Cambridge, Mass., MIT Press.

Chomsky, N.A. (1970) 'Remarks on nominalization', in R. Jacobs and P. Rosenbaum (eds) *Readings in English Transformational Grammar*, Waltham, Mass., Blaisdell.

Chomsky, N.A. (1971) 'Deep structure, surface structure and semantic interpretation', in D.D. Steinberg and L.A. Jakobovitz (eds) *Semantics*, London, Cambridge University Press.

Chomsky, N.A. (1972) *Language and Mind*, New York, Harcourt Brace Jovanovitch.

Chomsky, N.A. (1973) *The Backroom Boys*, London, Fontana/Collins.

Clark, H. (1970) 'Word associations and linguistic theory', in J. Lyons (ed.) *New Horizons in Linguistics*, Harmondsworth, Penguin.

Clark, R., Fairclough, N., Ivanic, R. and Martin-Jones, M. (1988) 'Critical language awareness', CLSL Working Papers 1, Centre for Language in Social Life, Department of Linguistics, University of Lancaster.

Cloran, C. (1989) 'Learning through language: the social construction of gender', in R. Hasan, and J. Martin (eds) *Learning Development: Learning Language, Learning Culture*, New Jersey, Ablex.

Cole, P. and Sadock, J. (eds) (1977) *Syntax and Semantics, vol. 8: Grammatical Relations*, New York, Academic Press.

Coleridge, E.H. (ed.) (1961) *The Poems of Samuel Taylor Coleridge*, London, Oxford University Press.

Cranny-Francis, A. (1987) 'Gender and genre: feminist rewriting of detective fiction', *Women's Studies International Forum*, November, 69–84.

Davidson, D. and Harman, G. (eds) (1975) *The Logic of Grammar*, Encino, Cal., Dickinson.

Dews, P. (1987) *The Logics of Disintegration. Post-Structuralist Thought and the Claims of Critical Theory*, London/New York, Verso.

Dixon, R.M.W. (1971) 'A method of semantic description', in D.D. Steinberg and L.A. Jakobovitz (eds) *Semantics*, London, Cambridge University Press.

Douglas, M. (1966) *Purity and Danger*, London, Routledge & Kegan Paul.

Douglas, M. (ed.) (1973) *Rules and Meanings: The Anthropology of Everyday Knowledge*, Harmondsworth, Penguin.

Downes, W.J. (1977) 'The imperative and pragmatics', *Journal of Linguistics*, 13, 77–97.

Elton, G.R. (1962) *The Tudor Revolution in Government*, London, Cambridge University Press.

Fairclough, N. (1985) 'Critical and descriptive goals in discourse analysis', *Journal of Pragmatics*, 9, 739–63.

Fairclough, N. (1988a) 'Discourse in social change: a conflictual view', Centre for Language in Social Life, Department of Linguistics, University of Lancaster.

Fairclough, N. (1988b) 'Register, power, and sociosemantic change', in D. Birch, and M. O'Toole (eds) *Functions of style*, London, Frances Pinter.

Fairclough, N. (1989a) 'Language and ideology', in M. Knowles and K. Malmkjaer (eds) *Language and Ideology*, English Language Research, University of Birmingham.

Fairclough, N. (1989b) 'What might we mean by "enterprise discourse"?' Research Paper 14, Centre for Language in Social Life, Department of Linguistics, University of Lancaster.

Fairclough, N. (1990) 'Technologization of discourse', Centre for Language in Social Life, Department of Linguistics, University of Lancaster.

Fairclough, N. (1991) 'Critical linguistics', in W. Bright (ed.) *Oxford International Encyclopaedia of Linguistics*, New York, Oxford University Press.

Fairclough, N. (1992) *Discourse and Social Change*, Cambridge, Polity Press.

Fillmore, C. (1968) 'The case for case', in E. Bach and T. Harms (eds) *Universals in Linguistic Theory*, New York, Holt, Rinehart & Winston.

Fillmore, C. (1969) 'Types of lexical information', in F. Kiefer (ed.) *Studies in Syntax and Semantics*, Dordrecht, Reidel.

Fillmore, C. (ed.) (1971) *Working Papers in Linguistics*, Columbus, Ohio State University Press.

Firth, J.R. (1957) *Papers in Linguistics 1934–1951*, London, Oxford University Press.

Fishman, J.A. (ed.) (1968) *Readings in the Sociology of Language*, The Hague, Mouton.

Fodor, J.A., Bever, T.G. and Garrett, M.F. (1974) *The Psychology of Language*, New York, McGraw-Hill.

Foucault, M. (1972a) 'Orders of discourse', *Social Science Information*, 10 (2), 7–30.

Foucault, M. (1972b) *The Archaeology of Knowledge*, trans. A. Sheridan, London, Tavistock Publications.

Foucault, M. (1980) *Power/Knowledge*, ed. C. Gordon, New York, Pantheon.

Fowler, R.G. (1982) *Linguistic Criticism*, London, Oxford University Press.

Fowler, R.G. (1988a) 'Critical linguistics', in K. Malmkjaev (ed.) *The Linguistic Encyclopaedia*, London, Routledge.

Fowler, R.G. (1988b) 'Notes on critical linguistics', in R. Steele and T. Threadgold (eds) (1988) *Language topics: Essays in honour of Michael Halliday*, 2 vols, Amsterdam, John Benjamins.

Fowler, R.G. (1990) *Language in the News: Discourse and Ideology in the Press*, London, Routledge.

Fowler, R., Hodge, R., Kress, G. and Trew, T. (1979) *Language and Control*, London, Routledge & Kegan Paul.

Freud, S. (1900) *The Interpretation of Dreams*, trans. J. Strachey, London, Hogarth Press.

Freud, S. (1901) *The Psychopathology of Everyday Life*, London, Hogarth Press.

Freud, S. (1905) *Jokes and Their Relation to the Unconscious*, London, Routledge & Kegan Paul.

Frow, J. (1985a) 'Discourse and power', *Economy and Society*, 14 (2), 193–214.

Frow, J. (1985b) 'Language, discourse, ideology', *Raritan*, V (1) Summer, 31–42.

Frow, J. (1988) *Literature and Marxism*, Oxford, Blackwell.

Giglioli, P.P. (ed.) (1972) *Language and Social Context*, Harmondsworth, Penguin.

Good, C. (1985) *Presse und soziale Wirklichkeit*, Düsseldorf, Schwann.

Greene, J. (1972) *Psycholinguistics*, Harmondsworth, Penguin.

Grice, H.P. (1968) 'Utterer's meaning, sentence meaning, and word-meaning', *Foundations of Language*, 4, 225–42.

Grice, H.P. (1975) 'Logic and conversation', in J. Cole and J. Morgan (eds) *Syntax and Semantics 3: Speech Acts*, New York and London, Academic Press, 41–58.

Gumperz, J.J. and Hymes, D. (eds) (1972) *Directions in Sociolinguistics*, New York and London, Holt, Rinehart & Winston.

Habermas, J. (1984) *The Theory of Communicative Action. Vol. 1: Reason and the Rationalization of Society*, trans. T. McCarthy, London, Heinemann.

Hale, K. (1971) 'A note on a Walbiri tradition of antonymy', in D.D. Steinberg and L.A. Jakobovitz (eds) *Semantics*, London, Cambridge University Press.

Halliday, M.A.K. (1967) *Grammar, Society and the Noun*, London, H.K. Lewis (University College London).

Halliday, M.A.K. (1967/8) 'Notes on transitivity and theme in English', *Journal of Linguistics*, 3, 37–81; 199–244; and 4, 179–215.

Halliday, M.A.K. (1970a) 'Language structure and language function', in J. Lyons (ed.) *New Horizons in Linguistics*, Harmondsworth, Penguin, 140–65.

Halliday, M.A.K. (1970b) 'Functional diversity in language, as seen from a consideration of modality and mood in English', *Foundations of Language*, 6, 322–61; also reprinted as chapter 13 in G.R. Kress (ed.) (1976a) *Halliday: System and Function in Language*, London, Oxford University Press.

Halliday, M.A.K. (1971) 'Linguistic function and literary style: an enquiry into the language of William Golding's *The Inheritors*', in S. Chatman (ed.) *Literary Style: A Symposium*, New York, Oxford University Press, 330–65.

Halliday, M.A.K. (1976) 'Anti-languages', *American Anthropologist* 78(3), 570–84.

Halliday, M.A.K. (1977) 'Text as semantic choice in social contexts', in T. v. Dijk and J. Petöfi (eds) *Grammars and Descriptions*, Berlin, Walter de Gruyter.

Halliday, M.A.K. (1978) *Language as Social Semiotic: The Social Interpretation of Language and Meaning*, London, Arnold.

Halliday, M.A.K. (1985a) *Introduction to Functional Grammar*, London, Arnold.

Halliday, M.A.K. (1985b) 'Dimensions of discourse analysis: grammar', in T. v. Dijk (ed.) *Handbook of Discourse Study. Vols 1–4*, London/New York, Academic Press.

Halliday, M.A.K. (1985/8) *Spoken and Written Language*, Geelong, Deakin University Press; Oxford, Oxford University Press.

Halliday, M.A.K. (1989) 'On the language of physical science', in M. Ghadessy (ed.) *Registers in Written English: Situational Factors and Linguistic Features*, London, Frances Pinter.

Halliday, M.A.K. and Hasan, R. (1976) *Cohesion in English*, London, Longman.

Halliday, M.A.K. and Hasan, R. (1985/8) *Language, Context-Text: A Social Semiotic Perspective*, Geelong, Deakin University Press; Oxford, Oxford University Press.

Harris, Z. (1952) 'Discourse analysis', *Language*, 28, 18–23; 474–94.

Harris, Z. (1957) 'Co-occurrence and transformation in linguistic structure', *Language*, 33, 283–340.

Hasan, R. (1978) 'Text in the systemic functional model', in W. Dressler (ed.) *Current Trends in Text Linguistics*, Berlin, Walter de Gruyter.

Hasan, R. (1979) 'On the notion of text', in J. Petöfi (ed.) *Text Versus Sentence: Basic questions of Text Linguistics*, Hamburg, Buske Verlag.

Hasan, R. (1984a) 'The Nursery Tale as a Genre', *Nottingham Linguistics Circular* 14.

Hasan, R. (1984b) 'Ways of saying: ways of meaning', in R.P. Fawcett *et al.* (eds) *Semiotics of Language and Culture*, London, Frances Pinter.

Hasan, R. (1985/8) *Linguistics, Language and Verbal Art*, Geelong, Deakin University Press; Oxford, Oxford University Press.

Hasan, R. (1986) 'The ontogenesis of ideology: an interpretation of mother-child talk', in T. Threadgold, E.A. Grosz, M.K. Halliday and G.P. Kress (eds) *Semiotics – Ideology – Language*, Sydney Association for Studies in Society and Culture, Sydney University.

Hodge, R. (1976a) 'Freud, Chomsky, and depth analysis', *UEA Papers in Linguistics*, 1, 46–64.

Hodge, R. (1976b) 'Linguistics and popular culture', in C.W.E. Bigsby (ed.) (1976) *Approaches to Popular Culture*, London, Arnold.

Hodge, R. (1977) 'Literacy and society: some consequences of linguistic modes of production', *UEA Papers in Linguistics*, 4, 1–17.

Hodge, R. (1982) 'Transformational analysis and the visual media', *Australian Journal of Screen Theory*, 7.

Hodge, R. (1984) 'Historical semantics and the meaning of discourse', *Australian Journal of Cultural Studies*, 2 (2), 124–31.

Hodge, R. (1985) 'Getting the message across: a systemic analysis of media coverage of a CND march', in P. Chilton (ed.) *Language and the Nuclear Arms Debate*, London, Frances Pinter.

Hodge, R. (1986) 'Song as discourse', in T. v. Dijk (ed.) *Literature Discourse and Communication*, Amsterdam, John Benjamins.

Hodge, R. (1988) 'Halliday and the stylistics of creativity', in D. Birch and M. O'Toole (eds) *Functions of Style*, London, Frances Pinter.

Hodge, R. (1989) 'Discourse in time', in B. Torode (ed.) *Text and Talk*, Amsterdam, Foris.

Hodge, R. (1990) *Literature as Discourse*, Cambridge, Polity Press.

Hodge, R. and Kress, G.R. (1974) 'Transformations, models and processes: towards a useable linguistics', *Journal of Literary Semantics*, 4 (1), 4–18.

Hodge, R. and Kress, G.R. (1982) 'The semiotics of love and power: *King Lear* and a new stylistics', *Southern Review*, 15 (2), 143–56.

Hodge, R. and Kress, G.R. (1983) 'Functional semiotics: key concepts for the analysis of media, culture and society', *Australian Journal of Cultural Studies*, 1 (1), 1–17.

Hodge, R. and Kress, G.R. (1986) 'Re-Reading as exorcism: semiotics and the ghost of Saussure', *Southern Review*, 16 (2), 38–52.

Hodge, R. and Kress, G.R. (1988) *Social Semiotics*, Oxford, Polity Press; Ithaca, NY, Cornell University Press.

Hodge, R. and Tripp, D. (1986) *Children and Television*, Cambridge, Polity Press.

Hofman, T.R. (1966) 'Past tense replacement and the modal system', *The Computation Laboratory of Harvard University, Report no. NSF-17*, Cambridge, Mass.

Huddleston, R.D. (1969) 'Some observations on tense and deixis', *Language*, 45, 777–806.

Hunter, I. (1984) 'After representation: recent discussions of the relations between language and literature', *Economy and Society*, 13, 397–430.

Hymes, D. (1964) *Language in Culture and Society*, New York, Harper & Row.

Hymes, D. (1968) 'The ethnography of speaking' in J.A. Fishman (ed.) *Readings in the Sociology of Language*, The Hague, Mouton, 99–138.

Hymes, D. (1972a) 'On communicative competence', in J. Pride and J. Holmes (eds) *Sociolinguistics*, Harmondsworth, Allen Lane.

Hymes, D. (1972b) 'Models of the interaction of language and social life', in J.J. Gumperz and D. Hymes (eds) (1972) *Directions in Sociolinguistics*, New York and London, Holt, Rinehart & Winston.

Jackson, N. (1969) *Fanny's Double Feature*, New York, Lancer.

Jacobs, R. and Rosenbaum, P. (eds) (1970) *Readings in English Transformational Grammar*, Waltham, Mass., Blaisdell.

Jones, D. (1973) *Before Rebecca*, London, Allen Lane.

Katz, J. and Postal, P. (1964) *An Integrated Theory of Linguistic Descriptions*, Cambridge, Mass., MIT Press.

Keddie, N. (ed.) (1973) *Tinker, Tailor . . . The Myth of Cultural Deprivation*, Harmondsworth, Penguin.

Kiefer, F. (ed.) (1969) *Studies in Syntax and Semantics*, Dordrecht, Reidel.

Klima, E. (1964) 'Negation in English', in J. Fodor and J. Katz (eds) *The Structure of Language*, Englewood Cliffs, NJ, Prentice-Hall.

Kress, G.R. (ed.) (1976a) *Halliday: System and Function in Language*, London, Oxford University Press.

Kress, G.R. (1976b) 'You name it, sort of thing . . . : some syntactic correlates of code', *UEA Papers in Linguistics*, 2, 36–42.

Kress, G.R. (1976c) 'Structuralism and popular culture', in C.W.E. Bigsby (ed.) *Approaches to Popular Culture*, London, Arnold.

Kress, G.R. (1977) 'Tense as modality', *UEA Papers in Linguistics*, 5, 40–52.

Kress, G.R. (1978a) 'Poetry as anti-language: a reconsideration of Donne's "Nocturnal"', *PTL*, 3, 327–44.

Kress, G.R (1978b) 'Towards an analysis of the language of European intellectuals', *Journal of European Studies*, 8, 274–91.

Kress, G.R. (1982) *Learning to Write*, London, Routledge & Kegan Paul.

Kress, G.R. (1983a) 'Linguistic and ideological transformations in newspaper language', in H. Davis and Paul Walton (eds) *Language Image and the Media*, Oxford, Blackwell.

Kress, G.R. (1983b) 'Media analysis and the study of discourse', *Media Information Australia*, 28, 3–12.

Kress, G.R. (1983c) 'The politics of newspaper language', *International Journal of the Sociology of Language*, 32, 43–58.

Kress, G.R. (1985/8) *Linguistic Processes in Sociocultural Practice*, Geelong, Deakin University Press; Oxford, Oxford University Press.

Kress, G.R. (1985a) 'Discourses, texts, readers and the pro-nuclear arguments', in P. Chilton (ed.) *Language and the Nuclear Arms Debate*, London, Frances Pinter.

Kress, G.R. (1985b) 'Ideological structures in discourse', in T. van Dijk (ed.) *Handbook of Discourse Study. Vols 1–4*, London/New York, Academic Press.

Kress, G.R. (1986a) 'Interrelations of reading and writing', in A. Wilkinson (ed.) *The Writing of Writing*, Milton Keynes, Open University Press.

Kress, G.R. (1986b) 'Language in the media: the construction of the domains of public and private', *Media Culture and Society*, 8 (4), 395–419.

Kress, G.R. (ed.) (1987a) *Communication and Culture*, Sydney, University of NSW Press.

Kress, G.R. (1987b) 'Educating readers: language in advertising', in J. Hawthorn (ed.) *Propaganda, Persuasion, and Polemic*, London, Arnold.

Kress, G.R. (1987c) 'Genre in a social theory of language', in I. Reid (ed.) *The Place of Genre in Learning*, Geelong, Deakin University Press; Oxford, Oxford University Press.

Kress, G.R. (1987d) 'Reading, writing and power', in C. Painter and J.R. Martin (eds) *Writing to Learn*, Melbourne, Applied Linguistics Association of Australia, Occasional Papers No. 9.

Kress, G.R. (1988) 'Textual matters: the social effectiveness of style', in D. Birch and M. O'Toole (eds) *Functions of Style*, London, Frances Pinter.

Kress, G.R. (1989a) 'History and language: towards a social account of linguistic change', *Journal of Pragmatics*, 13, 445–66.

Kress, G.R. (1989b) 'Texture as meaning', in R. Andrews (ed.) *Narrative and Argument*, Milton Keynes, Open University Press.

Kress, G.R. (1989c) 'The social production of language: history and structures of domination', in P. Fries and M. Gregory (eds) *Discourse in Society*, New Jersey, Ablex.

Kress, G.R. (1991) 'Critical discourse analysis', in W. Grabe (ed.) *Annual Review of Applied Linguistics*, vol. II, New York, Cambridge University Press, 84–100.

Kress, G.R. (1992a) 'English and the production of a culture of innovation: the case of the LINC materials', *English and Media Magazine*, 26, Winter.

Kress, G.R. (1992b) 'Genre in a social theory of language', *English in Education*, June.

Kress, G.R. (1992c) 'Participation and difference: the role of language in producing a culture of innovation', in P. Gilbert and A. Luke (eds) *Discourse* (Special Issue on Australian Discourses in Literacy), 12 (2), 123–30.

Kress, G.R. and Hodge, R. (1979) *Language as Ideology*, London, Routledge & Kegan Paul.

Kress, G.R. and Jones, G. (1981) 'Classifications at work: the case of middle-management', *Text*, 1(1), 65–83.

Kress, G. and van Leeuwen, T. (1990) *Reading Images*, Geelong, Deakin University Press.

Kress, G.R. and van Leeuwen, T. (1992a) 'Structures of visual representation', *Journal of Literary Semantics*, 21 (2), 91–117.

Kress, G.R. and van Leeuwen, T. (1992b) 'Trampling all over our unspoiled spot: Barthes' "punctum" and the politics of the extra-semiotic', *Southern Review*, 25 (1).

Kress, G.R. and Threadgold, T. (1988) 'Towards a social theory of genre', *Southern Review*, 21 (3) 215–43.

Kress, G.R. and Trew, T. (1978a) 'Transformations and discourse: a study in conceptual change', *Journal of Literary Semantics*, 7, 1, 29–48.

Kress, G.R. and Trew, T. (1978b) 'Ideological transformations of discourse: or, how the *Sunday Times* got its message across', *Sociological Review*, 26, 4, 755–76.

Kristeva, J. (1980) *Desire in Language*, trans. T. Gora, A. Jardine, L. Roudiez, New York, Columbia University Press.

Kuhn, T.S. (1962) *The Structure of Scientific Revolutions*, Chicago, University of Chicago Press.

Labov, W. (1969) 'Contraction, deletion and inherent variability of the English copula', *Language*, 45, 715–62.

Labov, W. (1972a) *Sociolinguistic Patterns*, Philadelphia, University of Pennsylvania Press.

Labov, W. (1972b) *Language in the Inner City*, Philadelphia, University of Pennsylvania Press.

Labov, W. (1972c) *Sociolinguistic Patterns*, Oxford, Blackwell.

Labov, W. (1973) 'The logic of non-standard English', in N. Keddie (ed.) *Tinker, Tailor . . . The Myth of Cultural Deprivation*, Harmondsworth, Penguin.

Lacan, J. (1977) *Ecrits: A Selection*, trans. A. Sheridan, New York, Norton.

Laing, R.D. (1971) *Self and Others*, Harmondsworth, Penguin.

Lakoff, G. (1966) 'Stative adjectives and verbs in English', *The Computation Laboratory of Harvard University, Report no. NSF-17*, Cambridge, Mass.

Lakoff, G. (1970) *Irregularity in Syntax*, New York, Holt, Rinehart & Winston.

Lakoff, R. (1973) 'Language and woman's place', *Language in Society*, 2, 45–80.

Lamb, S.M. (1966) *Outline of Stratificational Grammar*, Washington, DC, Georgetown University Press.

Leach, E. (1964) 'Anthropological aspects of language: animal categories and verbal abuse', in E.H. Lenneberg (ed.) *New Directions in the Study of Language*, Cambridge, Mass., MIT Press.

Leavis, F.R. (1963) *New Bearings in English Poetry*, Harmondsworth, Penguin.

Lees, R.B. (1960) *The Grammar of English Nominalizations*, The Hague, Mouton.

Lounsbury, F.G. (1956) 'A semantic analysis of Pawnee kinship usage', *Language*, 32, 158–94.

Luke, A. (1988) *Literacy Textbooks and Ideology: Postwar Literacy Instruction and the Methodology of Dick and Jane*, London, Falmer Press.

Luke, A. (1989) 'Open and closed texts: the semantic/ideological analysis of curricular narratives', *Journal of Pragmatics*, 13, 1.

Luke, A. and Baker, C. (eds), (1989) *Towards a Critical Sociology of Reading*, Amsterdam, John Benjamins.

Lyons, J. (1967) 'A note on possessive, existential, and locative sentences', *Foundations of Language*, 3, 390–6.

Lyons, J. (ed.) (1970) *New Horizons in Linguistics*, Harmondsworth, Penguin.

McHoul, A.W. (1986a) 'The getting of sexuality: Foucault, Garfinkel and the analysis of sexual discourse', *Theory, Culture and Society*, 13 (2), 65–79.

McHoul, A.W. (1986b) 'Why there are no guarantees for interrogators', *Journal of Pragmatics*, 11, 455–71.

McHoul, A.W. and Luke, A. (eds) (1989) *Journal of Pragmatics* (Special issue on Discourse Analysis in Australia).

Malinowski, B. (1923) 'The problem of meaning in primitive languages', in E.K. Ogden and I.A. Richards (eds) *The Meaning of Meaning*, London, Routledge & Kegan Paul.

Marcuse, H. (1964) *One-Dimensional Man*, London, Routledge & Kegan Paul.

Marcuse, H. (1968) *Negations*, Harmondsworth, Penguin; Boston, Beacon.

Martin, J.R. (1985/88) *Factual Writing: Exploring and Challenging Social Reality*, Geelong, Deakin University Press; Oxford, Oxford University Press.

Martin, J.R. (1986) 'Grammaticalising ecology: the politics of baby seals and kangaroos', in T. Threadgold, E. Grosz, M.A.K. Halliday and G.R. Kress (eds) *Semiotics – Ideology – Language*, Sydney Association for Studies in Society and Culture, Sydney University, 225–68.

Martin, J.R. and Rothery, J. (1981) *Writing Report No 1*, Linguistics Department, University of Sydney.

Marx, K. (1970) *Capital*, vol. I, London, Lawrence & Wishart.

Marx, K. and Engels, F. (1970, 1848) *Manifesto of the Communist Party*, Moscow, Progress Publishers.

Melrose, S. and Melrose, R. (1988) 'Drama, "style", stage', in D. Birch and M. O'Toole (eds) *Functions of Style*, London, Frances Pinter.

Mey, J. (1985) *Whose Language, A Study in Linguistic Pragmatics*, Amsterdam, John Benjamins.

Milton, J. (1955) *Areopagitica and Other Prose Works*, London, Dent.

Muecke, S. (1989) 'Body, inscription, epistemology: knowing Aboriginal texts', in S. Muecke, P. Roe and K. Benterrack, *Reading the Country*, Freemantle, Freemantle Arts Centre Press.

Osborne, J. (1958) *Look Back in Anger*, London, Faber.

O'Toole, M. (1985) 'Discerning criticism', in P. Chilton (ed.) *Language and the Nuclear Arms Debate*, London, Frances Pinter.

Passmore, J. (1961) *Philosophical Reasoning*, London, Duckworth.

Pecheux, M. (1982) *Language, Semantics, and Ideology*, trans. H. Nagpal, London, Macmillan.

Perlmutter, D.M. and Postal, P. (1977) 'Toward a universal characterization of passivization', in K. Whistler *et al.* (eds) (1977) *Proceedings of the 3rd Annual Meeting of the Berkeley Linguistics Society*, Berkeley, University of California Press, 394–417.

Piaget, J. (1932) *The Moral Judgment of the Child*, trans. M. Gabain, London, Routledge & Kegan Paul.

Pike, K.L. (1967) *Language in Relation to a Unified Theory of Human Behaviour*, The Hague, Mouton.

Poynton, C. (1985) *Language and Gender: Making the Difference*, Geelong/Oxford, Deakin University Press/Oxford University Press.

Pride, J. and Holmes, J. (eds) (1972) *Sociolinguistics*, Harmondsworth, Allen Lane.

Reid, I. (1986) 'The social semiotic of narrative exchange', in T. Threadgold, E. Grosz, M.A.K. Halliday and G.R. Kress (eds) *Semiotics – Ideology – Language*, Sydney Association for Studies in Society and Culture, Sydney University.

Reid, I. (ed.) (1988) *The Place of Genre in Learning: Current Debates*, Typereader Publications no. 1, Geelong Press, Deakin University.

Richardson, K. (1987) 'Critical linguistics and textual diagnosis', *Text*, 7 (2), 145–63.

Rosch, E. (1975) 'Human categorization', in N. Warren (ed.) *Advances in Cross-Cultural Psychology*, vol. 1, London, Academic Press.

Rosen, H. (ed.) (1974) *Language and Class Workshop*, 2. Harold Rosen, Language and Class Workshop, 41A Muswell Avenue, London N10 2EH.

Ross, J.R. (1969) 'Auxiliaries as main verbs', in W. Todd (ed.) *Studies in Philosophical Linguistics*, series 1, Evanston, Ill., Great Expectations.

Ross, J.R. (1970) 'On declarative sentences', in R. Jacobs and P. Rosenbaum (eds) *Readings in English Transformational Grammar*, Waltham, Mass., Blaisdell.

Sacks, H. (1972) 'On the analyzability of stories by children', in J.J. Gumperz and D. Hymes (eds) *Directions in Sociolinguistics*, New York and London, Holt, Rinehart & Winston.

Sacks, H. (1974) 'An analysis of a joke's telling in conversation', in R. Bauman and J. Sherzer (eds) *Explorations in the Ethnography of Speaking*, London, Cambridge University Press.

Said, E. (1983) *The World, the Text and the Book*, Cambridge, Mass., Harvard University Press.

Sapir, E. (1921) *Language: An Introduction to the Study of Speech*, New York, Harcourt, Brace & World.

Saussure, F. de (1966) *Course in General Linguistics*, New York, McGraw-Hill.

Schutz, A. (1970–3) *Selected Papers*, The Hague, Nijhoff.

Searle, J.R. (1969) *Speech Acts*, London, Cambridge University Press.

Searle, J.R. (1972) 'What is a speech act?' in P.P. Giglioli (ed.) *Language and Social Context*, Harmondsworth, Penguin.

Seidel, G. (ed.) (1988) *The Nature of the Right. A Feminist Analysis of Order Patterns*, Amsterdam, John Benjamins.

Seiler, H. (1971) 'Abstract structures for moods in Greek', *Language*, 47, 79–89.

Smith, C. (1961) 'A class of complex modifiers in English', *Language*, 37, 342–8.

Southgate, V. (n.d.) *The Enormous Turnip*, Loughborough, Wills & Hepworth.

Steele, R. and Threadgold, T. (eds) (1988) *Language Topics: Essays in Honour of Michael Halliday*, 2 vols, Amsterdam, John Benjamins.

Steinberg, D.D. and Jakobovitz, L.A. (eds) (1971) *Semantics*, London, Cambridge University Press.

Thibault, P. (1986a) 'Metaphor and political oratory in Ronald Reagan's acceptance speech', in R.M. Bollettieri (ed.) *US Presidential Election 1984: An Interdisciplinary Approach to the Analysis of Political Discourse*, Bologna, Pitagora Editrice, 149–68.

Thibault, P. (1986b) 'Text, discourse and context: a social semiotic perspective', *Toronto Semiotic Circle Monographs*, 3.

Thibault, P. (1989a) 'Genres, codes and pedagogy: towards a critical social semiotic account', *Southern Review*, 21 (3), 243–64.

Thibault, P. (1989b) 'Semantic variation, social heteroglossia, intertextuality: thematic and axiological meaning in spoken discourse', *Critical Studies*, 1 (2), 181–209.

Thompson, J.B. (1984) *Studies in the Theory of Ideology*, Cambridge, Polity Press.

Thompson, J.B. (1990) *Ideology and Modern Culture*, Cambridge, Polity Press.

Thorne, B. and Henley, N. (eds) (1975) *Language and Sex: Difference and Dominance*, Rowley, Mass., Newbury House.

Thorne, J.P. (1965) 'Stylistics and generative grammars', *Journal of Linguistics*, 1, 49–59.

Threadgold, T. (1986) 'Subjectivity, ideology and the feminine in John Donne's poetry', in T. Threadgold, E. Grosz, M.A.K. Halliday and G.R. Kress (eds) *Semiotics – Ideology – Language*, Sydney Association for Studies in Society and Culture, Sydney University.

Threadgold, T. (1987a) 'Rossi-Landi's higher dialectical level: alienation, relativity and ideology', *Il Protagora*, anno xxviii, Gennaio-Dicembre, IV Serie, per Ferruccio Rossi-Landi a cura di Susan Petrilli, 81–98.

Threadgold, T. (1987b) 'The semiotics of Halliday, Voloshinov and Eco', *American Journal of Semiotics*, 4 (3), 107–42.

Threadgold, T. (1988a) 'Changing the subject', in R. Steele and T. Threadgold (eds) *Language Topics: Essays in Honour of Michael Halliday*, 2 vols, Amsterdam, John Benjamins.

Threadgold, T. (1988b) 'Language and gender', *Australian Journal of Feminist Studies*, 3, 41–70.

Threadgold, T. (1988c) 'Review of Ian Reid, *The Place of Genre in Learning: Current Debates*', review article, *Southern Review*, 21, 3.

Threadgold, T. (1988d) 'Semiotics in Australia', in J. Umiker-Sebeok and T.A. Sebeok (eds) *The Semiotic Web: A Yearbook of Semiotics*, Bloomington, Indiana University Press, 231–72.

Threadgold, T. (1988e) 'Stories of race and gender: an unbounded discourse', in D. Birch and M. O'Toole (eds) *Functions of Style*, London, Frances Pinter.

Threadgold, T. (1989) 'Talking about genre: ideologies and incompatible discourses', *Journal of Cultural Studies*, 3 (3), 208–29.

Threadgold, T. and Cranny-Francis, A. (eds) (1989) *Feminine/Masculine and Representation*, Sydney, Allen & Unwin.

Threadgold, T., Grosz, E., Halliday, M.A.K. and Kress, G.R. (eds) (1986) *Semiotics – Ideology – Language*, Sydney Association for Studies in Society and Culture, Sydney University.

Trew, T. (1978) 'Theory at work', *UEA Papers in Linguistics*, 6, 39–60.

Trudgill, P. (1976) *Sociolinguistics*, Harmondsworth, Penguin.

v. Dijk, T. (ed.) (1985) *Handbook of Discourse Study. Vols 1–4*, London/New York, Academic Press.

v. Dijk, T. (1987a) *News Analysis. Case Studies in National and International News in the Press: Lebanon, Ethnic Minorities, Refugees and Squatters*, Hillsdale, NJ, Lawrence Erlbaum.

v. Dijk, T. (1987b) *Communicating Racism. Ethnic Prejudice in Thought and Talk*, Amsterdam, John Benjamins.

v. Dijk, T. (1988) *News as Discourse*, Hillsdale, NJ, Lawrence Erlbaum.

v. Dijk, T. (1991) *Racism and the Press*, London, Routledge.

v. Dijk, T. and Kintsch, W. (1983) *Strategies of Discourse Comprehension*, London/New York, Academic Press.

van Leeuwen, T. (1983) 'Levels of formality in the television interview', *Australian Journal of Screen Theory*, 13 (14), 59–69.

van Leeuwen, T. (1984) 'Impartial speech: observations on the intonation of radio newsreaders', *Australian Journal of Cultural Studies*, 2 (1), 84–98.

van Leeuwen, T. (1985a) 'Persuasion speech; the intonation of the live radio commercial', *Australian Journal of Cultural Studies*, 7, 25–35.

van Leeuwen, T. (1985b) 'Rhythmic structures of the film text', in T. van Dijk (ed.) *Discourse and Communication: New Approaches to the Analysis of Mass Media, Discourse and Communication*, Berlin, Walter de Gruyter.

van Leeuwen, T. (1986) 'The producer, the consumer and the state: analysis of a television news item', in T. Threadgold, E. Grosz, M.A.K. Halliday and G.R. Kress (eds) *Semiotics – Ideology – Language*, Sydney Association for Studies in Society and Culture, Sydney University.

van Leeuwen, T. (1987a) 'Generic strategies in press journalism', *Australian Review of Applied Linguistics*, 10 (2), 199–220.

van Leeuwen, T. (1987b) 'Semiotics of easy listening music: changed times, changed tunes', Sydney Association for Studies in Society and Culture, Sydney University.

Voloshinov, V.I. (1973) *Marxism and the Philosophy of Language*, New York, Seminar Press.

Warren, N. (ed.) (1975) *Advances in Cross-Cultural Psychology*, vol. 1, London, Academic Press.

Whistler, K. *et al.* (eds) (1977) *Proceedings of the 3rd Annual Meeting of the Berkeley Linguistics Society*, Berkeley, University of California Press.

Whorf, B.L. (1956), see Carroll, J.B. (ed.) (1956) *Language, Thought and Reality. Selected Writings of Benjamin Lee Whorf*, New York, Wiley.

Wodak, R., Nowak, P., Pelikan, J., Gruber, H., DeCillia, R. and Mitten, R. (1990) *Wir sind unschuldige Tater. Studien zum antisemitischen diskurs im Nachkriegsösterreich*, Frankfurt/Main, Suhrkamp.

Wootton, A. (1975) *Dilemmas of Discourse*, London, Allen & Unwin.

INDEX

Praise for *Inside the Minds*

"Unlike any other publisher – actual authors that are on the front-lines of what is happening in industry." – Paul A. Sellers, Executive Director, National Sales, Fleet and Remarketing, Hyundai Motor America

"What C-Level executives read to keep their edge and make pivotal business decisions. Timeless classics for indispensable knowledge." – Richard Costello, Manager-Corporate Marketing Communication, General Electric

"Want to know what the real leaders are thinking about now? It's in here." – Carl Ledbetter, SVP & CTO, Novell Inc.

"Aspatore has tapped into a gold mine of knowledge and expertise ignored by other publishing houses." – Jack Barsky, Managing Director, Information Technology & Chief Information Officer, ConEdison *Solutions*

"Priceless wisdom from experts at applying technology in support of business objectives." – Frank Campagnoni, CTO, GE Global Exchange Services

"Aspatore publishes the answers to every business person's questions." – Al Cotton, Director, Nypro Corporate Image, Nypro Inc

"Everything good books should be - honest, informative, inspiring, and incredibly well-written." – Patti D. Hill, President, BlabberMouth PR

"Answers questions that others don't even begin to ask." – Bart Stuck, Managing Director, Signal Lake LLC

"Unique insights into the way the experts think and the lessons they've learned from experience." – MT Rainey, Co-CEO, Young & Rubicam/Rainey Kelly Campbell Roalfe

"Must have information for business executives." – Alex Wilmerding, Principal, Boston Capital Ventures

"Reading about real-world strategies from real working people beats the typical business book hands down." – Andrew Ceccon, Chief Marketing Officer, OnlineBenefits Inc.

"Books of this publisher are syntheses of actual experiences of real-life, hands-on, front-line leaders--no academic or theoretical nonsense here. Comprehensive, tightly organized, yet nonetheless motivational!" – Lac V. Tran, Sr. Vice President, CIO and Associate Dean Rush University Medical Center

"Aspatore is unlike other publishers…books feature cutting-edge information provided by top executives working on the front-line of an industry." – Debra Reisenthel, President and CEO, Novasys Medical Inc

www.Aspatore.com

Aspatore Books, a Thomson Business, is the largest and most exclusive publisher of C-level executives (CEO, CFO, CTO, CMO, partner) from the world's most respected companies and law firms. Aspatore annually publishes a select group of C-level executives from the Global 1,000, top 250 law firms (partners and chairs), and other leading companies of all sizes. C-Level Business Intelligence™, as conceptualized and developed by Aspatore Books, provides professionals of all levels with proven business intelligence from industry insiders—direct and unfiltered insight from those who know it best— as opposed to third-party accounts offered by unknown authors and analysts. Aspatore Books is committed to publishing an innovative line of business and legal books, those which lay forth principles and offer insights that, when employed, can have a direct financial impact on the reader's business objectives, whatever they may be. In essence, Aspatore publishes critical tools—need-to-read as opposed to nice-to-read books—for all business professionals.

Inside the Minds

The critically acclaimed *Inside the Minds* series provides readers of all levels with proven business intelligence from C-level executives (CEO, CFO, CTO, CMO, partner) from the world's most respected companies. Each chapter is comparable to a white paper or essay and is a future-oriented look at where an industry/profession/topic is heading and the most important issues for future success. Each author has been carefully chosen through an exhaustive selection process by the *Inside the Minds* editorial board to write a chapter for this book. *Inside the Minds* was conceived in order to give readers actual insights into the leading minds of business executives worldwide. Because so few books or other publications are actually written by executives in industry, *Inside the Minds* presents an unprecedented look at various industries and professions never before available.

Utilizing New Media in Advertising

Industry Leaders on Integrating the Right Media Mix, Capitalizing on New Techniques, and Enhancing Brand Relation and Value

ASPATORE
BOOKS

Mat #40711770

CONTENTS

Advertisers Deliver a Message, But Customers Seek an Experience!

Jay Lenstrom

Chief Executive Officer

Radiate Group

Executing a Leadership Plan for Your Company

The leadership plan for our company centers around relevance. In our business, we must be relevant to employees, and employees/agencies must be relevant to corporations. In turn, the corporations must be relevant to customers.

We stay current by observing and listening to consumers at more than 2,000 global events each week. No publications, conferences, or studies can replace the awesome power of seeing what people across the world are influenced by as they work, learn, shop, and play.

These daily interactions, and the insights that we glean from them, allow our account teams and creatives to develop a unique vision when crafting new campaigns or tweaking existing ones.

This differentiates us from other companies in this space because we do not start out with predetermined answers, as advertising agencies or public relations firms do. Our solutions are customized and are derived from the intersection of brand insights and consumer actions.

To succeed in this loosely defined marketing space of "non-traditional media," companies must be willing to challenge the past communication methods used by marketers and find an advocate on the client side that is willing to make a bold difference.

It is not enough to just say that you are using non-traditional media; you must embrace it and continually search out new ways to leverage it for your particular brand or business needs. It is often too easy to become complacent with a thirty-second spot or a print ad. As consumers and marketers, we're all used to that. But it takes a determined and strategic stance to embrace new media to drive business objectives.

It should be fairly obvious that brands and marketers must use new media and their corresponding channels to reach increasingly fragmented and uninterested consumers. After all, they are the ones who are driving the new media space—whether it's virtual worlds, widgets, gaming, mobile technology, or digital content—and we as marketers do ourselves a great disservice by ignoring or diminishing the importance of these channels and new media habits.

Ensuring Your Company Generates Growing Revenues and Profits

To ensure that our company generates growing revenues and profits, we require focused direction and accountability from employees. We take market share away from competing agencies through in-depth insight generation and flawless execution. We manage 2,000 events a week, which requires a tremendous execution system and provides unparalleled access to gauging consumer behavior.

As CEO of a firm with multiple global divisions/units, the strategy of collaboration (teamwork) is unique to our industry and provides a competitive advantage. As our clients seek "breakthrough big ideas," it is important to have a process that will deliver on that objective. We believe that the development of great ideas is based on tremendous insight to consumers and brands. Most firms would list the same! However we then have three extra steps to proceed with:

- *Step 1*: Realize an individual's idea (CEO included) is not always the best.
- *Step 2*: Convince the other team members that their idea may not be best.
- *Step 3*: Encourage a uniquely diversified team solution.

(This process is clearly defined by Frans Johansson in his book, *The Medici Effect*.)

The fact that we are a global company allows us plenty of unique perspectives and insights. The international heterogeneity also gets a number of diverse viewpoints, behavior patterns, and local nuance included into the brainstorming. This gives us a much more robust and unique way of coming up with ideas, and the diversity that our international footprint gives us makes the ideas better, as opposed to a relatively homogenous approach that many agencies naturally have.

Big and breakthrough ideas are born out of differences, not similarities, especially when it comes to uses of new media. For instance, there are more cell phone users in India than there are Internet users. Clearly, mobile marketing campaigns are therefore more relevant and resonant there. There are more virtual world denizens in China than anywhere else in the world, making social networking and online gaming and commerce a key new media platform for consumer engagement. So gleaning insights from that country and incorporating them into our thinking elsewhere around the world gives us an edge for breakthrough ideation.

The Importance of Client Service and Feedback

I was a client for fifteen years, and I do *not* believe in the saying that is so often over-utilized: "The client is always right."

We respectfully challenge our clients with our insights and strategic thinking, and wish to be respected like in-house employees. Only through dynamic give-and-take can we develop a sharing relationship that strengthens our team.

We understand the importance of marketing feedback, which we are able to assess 24/7 because of the technology in use today by employees. We are fortunate to have cutting-edge technology clients such as SAP, Intel, Microsoft, and Samsung, so our global workforce is connected with ease to consumers and each other. We are able to act immediately to address two areas: crisis reaction and anticipated obsolescence.

Crisis Reaction

Our experience and large client base allows us to develop contingency plans for economic situations, inclement weather, natural disasters, company shutdowns, boycotts/protests, and a myriad of other issues that impact our space.

Anticipated Obsolescence

We know that if we don't reinvent our marketing programs on a quarterly basis, we will be imitated and lose our competitive edge. As one of the industry leaders, we and our work are often replicated in the marketplace by our competitors. (Imitation is indeed the sincerest form of flattery.) However, they lack the experience and scale to achieve the same results. Therefore, their actions create significant clutter in the marketplace.

Importantly, new technology, like handheld applications, bar code scanners, tablet PCs, digital audience counters, online and mobile tracking metrics, all allow us to gather and process information about a campaign in real time. We are therefore able to gauge the successes and shortcomings of a particular campaign incredibly quickly, and pass that information along to our clients. This is a drastic departure from creating a spot, buying the media for it, and waiting for the sales blip to appear weeks or months after the campaign has been aired. Just as processing speeds have skyrocketed, so has the speed at which we are able to assess and report elements of a campaign for our clients.

And although the technology has leapfrogged past agency practices, we still have to keep an eye on the basics for client services. In this regard, it is fairly simple to see how we are faring with our clients.

Forms of New Media Used over the Past Twelve Months

We are very open to all forms of new media. If it has been invented, we will analyze its relevance and applicability to our customer's brand planning and activation programs. Nothing is taboo. In this day and age of a disengaged and discombobulated consumer, we have to be media-agnostic. We are channel-agnostic as well, because of the new consumer demands and media habits—particularly the younger psychographics. Overall, new media address incredibly well the consumer need for compelling content, easy choice, and connected relevance from the marketers trying to engage them.

Consequently, we work with a number of forms. Obviously, the Internet is a heavy favorite. In this sphere, we find that viral video content is a great way to eschew the TV spots altogether. Why buy primetime when a branded video shot by a college student gets three million plays two days after being posted?

Video games—even simple arcade games—provide deep brand engagement if done in the proper way. Integrating brands and products contextually into video games will be the next big thing in advertising. One only has to look at the numbers behind gaming to see the enormous potential. Virtual worlds, such as Second Life, Neopets, and Sims Online, are also becoming a fertile ground for marketing messages, but most brands do not know how to live in these worlds and therefore lose their authenticity in the eyes of the virtual world denizens. It is a fine line to walk.

For instance, here are some examples to give scope to the opportunities that lie in wait for marketers willing to navigate the rocky shores:

1. World of Warcraft, a popular massive multi-player online role-playing game (MMORPG), surpassed 9 million worldwide subscribers in July 2007, an unprecedented subscriber base for a video game. (Thirty days of game play costs about $22.) More importantly, the virtual currency used in the game, Wow Gold, is regularly purchased with real dollar, yen, lira, and sterling on hundreds of broker sites across the globe. Some reports estimate that a virtual economy like Wow Gold rivals those mid-sized countries.

2. There are about 23 million "Residents" of Second Life, the virtual world developed by Linden Labs. This virtual world is exactly as the title purports: it is a virtual life for millions of people who assemble, trade, converse, eat, drink, work, and party in a virtual world—their so-called second life. The world's currency, the Linden Dollar, trades at about 266 to U.S. $1 on an open market, and is used to buy and sell services in the virtual world. A number of marketing agencies already exist in Second Life, as well as hundreds of brands and their shops. Each one of the 23 million Residents pays $14.95 per month to live somewhere else.

3. The launch of Halo 3—a Microsoft X-Box 360 game that uses live networking across the globe to play collaboratively—rewrote the rules of entertainment when it recorded an estimated $170 million in sales in the first twenty-four hours of its launch in the United States, beating previous records set by blockbuster movie releases like *Spiderman 3* and *Titanic* and books like *Harry Potter*. Microsoft has created a virtual world out of a video game, and it has become the most successful piece of entertainment of all time. And it's only the third version.

However, as a reminder, these shores are indeed rocky. Many marketers still do not understand how to enter new media spaces like virtual worlds or gaming. It's a new age, and new thinking must accompany it. First and foremost, however, is a need to be insightful and authentic.

Insights drive authenticity. Many brands entered the virtual world with the bravura of success in the real world and failed miserably. Some brands that entered Second Life found a somewhat skeptical audience. Brands that carried authenticity—or those that were already entrenched in the cultural currency of virtual world denizens and players—were embraced. American Apparel opened a virtual store to clothe the virtual avatars in Second Life. Anyone who bought clothes in the virtual store was able to receive discounts on clothes bought in the real world. Wells Fargo's virtual space in Second Life was called Stagecoach Island, where teens can party, mingle, and go windsurfing after accessing a Wells Fargo cash machine and taking a financial literacy test. Teaching teenagers about fiscal responsibility while giving them a thrill—only a virtual world can accomplish that. The key to any good branding, and any good marketing campaign, is in the insight that springboards it.

Unique insight and the positive word-of-mouth that accompanies it are the formula for authenticity. If you don't deliver, you won't survive. Many brands jumped on the bandwagon and opened virtual stores and showrooms in Second Life. Those brands were quickly dismissed and disparaged by Second Life residents because they were seen as interlopers who did nothing to ingratiate themselves in the community. They were seen as inauthentic to the Second Life experience. Moreover, residents in virtual worlds don't want a recreation of the real one. Why would they want to have the same experiences with brands in a world where they are trying to escape them?

Blogs and podcasts have also been highly effective in reaching micro-segments and niche audiences through authentic and credible voices to which people listen. It is said that a new blog is started every six seconds. This is an incredible development for both marketers and consumers. Blogs are not about writing. Blogs are about letting individual voices be heard by the masses and the ability to respond to those voices. Again, authenticity becomes paramount in this space. As has been evident in the debacles of major brands like McDonald's and Wal-Mart, inauthentic blogs are quickly discovered, debated, and disparaged by millions of consumers.

Of course, the mobile phone is a revolutionary device for us in the communication industries. From simple SMS (short message service) text messaging to video downloads, the cell phone is a massive opportunity to connect and engage brands with consumers. We have produced ring tones, cell phone games, videos, and mobile art. We have used the cell phone for text-to-screen campaigns at major concerts and club venues. We are working with GPS and navigational applications, as well.

For instance, imagine visiting New York City and walking up to the Guggenheim Museum from Central Park. There is a sticker or stencil or piece of out-of-home (OOH) advertising outside of the museum. Printed on the piece is a short code (SMS code) that you can dial in and receive a message. This code is specific to this particular location, as its coordinates match its GPS position. When accessed, the code releases a message associated with that location. In this case: "The Rothko Exhibit at the Guggenheim Museum is absolutely not to be missed." You go in, and find the show to be exhilarating. You punch in that code again on your cell phone and text in: "Fantastic. Worth every penny." The next time someone comes across that sticker or piece of OOH and accesses it through SMS, they will be able to read the original message and the one you left. With each experience, the dialogue builds. And pinpointing that dialogue to a particular place in the world is an exciting way to contextualize it and make it that much more relevant.

Consumers will always be enthralled by treasure hunts and global pursuits. GPS technology can be incorporated into marketing campaigns around that fascination and used to add to the experience. In 2007 Jeep was able to capitalize on this technology for a sweeps contest.

Paradoxically, new media only get newer. While most marketers are struggling to adopt and advance, the media they are appropriating are ever-changing. It is no secret that online advertising has surpassed radio and is set to cause some upheaval and transitional scurrying by the traditional shops. Some of the bigger ad deals and mergers of late have been centered on new media shops and online agencies. Still, the underlying notion of the new media landscape is in direct contrast to time-tested ad industry establishments. Consumer control is paramount in the new economy. Relevance and connectivity are gauges of brand-centricity.

Every marketing medium—including advertising—is a point of content. It is all content. And our company manages experiences every day that create new content! The objective for the content is the only parameter that changes, however sublime the differences may be. The same is applied to new marketing. It is a new medium to deliver compelling and contextual content. Importantly, that delivery mechanism isn't a derivation of a thirty-second spot. It should be an experience tailored to the real-time and immediate experience of the new media consumer. That experience is based on new, behavior-driving consumer prerogatives like content, choice, control, and context. It should be powerful enough that a customer tells another and another and another.

It takes a lot of practice to master the new media landscape. Clients must have long-term faith in the medium, which for the most part many already do, and confidence in the creative that is driving it.

The Impact of New Media on Advertising

We are in the midst of a major seismic shift in the communication industry, particularly with respect to marketing. We are progressing from an impression-based industry to one that is based on engagement with the consumer. In fact, even the term consumer is probably outdated.

There is a term that's been bandied around for a few years. The term is "prosumer." And although it may seem to be an ad-speak twist on the conventional term "consumer," we think the accepted definitions for the term can be seen as manifestations of never-been-seen-before consumer behavior. The definition of a "prosumer" is as follows:

1. A consumer who is an amateur in a particular field, but who is knowledgeable enough to require equipment that has some professional features ("professional" + "consumer")
2. A person who helps design or customize the products they purchase ("producer" + "consumer")

15

3. A person who creates goods for their own use and also possibly to sell ("producing" + "consumer")
4. A person who takes steps to correct difficulties with consumer companies or markets and to anticipate future problems ("proactive" + "consumer")

Let's take the first definition: this is all about that kid with two turntables and a microphone DJ-ing to his friends in the basement, who's using the same technical equipment as the top London DJ at the Ministry of Sound.

The second definition is applied to the so-called "mod" movement of online gaming. Many times, programmers and gaming experts are able to access the code for a published game and modify the gameplay. In many instances, the "mod" game is better than the original published game and often available for free download on gamer networks, wikis, and boards.

The third definition is perfectly embodied in the so-called sneaker heads, consumers who customize mainstream sneaker brands like Nike Air Force Ones and turn them into works of art. Nike recognized this trendy market several years ago and created Nike iD, an online shop and service to personalize their sneakers. Many sneaker designers create highly sought-after niche sneaker lines around brands like Nike (the perennial favorite), Puma, or Adidas. These are extremely pricey shoes and are treated with esteemed cultural currency by those in-the-know. One only has to watch an episode of HBO's *Entourage* to appreciate the cultural importance that sneakers, especially customized and sub-branded sneakers, have on the youth in both cities and suburbs.

And the fourth definition is probably the bitterest pill to swallow for marketers and brand managers who are oblivious to the fundamental shifts in consumer behavior: consumers are upset, and they are not going to take it anymore. More importantly, they have tools to deal massive body blows—if not death strokes—to any brand that gets in their way.

We are no longer pursuing eyeballs. We are in the business of connecting brands with people. And new media are at the heart of the imperative to engage with the consumer and create a dialogue instead of blasting out one-way messaging through traditional media channels.

Engagement through new media is integral in our industry because we are in the business of creating brand love. Defining brand love is a rather complex process. A better way to begin to explore the meanings of "brand love" is to ask what brands should do to generate love from their consumers. In this regard, here is a prescribed way to approach marketing campaigns:

1. Provide a clear and meaningful benefit—visceral, emotional, cerebral, and physical—in every marketing campaign directed to the target consumer. If you are not delivering a benefit to the consumer, you are only adding to the white noise of ad clutter, and your message will not only be ignored, it may also be desecrated.
2. Never underestimate the power of interpersonal communication. Mass marketing is good, but personal marketing is better. Brand love does not come from commercials. It comes from conversations.
3. Be authentic. Pine and Gilmore just wrote an entire book called *Authenticity*. In their estimation, only authentic brands that stand for something and deliver on it will exist in the near future.
4. Engage in the long haul. Engagement means years, not quarters.
5. Cuddle those who love your brand. Reward them *and* integrate them. Return the love, and embrace them back into the organization. Hire the true believers. There is a growing understanding that with the advent of consumer-generated media (CGM), marketers are more willing to listen and take direction from their consumers. This acceptance and appropriation by brands to listen to their loyalists and brand ambassadors can reawaken and reinvigorate a brand and its agency partners. New media make this happen. For instance, brand-centric videos can be recorded on cell phones and posted online immediately, allowing for both consumers and brand curators to simultaneously accept or reject the brand relevance and repercussion almost immediately. The power that brand loyalists have on the way that brand behaves is tangible. Loyalty rewards and special access are certainly effective ways to reach them and continue to delight, inspire, and influence them. But as marketers, we have to go beyond the conventional methods, like loyalty programs, to do so.
6. Conduct marketing campaigns only where and when the consumer wants you. It's more intuitive than scientific. We must use our head *and* our hearts. Consumer empathy is key. Ask yourself when crafting or

planning a campaign: would you want to be the audience? It's a gut check, but certainly an important barometer to the value of the brand experience we are trying to create, one individual person at a time.

7. Be innovative. There are only two ways to sell a product or service: market it well or innovate it.
8. Create entertaining experiences.
9. Stand for something and hold to it; again, the imperative for authenticity is paramount for any brand.
10. Make sure your employees are the first ones to demonstrate brand love. If you don't have the brand vanguard—the crack unit of brand loyalists and die-hards—on your brand team, you are in a very nebulous and disconcerting place. The apex brands, and challenger brands of the future, evoke a calling, a mantra, a kōan (a moment of spiritual insight or awakening) of understanding for the consumer. If that evocation isn't present within the core team, how can you possibly emanate it effectively to others?

As important as it is to engage consumers, it is equally important to engage the internal staff. From an experiential marketing vantage, this means creating compelling experiences for the internal teams to get pumped up, and staging contextual consumer immersions and events to get them informed and insight-driven. It is a long-term proposition and an integral part of a brand's emergence as a break-though entity that succeeds in a cutthroat marketplace.

Challenger brands like Axe or Scion have harnessed the internal insight-driven passion of their teams and agency partners to propel themselves into cult status brands, and established players like Apple, Jeep, and Nike continue to reinvent and reinvigorate themselves into perennial brand culthood.

All these imperatives for brand love rely on the compelling and contextual use of new media, such as the Internet and the cell phone. However, technology cannot replace the personal interaction. From an experiential marketing point of view, it cannot be used in the same framework as mass media. New media cannot mirror the top-down delivery of mass advertising. It must allow for personal interaction instead. Nothing can really replace the human interaction, and those marketers who think an

SMS blast will engage their customers are dangerously wrong in their assumptions.

The Response to the Use of New Media in Advertising

The reaction to new media is polarized: consumers embrace it, and traditional marketers reject it. From advertisers, there are two kinds of responses to the use of new media, and in a response one can discern what kind of company/firm this customer wants to be: does the firm exhibit half-hearted confusion or whole-hearted appropriation? The question is not about which industries will be transformed by the use of new media to enhance marketing/advertising experience, but only which will be first. Companies that do not recognize this change will perish. Those who see the necessity for change and embrace new media in advertising will be embraced in turn by the most empowered consumer base in the history of the world. The companies that are adopting the new media revolution are challenging the status quo and the long-held dominance of major brands and institutions.

Successful brands constantly seek out new opportunities to project themselves and their brand culturally, relevantly, and contextually outside of traditional messaging and traditional channels. For challenger brands, marketing campaigns are not judged by whether they are good ideas; they are judged by how far they push the idea into uncharted marketing territories.

Successful brands and the agencies that inspire them all relish the thrill of invention. They seek to create something new, rather than to piggy-back off something established. They yearn for the opportunity to delight their consumers at every touch-point, using innovating approaches and tactics to reach out to consumers in creative and compelling ways. We all rightly assume that the entire world is media, and the entire universe is the consumer base. The brands that will succeed in the future do not react; rather, they instigate. This forward thinking allows them to create their own culture and behavior, blaze their own unique trail toward their consumers, and lead the charge for breakthrough work. In all this, the use of new media is at the heart of the thinking.

Assessing When New Media Are Appropriate

I assess whether new media are appropriate for an advertising campaign by whether the client wants tangible sales results. In this day and with these tools available, it simply comes down to wanting clear results and success. The most compelling factors involved in assessing whether new media might be effective in an advertising campaign typically include the prospective audience and the brand's ability to be relevant to their lifestyle. Cost and type of campaign are outdated factors.

Under certain circumstances, new media should not be used in an advertising campaign, such as when the client demands a print campaign with no URL printed on the page. Otherwise, if you are not using new media to connect and engage with your consumer, you might as well retire to the bench, because you are not playing the right game.

The assessment of the success of new media in a campaign is simple. We measure sales impact and use that for our metric as success.

When persuading clients to use new media in their campaigns, I first show them the demonstrable results of more than five hundred clients. The problem for brand marketers today is simple. The basic value of mass media like television lies in its ability to deliver marketing messages through reach, frequency, exposure, and cost per thousand. It is a medium devoted to reaching as many eyeballs as possible at the least cost available. It is based on economies of scale. It is a perfect medium for a mass marketing consumer—except that the consumer no longer responds to mass marketing. Marketers can no longer effectively sell to a massive and anonymous crowd. They must now and forever sell to individuals instead. And the way to do so lies with the contextual and insightful implementation of new media, in concert with established media tactics, to reach the individual.

Jay Lenstrom has spent his entire business career in sports and entertainment marketing with some of the world's most experiential brands. His brand management, strategic insights, and negotiation team-building skills were developed while working at Miller Brewing Company for twelve years.

In 1991 Mr. Lenstrom joined GMR Marketing—an agency pioneer in music marketing. He joined a vibrant, tight-knit group of twenty-eight employees led by Gary M. Reynolds. As president, Mr. Lenstrom helped the company expand from a music agency to become the leading experiential marketing firm in the United States with expertise in sports, music, and lifestyle marketing, with a roster of more than eighty clients. As the marketing discipline expanded and continued to deliver results for national brands, GMR flourished.

In 1998, GMR was acquired by Omnicom, and consequently the agency enjoyed tremendous growth within the Omnicom network. In 2000, Mr. Reynolds and Mr. Lenstrom developed a unique business model that eventually became the Radiate Group.

Today with Mr. Lenstrom as chief executive officer, the Radiate Group has twenty-one agencies across the globe, 2,100 employees, and 400 clients that provide unique global solutions in experiential marketing.

Dedication: *To Max Lenderman.*

New Media—with Relevant Content—Offer Great Tools for Reaching Hispanics

Heberto Gutiérrez

Chief Executive Officer and Principal

INVENTIVA Inc.

Unique Selling Points: Differentiating Your Company in the Marketplace

My firm INVENTIVA Inc., was founded with a strong core vision, which, simply put, is to work with good clients, whom we define as those clients who are committed to multicultural marketing and who allow us to do great work.

As chief executive officer and principal of INVENTIVA, I am committed to remaining closely tied to the operation and product of our marketing firm. That is my motivation: the passion for working in close contact with our clients, our products, and our operation is the reason I got into this business in the first place.

In the business world, it is often challenging to stay true to the integrity and vision of your company, but I have found that it is absolutely essential to do so if you wish to achieve the type of company you envisioned. Often, the ability to stay true to the original vision is what sets a company apart from competitors and serves as the company's unique selling point. In my firm, senior management, I especially, remain closely involved with every client. We also provide customized services to meet each client's unique needs, from assessments to plans to implementation, including full-service advertising. "INVENTIVA" means "ingenious" in Spanish, and that is exactly how we try to approach client needs and assignments. Clients appreciate this, and I believe this approach is different from the one taken by many other firms in this space.

Ultimately, we believe that the quality of client service is as important as the quality of our marketing and creative output. Being personally involved with every client at least weekly keeps my finger on the pulse of everything that affects my clients' satisfaction with our firm and helps set us apart from competitors.

While we do not consciously try to take away market share from competing agencies, choosing instead to remain focused on the work so we can indulge our professional passion, dissatisfied companies tend to look actively for alternatives. Periodically, we get phone calls from some of these companies, and we see where that leads. Our way of qualifying potential clients is to determine not so much what their monthly billings will be, but whether they are indeed committed to multicultural marketing and whether they will allow us to do good work on their behalf.

I speak to many audiences around the country on the subject of multicultural marketing because that is my passion, and very often that generates a call or two from potential clients. In these ways, following my passion and remaining true to our company's vision provide the added value of generating greater market share.

Adding Financial Value to the Company: Generating Revenues and Profits

As long as we attract and keep good clients and focus on our firm's output, which is built on great thinking, outstanding creative, and excellent client service, the revenues and profitability will largely take care of themselves. Producing good results for our clients produces good results for INVENTIVA.

The most important thing I do that has a direct financial impact and adds value for the company is to communicate directly with our clients, either by phone or e-mail, at least once a week. I am committed to incorporating their feedback into our operations. Next, I am dedicated to taking care of my people. Employees who feel appreciated produce higher-quality, more consistent work. Finally, I drive the quality control process, which includes reviewing plans, research, creative, recommendations, and other activities. Nothing this firm produces goes to the client without my review. This is consistent with my leadership plan because it helps retain good clients who are committed to multicultural marketing and who allow us to do great work. It is in this way that I indulge my passion for the work. If I am excited and involved, my employees know it and respond in kind, and my clients recognize and appreciate it.

With respect to personally developed strategies as CEO for helping the company grow and achieve more profit, I am committed to:

1. Ensuring ongoing senior management involvement. Senior management must be personally invested in the business, and that involvement is what I love about the business.
2. Making sure that each client knows it is important to us. We don't just tell them that; we're also available to them when they need us, and we move quickly to do whatever is necessary. I love meeting a client's demands with amazing speed and quality, and then asking them if their old agency (which is always bigger) could move that quickly for them or be that innovative.
3. Producing great, on-target creative work and excellent service. I firmly believe that client service is as much a product of the firm as the marketing plans, advertising, and promotional materials we produce; being available whenever clients call, moving very quickly to address urgent needs, and helping them think through difficult situations are all very important to clients. Quality control extends to how we treat clients, in addition to the things we give them. I believe in treating our clients the way *I* would like to be treated. And I'm a very demanding guy.

While these strategies are clearly not rocket science, they are often overlooked. Unfortunately, high-quality service isn't as prevalent as it used to be in many industries, not just marketing and advertising. It seems some owners and CEOs focus primarily on the financials of their business and delegate day-to-day operations—including quality control—to others.

The ethnic composition of the U.S. population is changing, and ten, twenty, or thirty years down the road, this country will look significantly different. We made a conscious decision several years ago to focus on multicultural marketing, the fastest-growing segment of the U.S. market, to help companies understand, prepare for, and realize the potential opportunities these changes will offer.

Measuring the Success of the Company and Its Services

The most important measure of success is whether and to what degree we have been able to move the needle for the client in the marketplace. This simply answers the questions of whether our work did what it was supposed to do and whether we achieved or exceeded objectives. If we did, all the other measures take care of themselves.

Furthermore, listening to customer and market feedback is an excellent indicator of where we stand. Delivering feedback is a dynamic process. There is no substitute for talking to the target audience, and I make it my job to converse with various groups with great attention and understanding. I am then empowered to educate my clients on what their target audiences think and, more importantly, why they think that way.

Because I am in touch with every client at least weekly, I listen to them carefully and personally discuss their feedback with our staff. Nobody wants to hear the client say that it does not like something that we did, but personally I also hate to hear a client say that our service is "OK." "OK" is simply not OK with me. I very much want clients to say that what we did for them was excellent; if I do not hear that, we will redo it and make it excellent. This is the way we ensure client satisfaction and growth for our firm. Incorporating client feedback, as well as what's going on in the marketplace, is much easier when you do not have to go through layers of supervision and a large bureaucracy.

Targeting New Media to the Hispanic Market

As a label, the term "new media" that describes today's growing range of Internet-based interactive communication tools, such as interactive campaigns and social networking, cell phone texting, keyword marketing and pop-up and banner advertising, misses the mark. "New" media might more properly be called "participatory" media, because the important thing is not that these tools are new, but that they give users an unprecedented ability to participate in the communication or entertainment experience. Users can exercise more choices than ever in terms of what to look at and when, and their choices determine what they see subsequently. The key is that today's participatory media create a two-way connection instead of a one-way broadcast.

Hispanics represent one of the most attractive markets for the new participatory media because of four converging factors:

1. Hispanics are the largest and fastest-growing segment of the U.S. population.

2. Hispanics' access to the Internet is growing daily, and almost two-thirds of online Hispanics have broadband access from home.
3. Hispanics are much younger on average than non-Hispanics.
4. Hispanics pay more attention to Internet advertising and have a greater connection to Internet content than the general population, according to several research sources, which will be explored later in this chapter. (In addition to what we already know because we're Hispanics ourselves, we are voracious consumers of secondary research on Hispanic attitudes, perceptions, and behaviors that is conducted by a wide variety of organizations. We think it's important to get information from a variety of sources to avoid getting tunnel vision about the subject and target audience. We conduct both qualitative and quantitative primary research, but it's usually client- or product-specific.)

With all of its electronic opportunities, new media are becoming increasingly important to U.S. Hispanics and will only continue to do so as the population grows and prospers. Advertisers who ignore targeting new media to Hispanics—whether to gain competitive advantage or to protect against competitive loss—do so at their own peril.

Because of language, culture, and immigration experiences, Hispanics receive and process information through a different lens than the general market. If advertisers understand and appreciate this, and then construct their Hispanic campaigns properly, they will assure themselves of a robust and loyal customer base for years to come.

Size of the Hispanic Opportunity: Forming a Relationship with Young Consumers

Hispanics present an extremely attractive market opportunity, if for no other reason than size. The Hispanic population is growing much faster than Anglos or the general population. Every sixty seconds, the United States gains 2.5 new Hispanics, compared to just 0.5 new Anglos.

According to the U.S. Census Bureau, there were 44.3 million Hispanics in the United States in 2006, approximately 14.7 percent of a total population of 301 million. But while the total U.S. population grew 7 percent from 2000 to 2006, the nation's Anglo population grew less than 1 percent, from

195.5 million to 197.1 million. During the same period, Hispanics grew more than 24 percent, from 35.7 million to 44.3 million. In fact, the United States is now the second-largest Spanish-speaking country in the world after Mexico, and the number of U.S. Hispanics is now greater than the entire population of Canada. The U.S. Census Bureau projects that by 2050, 25 percent of the U.S. population will be Hispanic, and while Anglos will still be the largest group at that time, they will no longer be the majority of the population.

Hispanics today represent $863 billion of annual buying power. Furthermore, the Hispanic audience is a significantly younger group than most. Hispanics are the youngest demographic group in the United States; the median age for Hispanics is 27 compared to 39 for non-Hispanics[1]. The importance of this fact is that a much larger percentage of this audience was born and came of age during the "digital age" than with other demographic groups. Because of their exposure to computers beginning in their earliest school years, they are more "digital natives" than "digital immigrants." Like immigrants' children, who pick up a new language much faster than their parents, digital natives pick up the language of the Internet much faster and to a much greater degree and comfort level than digital immigrants who try to acquire these skills as adults.

Further, Hispanic households are larger than non-Hispanic households, with 3.7 members in Hispanic households compared to 2.6 members in non-Hispanic households[2].

Internet Access

This growth and these demographics have a great deal to do with new media. This is largely because more Hispanics than ever before, especially second- and third-generation, have greater levels of education, higher incomes, and more professional occupations. Education and English-language proficiency are the greatest predictors of Internet usage[3], and both are at all-time highs and constantly growing.

---

[1] Nielsen Media Research.
[2] Ibid.
[3] Latinos Online, Pew Hispanic Center, 2007.

Hispanics are also wired today to a much greater degree than many people realize, and they are rapidly acquiring broadband access. According to the Pew Hispanic Center[4], 67 percent of Hispanics between the ages of 18 and 29 use the Internet. For ages 30 to 41, 61 percent of Hispanics use the Internet. Other studies help round out the picture of Hispanic Internet usage:

- Nearly one of every two Hispanics ages 18 and up has Internet access.[5]
- Approximately one million new Hispanics go online each year, and that pace is expected to accelerate.[6]
- Seventy-nine percent of Hispanic homes have Internet access, and 61 percent of those have broadband at home.[7]
- Internet penetration among Hispanics is growing at eight times the rate of the general market.[8]

Perhaps because first-generation Hispanics did not have many information sources in their countries of origin, or perhaps because lower-income Hispanics over the years have not been the targets of direct mail and other product and service promotions, Hispanics today are "information-starved" compared to the general population. The sheer volume of product variations represented by SKUs (stock-keeping units—the barcodes on every product label) is much greater in the United States, and Hispanics want information to help them choose what is best for them. As consumers, they understand the value of making an informed decision. For example, look at the choices offered in just one product category: pain medications. There are tablets, caplets, gel caps, powder, regular-strength, extra-strength, timed-release, brand names and generics, etc. How are they different? Which is best? Multiply this by the number of products available, and you begin to see why Hispanics actively seek more information.

As a result, Hispanics pay more attention to the information and promotions directed to them. When they go online, they are more inclined than most consumers to click on banners and display ads and to read the

---

[4] Ibid.
[5] Simmons National Consumer Survey, 2005
[6] eMarketer, 2006
[7] Simmons Custom Research, 2006
[8] Simmons National Consumer Survey, 2005

content they subsequently receive. What further enhances the online experience for many Hispanics is the opportunity to access Spanish-language Web sites. Spanish-preferred Internet users lean toward getting information and conducting business over Spanish Web sites. Even fully bilingual Hispanics often feel more comfortable going online in Spanish. Especially for first-generation Hispanics, Spanish Web sites evoke positive connotations and a greater degree of personal comfort because the sites connect them to home, meaning their countries of origin.

Furthermore, online usage is tied with radio as the second-most consumed medium by Hispanics, surpassing print by 80 percent.[9] Information such as this is invaluable to advertisers trying to reach this audience via the most effective and prevalent media possible.

There is truly an emotional connection for Hispanics that occurs online. Online Hispanics agree with many statements regarding Spanish-language Web sites.[10] For example, 90 percent agree with the statement: "Spanish-language sites give me a connection to my culture," while 74 percent agree with the statement, "I feel more emotionally connected than with English-language sites." Finally, 79 percent of online Hispanics agree that "I can express myself better on Spanish-language Web sites."

In addition to this emotional connection, there is also an information connection that takes place. Of online Hispanic users, the following percentage agreed with these statements:

- Spanish-language sites are an important educational resource for the Hispanic community. (95 percent)
- They are a way to get news and information on my country of origin. (91 percent)
- They help me stay informed on Latino entertainment trends. (88 percent)
- I feel more comfortable getting health information from Spanish-language sites. (79 percent)
- I feel more comfortable getting financial information. (69 percent)

---

[9] Hispanic Internet Usage & Engagement Study, Simmons Custom Research, 2006
[10] Ibid.

Even more important to providers and users of new media, two-thirds of online Hispanics say they are more likely to click on ads on Spanish-language sites than on English-language sites (online Hispanics vs. non-Hispanics online). They are[11]:

- Twice as likely to feel Internet ads are easy and clear to understand.
- Five times more likely to click on Internet ads to get information.
- Seventy-seven percent more likely to find Internet ads informative.

The interactivity of new media and its 24/7 availability make new media a personal experience for Hispanic users, and sophisticated marketers are beginning to get the message.

"The objective is to make interactive the center of the marketing strategy so that consumers can be spoken to individually," said Julie Roehm, director of marketing communications at Chrysler Group and self-described "ROI fanatic."[12]

Best Practices: How to Do It Right

Instead of focusing on the latest technology being employed to attract Hispanic attention, it is more helpful to consider how you will treat that attention once you get it, since the technology will continue to evolve.

Today's new media are increasingly successful because interactivity creates such a personal connection between advertiser and viewer. There is a much greater sense the advertiser is talking *to me*. And the corollary thought—"because I matter"—makes this encounter extremely powerful to Hispanics.

Therefore, advertisers should consider eight steps for utilizing new media to create the interactive experience necessary to convert online Hispanic viewers into customers:[12]

---

[11] Ibid.
[12] AdAge.com, April 18, 2005

1. In-language communication

- Advertise in Spanish. This is the most effective way to communicate with Hispanics: it is 61 percent more effective than English ads at increasing awareness, 57 percent more effective in building message comprehension, and 4.5 times more persuasive than English advertising.[13]

- Write directly to the target audience. Textbook Spanish does not work any better than textbook English, and Hispanics are no more homogeneous than American Anglos. Most advertisers to Anglos would tailor a message differently for audiences in New York, Miami, Dallas, and Los Angeles. This is also true with Hispanics: they come from Mexico, the Caribbean and Central and South America, as well. Be aware of the differences.

- Adapt copy; do not translate it. Conveying the proper meaning is as important as using Spanish words. One of my clients is the American Quarter Horse Association, which uses the term "forking" a horse, meaning to climb into a saddle with a leg on each side of the horse. A professional translator they used before we began working with them translated the word "fork" as the eating utensil, so the meaning of the phrase became "jabbing the horse with a fork." To avoid confusion and potentially offending the audience, work with a team of Spanish speakers that adapts message content and checks each other's work.

- Plan for more space on your display ads, banners, and pop-ups, as well as pages on the Spanish version of your Web site because it takes about 25 percent more words to say the same thing in Spanish as in English. If you are trying to drive calls to your telemarketing center, be prepared to have reps spend more time with each Spanish-language call. Obviously, it is necessary to have Spanish-speaking call-takers. Time spent per

---

[13] Roslow Research Group, 2000
[14] Some of the ideas in this section were crystallized thanks to a presentation by Lee Vann, founder, Captura Group, at Direct Marketing Association's Directo Days Conference, April 2007

call is an important metric for telemarketers, but Hispanics act differently than Anglos when they call an 800 number. For example, when Anglos call, they tend to know which items they want, how many of each, and in what sizes and colors; furthermore, they have their credit cards ready. Hispanics, on the other hand, want more information so they feel confident that they are making a good decision before they place an order. There could easily be multiple family members on the call, each contributing questions and opinions.

- Unlike English, Spanish has the formal and informal voice. It is a sign of respect in the Hispanic culture to use the formal voice when you meet people, until you are invited to address them informally. For example, "It's nice to see you, Mr. Smith," is a formal address, while the response, "Please, call me 'John,'" is an invitation to use the informal voice. A way of showing this type of respect in a company's marketing efforts might be done by having the first two or three advertising or communications efforts address the Hispanic audience using the formal voice, and later switching to an informal voice after establishing a relationship of sorts.

- Also unlike English, Spanish has gender-specific words, and advertisers must choose their words carefully. A great example is Anheuser-Busch's discovery that their slogan for Budweiser —the "King of Beers"—does not work in Spanish-speaking countries because cerveza (beer) is a female word. If Anheuser-Busch insisted on a "royal metaphor" to promote Budweiser, it would of necessity become the "Queen of Beers," perhaps to the dismay of the beer's macho image.

2. *In-cultural relevance*

- Language communicates, but culture connects. Not all Hispanics prefer to read Spanish Web pages. Some Hispanics prefer to speak Spanish; some prefer to speak English; and some are equally comfortable with either language. Therefore, connecting with Hispanics goes "beyond español" to utilizing proper cultural references and "touch points." Spanish-language advertising connects especially well with older and first-generation immigrants, but in-cultural advertising connects with all Hispanics.

- Everybody knows that family is very important to Hispanics, but family is important to Anglos, too. It takes a deeper understanding of emotions and aspirations to explain why and how Hispanics are different. For example, while Anglos want to do better in life than their parents and grandparents, Hispanics also want to make a name for their families and themselves. And while Hispanics also want to be the first in their families to move ahead, they place greater emphasis on improving life for the whole family.

- Another difference is what each group looks for in the way of customer service. While Anglos prize speed and efficiency (high tech) in how they are served, Hispanics value highly personalized service (high touch) as a sign of respect.

4. Accessibility

- Make it easy for Spanish-preferred Hispanics. Give them a Spanish version of your Web site and provide them with a language option that allows them to switch easily between Spanish and English. This language "toggle switch" needs to be highly visible. The degree to which a Web site makes a Spanish version of the site accessible answers this question in their minds: "Am I important to you, or am I an after-thought?" As an advertiser, do not play hard-to-get; that is, do not make users hunt for information.

- Between 50 percent and 60 percent of "click here" links on Spanish pages take people to English ads, pages, or sites. This is true of hot links, banners, pop-up ads, and other tools. Advertisers need to go the extra step: "click here" links on Spanish pages need to be in Spanish and need to go to Spanish ads. If you are going to send them to an English site, let them know up front, so they will not feel betrayed.

4. Ease of use

- Be sure documents are in printer-friendly layouts and are easy to read with a comfortable font and point size.
- Be sure that computers and printers can "habla español"; that is, that they can read and print orders and communications sent to them by Spanish-speaking readers. I have seen this cause problems in terms of strange characters that ultimately required software upgrades. The entire IT system needs to be capable of reading and printing Spanish.
- An advertiser's most important forms should be available in both Spanish and English for viewing and printing. Our client, The American Quarter Horse Association, offers the necessary forms to complete registrations, transfers, membership applications, stallion breeding reports, DNA reports, and applications to compete in specific shows in both Spanish and English.

5. Make Spanish Web sites more educational and instructional

- Hispanics want more information and less promotion. One reason our efforts for our client Beneficial Finance were successful was that we told Hispanics, "When you are applying for credit, here is what we look at"; we then provided them with specific metrics, such as, "Have you paid your bills on time?" and other qualifiers.
- Tell them what they need to know clearly and succinctly. Err on the side of caution, and explain everything. When we worked for Household International, we had them say, "Here is what we mean when we talk about your 'credit score.'" Furthermore, avoid acronyms; do not assume your audience knows what you are talking about.
- Fully explain your product or service. Hispanics need to be educated before they agree to buy. Convey benefits based on a full understanding of the product or service.

6. *Consider whether the deal you offer in Spanish is as good as the one in English*

- The Spanish offer needs to be as good as the one offered in English because the Hispanic audience absolutely will compare. Spanish viewers will often get someone to compare the information for them if they cannot compare the two languages themselves. They are suspicious, based on experience. If they think the Spanish offer is inferior to the English offer, it demonstrates a lack of respect and hurts your credibility.

- When advertisers update English pages, they need to update their Spanish pages at the same time. They should never update English this week and Spanish next. If the Spanish site is not updated as frequently, it sends the message to them that "Anglos matter more to this company than I do."

- Do not assume all Hispanics are alike. Hispanics are not one homogeneous group. There are differences based on their level of acculturation (e.g., second-, third-, or fourth-generation), as well as their country of origin.

7. *Real-time assistance*

- Advertisers should consider offering real-time assistance whenever possible for maximum effectiveness. I love using Continental Airlines' Web site, which offers real-time assistance with a live person via chat to ensure customers get the assistance they need.

8. *Measurement*

- At its core, new media represent another form of direct marketing, and the mantra of direct marketing is "test, test, test." If something fails to elicit the response for which you were looking, adjust your efforts and try again, just as you would with direct mail.

- It is always important to calculate return on investment, and metrics for new media are getting better all the time. Always keep in mind there is a difference between process metrics, such as clicks, time spent on each page, etc., and results metrics, which include number of orders placed, items per order, revenue, margins, and other data. Process metrics are indicators of problems or opportunities, but results metrics are more useful in calculating ROI.

- Sometimes measurements have to be different for different audiences, such as length of time spent handling each call. For reasons explained earlier, Hispanics take longer than Anglos to make a purchase. New products and new information also take longer for viewers to analyze and respond to.

- When calculating ROI, never underestimate the value of exposure as an indicator of business down the road. This comes in a variety of ways, such as TV coverage at rodeos (or Mexicans' *charreadas*) or other events, news announcements, or banner ads in trade show Web sites.

- Also when calculating ROI, do not sell your efforts short by looking only at current-year revenues. There is a lifetime value of each customer that may be far more considerable.

Case Study: INVENTIVA's Work with American Quarter Horse Association

An excellent example of using new media to reach the Hispanic audience can be seen by the work we have done with our client, American Quarter Horse Association (AQHA). Our objectives were to identify ways to improve service to AQHA's existing Hispanic membership and grow AQHA's Hispanic membership in the United States, in Mexico, and throughout Latin America.

The specific situation we were facing with this client is that AQHA, the premier American quarter horse association in the world, wanted to do a better job of serving Hispanic quarter horse owners in the United States, Mexico, and Latin America; however, they did not know how or where to start. We defined the target audience to be U.S., Mexican, and Latin American Hispanic owners and breeders of American quarter horses, including recreational, work, racing, show, and *charro* (Mexican rodeo) horses. AQHA's target audience is spread throughout the Western Hemisphere, making it very difficult to reach out to them cost-effectively.

The client knew that many American quarter horse owners in Mexico and Latin America did not see the benefits of becoming members of AQHA, and therefore did not register their horses with AQHA. Further, improving the quality of service would improve AQHA's image among Hispanics, which would lead to increased membership and revenues.

In response, INVENTIVA developed clear strategies and a solid action plan to achieve the desired results. Our strategies were to use the Internet and new media methods to reach out to geographically dispersed Hispanics and to utilize the Internet and new media methods to make AQHA services more user-friendly to Hispanics.

The specific actions taken by INVENTIVA included:

- Conducting both internal and external audits of AQHA's operations, especially the ways they supported and interfaced with Hispanic members and prospective members. In the process, we conducted more than one hundred interviews with the target audience in several countries
- Preparing a gap analysis that identified many areas where Hispanics felt that they were of little value to AQHA, as well as where Hispanics felt that the services available to them were substandard compared to those of Anglo and European members
- Making a variety of recommendations for changes to internal processes and how AQHA reaches out to Hispanic prospective members
- Developing a Hispanic marketing plan based on our recommendations
- Dramatically increasing AQHA's participation in Hispanic events, including operating booths at which members and prospects could conduct AQHA business in person
- Helping AQHA hire an in-house Spanish speaker to adapt English communications
- Assisting AQHA to expand its member services call bureau (primarily inbound calls) with the addition of fifteen Spanish-speaking call reps to put a human, personal face on AQHA for this audience

- Creating and instituting a long-term strategy of driving more of AQHA's business with Hispanic members and prospects to the Internet by:
  - o Launching AQHA's Spanish-language Web site
  - o Adapting more than seventy business forms to Spanish (for example, membership, horse registration, transfers, DNA, and stallion breeding reports) and making them immediately downloadable from AQHA's Web site
  - o Creating and launching a free Spanish-language e-newsletter "*Boletín*" for all members and prospects who request it

Our results were clear: the strategy was a success, and this scenario has come to serve as a strong case study for the effectiveness of new media in reaching the Hispanic population. Our results are as follows:

1. AQHA's Hispanic membership is reacting positively to AQHA's outreach efforts.
   - The number of Spanish calls received by AQHA's inbound call bureau has grown 110 percent since the program launch in 2003:
     - 2006: 7,882
     - 2005: 6,390
     - 2004: 5,494
     - 2003: 3,748

   - The number of Spanish pages on AQHA's Web site has grown from 48 in 2004 to 115 in 2006, and the number of Spanish page views has grown dramatically. Spanish pages viewed:
     - 2006: 252,058 (59,013 unique visitors)
     - 2005: 161,327
     - 2004: 43,150

2. AQHA's Hispanic membership in both the United States and Latin America is up 20 percent:
     - 2005: 946 members
     - 2004: 872 members
     - 2003: 782 members

3. Horse registrations, transfers, and revenue from Hispanic memberships are up dramatically, as revealed by the data below:

> Hispanic new registrations
> 2005:   1,096 registrations
> 2004:   1,046 registrations
> 2003:   927 registrations
> *More than 18 percent increase*
>
> Transfers into and out of Mexico
> 2005:   1,021 transfers
> 2004:   843 transfers
> 2003:   684 transfers
> *More than 52 percent increase*
>
> Transfers within Mexico
> 2005:   621 transfers
> 2004:   597 transfers
> 2003:   512 transfers
> *More than 21 percent increase*

4. Readership of the *"Boletín,"* AQHA's Spanish e-newsletter, is up to 3,000 monthly from zero over the span of just two years.

5. Based on Web site metrics, an ever-increasing number of visitors to AQHA's Spanish Web site are coming through *Boletín* links.

Conclusion

The bottom line is that today's new media are interesting and creative, but they are ultimately just tools. New media get advertisers to the viewer's "front door," but whether you get invited into the Hispanic viewer's home, heart, and mind depends on the content more than the technology.

Connecting with Hispanics offers great business opportunities because of the size, age, and Internet access of this market, but creating connections requires a lot of thought and planning about message content and delivery.

If Hispanics believe advertisers are making a sincere effort to understand and respect them as people, rather than being after their money or out to make a sale, then the companies will make friends and customers. The more that advertisers come to understand the Hispanic culture and improve the Spanish-language options they offer, the more successful they will be for the long term.

I strongly suggest that advertisers seek help from knowledgeable communicators with experience both in language and in culture, rather than trying to figure it out by themselves. What seems logical to you will not always seem logical to Hispanic audiences, even if you get all the words right. You must understand more than just the Spanish language to genuinely communicate with this group, and a true understanding of each client will come only from extensive research, an open mind, and a flexible approach.

As a first-generation American himself, Heberto Gutiérrez doesn't just understand the multicultural experience—he lives it. Born in Mexico, he came to the United States at age 4, and became a U.S. citizen at age 16. After graduating from college and enjoying a successful business career that included serving as general manager of Univision's TV station in San Antonio, he started INVENTIVA, a multicultural marketing, consulting, and training firm, in 1990.

Since then, Mr. Gutiérrez has helped many industry-leading companies get started in and navigate the multicultural waters, including Prudential Insurance, PacifiCare, R.J. Reynolds, AT&T, Motorola, Household Finance, American Electric Power, Chase Mortgage, Arby's Restaurants, Delta Faucets, American Quarter Horse Association, Justin Boots, Tony Lama, Wonder Bread, and United Export Trade Association. INVENTIVA's success comes from learning everything it can about its clients, and then teaching them everything it knows about successful multicultural marketing.

Mr. Gutiérrez and INVENTIVA have been recognized by industry and government for making a difference at the grassroots level. Most importantly, he has won a national Gold EFFIE Award for ethnic marketing effectiveness from the American Marketing Association, and the American Advertising Federation's Silver Medal Award, its highest individual honor. Mr. Gutiérrez has been appointed twice by the governor of

Texas as a state commissioner on the Texas 9-1-1 Emergency Communications Commission.

Mr. Gutiérrez has also conducted workshops, presentations, and Webinars—domestically and internationally—to such organizations as Five Star Speakers, American Advertising Federation, Strategy Research Corp., Advertising Specialty Institute, BankersOnline.com, Arkansas Bankers Association, Texas Bankers Association, U.S. Livestock Genetics Inc., Free Trade Alliance (Mexico), and American Quarter Horse Association.

Dedication: *To Lia, my partner in life and business; she taught me to enjoy life, one breath at a time. And to my mother, Juanita Villarreal, who inspired me to embrace both of my cultures.*

Our Promise: The Client...First!

Mireya Valero
President and Chief Executive Officer
Spanish Marketing Inc.

The Company

We approach business confidently, yet cautiously. Having the capability to surpass our clients' expectations is our first consideration. Our promise says, "The Client ... First." We know our market; we listen to the clients' needs and determine whether our promise is applicable. We assess clients' expectations and feasibility. Upon this analysis, we establish our ability to perform and deliver according to our promise.

In keeping our promise, we are guided by our responsiveness policy. Prospective client calls are handled by key staff that is knowledgeable, engaged, and proactive. An employee who is knowledgeable about the agency is one who can explain its capabilities and determine whether there is a match between the prospect and Spanish Marketing Inc., or SMI. An engaged employee is one who is committed to the principles of service to the client and is excited about serving. The last characteristic of the responsiveness policy is that the employee handling the screening process is proactive, which speeds up service delivery.

For example, we were contacted by MADD (Mothers Against Drunk Driving), a nonprofit organization with national recognition, to participate on a national campaign targeted to the foreign-born Hispanic market. The requirements were to send an impacting message across socio-economic levels and gender. Other agencies had declined the offer because of the lack of funds. When SMI was contacted, a meeting was arranged the same day in MADD's office. The client explained her vision and ideas. SMI staff listened politely, shared the company's strengths, and arranged for another meeting.

Returning to the SMI office, our team set up a brainstorming session, and in comparing notes, they agreed that the client's definition of the market and the message were conflictive. The client was informed about it diplomatically. The nonprofit organization accepted SMI's ideas and asked for a presentation. SMI prepared a proposal that was accepted. The client has returned multiple times with additional projects.

Our philosophy is to deliver beyond expectations, creating long-term relationships building trust and confidence that we will do the right thing every time. Passion and belief in the cause were major contributors for success in this case. We created a win-win situation and continue to work together. We delivered beyond the client's expectation with their budget leveraged with pro-bono services mainly because we believe in MADD's cause, and the national recognition of their name would bring us to the next level in the industry.

We are agency of record for Pizza Patron, a national franchise company. Our relationship generated from a lead after reading an article in a business journal. The CEO was attempting to penetrate hard and heavy into the Hispanic community. Their branding needs were specifically what our tactics could meet. Confident about our services and the certainty that we could deliver, we contacted the client multiple times to arouse their interest. Eventually, we received a call-back. We were told that five agencies would be bidding for the project. We would be the fifth if chosen after the initial meeting. We guided ourselves by pricing, presentation, professionalism, persistence, and profit—we seldom go wrong with this policy. We secured the account, and we now are the agency of record for the company.

My leadership style is simply "hands-off." I have an open-door policy. The plan clearly communicates inter-accountability from the team in an autonomous environment. We are all accountable to one another. This method works well for me as the leader of the company, and for the organization, as well. We have survived a couple of fluctuations in the market, including the 9/11 catastrophe, which affected most industries.

We are an infant in the field compared to the giants in the industry; we began in mid-2001 with a limited operations budget. SMI is a byproduct of the recession of 2000, when the economy was suffering and so were the advertising budgets. This was a critical time for the Hispanic-owned business and a great opportunity for me. From the beginning, SMI had to operate utilizing mean and lean measures.

Not far behind was the 9/11 tragedy, which also caused uncertainty, to say the least. Many small companies did not survive the financial pressures; however, we have been able to gradually grow.

We are driven by our vision statement, which reads: "Our vision is to become a successful marketing organization by helping our clients succeed." By centering on the success of our client, we prosper.

We conduct weekly meetings to review project reports, discuss internal and external business matters, and acknowledge each of the team members' contributions for a job well done or provide support when needed. This supportive environment gives new employees a platform to develop new skills and grow professionally. Each leading function in the company is headed by a seasoned professional who operates autonomously. We want to create marketing and advertising gurus.

Forecasting and projecting are critical in ensuring that we continue to grow. We update records and accounts daily to ensure that we stay on target. Budgeting helps us measure the profitability that we want to achieve. We review these figures consistently to identify any changes or make adjustments when necessary.

Adopting and operating by the following three principal strategies has had long-term positive impact on the company:

- *Knowledge-based:* We want to be known as a knowledge-based organization with extensive experience in our industry. We are spending a great deal of human intellect and tangible resources to ensure that our internal culture is lived daily. Our personnel know the mission, vision, culture, and values. We have an all-staff retreat each quarter to evaluate past performance and to review internal procedures and processes. These quarterly meetings give us an opportunity to bond, to value each other's input and feedback, and to respect collective contribution.

- *Niche-oriented:* When SMI was established, the vision was to serve the Hispanic population. We know our target, because *we are* the target. When reaching the Hispanic market, you are targeting the human element of the people. You are touching their heart and soul! Our Hispanic clients know that we have their best interests at heart. We give them an honest, real perspective of our analysis and show them real outcomes with which they can identify. In the general market, our client is convinced that we know our market, usually during our first presentation.

- *Mean and lean:* Adapting a mean and lean approach to the financial management of the company is proving of highest value to the company. This approach allows us to keep thriving in a very competitive market. We have a good banking relationship and guard our credit zealously. We keep a balanced portfolio of small and large clients to give us a proportionate cash flow and to help us avoid becoming over-dependent on either.

I am guided by the following three statements, which keep me focused and assure me that we are moving forward continuously:

- A leader leads by example, living a simple lifestyle conserving for future opportunities or threats.
- A leader manages resources cautiously, planning, budgeting, reviewing, and reconciling continuously.
- A leader stays abreast of the constant changes in his environment and adapts to those changes to survive and even to thrive.

We are thrifty and sacrifice when necessary, and all benefit when there is plenty. When thriftiness is required, I lead by example. A leader keeps his team informed. New staff learns quickly how we operate, and they either commit or move on. Our combined intellectual capital keeps revenues steady.

Service and Success

Client service and attention are of utmost importance to the company. We are responsive, attentive, and flexible. We customize solutions for our clients, adapting to their needs.

For example, when we visited with MADD, they had ideas of how they wanted to launch their campaign and the message they wanted to send. Based on our cultural experience, we knew that the message would not resonate well and definitely would not be accepted among the Hispanic target. Our expert knowledge gave us the confidence to address the reasons the meaning would be lost and present the client ideas that would create the most impacting and impressive campaign. It is of utmost importance to justify and support the proposed solution, ensuring the desired results.

The best way for us to serve our client is by keeping up with best practices and trends of the omnipresent change and the evolution of the advertising industry. Much of this change is driven by the market requiring an immediate and proactive response.

We incorporate market and client feedback by creating a strategic plan with benchmarks for the clients. We monitor results from all activities that we design for the client. In 2001, we secured a used car sales distributorship with multiple locations in Dallas and Houston. The client spent a considerable amount of funds on radio and TV advertising. The key elements in this relationship were honesty, trust, and constant communication. We received sales and activity reports before the campaigns, during, and after. We monitored sales from all locations daily, weekly, and monthly to the point where we were able to derive a cost benefit analysis formula to determine return on investment. We had a well established communications system via an 800 number to capture contact information and achieve sales goals.

We know our market. We are gaining recognition in the industry, and when clients knock on our door, we are ready. This is a highly competitive industry, and we play the field. This all contributes to taking away market share from the competition. Our goal is to continue to grow steadily but cautiously. Focusing on SMI's Five Ps—pricing, presentation, professionalism, persistence, and profit—has produced positive results.

Companies need strategic direction to keep focused during fluctuations in the internal or external environments. Direction is generated from the top leader. Our mission and vision give us that direction. Confidence in our identity allows us to perform at the highest level possible. Each employee knows and lives by our internal culture and values. We conduct quarterly workshops for all the staff to ensure that we are following our strategic plan. We review past performance; project future activity; and evaluate the effectiveness of our current policies.

Below is a summary of our mission, vision, culture, and values:

Our mission is to increase our clients' overall sales opportunities through a systematic, well planned and executed marketing program, utilizing our *unique* firsthand knowledge, *diversified* experience, and *sincere* personalized attention.

Our vision is to become a successful marketing organization by helping our clients succeed.

Our culture: We embrace a culture that nurtures respect, supports and enhances knowledge, and encourages effective teamwork.

Our values drive our business...

- Ethics. We serve our clients with the highest ethical standards.
- Integrity. We value integrity as a way of doing business.
- Community-oriented. We give back to the community.
- Responsibility. We fulfill our commitments.

Our internal operations are simple. We want to continue to increase sales, but retention is important. Retention brings referrals generating our expected growth. Past performance is our best benchmark. Success for SMI is the success of our clients. Our greatest achievements are generated in branding, which creates the foundation for business success and productivity.

Understanding and Evaluating New Media

In my opinion, the response to the use of new media in advertising is phenomenal and enthusiastic among corporate America, and especially the youth. New media are the innovative channels of communication, audio and visual productions brought about with electronic communications and technology such as the Internet.

Media are continuously changing, moving faster than ever. For decades, radio, TV, and print media were the principal channels of marketing and advertising. Social media have revolutionized the communications field, allowing people to do their own advertising and marketing using blogging, podcasting, Web site development, and broadcasting. Channel integration is producing better than expected results. Keeping up with the learning curve of new technology and resources gives us an upper hand in the industry. Key personnel take continuing education classes in computer technology, not necessarily to become experts but to understand the basics of the new technology. The objectives of this education are to conceptualize the execution of the software application that generates the final product and to intelligently explain and recommend the right solutions to the client. This is also true for using the latest software applications to produce top-notch audio and visual collateral. Our equipment has the capacity to store and compatibility to manage these applications.

We also learn about new products and opportunities in the new media industry from vendors and research. We have a good relationship with some advertising giants whose best interest is to keep us updated of changes and opportunities.

In the twenty-first century, the advertising and marketing industry is driven by innovation and creativity. When you think the industry has reached the pinnacle of innovation, something not yet conceivable is in the planning stages or on the market. Research and education are the keys to maintaining the learning curve at its peak. PR Newswire, PRWeb, and Vocus have constant, ongoing training to ensure that we are exploiting all the capabilities of the services to benefit our clients.

We receive ongoing invitations to participate in conferences, Webinars, and teleconferencing from software vendors and service providers whose best interest is for us to keep up with changes and upgrades. We also receive Webzines, newsletters, white papers, etc., that keep us informed, as well.

The software, gaming, and music industries have encountered great challenges and conflict within the new media, allowing the client to tap into beta products, yet avoid piracy. Creative advertising has allowed these industries to adapt and achieve a balance, allowing the customer to try/test the product and prevent abuse.

We have not been directly involved with any of our customers in the software, gaming, or music industries to fight these particular challenges. It is equally important for SMI to operate on the principles of protecting the client's intellectual rights and maintaining confidentiality and non-disclosure agreements in place.

NAPSTER is an example of a company that had to adjust to the needs of the market to minimize the effects of user abuse. Software companies adapted by providing licensing rights for a fee to avoid duplication and multi-use of one copy, thus greatly impacting the bottom lines of their companies' financials.

The specific media channel we use is selected based on the target audience and desired results. When the target audience cannot be captured using the new media outlet, we would not use new media in a campaign. For example, creating an interactive Web site would not be the best advertising and marketing channel for a bakery in the Mexican barrio. Most of their clients will read the weekly Spanish newspaper or the flyer in the beauty shop. The campaign must meet the client's desires for exposure.

The most compelling factors in considering the effectiveness of utilizing new media in a campaign depend on the goals and objectives of the campaign. Facilitating access by the target market is of critical consideration. In some cases, channel integration may be the most effective, rather than the one, means of communication. Channel integration is launching a campaign that utilizes a combination of a series of media, such as an advertisement in the *Wall Street Journal*, in *The Economist*, on a Web site, and on Bloomberg TV, and perhaps a ten-second spot on National Public Radio.

New media in advertising and marketing are giving our company more options to offer. Knowledge, planning, and placement determine the effectiveness of the various channels of new media. With the limited experience that we have with new media, as you can see by the dollars spent on the Internet (below), our measurements for success on the Internet are the standard measurements available in the market—number of visits, time spent on site, etc. In the public relations area, the service provider sends reports and alerts and accumulates data for analysis.

Using New Media

We recently added Public Relations Services to our scope of services. In the electronic media, channel integration has been the most valuable in implementing this strategy. We use PR Newswire, Vocus, and PRWeb. We do not use traditional tools, such as press kits. They have become obsolete for us. Today, we deal directly with the media representatives, which is a more efficient method. The human element of the relationship is more effective. It is easier to negotiate.

We use Internet advertising and podcasting via a vendor, and we are in the execution stage with one of our clients to include blogging on his Web site. We are in the process of developing our first interactive Web site. We are eager to launch it and monitor the results. We advertise on Google and Yahoo. As we become more knowledgeable in new areas and are confident that is the right solution for our client, we jump to that level in the playground. The most effective forms of new media in the last year have been Web presence and Internet-driven products.

These are the percentages that we currently place in various media channels:

- Newspaper, 15 percent
- Magazine, 5 percent
- Radio, 25 percent
- TV, 49 percent
- Internet, 6 percent

Our SMI team is composed of seasoned experts and new gurus in our industry. We cross-train in areas of responsibility for timely delivery and meeting our commitments. We have a blend of training. Some of the training is structured in quarterly retreats for one day, where we teach about management and marketing strategy, sales, media, economics, and human relations, etc. All training has a purpose, whether to improve our internal performance or to improve our external performance: delivery to the client.

Experience and past results allow us to determine the best use of the type of media to utilize. Weekly meetings and frequent communication with our clients and media contacts are the best means of staying abreast of results. We get direct feedback from the client to verify direct impact and benefit. Media reports when applicable are very useful to us and for the client. Vendors provide education and technical support. They introduce new products and spend a great deal of resources to capture market (agencies similar to SMI). We buy media time from the major communications giants, and they educate us. We buy software, hardware, and services. They educate us as well. Everyone is interested in maximizing the utilization of their product or service.

Clients who are used to, or prefer, more traditional advertising methods may be reluctant to use new media in their campaigns. Our standard practice is to present to the clients various options and the results expected from each. If the proposal includes an option unfamiliar to the clients, then we introduce the new service or technology and the advantages.

We utilize industry best practices when implementing new media in our campaigns. For example, the Direct Marketing Association has published its fifteenth annual *Multichannel Marketing in the Catalog Industry*, which found "successful multichannel marketers have consistent and integrated standards across all channels. The study—which is a comprehensive roadmap for best practices and trends in channel integration within the catalog, retail, and e-commerce infrastructures—also reveals that nearly 70 percent of respondents reported increased multichannel sales over the prior year, and 59 percent reported increased catalog circulation in 2006. These findings are consistent with our experience in the market.

A good example is the Uniform Store located at the downtown mall. They have an interactive Web site where the client can order, request quotes for volume purchases, send credit applications, pay online, request a catalog, or perform other activities from anywhere in the world. The best practice is the confirmation that based on data collection and analysis and a blend of various e-commerce activities, the store is out of touch but within reach.

Lack of access to new technology in a particular segment represents a barrier for some advertisers. This is the biggest challenge we have encountered in using new media. However, traditional methods are equally effective in those segments, particularly when targeting a large market segment.

Return on investment for our client is the most careful consideration when selecting any product or service. We are results-driven. Our in-depth expertise in the industry gives us leverage to negotiate the best terms for our clients. We seek added value on their behalf. It is important to determine the objectives initially to place the campaign using the correct channels for exposure.

Positive return on investment for most companies is an increase in revenues, but it can also include a greater number of clients and contacts or developing more solid relationships, depending on the objectives of the investment infusion. The benefits sought can be extrinsic or intrinsic.

Mireya Valero has been in the Hispanic radio and marketing industry in the United States since 1988. She started her career as a copy writer with Rodriguez Communications (RC). She has worked on accounts such as Bank One, Blue Cross/Blue Shield, First Bank, Chase Bank, City of Miami Beach, Fiserv, HEB, Pepsi, and Wrangler to name just a few. She traveled throughout the country as RC acquired more radio stations. Her assignment was to set up and train the traffic department. Another assignment at RC was to create and co-ordinate all the station promotions.

While working in sales for RC, Ms. Valero realized she had a higher calling. Working one-on-one with small Hispanic business owners, she saw the need to educate this ever-growing entrepreneurial segment on how to market their products or services properly and not to be at the mercy of the media. It was this insight that led her to create Spanish Marketing Inc., of which she is president and chief executive officer.

Ms. Valero was born in Tampico, Tamaulipas, Mexico, and now resides in Dallas with her two sons, Michael and Alex.

Dedication: *To my sons, Alex and Michael…my guiding stars!*

Acknowledgements: *My deepest gratitude for their contribution on shaping SMI—Chuck Brooks, CEO, Texas Broadcasting and TORO Homes; Yolanda Castillo-Crosley, IFT Consulting; and the SMI Team.*

Hispanic Marketing and Advertising

Lauren Boyle

President

Grupo Exito

Effective Group-specific Marketing

At Grupo Exito, we focus primarily on delivering effective results to our clients. As a result, we differ from many other agencies in that we do not try to fit a square peg into a round hole. Instead, we work hard to understand and then fulfill the very specific needs of our clients.

Many agencies focus on offering creative and media-buying services as they deliver high revenue drivers for their companies. Some use their clients to realize award-winning creative projects for the agency, and do not put the clients' needs first by putting together ads that resonate with a target audience or deliver real results. This approach often results in off-strategy advertising for the brand that is both inefficient and ineffectual.

We are a competitive company because we look at specific client needs, but also because we specialize in Hispanic marketing and PR, which sets us apart from mainstream competition. The basic principles that apply in communicating with average market consumers generally work just as well when dealing within a specifically Hispanic market. The cultural approach that needs to be taken, however, is notably different.

Demographic characteristics provide only a foundational knowledge in concern to the U.S. Hispanic market. To succeed with this population, one must go deeper than surface demographics, taking into consideration factors such as language, country of origin, culture, level of assimilation, traditions, and socio-economic characteristics. All of these combined factors must be understood to effectively target this very complex market.

We generate revenue by researching clients that need help in our specialty, the U.S. Hispanic market. We remain successful, again, because we work diligently to understand client-specific needs. This may seem simple, but it is nonetheless true: if you listen and work together with your clients, your business will continue to thrive. In this vein, communication with our clients is a key component of our success. Facilitating communication means retaining accounts based on specific needs and details, and offering expertise and solutions in line with these details. Following through with these basic processes ultimately delivers results.

Company and Leadership Structures

Grupo Exito consists of a group of high-level, award-winning executives. Everyone is an expert in their specialty, which enables professionalism and teamwork to shine through.

We also work as a virtual office team with one meeting location. In doing this, we find that we work more efficiently and keep our overhead low. We do not maintain any expensive downtown office space that ultimately gets charged back to the client.

Networking is another component, which is key to any business's success.

Competition and Client Service

We believe that there is enough business demand in the market right now for companies to be successful. We also believe in karma. Thus, we do not actively pursue any other agency's accounts; if a client comes to us unsatisfied with their current agency, however, we do speak with them and offer guidance.

Client service is the most important aspect of running any business. We excel in client service because we continually communicate with our clients; we listen to their needs; and we provide effective solutions. Servicing our clients with great communication is the backbone of our business because without positive, effective service, we would lose many of our best customers.

In line with this, we are always researching relevant markets for our clients, and we request client feedback as often as possible. Both research and client feedback serve in analyzing the challenges we face in the market, as well as within our own company. Having gathered and analyzed our research and feedback, we take immediate action in incorporating or adjusting our campaigns.

Client feedback is also important in benchmarking our success as a company. We primarily measure our success in terms of our clients' success; because our existence depends on our clients, their success is our success, too. Feedback lets us know how well we have served our customers and how well we are doing business. Of course, we also measure success by our profit margin and our level of employee satisfaction. Our method for determining employee satisfaction is our open-door policy—we always communicate with one another.

The "In-Culture" Two-Step Marketing Strategy

Strategy 1: Cultural Relevance

A product or service that already advertises in the general market must first look at its Hispanic marketing objective and determine the target market. The most obvious and effective way to reach the Hispanic market is, of course, through Spanish language media. But this is more complex than just translating a message into another language; that only produces words without real *meaning*. You must have *meaning* to effectively make an impact.

Important points to consider when assessing clients and clients' brands:

- Who represents the client or brand's general market consumer?
- Who is the competition, and what are they doing?
- Is this a national, regional, or local client or brand?
- Does the client/brand's distribution effectively reach the Hispanic consumer?
- Is the product marketable to the overall Hispanic population, or is it targeting only, say, men ages 25 to 49?
- What is client/brand's message, and how is it relevant to the Hispanic market?
- What is the price point?

Once our target population has been thoroughly evaluated, we then develop the appropriate brand message and strategy. The message must reflect the population evaluation with its relevant meaning or cultural relevance. From here we determine the creative outlets necessary in relaying these culturally relevant messages.

Strategy 2: Market "In-culture"

After the culturally relevant message and overall strategy are completed, following the previous strategy, the next step is to deliver the final message "in-culture."

In the beginning it is crucial to identify the brand's key objectives for the Hispanic market, and then to take into consideration the target consumer, country of origin, language usage, age, socio-economic status, acculturation level, and so on. Another important factor to consider is when families in the specific market migrated to the United States. Also, consumer behavior, traditions, religion, and values can all vary dramatically from a Texas-born Hispanic to a Venezuelan-born Hispanic.

All this information provides the intelligence that is needed to successfully reach a multifaceted minority market. Once this intelligence has been effectively evaluated, we then compile the appropriate media outlets to deliver the specific "in-culture" message to our specific target population.

New Media in Advertising

Over the past twelve months, our company has utilized Internet ad banners, blogs, social networking sites, MMS text messaging campaigns, and e-mail marketing.

There is no question that Internet usage in general has changed the world as we know it. At any time, and without any thought, virtually anyone seeking information can now look to the Internet for a quick solution. Whether it is on their cellular phone or other mobile device, information and technology are now at the world's fingertips. Accordingly, these technologies are essential to an effective modern marketing campaign.

There is no exception to the Internet proliferation relative to the U.S. Hispanic population. The U.S. Hispanic online market is the fastest growing segment online, as described by Nielsen (Advertising Age, 2007). As the group's population increases, so too will the need for more target-specific Internet services increase. Strategies and tactics in U.S. Hispanic media today should include Web site development and online marketing; and for companies looking to reach more affluent U.S. Hispanics, the online world offers a cost-efficient opportunity when compared to traditional radio and television advertising.

Some companies and advertisers have underestimated Hispanics' Internet usage and have not offered Spanish language versions of their Web sites. This is indeed a gross mistake. According to *Advertising Age*, what they have overlooked is that approximately 65 percent of U.S. Hispanics own a computer (Pew Internet, 2007)—a very high number for a group who have, until recently, been underserved by the online world. And with the growth in Hispanic Internet usage, online video advertising is growing at a rapid pace with increased brand awareness.

I have personally noticed an influx of digital media detracting from radio, television, and traditional print sources. The ability to be seen and heard is now a greater challenge. Corporations looking to reach Hispanic consumers are jumping onto the Hispanic bandwagon, where there is tremendous growth opportunity for new media online, or through mobile and integrated advertising. Spanish language television and radio stations are utilizing their Web sites to promote their events, programming, clients, and contests. Univision radio and television are excellent examples of this (Univision.com and yahoo.telemundo.com).

Internet TV is also an important revenue driver in U.S. Hispanic media. Terra, one of the largest Spanish language online portal companies, generated 17 percent of its online advertising revenues in 2006 by Internet TV. Terra has more than 8 million unique visitors per month and offers a variety of services and resources.

Also, Telemundo/NBC is trying to capitalize on the popularity of its telenovelas by repurposing its Web site content in creating discussion forums around the programming, where Hispanic viewers can exchange feedback and commentary, download clips, and view excerpts from the shows. Additionally, Telemundo is introducing interactive ways for engaging Hispanic viewers with their programming online. They are inviting people to send in videos interpreting some aspect of the popular hit telenovela, *Zorro*, through song, dance, or other interpretive form, and posting it on the Web site.

In 2007, Univision also launched a video portal on Univision.com, where users can access clips from their TV shows, celebrity interviews, music videos, news clips, and now even program viewing. They are also launching a social networking service in addition to a wireless video subscription service through their new mobile initiative, Univision Móvil.

The marketplace has diversified as television and radio options continue to grow, and marketers are seeking new and innovative avenues to reach U.S. Hispanics. As lives in America continue to become more hectic, and people spend less time in front of the television and more time online, marketers will continue to move toward a digital and integrated advertising approach.

The Response to New Media Approaches

Most clients respond to the new media with open arms, while others assume that Hispanics do not use computers. But as far as new media marketing results, the response is quantitatively excellent.

An article published recently on Portada.com, a leading Spanish language Internet research and blog site, states that Hispanic teens have an affinity for cutting-edge technological features. It also states that the fastest emerging platform to reach them through is mobile marketing.

Statistics from MTV network's Slivered Screen research demonstrate that 63 percent of Hispanics in the United States own a media-capable cell phone and are 23 percent more likely to use them to watch video content and programming than the general population. This is a very high number as compared to the non-Hispanic percentage of 46 percent.

Responding to such compelling data, MTV Tr3s launched a multi-carrier, bilingual mobile channel for Hispanic youth in March 2007 that includes ring tones and video content from popular Latin artists.

Obviously the U.S. Hispanic online market is expanding at an incredibly rapid pace. For companies looking to reach more affluent U.S. Hispanics especially, the Internet offers a cost-efficient and highly effective opportunity. To succeed with online marketing efforts, though, developing an integrated Hispanic online marketing program that delivers the customer value and achieves business objectives is imperative. The aims and goals of the traditional marketing campaign should not be abandoned simply because of changes in technology and advertising media.

New Media Opportunities

The year 2007 presented many new Hispanic-targeted Web site offerings, with a variety of services and content. A report on Portada online in June 2007 lists many new online initiatives from health-related social networking sites, banks, and financial Web portals to larger and more mainstream sites from companies such as Best Buy, Dell, MySpace, and BabyCenter. My company uses Internet banners almost as often as we use radio, and usually in tandem with radio. We also utilize television, print, e-mail marketing, and blogging, all of which have been successful for our clients.

Today, traditional marketing tools account for about 20 percent of our strategies. We have working business relationships with the majority of the media companies we work with, so we normally submit avails and RFPs and then go from there.

In contrast, at least 15 percent of our marketing strategy utilizes new media, such as blogs, banners, and social networking sites. Interestingly, social networking among adults has become a popular phenomenon.

A report by Forrester Research indicates that social online networking among Hispanics tripled between 2005 and 2006. The report demonstrates that half of online Hispanics are involved in at least one of five social Internet activities, including blogging, personal Web pages, and involvement on discussion boards. According to the study, MySpace ranks first, with 31 percent of Hispanics visiting at least once monthly.

Convincing the client who is skeptical of new media is a challenge, and the best defense is research and empirical proof of effectiveness. For clients that have grown used to traditional advertising over the years, good research, success stories, and great ideas are also key to persuading them toward the benefits of the new media—but I cannot emphasize enough how important research is for this purpose. When your client sees the numbers produced by Internet users, they usually take a favorable stance.

In reality, it is difficult to imagine a circumstance where new media would not be a viable or even an essential component to an advertising campaign. Ignoring new media is comparable to thinking that not everyone benefits from television advertising—it is just not a good idea. Unless your core target demo is primarily over the age of 70, new media can always be a relevant tool.

Utilizing New Media Opportunities

Complete integration of the strategic platform is crucial to implementing successful advertising campaigns within the Hispanic market. The key industry buzzword in 2007 was "integration." The message needs to be clear and consistent while it is integrated with the appropriate media mix for the target consumer.

Trade resources and the Internet are the best tools for discovering ways to market using new media. Industry trade publications and trade conferences are also tools that we make use of at our company in looking for ways to expand our technologies and marketing possibilities.

Vendors also play a large role in helping to implement new media. Outsourcing is key to keep costs down in that area—especially for maintaining sites and tracking results. Maintaining full-time staff for these areas increases overhead, which eventually gets charged back to the client.

Another advantage of most new media campaigns is that they can be tracked instantaneously. We utilize as many tools as we can to track the number of hits and click-through rates to assess effectiveness. Our clients like to be "in the know" about the effectiveness of their campaigns. Providing data and facts to them more frequently increases the communication flow between agency and client.

Key Players in the Current New Media Business

A case study presented by Conill Advertising Inc. in New York at the Association of Hispanic Advertising Agencies Conference in Chicago in 2007 shared the ideation and strategy implemented in the 2006 Toyota Yaris launch. Conill helped take the car from unknown status to a 30 percent share of the entry-level subcompact automotive segment in the Hispanic market. He did this by targeting young Hispanics who view themselves as trendsetters leading the way in a new and multicultural world.

The Yaris launch partnered with Telemundo, Univision, Mun2, SiTV, and Batanga as the integrated campaign utilized online, TV, and print, and focused on English-language outlets that reflected Latino lifestyles, such as SiTV and *Urban Latino* magazine.

MundoYaris.com was the site that Conill created where visitors could mix music and create ringtones; it also included a Yaris Design Lab for making films, music, and art. A sweepstakes was also added for participants to try to win a performance at home by the Afro-Latin band Ozomatli.

This campaign is an example of how integration was achieved, by specific targeted messaging, utilizing traditional media mixed with new media, and it delivered for the client. The message resonated with the Latino consumer, as it was modern, appealing to the young demographic, but also "in-culture."

Digital media will continue to detract from traditional media, especially in the Hispanic market, as it becomes more mobile and continues to grow. There are already many new media choices targeting U.S. Latinos, but the key to success with integrating new media, as with any media, is that your message is in-culture and culturally relevant.

References

Advertising Age Hispanic Fact Pack, 2007. *Use of Technology.* http://www.adage.com/images/random/hispfactpack07.pdf.

Hispanicprwire.com, September 27, 2007. "BabyCenter Gives Birth to a New Spanish Language Website, BabyCenter(R) en Español." http://www.hispanicprwire.com/news.php?l=in&id=9611&cha=8.

Nielsen.com, November 6, 2007. "Spanish-Language Ad Spending Remains Strong, Nielsen Reports." http://www.nielsen.com/media/2007/pr_071106.html.

PewInternet.org, March 14, 2007. *Latinos Online.* http://www.pewinternet.org/pdfs/Latinos_Online_March_14_2007.pdf.

Portada-online.com, May 21, 2007. "Hispanic Internet TV to Grow Substantially in '07." http://www.portada-online.com/productdetails.aspx?productID=2309

Portada-online.com, September 4, 2007. "Social Networking among Hispanics tripled between 2005 and 2006." http://www.portada-online.com/productdetails.aspx?productID=2446.

Portada-online.com, March 14, 2007. "Telemundo Repurposes Broadcast Content Online." http://www.portada-online.com/productdetails.aspx?productID=2219.

Portada-online.com, June 18, 2007. "Univision launches Video Portal." http://www.portada-online.com/productdetails.aspx?productID=2367.

Shields, Mike, November 5, 2007. "Telemundo to Offer Full Shows on Yahoo." http://www.mediaweek.com/mw/news/interactive/article_display.jsp?vnu_content_id=1003668189.

Lauren Boyle's knowledge of and experience in the Hispanic culture goes back to her childhood, when she lived in Mexico for many years. It was there she adopted the language and the Hispanic lifestyle and culture.

Ms. Boyle, president of Grupo Exito, holds a Master's of Fine Arts degree in broadcast media from the University of Arkansas and has served as a professor at the University of Texas Arlington in marketing and promotions management. Currently, she is a professor of Spanish language media in the University of North Texas's Radio/TV/Film department and is a well-known specialist in Hispanic marketing and advertising consulting for brands in the Dallas-Fort Worth market and nationally.

Having worked in the U.S. Hispanic media for fifteen years, Ms. Boyle has held positions in national sales and promotions management for Hispanic broadcasting (Univision Radio), Z Spanish Radio, and Radio Unica. In addition, she has worked with many blue-chip accounts, such as Durex, Coca-Cola, L'Oreal, Clearasil, British

Telecom, X-Box Live, H&M, McDonald's, Motts, Visa, Lowe's, Coors Light, Heineken, Motorola, and Kraft.

Ms. Boyle has served as the director of promotions for En Vivo, an Omnicom Hispanic experiential and activation company, where she developed the Visa and Lowe's Hispanic Ambassador Programs nationwide.

Prior to En Vivo, Ms. Boyle was the head of Momentum, a McCann Erickson Worldwide agency, working in Ireland and the UK, where she won five European APMC awards for her work on Durex, Clearasil, and Motorola.

Disrupting the Health Care Space

Anne Devereux

Chairman and Chief Executive Officer

TBWA\WorldHealth and LyonHeart

Leadership

We believe that growth and profitability come from establishing a strong, positive corporate culture, rather than the other way around.

We do not settle for our clients being "satisfied"—we expect ourselves to be constantly challenging the norms and pushing both our clients and ourselves to approach marketing challenges in ways that redefine the marketing paradigm

I am a strong and decisive chief executive officer, but my style is to find ways to empower everyone who wants to take on greater responsibility.

When I joined LLNS, which became LyonHeart in 2007, and TBWA\WorldHealth almost two years ago, I was challenged by Omnicom to take what had been a steady, stable but "old school" health care marketing organization and turn it into a dominant player that shapes the future of our industry.

While that challenge sounds daunting, it did not feel that way, because joining the TBWA network meant I inherited a unique and proprietary process for developing visionary ideas and changing the game.

That process is called "Disruption." Disruption literally means evaluating and challenging preconceived notions (of marketing, business, industry, etc.), thereby discovering kernels of insight and opportunity that allow us to create a new vision for our future and redefine the market in our favor. The concept and process of Disruption was created by Jean-Marie Dru, chief executive officer of TBWA Worldwide and a cadre of smart, creative, non-traditional thinkers. (See his series of books on the topic.)

The "disruptive idea" is that the one which reframes the opportunity gets us there.

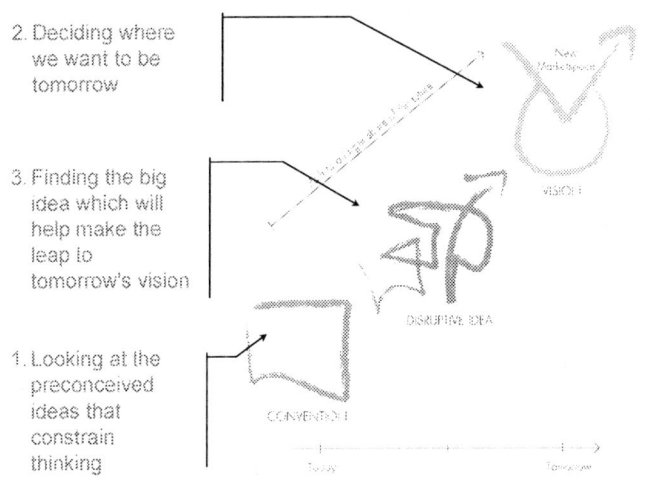

For our TBWA client, Pedigree, Disruption meant helping them realize that they were stuck in a conventional marketing rut—comparing ingredients in their dog food with ingredients in competitors' dog food—and ingredient comparisons made them a commodity. Using Disruption, we helped them discover that the common truth about all dog-owners was not their search for ingredients, but their *love of dogs*. In fact, we helped Pedigree create a vision to become a dog-loving company instead of an ingredient-selling company—and that helped them achieve quantum growth and market dominance.

We did the same for clients across the spectrum of health care accounts as well, doing so through our flagship health care agency, LLNS.

So when I needed to develop a vision for LLNS, I decided to launch Disruption on ourselves.

I started by assembling a group of strategists, account executives, and creative directors, and we began to do our homework. Specifically, we assessed the competition and the trends in our marketplace. We interviewed current clients, clients who had fired us, and clients with whom we hoped to work. We interviewed employees and those who had left the agency. We conducted surveys that compared our performance (in terms of bottom line growth, profitability, retention, employee satisfaction) with other agencies within our network. We took a very honest look at our strengths and weaknesses to develop true perspective.

But the most important thing we did as a company, and I did as a leader, was to enroll and involve *all* levels of the agency in our introspection and quest. Anyone who wanted to be part of our rebirth was encouraged and nurtured. They served on committees, conducted interviews, and developed ideas. More than fifty agency personnel participated in our formal two-day off-site Disruption session. A cross-disciplined group wrote a new set of values and our mantra. And some of the most junior staff helped create a new name (LyonHeart), which effectively captured our heritage: Mike *Lyons* was a founding partner and creative director of the original agency, and the "*heart*" communicates the new, revitalized spirit built as a result of our own Disruption.

My first job as a leader was to create an environment that fostered and nurtured this introspection, participation, and aspiration.

My second job as a leader was to take this input and translate it for the entire company, and for our client base, in a way that could be experienced and measured. That meant creating a forum for ongoing communication and measurement, as well as creating a new "brand personality" that would guide our communications, hiring decisions, and values.

The communication outputs that resulted from that challenge included:

- The development of committees and initiatives to continually bring fresh ideas to ourselves and our clients.
- The creation of a corporate mantra that communicates our values and personality in a way that is motivating and relevant to the creative people who work in advertising.
- The use of new media tactics to create interest and intrigue. We created an unbranded site called jointheuprising.org, an attempt to rebel against the rote processes that were practiced by the majority of marketers in

our industry. We bought space on phone kiosks surrounding our clients' offices and ran ads driving them to the site. We created viral e-mails and wrapped the *New York Daily News* with our Web address, handing out the papers at client locations to drive interest. The development and launch of the unbranded campaign captured the non-traditional and progressive approach of our new agency and communicated it to our industry.

- Launching a branded ad series after seeding the market, which demonstrated our understanding of the challenges our clients face, as well as our non-traditional approach to developing solutions. It also incorporated the icons from our Web site to begin to build our visual brand.

- Hiring people with experience beyond the traditional bounds of our industry, including health care copywriters who had been screenwriters and anthropologists, and a strategic planner who had been a news reporter.

- Making a corporate commitment to a philanthropic cause where we can all participate and see the direct benefit of the good work we do. (In our case, it was a commitment to iHUG, a new not-for-profit organization that is bringing education and medical care to Kabalagala, a small town in Uganda predominantly inhabited by children orphaned by AIDS, tuberculosis, and malaria.) Teams within the agency contribute to the organization's development of educational materials, fund-raising efforts, and news dissemination.

- Creating vehicles to accept and foster ongoing suggestions and input on how we are doing from all members of the staff.

- Measuring ourselves against other Omnicom agencies through participation in an annual employee satisfaction survey. That survey was created based on the understanding that growth and profitability are directly correlated to employee satisfaction and positive corporate culture.

There are several things we do that have a direct financial impact and add value to the company. The first is offering to clients that we will work with base compensation that is accelerated based on the achievement of measurable performance objectives (putting money where our mouth is). Next, we create an improved process for generating and sealing new business—all fueled by our Disruption process and relentless approach to the work. Finally, we make all senior people conscious of and responsible for the profit and loss management of their departments, including creative directors, who are not normally taxed with such issues.

I believe that:

1. Developing all members of the organization into leaders strengthens the agency and helps facilitate succession planning.
2. Giving creative people a sense of cost/profitability implications helps curb excessive spending and makes everyone accountable.
3. Valuing work that grows clients' business over work that wins awards ensures that our business is aligned with our clients' objectives and that more assignments come our way. For example, we value our Effie awards (which measure campaign effectiveness/business results) even more than we value our Cannes Lyons, which measure creative alone.
4. Offering to have part of our compensation be based on actual performance objectives demonstrates our confidence in our work and our commitment to our clients' business. It also helps fight the perception that we are in a commodity business. We are differentiated by our superior and valuable ideas.

Success

Client service is crucial, but it is not sufficient. In our business, superb client service is actually an entry point—a cost of doing business. Superb listening skills and the ability to execute were what our original agency (LLNS) was known for, and we did it well. But good service on its own leads clients to expect that we are "responsive doers," but not "valued thinkers." (We want to be partners, not just vendors.) In our reinvention, LyonHeart used LLNS's superb track record of service as a base, and added incremental levels of proactive ideation, non-traditional media initiatives, and customer cross-fertilization to really move the needle.

Client feedback and how we incorporate it are immediately apparent in our new business win-rate, employee and client retention rates, industry awards, and the general day-to-day management of our business. For example, clients in the early stages of our pitch process had lots of questions about the management structure of the organizations and how, with two different names and locations, we could ensure complete and seamless integration. It quickly became apparent that either I needed to physically attend each pitch, or we needed to include charts explaining our organizational structure (that both pieces report in to me) to give clients confidence that one person was ultimately being held responsible and could effect change throughout the network.

We also ask our senior staff to ask clients on an ongoing basis about how well we are meeting their needs, and have scheduled meetings twice a year for executive management to do brand reviews on every key account to uncover opportunities to add more value to the business.

What's more, we also made our executive staff more informed on (and therefore more responsible for) the overall profit and loss management of their accounts. They help craft how we staff business to provide the service our clients need while still achieving company profit targets. Same with organic growth: they are rewarded not only on their superb management of existing business, but also by their ability to grow those assignments beyond the existing scope.

We fully believe that by investing in our people, business results will follow. (See books by Len Schlessinger, *The Service Profit Chain,* and David Maister, *Managing the Professional Services Firm,* to get background on the correlation between strong corporate culture/valuing employees and bottom line profitability and growth.)

We manage our business tightly, turning down any assignments that do not meet two basic criteria:

1. They will allow us to do good work.
2. That we can make a fair profit.

We do not worry about competing agencies or taking away market share from our competitors. We do what we do exceptionally well, keeping our "eye on the prize, not on the competition." The only time we look at the competition is to see whether they have snippets of ideas that we can learn from, or take and make better.

Our benchmarks for measuring success for our company include:

1. Employee and client retention
2. Organic growth
3. New business wins
4. Profitability
5. Employee satisfaction (measured by the Maister survey conducted annually by Omnicom, as well as ongoing feedback in message boxes and one-on-one conversations with the CEO)

Understanding New Media

We have also seen how the use of new media has impacted the lives of consumers. Five years ago, patients had significant mistrust of both health-related information available on the Internet and their privacy dealing with health-related issues online. Today, the environment has changed dramatically, with the Internet being the first place patients and their loved ones turn to research diagnoses and treatment options, as well as to connect with other sufferers. Further, industry research reports that consumers now trust information obtained through the Internet more than they trust information received from their physicians! As a result, the length of time people spend online and the depth of their searches have increased exponentially—and, in parallel fashion, the average time a person has with his or her doctor continues to decrease because of pressures from managed care organizations and decreased revenue among many practicing physicians.

New media tools connected with the online space are welcomed additions, and allow for both personalization and privacy. Within the health care space, reminders for refills and alerts to take daily medicine are welcomed, and many forms of new media (cell phones, PDAs and e-mail reminders) are being used to improve adherence. New media allow for personalized messages that reach patients in the way they want to be reached, and tools that help link them back to their doctor to track their progress will dramatically improve health outcomes. New media will also continue to link the patient and the physician more closely so that adjustments to regimens can be made on an ongoing basis and results reported back.

Within the general advertising space, the current question is how consumer-generated content will evolve and affect marketing practices. Most marketers are now experimenting with ways to introduce their products onto consumer-generated sites like YouTube and Facebook in ways that will not feel forced or foreign. Further, a number of companies are springing up that are looking to create communications tools that make communications more personal and relevant for individual users. Marchex, for example, has purchased all U.S. Zipcodes.net, and is creating a local network where small businesses can finally afford to reach out to customers, and local customers can rate and rank their experiences on a one-by-one basis within their community. The incremental volume generated on these sites (and the customer satisfaction achieved) can be tracked down to an individual level and compared against other lead-generation tools. This is micro-marketing and customer engagement at a totally new level.

Evaluating New Media

Assessing the effectiveness of the new media in advertising depends on the media vehicle and the objective. Measurements like redemption rates, hits, pass-along, enrollment, phone responses, and purchase conversion are all common.

We study the ways that others use the new media in advertising campaigns, to learn about new developments. Omnicom has a series of programs where the most recently acquired companies within the family that have developed new technologies take their shows on the road and present those capabilities to the other companies. That keeps our knowledge fresh. We also have directors of new media on staff consistently looking to present new opportunities to us.

New media need to reach the target when they are most disposed to receiving and acting on the message and different clients use different tools to determine which media are most relevant. Some cross-reference consumer database information with proprietary research to see which media index most highly. (We call this "Connections Planning.") Others take experience within their field of expertise and extrapolate that knowledge for the new brand. Still others are sold on new technologies by reps and want to be the first to try them.

Within our agency, we consider several factors to assess whether new media might be effective. These include the prospective audience, the cost, and the type of campaign being planned. Our media philosophy is to first understand the behavior change that is warranted, and then find the most effective vehicles to accomplish that change. Media tools being used to generate awareness are usually very different from tools used to get someone to ask their doctor a question or the tactics needed to get someone already on therapy to comply with the prescribed regimen. Further, media choices differ based not just on audience, but also on disease state.

For example, women suffering from symptoms of menopause do not discuss their issues with their families, and often feel that doctors are unsympathetic about their symptoms. But they do trust other women who are suffering symptoms themselves. So viral media that allow them to share stories, anecdotes, and solutions with each other make sense.

A diagnosis of cancer presents a very different media scenario. From the moment of diagnosis, not only is the patient involved, but a wide range of family members and friends go online to do research, investigate treatments, seek second opinions, and provide support to each other. At the same time, patients need privacy to recover or cope. So Web sites that allow loved ones to tell each other about progress without bothering the patient have become very popular and are used as a focal point for sharing news and information.

There is no universal rule for when not to use new media in an advertising campaign. We still would tend to skew new media toward more savvy audiences and those who can afford to use the new technologies. Older consumers, especially those who do not actively use either the Internet or cellular technology don't make sense for this type of initiative. Further, audiences who seek information and are very active in managing their health will be much more receptive to receiving communications from non-traditional sources, while those who are not connected with their illness might consider such marketing intrusive.

In addition to age and interest skews, media effectiveness varies based on the marketing objective, target audience, message, and many more factors; no single tool can be deemed most effective. In fact, our experience is that no single tactic is as effective as an integrated set of activities that approach our target audience from different angles. For example, a TV spot that drives awareness and sends consumers to a Web site where they can get more information, use viral tools to share that information with friends, use that site to communicate with their doctor, and then track their progress online is far more effective than any of those elements on their own.

Tools that track the number of site hits, length of time, or depth of interaction are helpful, but our ROI is ultimately determined by projecting a "normal" growth pattern for the brand and then tracking the incremental volume that appears to be gained from non-traditional efforts. Sometimes we can get more specific information connected to each initiative. But within pharma, patients have to opt-in (agree to have their information tracked) before we can do so. So ROI is often still an estimate.

Using New Media

We offer employees training in new media on a variety of levels. When there is a specific new technology, like e-detailing, our partners in execution generally provide training for our key staff. This is currently happening with ProScape, a technology provider that specializes in this space. They train our people so that we can create good work using their technology. It's a win-win.

Further, Omnicom offers a number of educational opportunities that include the new media space. They are taught by a combination of professional educators and experts from within our organizations. In fact, we make a concerted effort to present credentials and capabilities of all new members of the Omnicom network to our senior staff and to train anyone necessary. We also provide reimbursement for courses our employees want to take in the new media space as long as those courses augment their contributions to the company.

We do not use blogs in advertising campaigns. Blogs cannot be sponsored by prescription drug manufacturers because there is a significant risk of inaccurate information being given. However, blogs can and do connect patients and caregivers with each other to discuss experiences, doctors, treatment regimens, and coping mechanisms—and that is a good thing.

It can sometimes be a challenge to persuade clients who are more used to traditional advertising to use new media in their campaigns. It really depends who the client is. Some of the more progressive marketing directors ask us to propose non-traditional solutions as part of our briefing. Others are persuaded when we approach our plan by looking at the communications goals and the best vehicles to reach those goals. The biggest challenge comes from clients looking to measure specific ROI for every given program. Not all new media are measurable in the traditional way, and that is sometimes hard for clients to sell to their management to justify a non-traditional approach.

New media often include the use of global asset management systems, where clients or agencies in individual countries can access assets and reproduce them in the most valid way within their marketing environments. Assuming everyone adheres to brand standards, this is a great thing, saving clients the expense of conducting the unnecessary research or recreating work. It also is often abused when there is no one with the authority to manage or limit the use of assets on a country-by-country basis, and the work begins to become less integrated and more variable.

We are vigilant about not allowing contributions to branded marketing messages by anyone other than the core marketing team. All pharmaceutical marketing is vetted and approved by an extensive number of players, including marketing and sales teams, legal, medical and regulatory affairs, and sometimes the FDA itself. Any media tool that allows community participation cannot be done under the banner of a branded message because there is very significant risk in the conveyance of inaccurate, un-proven, or off-label information.

I would say that the use of cultural anthropology to understand the difference between what consumers say they do and what they really do has unleashed a range of new media, offers, and dialogues.

For example, traditional market research was built on the assumption that people who are watching TV are open to hearing sales pitches. Market research therefore measures which of the spots are best at communicating in that venue. However, traditional research does not measure whether people are open to hearing messages on TV at all. Further, if they *are* interested, it does not tell us when they will best hear it, when they will act on it, and what we should say. Conversely, if they are not open to TV messaging, traditional research does not tell us which alternate media will work better.

On the other hand, behavioral (anthropologic) research tells us that while people are still watching TV, they are doing it differently. They may be multi-tasking (also using the computer, phone, and iPod at the same time), or they may be watching with the sole purpose of unwinding and therefore be completely closed to hearing any messaging at all. DVRs (digital video recorders) exacerbate that phenomenon, allowing viewers to fast-forward past anything irrelevant to them.

Via new media, we need to take advantage of information gleaned from behavioral research, and use those personalized moments when our target is most open to receiving information, to give them the opportunity to act before their interest in acting has passed. This is especially important in health care. We cannot rely on people remembering our messaging when they get to a retail environment, because generally they need to be under a doctor's care to receive a prescription. So using new media to further educate (making our patients smarter so they can ask the right questions of their health care provider) or giving them tools to help make them better patients (more compliant with therapy or more adherent to a diet and exercise regimen) is key.

A leader and visionary in health care marketing, Anne Devereux is responsible for the continued evolution of the agency and the worldwide network as it continuously strives to help clients build world-class brands. Prior to joining LLNS, Ms. Devereux was BBDO's chief integration officer, as well as managing director of all health-related assignments within BBDO New York. While at BBDO, she built one of the fastest-growing health care units of a major advertising network.

Before joining BBDO, Ms. Devereux was president and founder of Consumer Healthworks, which then became Merkley Newman Harty Healthworks, one of the first agencies to specialize in direct-to-consumer advertising for health care brands.

A Wellesley College graduate, Ms. Devereux is the proud mother of two daughters, Lauren and Ciara. In her spare time she can be found at the gym, in the garden, or at her kitchen table designing jewelry.

Brands without Borders

Yuri and Anna Radzievsky
Chairman and Chief Executive Officer;
Chief Creative Officer and Executive Vice President
GlobalWorks Group

The Company

Some twenty-five years ago, long before the advent of virtual teams, we began to develop a worldwide network of journalists, academics, marketers, and researchers. These experts provided instant, on-the-ground intelligence about any culture, demographic, or value- and mind-set, in any marketplace, around the globe. The network gave us ready access to many of the best minds and top authorities. Our competitors operated instead vast, costly, cumbersome agency networks, whose individual entities did not always work toward common cause.

Think of it: One meeting versus many, to collaborate on a global initiative. One group to uphold brand integrity, market by market. One team to ensure brand consistency, worldwide. One group to create and deliver a clear, coherent brand voice to audiences everywhere. The lean, virtual, borderless network offered a singular level of management control, efficiency, and economy. As complexity became a byproduct of globalization, our simplified approach won many proponents.

As powerful as the approach was, and as marketplace intelligence evolved into brand content, demand mounted for a better way to create, manage, share, and distribute content. A digital technology platform we originated and offer to clients, together with our extensive package of Web globalization services—we call it Orchestrate™—supplied the missing link. Imagine a client with scores of Web sites, in a dozen languages, fueled by hundreds of content creators, in fifty or more countries. The challenge is not only about differences in language and culture; it is also about differences in technology. In many cases, old systems cannot talk with new ones. Or software built around one language is incompatible with another language. The result is digital chaos.

Call our Web-based services and systems "technology without borders." We have developed digital tools to overcome the incompatibilities. The technology helps clients create a borderless, collaborative environment. Think about the endless reviews and approvals needed to create global brand content. How do you manage the process, the sharing, and distribution? The hosted Web services we provide allow clients to pull everything together. Result: The entire branding, marketing, communications chain operates seamlessly and globally. The technology differentiates us as much as our borderless creativity.

If you are in the branding and advertising business, as we are, leadership assumes many guises. We are, in many ways, both a laboratory and factory of innovation. It is not only that we must unrelentingly be creating new ideas. In our case, the ideas need to cross the divides of language, culture, and geography. Our own platform as an agency is the resonant phrase, "Brands without borders." Such brands succeed in attracting consumers everywhere. Internally, our mantra is: "It takes an agency without borders to build brands without borders." The question then becomes: How does leadership imbed and express that idea, not just throughout the organization, but also amid the all-important client community?

Leadership is, for us, all about collaboration. We are a different kind of global agency. Everything we do, we do under a single roof, rather than via a network of regional offices. Our staff, headquartered in New York, represents some forty nationalities. We also created over the years a virtual network of five hundred experts around the world. An agency without borders is exactly that. Our approach is what we call "open-source." We believe that when the minds of many different cultures focus and interact on a common creative challenge, the solution is often better, richer, and deeper than if the limits of a single culture were brought to bear. Leadership, then, is about nurturing a climate of equality. This enables our creative people to speak a common language, to harness and express the best ideas, emanating from not one but many cultural backgrounds.

Interestingly, clients want what we offer, but either do not realize such an approach exists or—because tradition weighs so heavily—have not recognized the approach as a solution. We go to great lengths, especially in initial presentations, to demonstrate that we have not only better ideas (which all agencies must do), but also a better way of doing things. We have developed digital tools to streamline collaboration on and sharing of brand content worldwide. The technology embodies the thrust of brands without borders. Leadership's role is to endlessly reinforce the advantage of the better way and the better idea, and how the two, working in harmony, produce on every level a better outcome.

Put Orchestrate to work for Avaya, and you can see how our Net-based solutions illustrate that role. The service, focused on managing brand content worldwide, enabled Avaya to launch eleven Web sites across Europe and North America in the first year alone. Orchestrate powers all brand-defining visuals, among them thousands of banners and hundreds of interactive Flash modules, movies, and podcasts, all in eighteen languages. The solution helped expand unique global visitors to Avaya.com by 20 percent. Increased content satisfaction leaped twenty points, from 59 percent to 79 percent.

Growth, Profit, and Success

How can your company grow and generate increasing revenue? First, diversify your revenue stream. Owing to the volatility of the business, you will not remain for long a one-trick pony. As much as we innovate for our clients, we also innovate for ourselves. We not only do what we all refer to us as traditional advertising, but we are also resourced to provide a full realm of net-related and net-supported services. Orchestrate, mentioned above, a Web-based brand-management solution we created, embodies the approach. It's an easy-to-use, hosted service for worldwide management of branded content. We and clients use Orchestrate to harmonize how we create, share, revise, and publish content across multiple channels, languages, and cultures. Thus, technology has become an important and growing revenue source. Because we are so deeply immersed in language and culture, we are positioned to create and recast advertising, corporate ID, and branding in other languages, adding yet another financial stream.

Second, we cast a wide net for business—which is to say, there is virtually no category of business beyond our reach. We may, on the one hand, be heavily responsible for Avaya's Web presence around the globe, a task involving myriad languages, volumes of content and extensive technological tools and platforms. On the other, we can create award-winning TV advertising for Cablevision focused on the Hispanic market, yielding among the segment the brand's best response ever.

Third, we believe that communicating for ourselves is as imperative to the vitality of the business as is communicating for clients. We use all the tools—interviews, speeches, articles, white papers, and newsletters. More than anything else, we use our Web site to spotlight and differentiate our point of view. The site is as much about us as it is a showcase for clients. As an agency, we have a story that takes a little longer to tell. It is one thing to talk about your thinking, which departs in our case radically from tradition. But what the site provides beyond anything else is how that thinking translates into execution. We update constantly and see the site as both a gateway and an engine for continuing growth.

We champion inclusion, inspiration, and innovation. It is a three-part role and embraces everything we do as an organization. The role focuses on what we call the building blocks of the agency. One grows essentially out of the other. My job is to see that the sequence is clear to all, including clients, and that the outcome benefits not just clients, but the entire enterprise, especially the bottom line.

Inclusion refers to the signature diversity of our human capital. We hail from all over the world, and always have. We recognize our commonalities, celebrate our differences, and approach the global marketplace with the same point of view. Our diversity enriches and deepens the pool of ideas we draw from.

That brings us to inspiration. Because we champion inclusion, we bring to creative challenges the spark of many languages, cultures, and nationalities. Imagine what it is like when the backgrounds and brainpower of people from a dozen countries confront a brand challenge. The number of possible solutions multiplies beyond anything a single culture could provide.

Out of inclusion and inspiration springs innovation. This is what clients pay for—ideas that work. Not just any ideas, but the kind that surprise in their originality and impact. For one of the country's biggest cable companies, our research showed that Hispanics and African-Americans in the Northeast were unconvinced they needed digital TV, broadband, and voice services. Via TV, radio, print, transit, and direct mail, we humorously positioned the services as better choices versus the competition. More importantly, perhaps, we underscored that peers and neighbors clearly thought so, because—and this was the critical insight—they themselves were already enjoying the services. Result: response rates were 200 percent higher than any comparable campaigns in the past.

One of the world's largest professional services firms—and a client for many years—sought a more penetrating digital path into the C-suite. Business may not be sport, but that didn't stop CEOs from playing a strategy game on the Internet, geared to their specific industries. We created a kind of strategic IQ challenge, focused on key sectors like energy, automotive, pharma, and mergers and acquisitions. The games boosted C-suite traffic to the client's Web site by 165 percent, produced more than a thousand downloads of critical articles and research, and generated more than one hundred face-to-face sales meetings with always-elusive captains of industry.

Nothing we do to create value is as important as creating a climate where the forces of inclusion, inspiration, and innovation can thrive and attain their fullest potential.

If the agency business were a science, discussing questions of capturing market share, incorporating feedback, and measuring success would be easy and straightforward. But the business, we think most of my peers would agree, is much more art than science—or so it often seems. Pulling market share from competing agencies? We see giant brands give creative assignments to smaller shops. We see bigger shops suddenly grabbing business from smaller ones. We see years of loyalty thrown out the window, when new management enters the picture, or there is a market downturn or a loss of share. Sure, you can endlessly throw spec work at a target account or promise to do more for less. The reality is anything but predictable. In an agency shootout, between an outside agency and the incumbent, you may— as the winner—gain someone else's market share. But it is not market share as such. It is simply part of the relentless churn of the business.

Not to sound cynical, but we would argue that the best client service is the service that ensures the best outcome. We all become expert at hand-holding. But the way to hold on to business is to deliver results out of all proportion to client expectation and investment, because in truth, that is what gives you staying power in this business. Our chief measure of success is how much follow-on business we win. We may do an outstanding job in the Latino market, and the client may ask us to target other culturally unique audiences. Or we may be invited to provide more than global brand content, when a client recognizes we have the technology to streamline, on a global scale, the entire brand collaborative process.

If optimism is a strategy, then we have made it a strategy we try to pass on to every member of the agency, and clients as well. We always believe we can do better, and do more. How? By nurturing a culture of innovation and the belief that, as a team, we have the desire and capacity to bring clients something extraordinary.

To cite but one example, we have worked for years with a client called Hughes. We helped management redefine the company's brand identity, as it evolved from manufacturing into a service-oriented enterprise. We were there when it spun off from General Motors, needing to re-brand itself as an independent entity. When Rupert Murdoch bought DirecTV, which was part of Hughes, we not only continued to believe in the company's prospects, but collaborated with management to re-shape the new image of the company for its many audiences, from Wall Street to Main Street.

Today, Hughes is the largest provider of broadband by satellite. We remain its brand champion.

New Media in Advertising

There are, of course, no hard and fast rules about who will use new media, or when to use it, or what percentage of budget it should represent. Web design and development have played a major role in our work for clients during the past twelve months. So have online-rich media and online games. To the mix, we can add e-card tools, kiosk multimedia, e-mails, and multimedia DVDs. The context is entirely fluid. And clients are much more likely to either evaluate or agree to add new media and to do so more frequently.

Thanks to new media, the relationship between customer and brand content has become much more openly transactional. Now, much has been made about how the customer, rather than the brand, controls the game— words, time, and space. The price of that ownership is a willingness to let the brand into every corner of digital life. It is not the brand presence so much as the brand's ability to monitor, on an unparalleled scale, customer life online. We can follow keystrokes as users navigate Web sites. Interests and passions. Chatter and buzz. We can keep tabs on preference and criticism. Purchase behavior and social interactivity. We can, with this intelligence, re-contour and personalize the brand experience as never before.

But the way things are moving, that last idea may already be an understatement. Brands will soon be able to track the customer's steps across the entire electronic frontier. They will be able to see what you see, hear what you hear, follow you to concerts, accompany you 24/7. The customer world will accept this in exchange for free, brand-sponsored content and media: music, DVDs, events, free-calling, video, cell phones, games, and software.

What will come of it all? Brand and customer will get to know each other more intimately; that is, brands will understand customer needs and wants, values, and behavior far better than ever before possible. This in turn, we hope, will lead to ever richer levels of brand personalization, especially in media and message. The trend should ignite new levels of innovation, as brands seek to integrate what they learn into better products or heightened brand experiences.

Connectedness will be the goal, every device linked to every other device. Brand content will travel the network like so many electrons. It will become part of global collaboration. People will share brand experiences, reviews, recommendations, and purchases, in a non-stop conversation. Brand connectedness will transcend language, culture, and geography. In the process, traditional media like print and broadcast will continue to be part of the dialogue, but in digital form.

It is impossible today to be a global brand without a multi-dimensional footprint on the Web. Appropriateness is not the issue. New media are no less a component in the marketing mix than traditional media. The core challenge is deciding among the many new brand channels springing up, nearly every time you turn around. In this environment, brands need to be open to more testing and exploration. The great thing about new media is the relatively low cost of experimentation.

The divide between generations, digitally speaking, plays a key role in the use of new media. We as an agency throw our weight behind—no surprise—online initiatives targeting a younger, non-boomer demographic. You go where your audience is—or, to put it another way, where your audience these days takes you. One more digital generation, and the brand world is likely to open its embrace to an older segment, which, unlike its forebears, grew up with computers, MySpace, and Second Life.

We see new media as high-leverage media. Because we can track results so quickly and precisely, the risk is far lower than with traditional media. New media, like direct response, are much more measurable, especially in terms of purchase information.

One benchmark we like to use, if a client is willing to share the data, is how Net-driven purchases compare with direct advertising using mail, print, and broadcast. Online is most often the low-cost producer.

Our people come from all over the world. As a demographic, they tend to mirror our markets. Like those markets, they are Web-savvy and ever curious about the next new thing coming down the digital pike. Openness to the new takes the place of formal new-media training. Because of their global exposure, they are much more likely to suggest new-media ideas that transcend any one culture or country. The globe, we find, is the best training and proving ground of all.

Yuri and Anna Radzievsky founded GlobalWorks in 1999, an agency fusing branding, culture, and technology for the global, borderless marketspace. Mr. Radzievsky is chairman and chief executive officer, while Mrs. Radzievsky serves as executive vice president. For three decades, he has been a trailblazer in global branding, multicultural marketing, and digital communications. She is recognized for combining award-winning creativity with relentless entrepreneurial drive, leading to the launch of three highly successful advertising agencies.

During the Soviet era, Mr. Radzievsky was born and reared in Moscow, where he hosted one of the USSR's most popular TV shows and wrote for Soviet TV, radio, and stage. Mrs. Radzievsky came from Riga, the capital of Latvia. Born in Riga, on the Baltic

Sea, she grew up in the multicultural environment of the former U.S.S.R, where consumers spoke in more than one hundred languages and dialects.

Mrs. Radzievsky graduated from the University of Latvia with a master's degree in chemical engineering. Her interests took her into the communications realm, and she became involved with TV production in Moscow. Both with advanced degrees in engineering, their real passion lay in the arts and communication. They met while he was host of the TV show, and she became immersed in TV production. The polyglot world of Russia placed them at the center of an evolving, multilingual, multicultural universe.

The couple immigrated to the United States in 1973 and founded Euramerica, a pioneer in multicultural marketing communications, which quickly grew to be the largest in the field. They launched a second agency in 1990, Y A R Communications, building it into a leader with billings of more than $200 million a year. After founding GlobalWorks, they combined the agency with Internet-focused Liquid Digital, in 2000, absorbing its cutting-edge technology to form GlobalWorks Group LLC.

The Radzievskys' clients have included AT&T, General Electric, Discovery Communications, CNN, EDS, and Walt Disney. Current clients include Hughes, Ernst & Young, Cablevision, AlcatelLucent, Avaya, and other leading global brands. In the decades the couple has been in business together, their agencies have created, adapted, and recast advertising for business and consumers, in more than eighty languages, and for more than one hundred countries, including the United States.

Effective Creativity

Court Crandall
Creative Partner
Ground Zero

Client Service

Ground Zero has always been described as a creative agency because we win lots of creative awards and take rather unconventional approaches to our clients' business problems. But the fact is we are extremely strategically focused. We spend a lot of effort just trying to figure out what exactly a client hopes to accomplish in the marketplace, and then try to create a custom solution to accomplish that goal. It is almost viewed as a given that there will be a strong creative component, but we do not make that a goal in and of itself.

I think nowadays, the value of client service has changed. Most good clients do not want someone who just organizes meetings and gets them Lakers tickets when they are in town. They want smart people helping to drive their business. And they know they are paying for each person who is working on their account. So if your name is on the spreadsheet, you need to be adding value to the client's business.

This means you have to be contributing ideas. Increasingly, clients are looking not just for an ad agency, but a partner who can make suggestions about everything from how to improve the packaging to how to tweak the menu mix.

Client and market feedback are valuable to us. We actually have a focus group area built into our building so that we can easily focus test our strategies and our creative. The key with incorporating both market and client feedback is to figure out what each party says they need, rather than just giving them what they ask for. Left to their own devices, focus group respondents would create the worst advertising in the world. But this does not mean that you cannot learn from where they are getting hung up on a particular idea and figure out how to better present your thoughts. For instance, with our anti-smoking account, we'll often learn that a particular fact about the toxicity of secondhand smoke or the manipulative actions of the tobacco industry are particularly compelling to the audience, but they just don't love the way we've served it up creatively. So rather than asking them to write our commercials, we use them more as a litmus test to see whether we're making the most of our communication opportunity.

To take away market share from competing agencies, we work harder, faster, and smarter. You have to have more people doing more things—strategic planning, interactive, guerilla marketing, package design, and event marketing. In short, if the marketing director will be in his or her job for an average of eighteen months, he or she needs to know that you have the dedication and resources to make a profound impact on the business immediately.

It's a competitive industry, and the only way to grow as an agency is to take share from someone else. We don't like to talk about this at our advertising events while we're eating shrimp and patting each other on the back, but it's a fact of the business—there simply aren't enough new brands generated every year to make it an industry where you can be successful without grabbing a few of someone else's clients and simultaneously defending your own.

Leadership and Growth

Generating growing revenues and profits is not easy. We try to take the right business and not take the wrong business. After fourteen years of running the company, I have found the business you turn down has at least as big an effect on growth as the business you take on. If you convince yourself that even though a client does not really want what you do, but is appealing just because they have a large budget, you will ultimately do your agency a disservice and slow its growth.

The tricky part, or course, is figuring out which are the right clients. For us, we have two very basic measures. First, do they believe that if you do good things, good things can happen? In other words, do they have their eyes set on achieving a goal rather than just avoiding being the person who made a misstep? (This probably seems obvious, but you'd be surprised how much of middle management is just looking to avoid risk these days.) Second, are they the kind of people you'd want to go have a beer with at the end of the day? The premise here is that if they're nice people, there's no marketing problem you can't solve together.

Growing our company and achieving more profit have included the strategy of developing businesses outside the traditional adverting channels. For instance, we bought the U.S. distribution rights to a flavored vodka brand called Pinky. We have since redesigned the packaging and logo, aimed the product specifically at women, and taken on a large financier. We are now both client and agency.

In addition to this providing an additional revenue source for the company and creative opportunities for our staff, I think the endeavor is appealing to marketing directors of other brands because it shows that we know what it means to deal with things like distribution, motivating a sales force, and making sure the scanner can read the UPC codes.

Our company is based around two words: "Out think." This is an internal mantra, as well as a description of what we try to offer our clients. As such, we place little emphasis on titles, ego, or tradition. Rather, we encourage every employee in Ground Zero to behave like a creative thinker—finding solutions to business problems.

We focus on three key strategies that have a direct impact on our finances, draw customers to us, and help us keep those customers:

- Keep our expenses under control in pitches. A lot of agencies invest tens to hundreds of thousands of dollars into a speculative pitch. We cannot and we will not.
- Produce the kind of work creative-minded people want to be part of. You would be surprised how much less important salary becomes when people are doing the kind of work they are proud of.
- Do not create an environment where people think it is OK to be cavalier about the company's money.

Why are these strategies important? An ad agency is a small business. So everything you do as management will immediately impact the bottom line of the company and the behavior of the employees. If you don't fly first class to the shoot, it's hard for the junior copywriters to say they should.

Understanding New Media

The response to the use of new media in advertising has been somewhat slow, and clients have been treading slowly and carefully. The companies that have been earlier adopters of new media have been leading the way for others in terms of lessons to learn. However, the early adopters have been able to be more on the forefront of trying new things and from it learning valuable lessons that have not been shared with everyone. This provides them an advantage as technology changes, allowing them to move more fluidly with it than the advertisers that are late in trying new media.

Since adoption has been slow, there still are many lessons to be learned and creative campaigns that have not been done yet. It is still in the growth phase, where the clients that are willing to take those risks are benefiting the most in the short term, but more for long-term learning. If you think about it, only a handful of companies are fully taking advantage of new media and creating integrated campaigns addressing DVRs, on-demand, ITV, mobile, Bluetooth, etc. It appears many companies are waiting for critical mass to collect before incorporating new media into their campaigns. It should happen earlier, so that it can be tested more efficiently, so that creative and media can learn from each campaign before it hits critical mass.

New media, no matter how much or little it has penetrated the industry, is changing advertising. Mostly this is because clients are rethinking all the traditional constructs—TRPs, reach, frequency, what the purpose of an ad is, what will make an ad successful. It is pretty exciting.

New media are moving toward centering on the PC, with the PC being the network to unify multiple devices to work as one. Advertising campaigns will soon involve more of a push/pull model, where advertisers will be pushing a message, hoping that consumers will pull it through to all the channels, from PC to TV to mobile to video to other consumers. When this happens, the best campaigns will then be spread by consumers to view in all new emerging media forms. Advertising campaigns will become more of a 360-degree cycle, where along the way it will be viewed on each new medium. Advertising will become its own form of entertainment, where consumers will be able to interact with the creative/content in some form. Consumers will be able to instantly interact and communicate with the advertising company for any additional information and comments.

Typically, we learn about new media being incorporated in advertising campaigns when there are good case studies to read about. Usually it is when an advertiser has been able to successfully use that new medium.

I actually believe we were one of the first, if not the first, to use the Internet to perpetuate a hoax that got our client lots of attention. Years ago, for the launch of Sega's online game, Heat, we decided to dump the conventional wisdom that video games perpetuate violence on its head and created a campaign all around the bogus concept of "Cyberdiversion." The idea was that by taking your innate urges to kill onto the Internet, where they can't hurt anyone, you were doing mankind a favor. We created the Cyberdiversion Institute that espoused this philosophy and a dozen fake Web sites that ranged from the London Cyberdiversion headquarters to Mothers Against Cyberdiversion. In the end, the campaign got loads of press and was featured on Fox News.

Because the use and implementation of new media in advertising is so new, sometimes it is necessary to persuade clients who might prefer to stick more familiar, traditional advertising methods in their campaigns. The way to handle that is to tell them why the path you are suggesting is more likely to be successful than a more traditional approach. In the end, all these new media options are really nothing more than tools. If you spend your energy explaining to your clients what you are trying to build, they probably will not object to the tools you choose to build it.

Using New Media

To assess whether new media are appropriate for an advertising campaign, first you have to ask whether it helps the client accomplish the stated business goal. Then you have to be as honest with yourself as possible and ask, "Is this likely to be something that gets spread around the Internet and picked up by other news sources?" If the answer is yes, chances are it is worth the media and production expenditure because you will get all sorts of free exposure beyond what you pay for.

The top factors that are assessed in deciding whether new media will be effective are, first, the prospective audience; then, the type of campaign; then cost, especially if budgets are very tight. We look at the business objectives and the available dollars. Typically, it is not an all-or-nothing proposition. Because a lot of new media are relatively cheap in comparison, we are typically able to allocate a portion of the budget to new media or create a campaign where the new media and traditional media feed off one another. For instance, for ESPN College Gameday, we have just created a series of fifteen commercials based on facts about the show that are either true or false. The viewer is then guided to the Web site, Collegegameday.com, to find the answers.

There are times when new media should not be used. Usually this is when it does not make sense, based on the marketing objectives that the client wants to achieve.

The biggest challenge in using new media has been to persuade clients to be one of the first to try new media. It is difficult to convince clients they should take a small portion of their TV budgets to test new media.

Vendors play a vital role in utilizing new media. They have the most experience with the new media; thus, they are able to provide valuable insights to how best to execute creative to match the medium. They are also important to help bring ideas together, even if it requires vendors to adapt their product to the creative concept so that it works the most effectively. Some of the best campaigns have been through a collaborative effort between agency and vendor.

New media can encompass a variety of formats. Below is a breakdown of media used in our campaigns by volume:

- Broadcast, 60 percent
- Print, 15 percent
- Outdoor advertising, 8 percent
- Interactive, 12 percent
- Guerrilla, 5 percent

We do not create blogs for our clients, but do pursue user-generated content and monitor and respond to chat room, blogs, RSS feeds, and consumer postings, etc. We basically use any way we can to incorporate relevant communication platforms that resonate with the consumer. Our best practices in utilizing new media in our campaigns are as follows:

1. Have a clearly identified marketing objective and translate that into a media objective.
2. Have a clear understanding of the audience and their characteristics and behavior.
3. Identify the new media that best fit the objectives and the audience profile and the applications of each new medium that matches the audience usage patterns.
4. Map the customer journey to get to the message: How hard or easy is the process? Will it differ at all based on any external elements?
5. Identify different ways to target the audience so it is more defined, whether it is by day part, functionality, location, etc.
6. Consider the placement of the message within the medium: First position, top position, last position, only advertiser, etc.
7. Creatively design an ad that best suits the medium and how the consumer uses the new medium. Find ways to engage the consumer that are natural.
8. Establish the frequency of the message and how many executions of the message are required.
9. Establish the metrics for success before the campaign begins, and keep focused on its objectives. Work with vendor to provide affidavits and audits if the new media are not measured by a third-party source.
10. Optimize based on learnings—learn from the mistakes.

Evaluating New Media

Adidas has done a good job of identifying new media opportunities for the appropriate audience. They have made strong use of mobile programs abroad, where new media are accepted quickly by the consumer. The most exciting of these were in Tokyo, where people were actually suspended from buildings by bungee chords and played soccer games on the sides of the structures.

With new media, there are minimal benchmarking components, since it is new. If there is any type of auditing or measurement system in place, this is used as a benchmark, along with any kind of case studies available. With new media, it is sometimes difficult to be so scientific about the approach. Many times benchmarking is based on pure gut reaction. This is the approach Steve Jobs takes on many of his media approaches. Look at where he is today.

Assessing the effectiveness of the use of new media in advertising is dependent on the media. If it is something that is "trackable," there is usually an ROI analysis built into the whole process, depending on the overall objective of the campaigns. If it was a purely branding campaign, it is difficult to measure unless there was testing with a control group to gauge some sort of measurement.

Determining the ROI also depends on the medium and the objectives set before the campaign commences. If it is a direct-response client and there are trackable means that lead back to the specific medium, we do an acquisition-to-sales analysis where we can pinpoint the efficacy of the medium. If it is a branding campaign, without any testing parameters, we would do some type of branding recall study to see whether there was any type of lift.

I interpret "new media" as emerging technologies—but new media can be defined as anything new for its time, such as all the new OOH (out-of-home) applications occurring in the past few years. In the last year alone, we have created Web sites, online banners, a video that was distributed YouTube-style, a proprietary "Sandman" building competition on the beaches of California at Christmas for our Kohl's client, a short film for ESPN and Dominos, and a variety of events for our Pinky Vodka. Interactive promotions have generated a great deal of word-of-mouth (WOM) and impressions on a global front. Guerilla events, Bluetooth/cell phone integration, and WOM have acted as good extenders of our brands on an intimate, small scale, but the awareness levels are just not available yet.

Inevitably, this will change over time as consumers go to the computer, phone or yet-to-be-created device as their primary entertainment or communication portal. Until then, the key is finding the right mix of traditional and non-traditional media vehicles to solve whatever the business problem is at hand.

As a partner of Ground Zero, Court Crandall has spent the last nine years creating award-winning advertising for a variety of clients, a children's book called Hugville released by Random House, two actual children, the DreamWorks movie, Old School, and the independent film, A Lobster Tale.

Before forming the agency, Mr. Crandall's accomplishments as copywriter and creative director included launching the new Lexus Coupe with an advertising campaign that created a six-month wait-list for the car, won a Gold Effie for effectiveness and a Kelly nomination as one of the top twenty-five magazine campaigns in the country, and earned him ADWEEK Magazine's title, "Creative All-Star of the West Coast." He and former partner, Kirk Souder, were also recognized as the most award-winning creative duo in Los Angeles for four years and named "Creative Directors of the Year" by ADWEEK.

Mr. Crandall continues to believe that being creative is no excuse for being lazy, self-important, or uninterested in your client's business—a philosophy he has attempted to instill through not only the creative department, but the industry as a whole.

Dedication: *To all the clients who have entrusted us with their business over the last fourteen years.*

The Power of Engagement

Renee White Fraser, Ph.D.
Chief Executive Officer
Fraser Communications

Unique Elements of the Business: Setting Your Firm Apart

The advertising business is going through a pivotal time of change. New media and the Internet are giving consumers new ways to interact and absorb messaging. We are no longer in a world of reach and frequency alone; we are in a world in which *engagement* is key. Advertising agencies have to find better, more meaningful ways to engage consumers and clients.

Fraser Communications was established as an advertising firm driven by two fundamental tenets:

1. Strategic research is key to improving the effectiveness of advertising campaigns.
2. Socially responsible work will help the agency prosper.

When I started the firm in 1992, I witnessed many ad agencies cutting staff and even the larger agencies offering senior-level talent at the original meetings and very quickly assigning more junior staff to pitch clients. Clearly they were limiting the opportunities for engagement with clients and not delivering on the value proposition the agencies stood for. I was determined to develop a company of senior-level, smart people from all disciplines who would be involved on a day-to-day basis with clients. This seems to be a more popular model now, since so many large agencies have made significant cuts in upper management. However, at Fraser Communications we have the advantage of a team that has worked together and knows how to create synergistic campaigns to build our clients' businesses.

As a social psychologist, I saw how research could help delve into the consumers' minds and, just as important, how research could be used to demonstrate the return on investment (ROI) from advertising. No other agencies in the small and mid-size categories offered this perspective. Few ad agencies were run by women, and no ad agency was run by a psychologist/researcher. In fact, this is still the case. There are no ad agencies run by research professionals, but there are more agencies run by women, thankfully. Research is typically a capacity that large ad agencies bring to clients. Rarely, if ever, do the independent agencies make it one of the core competencies of the agency.

In the business world, where ROI questions are asked routinely about most line items, advertising is under more scrutiny than ever. Fraser Communications is not afraid of this. In fact, we embrace it. Research is a tool that can make the communications efforts smarter and more valuable.

Psychological insights can help generate powerful creative strategies that reach more deeply into behavior, and actually even motivate it. It was psychological research on the Toyota brand that led to our opportunity to work with Toyota on advertising in 2003, and research plays a role in the advertising we do for them to this day.

A more recent example is our California statewide campaign called Flex Your Power. This campaign is focused on motivating people to reduce their use of electricity through more efficient behaviors in their homes. There is a complementary effort directed at businesses, but our program was focused specifically on homeowners and renters. The program began in 2000 as a result of limitations in the power grid serving California. Californians have made great strides in efficiency.

> "Today the state (CA) uses less energy per capita than any other state in the country, defying the international image of American energy gluttony. Since 1974, California has held its per capita energy consumption essentially constant, while energy use per person for the United States overall has jumped 50 percent." (Steven Munson, "In Energy Conservation, Calif. Sees Light," *Washington Post*, Saturday, February 17, 2007.

See the chart on the next page for an illustration of the differences in energy consumption in California versus the rest of the United States.

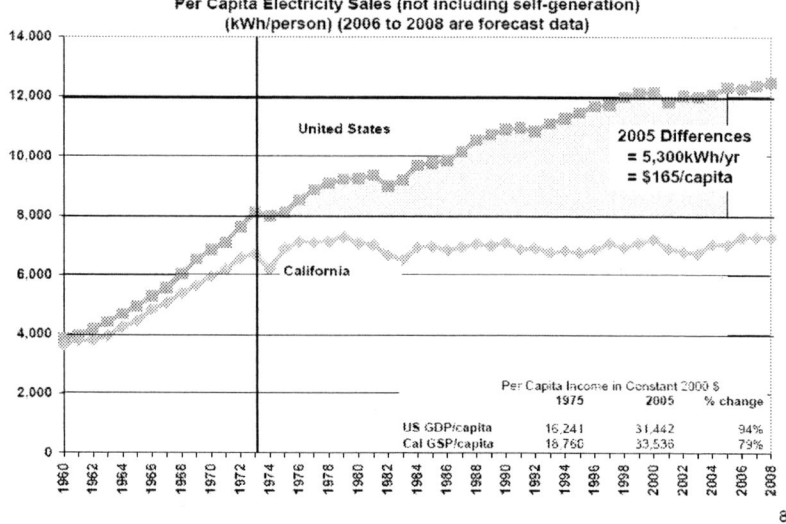

(Source: California Energy Commission)

This is true even though people have added an average of six electrical products to their homes in the last thirty years. Our campaign in 2006 improved people's proclivity to reduce their use of electricity, but it was clear when looking at the pre-post studies that attitudes were stalled. People felt that they were already doing enough. Working with our partners, McGuire and Partners and Brainchild, we designed and conducted research into the attitudes and lifestyles of consumers from different segments across the state.

This research was conducted in the spring of 2007. Utilizing focus groups and in-depth interviews, we probed into the lifestyles of people and asked them about their beliefs regarding climate change and the environment.

Questions included: What are the major issues facing us in the state (to see where and when energy conservation came up)? Why do you conserve energy and how much do you do? Could you do more? People seemed connected to the earth and concerned about the consequences of their own behavior. Making them aware of the connection between their own electricity consumption and greenhouse gases created a sense of alarm. In fact, this research provided the insight that drove our creative development process. Brainchild developed an integrated campaign that made salient the legacy we are potentially leaving the next generation and future generations. The television ads show pictures of children playing and an image of a grandparent or parent plays on a video screen in the room or in a window as the parent reads their last will and testament.

As the executions were developed, we insisted on both positive and more negative executions. Our research had determined that people needed hope and credit for what they had committed to thus far. The campaign was very powerful. In the positive television execution, the voice-over says:

> *To my children, Patrick and Erin, I leave the California I know. The mountains, the streams, the smell of the woods when you go hiking. I want to give you everything that I had to enjoy. The best of all possible worlds. I promise to take responsibility for the California that I leave my children.*

Knowing that some people needed to be prodded to take action with a more severe message, we rotated into the schedule another television ad with this negative message:

> *To my children, Andrew, Audrey, and Bradley. I leave floods and homes underwater and the landscape that isn't the same. I think about you every day, of being with you. I'm truly sorry, guys. I love you. I should have done better. I promise to take responsibility for the California I leave my children.*

In the research, we also noted that people wanted to know what they should do. In response, we included highly specific actions people could take and the amount of greenhouse gases they would eliminate by taking those actions. For example, we asked people to replace traditional light bulbs with CFLs (compact fluorescent light bulbs), using a key fact: "If all California households replaced five regular bulbs with CFLs, it is like taking 400,000 cars off the road," or, "If all Californians replace all old air conditioners with efficient ones, it will be like taking 275,000 cars off the road."

The research clearly informed the creative approach.

Most importantly, we have seen the impact of this work. In a pre/post study of Californians, we witnessed a significant shift in willingness to take specific actions to reduce use of electricity; impressively, in the hottest periods of the summer, we saw a 1,500-megawatt savings as people all over the state reduced or shifted their use of electricity.

Making research an integral part of the discussion with a client changes the conversation. It means we share a common interest in effectiveness and that we want to learn together. In other words, it enhanced the engagement opportunities, and the engagement was strategically relevant to the client's business and professional goals. I believe it signals a respect for learning from the consumer and a willingness to engage in an active learning process with the client, all of which further enhances the client bond and creates a fertile and productive working relationship.

Leadership Style and Making a Profit: Bringing Added Value to the Business

Like every good business person, I make a point of hiring smart people and delegating responsibilities. I see my role as conductor and cheerleader; I have to keep the agency running smoothly while focusing on growth and profitability. I believe that if people feel valued in a firm and want the organization to grow, they will constructively participate in that goal. This means that they will help keep costs down, find ways to work smarter, and help the agency get new business in new and different ways.

My philosophy is to reward and recognize good work as often as possible and to encourage innovative thinking. Simply being right is never my goal; in fact, I want others to be right and smart about new directions we offer our clients. As we approach what we call "new media," this is critically important. The industry is changing, and we need to be on the leading (not bleeding) edge of that change. We have made significant strides in interactive and experiential media, which are explored later in this chapter.

Growing the Agency

In order to grow the business, my most important role is actually outside of the agency. I have to be a visible symbol and spokesperson for our work and our way of doing advertising. New business comes to us through reputation and referrals.

Acting in a socially responsible way seems to have been ingrained in me from an early age. My father was in the advertising business, and I recall being impressed with the creativity and intelligence of his colleagues at Young and Rubicam in New York City. But as a young person, I was also determined to make this a better world, and it was discouraging at the time to see all those bright people not working to improve lives or the condition of the world. As a result, when I started my own company, I focused on doing good, as well as being profitable. Social responsibility was a core value of the company, but I was aware that we needed to build a profitable business to sustain the work. These two things do not have to be mutually exclusive. In fact, I believe that our profitability and growth have been helped by this sense of social responsibility.

Social responsibility means several things. As a leader in the community, I believe it means participating in important local issues and in social service; therefore, I sit on several boards. I am most proud of the work I have done as part of the United Way of Greater Los Angeles board and the Volunteers of America board. Our work for United Way has helped make it more of an impact leader in Los Angeles. United Way in Los Angeles has led the country in defining specific needs and "pathways out of poverty" to make a serious impact on things like the high drop-out rate and homelessness.

Most recently we have developed a campaign for United Way that very explicitly asks people to engage in fighting poverty in Los Angeles. A large, very spread-out area, the county includes 82 different cities and covers 4,084 square miles. Consequently, most people and potential donors do not see or feel the issues of poverty. There are 1.6 million people who live in poverty, so we had to find a way to make this visceral.

The campaign asks people to take responsibility: Together we can fight poverty, United we will win.

Participating on these boards helps one become much more familiar with the complexities of issues facing our community. It also provides exposure to CEOs and CMOs of prominent companies, and business opportunities emerge from these relationships. Working with clients that are large medical systems, like Cedars-Sinai and UCLA Healthcare, increased my understanding of the need for health care for all people. Consequently, I have been very involved in efforts with Governor Schwarzenegger to create universal health insurance in California and at the federal level.

Reflecting our concern for making a difference, the agency has taken on environmental causes. In fact, we have a reputation for being one of the premier "green" communications firms in the United States. In 2000 we created an award-winning campaign for the largest water provider in the world, Metropolitan Water District. They re-sell water and maintain a reliable supply for all of Southern California. MWD is a consortium of twenty-six cities and water districts that serve nearly 18 million people, covering Southern California. For the first time in water conservation social marketing, we used humor to engage people. The campaign was based on the line "You may be suffering from an overactive sprinkler." The campaign used interactive, radio, newspaper, and TV vignettes to persuade people to reduce their outdoor watering. Results were dramatic: we saw a 5.5 percent reduction after one year. The client measured this utilizing sophisticated measurements developed by their engineers and analysts. This campaign was followed by the Flex Your Power campaign described earlier. We are also currently engaged in groundbreaking social marketing for the County of Los Angeles, which is discussed in detail in the new media section of this chapter.

In this context, the evaluation of success is defined by several elements. Success incorporates client satisfaction, results, and profitability. We have found that if you have the first two, you gain the last. In fact, as our work for clients like Toyota, East West Bank, Cedars Sinai, and ProMax demonstrates, clients increase their budgets when they see that advertising is working. (It is a complicated combination of measures including client interviews annually, asking for letters of reference, and actual studies that measure the impact of advertising.)

New Media in Advertising

In the last twelve months we have used more than a dozen forms of new media, and I project that this figure will only grow. More importantly, I see the percentage of the budget devoted to new media increasing. As an industry, we have been focused on awareness building, for which the essential formula is reach and frequency. However, new mindsets are surfacing as the consumer is offered many more choices. Consumers can ignore, time-shift, censor, and multi-task themselves away from our messages, and as the Nielsen ratings demonstrate, more and more people are watching less television and traditional media. The new role of media and advertising is engagement. The shift in viewing is powerful and particularly strong in men and women ages 18 to 34.

Adults Spend More Time with Television Each Day Than They Do with Any Other Medium

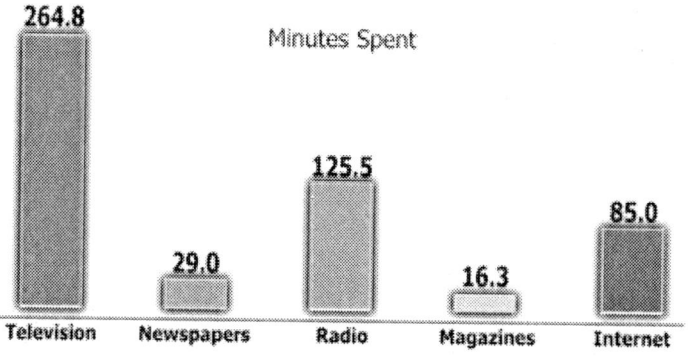

Adults: Time Spent Yesterday in Minutes with Major Media

Adults	Television	Newspapers	Radio	Magazines	Internet
Age					
18+	264.8	29.0	125.5	16.3	85.0
18-34	246.7	18.0	135.8	17.9	109.3
18-49	247.1	21.0	146.6	15.7	104.5
25-49	248.2	21.4	145.1	15.1	101.3
25-54	256.0	22.6	144.0	14.7	98.2
35-64	273.2	28.4	137.4	16.0	90.7
65+	271.7	51.2	67.5	14.1	21.1
Household Income					
Under $25K	305.3	23.3	142.6	14.7	56.1
$25-50K	291.4	25.6	118.8	15.0	60.9
$50-75K	239.5	30.9	150.3	14.4	83.2
$75K+	229.1	31.9	117.5	16.6	126.3
$100K+	214.7	32.5	109.8	19.8	143.0
Education					
HS Grad	307.9	24.1	140.6	14.3	60.3
Some College	276.7	31.1	138.8	14.1	87.7
College Grad +	219.3	31.7	107.3	19.8	109.5
Occupation					
Prof/Tech/Mgr/Owner	214.3	25.7	126.2	16.3	115.6
Admin/Clerical/Sales	272.1	25.6	183.9	15.7	118.2
Trade/Service	248.3	25.8	160.6	14.5	49.3

Source: TVB, Nielsen Media Research Custom Survey 2006

We see new media as fresh ways to *engage* the consumer and entice them to become more involved in the relationship with our clients' brands. Ultimately, that is what a brand is: a relationship with the consumer. A brand is the feelings and associations that are created in the mind and heart.

> "Every advertisement should be thought of as a contribution to the complex symbol which is the brand image."
>
> —David Ogilvy

New media is a broad category. It includes all the new ways of reaching people with the Internet, as well as new means of reaching people in their lives; essentially, it is experiential media, which includes:

- Text messaging on people's phones
- Street teams: people dressed up on street corners/public spaces
- Coffee sleeves
- Cocktail coasters
- Postcards at bars
- Sidewalk chalking
- Posters in clubs
- Mirror clings in public restrooms
- Floor ads
- Talking billboards above urinals
- Parking lot stripes painted with ads
- Pole ads in parking lots
- Ads in any unexpected place

These media approaches rarely provide reach; however, while it is difficult to reach millions of people through these media, you can use them to create buzz or word-of-mouth. That is probably the most valuable form of advertising. Being in an unexpected but unobtrusive place is engaging, and *engagement* is what it is all about. In a recent campaign for AIDS Healthcare Foundation, we had to reach men who have sex with men, or MSMs. The campaign also had a very specific geography in Los Angeles. Our goal was to persuade MSMs to use condoms and to be treated for HIV twice per year. Past social marketing campaigns in this arena had been problematic.

They have been criticized for being guilt-inducing or negative in terms of the stereotypes they use. In some cases, the campaigns had been offensive to men who are HIV positive, who were actually part of our target audience.

The advertising campaign we developed was based on understanding what is valued by gay men. We know from qualitative research that they value their appearance and their healthiness. Utilizing MRI (Mediamark Research Inc.), we found that they index high on using gyms and body/personal care products. They also enjoy a fun lifestyle with lots of partying and socializing. The agency account planners and account service people went out and observed many of the locations that are popular for MSMs. Our strategy was to embrace the lifestyle and normalize testing and to diligently avoid including any blame or negative consequences of AIDS.

The campaign taglines were:

Be Happy. Stay Negative and Be Healthy. Stay Negative.

The campaign included interactive, print, and a great deal of "out of home" bus shelters, as well as eight sheets (a form of outdoor advertising that is found on city streets and is more visible from sidewalks than the larger spectacular boards often used on highways and heavily trafficked streets), coffee sleeves, coasters, mirror clings, and similar creative tactics.

Positioning advertising in unexpected places is a key element of success. That is why we had condom coasters in clubs, coffee sleeves in coffee houses. We surrounded the target audience. In the new media area we also designed a "float" for the gay pride parade. Men and women wore T-shirts and marched in line forming a "human ad." They handed out colorful strips that mimicked the ads but had real condoms on them. They carried the banner that represented the ad. It was a great way to get the message out. More than 80,000 people "got the message" that day. The local media did a crowd count.

Another element of the campaign was the "Be Healthy. Stay Negative." component. For this we utilized a lot of out-of-home, or advertising that includes billboards, posters, etc. The message could be seen and appreciated by everyone. Whereas the condom ad message might have been offensive to someone driving down the street, these ads were well accepted. They featured attractive young men with their shirts on and off. In each case the ad simply stated healthy things they did and included twice-a-year AIDS testing as one of them.

To make the message even more relevant, we placed ads in gyms and clubs in the area, but not the way you would expect. We placed decals on weights so men saw them as they lifted. When they went to the changing room, they saw the ads on the mirrors. The messages became a part of their lives. We truly did not get any negative feedback. We were careful, and the ads with the condoms ran only in gay publications or were in gay coffee shops, etc. There is so much AIDS awareness advertising, it is surprising how open people are about condoms. This may be more the case in California than other parts of the United States.

This concept was also used in interactive ads. They expanded as you rolled over them, so you got all the information you needed. They ran on Gay.com and PlanetOut.com, which gay men frequent.

This campaign lasted three months and broke records for effectiveness. A post-only study was conducted to determine engagement. The client's budget was limited, so a pre-measure prior to the advertising was *not possible*. Even though this was a post-only, it was evident that the campaign had a powerful impact. We were pleased to see 76 percent awareness of the campaign. This level of ad campaign recall is unheard of. It is especially notable since the campaign ran for only three months, and the budget was not high (less than $300,000).

In another study conducted while the campaign was running, MSMs were interviewed about campaigns related to men's sexual health; 59 percent of those interviewed cited a campaign called the Stay Negative campaign by name. They reported seeing the taglines and played back the ads when asked in an open-ended question "What campaigns for men's sexual health have you seen or heard in the last three months?

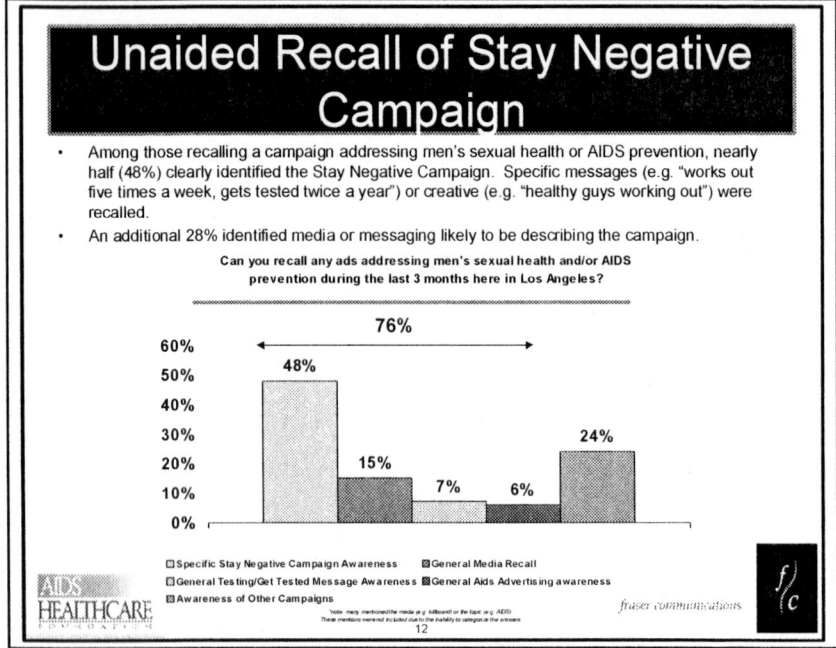

Unaided Recall of Stay Negative Campaign

- Among those recalling a campaign addressing men's sexual health or AIDS prevention, nearly half (48%) clearly identified the Stay Negative Campaign. Specific messages (e.g. "works out five times a week, gets tested twice a year") or creative (e.g. "healthy guys working out") were recalled.
- An additional 28% identified media or messaging likely to be describing the campaign.

Can you recall any ads addressing men's sexual health and/or AIDS prevention during the last 3 months here in Los Angeles?

☐ Specific Stay Negative Campaign Awareness ☒ General Media Recall
☐ General Testing/Get Tested Message Awareness ☒ General Aids Advertising awareness
☒ Awareness of Other Campaigns

In the post-study conducted for this campaign, respondents were asked whether the campaign was relevant, appealing, and motivating for several actions. In all of these areas it achieved ratings in the 70 percent to 80 percent range. Notably, the campaign was appealing and relevant to HIV positive *as well as* HIV negative men, and it appealed/motivated across Latinos and African-Americans.

Interruptive experiential media were a key part of the effectiveness of this campaign. In fact, the respondents mentioned specifically some of the unusual places they saw the messages.

Another example of new media is provided by the campaign we ran to reach young women of color in Los Angeles in which we utilized text messaging in a unique way. This campaign was designed to increase awareness of STDs and to encourage young women to be tested regularly.

After extensive research, we found that forcing the consequences of STDs did not motivate testing. Women wanted to be told by a peer, and they did not want to be stigmatized. We turned that around and created a campaign called "Don't Think. Know." The creative approach showed bold and attractive young women representing aspirational peers proudly saying, "I know." Then we put the message out in the environment on bus sides, inside buses, on bus shelters, in hair salons, on postcards and posters in nail salons, in clinics, in dress shops, and other similar locations. We placed the message in places where young women congregate and could consider a personal subject: places where boys would not be seen.

We wanted the girls to get tested, so we bought the code for "I know." If they texted the code, they would receive the address and phone number of the nearest free testing location. We worked with a vendor that manages text messages and purchased a certain number of message impressions—so we crafted the message to go out to girls. We also purchased the service that allowed for them to text "I know" into their phones, and the nearest location for a free test is sent to them right away. There were no questions and no stigma—just action.

Assessing When New Media Are Appropriate

Simply put, new media advertising is appropriate when it is an effective way to reach an audience. If the medium is an important part of their lives, and the message can be conveyed well, then it should be included. In most assignments, we need to reach large numbers of people. The Internet does not provide strong reach without very large budgets and a long campaign effort. Right now, the Internet is usually not the main medium utilized. We use more traditional media to create a foundation of awareness and interest. The Internet is a tool we use to engage people and ask for their involvement. In cases where we want them to go to the Web site, we offer users a click-through. In others, where we want them to gain information, we create expandable banners that allow them to get the information quickly. The latter approach is preferable because people do not want the flow of their user experience interrupted.

As an example, we are advertising energy conservation as part of Flex Your Power. Some of the banner ads remind people they can make a big impact on global warming by buying energy-efficient appliances. When they scroll over the banner, they see facts on how efficient certain appliances are. If they hit the link, they go right to a buying guide to help them find the most energy-efficient product they are seeking.

Because it is unconventional and inventive, new media present a powerful set of tools to help realize our fundamental tenets: socially responsible work does indeed help the agency to prosper, and strategic research, as illustrated by the power of our new media campaigns, is key to improving the effectiveness of advertising. At this stage, the possibilities seem endless and present inspirational motivation for those of us in this field to continue engaging with consumers and clients in new and innovative ways.

Under the leadership of founder Renee White Fraser, Fraser Communications has developed into the third fastest growing, woman-owned business in the Los Angeles area, with more than $42 million in sales, and is ranked thirty-sixth nationwide by Entrepreneur Magazine in the category of fastest-growing woman-owned businesses in the United States.

Since 1992, the full-service advertising and marketing agency has attracted a broad spectrum of local and nationally recognized clients, including Toyota, Cedars-Sinai Medical Center, AIDS Healthcare Foundation, East West Bank, The United Way of Greater Los Angeles, Flex Your Power (the California State Energy Conservation Campaign), Promax, Rainbow Light, and Los Angeles World Airports (LA/Ontario International and LA/Palmdale Regional Airports).

Having earned her Ph.D. in psychology from the University of Southern California, Ms. Fraser is a consumer psychologist who also serves on several non-profit boards. Most recently, she addressed the West Hollywood Women's Leadership Conference and gave the keynote address of "Women Lead Differently—We Walk Shoulder to Shoulder" at the 2006 International Forum of Outstanding Women Entrepreneurs in Shanghai. She serves on the faculty of University of Southern California and is currently featured on American Airlines' The Insider Exclusive program in a segment called "L.A.'s Most Influential Women."

Honored by Advertising Age as one of the "Ten Brightest Women in Advertising," Ms. Fraser was the recipient of the 2003 Los Angeles SBA "Women in Business Advocate of the Year" Award and the 2004 LA Business Journal "Woman CEO of the Year" Award. Throughout a career that has included being president and general manager of

Bozell Inc./Pacific Region, she has established a reputation as a brand builder. She distinguishes herself as a research expert and leads a team of experts in qualitative and quantitative research, which results in thoughtful and effective campaigns for her clients. Ms. Fraser is currently featured, along with fellow entrepreneur and business leader Betsy Berkhemer-Credaire on 2MinutesWith.com, a new business radio talk show and Web site. The newly launched program finds her and Ms. Berkhemer-Credaire sharing their experiences and interviewing high-level executives to encourage and inspire entrepreneurship among listeners.